D0349266

REGENT'S
UNIVERSITY LONDON

Park Campus
Library

Telephone: 020 7487 7449   **Email:** library@regents.ac.uk
renew online: www.regents.ac.uk/libcat

This book is due for r

THE SWORD DANCE

Lady Sarah Lennox and the Napiers

Also by Priscilla Napier
A LATE BEGINNER

Sarah Lennox, Susan Fox-Strangways
and Charles James Fox

THE SWORD DANCE
Lady Sarah Lennox
and the Napiers

Priscilla Napier

'*I remember William Napier as I first saw him in youth, leading his men into battle at Busaco*, en sabreur, *as for a dance.*'

REGENT'S
UNIVERSITY LONDON
WITHDRAWN

London

MICHAEL JOSEPH

REGENT'S
UNIVERSITY LONDON

First published in Great Britain by
MICHAEL JOSEPH LTD
52 Bedford Square
London, WC1
1971

© 1971 by Priscilla Napier

All Rights Reserved. No part of this
publication may be reproduced, stored
in a retrieval system, or transmitted, in
any form or by any means, electronic,
mechanical, photocopying, recording, or
otherwise, without the prior permission of
the Copyright owner

7181 0830 2

Set and printed in Great Britain by
Western Printing Services Ltd, Bristol in
ten on twelve point Times Roman on
paper supplied by P. F. Bingham Ltd,
Croydon, Surrey and bound by James
Burn at Esher, Surrey

To My Daughter
Lavinia

Contents

List of Illustrations
9

Foreword
11

Part I
The Ninth Diamond
13

Part II
Summer in Kildare
93

Part III
Full of Promise
187

Part IV
A Rain-washed Country
345

Short Bibliography
371

Family Tree: The Lennoxes
facing page 372

Family Tree: The Napiers
facing page 373

Index
373

List of Illustrations

Frontispiece
Sarah Lennox, Susan Fox-Strangways and Charles James Fox

Plates 1–4 facing pages 48—49
The Four Lennox Sisters: Caroline, Emily, Louisa and Sarah

Plate 5 facing page 96
Henry Fox, 1st Lord Holland

Plate 6 facing page 96
Sir Charles Bunbury

Plate 7 facing page 97
Susan Fox-Strangways

Plate 8 facing page 97
William O'Brien

Plate 9 facing page 128
Celbridge

Plate 10 facing page 128
Castletown

Plate 11 facing page 129
Tom Conolly

Plate 12 facing page 129
Edward Fitzgerald

Plate 13 facing page 240
Louisa Conolly

Plate 14 facing page 240
Sarah Napier

Plate 15 between pages 240–241
British Light Troops fording the Esla

Plate 16 between pages 240-241
The Battle of Salamanca

Plate 17 facing page 241
Charles Napier

Plate 18 facing page 241
George Napier

Plate 19 facing page 241
William Napier

Foreword

This is the second volume, the first to be published, of an intermittent account of the Napier family between 1068 and 1940. Into this in the late eighteenth century a charmer called Sarah Lennox impinged so effectively and with so thorough a documentation that it is obligatory to tell her tale.

The thought of a family history causes the stoutest literary heart to sink. Will it be snobbish? Why ask: of course it will. In everybody's pedigree there is a Mary Ann Snooks from the cottage under the hill, from whom we draw exactly the same number of genes as we do from the patrician head of the house; but Mary Ann Snooks does not keep journals or write letters and history must be drawn from those who do.

The tidal centuries roll us up and down, hither and yon; there are brimmings of intelligence, mirth, courage, and great stretches of blank but fertile ebb. But the history of one family is in some sort the tale of all: in the generations between now and the Conquest we have all had over a thousand million ancestors, and as there were only five million people in England even at the time of Queen Anne, we are all much more closely related to each other than some of us would like to think we were. So that perhaps the interest may be general and not confined to clan.

My thanks are due to the following who have kindly given permission for the use of the pictures illustrating this book: Sir William Napier Bunbury, Bt., for Plate 7; Lady Galway, for the Frontispiece and Plates 2, 4, 6, 8, 9 and 13; The Trustees of Goodwood House, for Plates 3 and 14; The Hon. Desmond Guinness and the Irish Georgian Society, for Plates 11 and 12; Victor McCaughan, for Plate 10; The Trustees of the Victoria & Albert Museum, for Plate 5; and Mrs Wynne-Roberts, for Plate 15. I would also like to thank Duckworth & Co. Ltd, for permission to quote from *Cautionary Tales* by Hilaire Belloc.

Foreword

And finally, my grateful thanks in this and other volumes to all who have kindly risked the post and lent me letters or unpublished memoirs, particularly to Mr Ivan Napier, Lord Napier and Ettrick, Sir Joseph Napier, Bt., Captain Lennox Napier, Royal Navy, Lady (William) Luce, and my son, Miles Napier. Gratitude also to the Bodleian Library at Oxford, so superbly beautiful and peaceful; and to that miracle of speed and efficiency, the National Library at Edinburgh.

Part I

The Ninth Diamond

I

Henry Fox, a failed politician but doing nicely as Paymaster-General, was not ill-pleased when his young sister-in-law arrived from Ireland on a bleak November day to make her home in his house. Immensely unpopular as a statesman, he was a warm family man and came of optimistic stock. His father Stephen Fox, deciding at the age of 77 that his first batch of children were not quite up to snuff, had married again and had four more, including twins, of whom Henry Fox, born when his father was seventy-nine, was one. Henry was a noted tease, and he and his wife Caroline had no daughter upon whom to practise. A fourteen-year-old aunt would be just the thing for his three sons: they could safely fall in love with her and it would keep them out of trouble. Stephen, called Ste, was at Eton, quiet and plain and much liked by all who knew him well; Harry was a stout apple-cheeked little boy who looked just like turning into the capable humorous soldier he afterwards became; and the middle son, Charles James, was the problem one; moody, sparky, up and down, handsome but inclined to fat, irrepressibly funny and generally so at the wrong moments.

'Charles is dreadfully passionate, what shall we do with him?' Caroline would wonder; but Henry thought him so sensible that he would probably cure himself. He spoiled this clever boy out of measure.

Henry Fox had bought Holland House ten years back; built for Sir Henry Rich in Charles I's day, it was rural still with its park and farm and hayfields: the garden was neglected until Henry Fox had it laid out and terraced by William Kent, and while insisting that he didn't know an oak tree from a gooseberry bush, had it planted with 'sixty sorts of shrubs that can abide our climate'. Throughout its history it was lived in by people who liked to entertain lavishly and amusingly: there were probably more jokes made there to the square yard than at any other terrain in London. Sarah Lennox had been there before as a very small child with her mother.

She had been born on St Valentine's Day in 1745 and was now going on fifteen; tall, shy, and a thought awkward; seeming to carry, as is usual at that age, more than the normal complement of elbows. Henry Fox thought her ravishingly pretty, but he was fifty-four and vulnerable: would others share his view?

'Her beauty is not easily described,' he wrote later, 'other than by saying she had the finest complexion, most beautiful hair, and prettiest person that ever was seen, with a sprightly and fine air, a pretty mouth, and remarkably fine teeth, excess of bloom in her cheeks, little eyes,—but this is not describing her, for her great beauty was a peculiarity of countenance, that made her at the same time different from and prettyer than any other girl I ever saw.' In time Henry Fox came to like her almost more for her courage and humility, for her sweet temper and ready wit.

It was not long before he found that his admiration for Sarah was widely shared. From the start the young King 'always talked to her with looks of pleasure and admiration; and as the crown neither lessened her beauty nor his sense of it, this still continued'. Nor did the fancy pass. Time after time as the year 1760 rolled on Henry's wife Caroline returned from Court to tell her husband that the young man had no eyes but for Sarah and talked to her to the exclusion of all others, his blue eyes flashing love as brightly as a lighthouse. Henry Fox's attention was really caught and he applied himself in full; for of all prime ways to make friends and influence people, a sweet pretty sister-in-law sharing the throne of England is beyond compare. What a poke in the eye for Bute, that bossy Scot!

But would Sarah play? For the young, as Henry Fox well knew, having children of his own, are kittle cattle when it comes to ful- filling parental ambitions. If Sarah would only take direction, the Fox family, and the Whig cause with it, would be home and dry for years. A charming sensible wife, who would keep George III's feet on the ground, and abate his grandiosity! Keep your head, darling girl, and we may hang on to the American colonies; or at least part friends.

No such luck: and only the fortunate Napiers were the gainers. It was in 1781, twenty years on, that this gay and gusty element breezed into their family, flickering over its puritan rock in a warm impulsive glow, not to mention a sharp flame of continental worldliness and general know-how. Donny Napier, who married Sarah Lennox in the summer of this year against a background of continuous disapproving murmurs from all quarters, had a personality as strong as hers: through their five sons they had a lasting influence on all who shared their name.

The Napiers came from Northumbria and appear to spring fully characterised from the brow of history in the person of Archill, a nobleman of that area, fighting at full stretch for a cause well and truly lost two years back. An illegitimate Scandinavian duke, domiciled in Northern France, had landed in the south of England and actually had himself crowned at Westminster; and Archill, 'potentissimus Nordohimbrorum', fighting for the rightful Saxon heir, Edgar Atheling, against this intruding William, had presently to effect a rapid transit over the border into Scotland in 1068. Here he married the daughter of the Celtic Mormaer of Lennox, a region around Loch Lomond drawing its name from the Gaelic word *Levenax*—the field of the quiet stream. By David I's time Archill's grandson was recorded as earl of Lennox, and the Napiers in fact were Lennoxes and drew their surname from a flattering legend originating circa 1150, in which Donald, younger son of the second earl of Lennox did so well in a battle that the Scots King assured him, 'Lennox thou hast nae peer.' This pleasing tale, rather more firmly based in fact than seems likely on the face of things, has jollied them along very happily for 800 years.

The pattern varies little. In 1298 John Napier, as lieutenant to Sir William Oliphant, was defending Stirling Castle, last Scots stronghold not in English hands, against Edward I, that firm protagonist of the doctrine that non-Caucasians begin at Berwick-upon-Tweed. But Wallace was captured in this year, and hung, drawn and quartered in London for breaking an allegiance he had never made; and Stirling was starved into surrender, the garrison, though spared the indignity of chains, was obliged to trudge south over the Border hills into English captivity, with their stomachs doubtless still deranged and groaning, and John Napier was mulcted three years' rent of his lands, and lucky enough to survive. Malcolm of Lennox, a noted partisan, was still in action for Robert the Bruce against the English and the collabos of eastern Scotland; but by 1488 the earldom of Lennox had petered out into three daughters, and Archibald Napier of Merchiston, Menteith and Rusky, put in a claim as senior grandson of the middle daughter and a Lennox by male descent anyway. Not only was there a lot of land involved, but the 'honour of Lennox', the title of earl, had gathered to itself a kind of romantic aura, based mainly on antiquity and on Malcolm, 4th earl, the resistance hero, one of the only two Scots earls brave enough to swear in at Robert the Bruce's crowning (the other being Atholl, who was captured, hung, drawn and quartered), and putting his name to that famed Scottish document, the Declaration of Independence signed at Arbroath in 1320.

But the youngest Lennox sister had been married to a Stewart whose descendant, called Lord Derneley, also claimed, and as the King by this time was also a Stewart, Napiers and Haldanes (also descended from the middle sister) lost and Derneley won. Title and half earldom went to him, Napiers and Haldanes getting a quarter each. This decision was arrived at in 1492, but the protagonists, still arguing hotly about whose mother or whose grandmother had been the eldest sister, had no time to look over their shoulders and notice that America was being discovered. The Napiers accordingly remained plain Napiers and were probably none the worse for this, as the Derneleys, carried away by the whole thing, married their descendant to a Plantagenet of sorts, thus qualifying their great-grandson, the luckless Darnley, for a marriage with Mary Queen of Scots, and causing this unpopular character to be blown sky high at Kirk o' Fields in 1567 by person or persons unknown.

The Napiers meanwhile continued with monotonous regularity from father to son to be killed in the noon of life fighting for their kings—those accident-prone Stewarts—at Sauchieburn, Flodden, Pinkie Cleugh, etc; and but for the joining of the two kingdoms under James VI and I in 1603 would probably not be with us yet. There were exceptions. William Napier, governor of Edinburgh Castle in 1401 and repelling yet another English assault upon this frontier fortress under Henry IV, made, for all we know, old bones. During the fifteenth century the magnificent crown spire of St Giles's cathedral was slowly rising on Edinburgh's great central ridge: maybe it was in thankfulness for reaching the ripe age of fifty that Sir Alexander Napier built its chapel of San Salvator, putting his own head on the corbel of the half pillar near the high altar. So small and high up that not even the Covenanters would reach up to scrape it off, his long countenance reposes above the Lennox arms; arched eyebrows, beak nose, and an extremely cynical expression, improbably poised upon a pair of cherub's wings. Archibald Napier, born 1534, was taking no chances on extinction: married at fourteen, he had three children before he was twenty, and an eldest son at a university by the time he himself was twenty-eight. Since 1400 those of the Napiers that had survived a soldiering youth had been ambassadors, provosts, 'Maisters of Houshald' to the kings, Vice Admiral of Scotland in 1461; all of which must have sharpened up their intelligences, and when in the 1570s Archibald Napier went on a mission to London 'his witt and knawledge was wonderit at be the Englischmen'. John Napier, born in 1550 to a fifteen-year-old father and a mother scarcely older, invented logarithms, which caught on, and tanks and submarines, which fortunately did not. (These to confront the Spaniards, said to be brooding a second Armada.) He also invented the decimal point, a useful little device which he neglected to patent. Between this and writing a Latin treatise in scientific terms on the Revelation and another on the Trinity, he found time to be an efficient landlord and to father twelve children, six of each; mathematical precision obtaining here as elsewhere. There was a blood feud with the Scotts, and John's younger half-brother, Alexander Napier of Loriston, had a terrible feeling that it was going to drop. Must Scotland, glad land of vengeance and the free for all, lapse tamely into civilisation?

'Never embrayce dishonorabill agreyment,' Alexander urged in 1600, but elder brother John's attention was distracted by the Trinity and the decimal point, the arrangements for the marriage of his youngest sister with Lord Ogilvie of Airlie and measures to circumvent the perennial Campbell-Macgregor troubles that banged on around Loch Lomond. Revenging Scotts had killed a younger brother under the walls of Holyroodhouse, 'hard by the palace, under cloud of night, in outright felony, by the number of seven, armed with sword, spear and pistolets, with which all he was slain being a young man not yet twenty-two years for no more cause but that he defended himself against their brother', and Alexander Napier's anti-Scott rage bites into the paper. But philosopher John was into his fifties now and shrewd enough to finish inventing his logarithms before taking on the bold Buccleuch. 'Make use of this treatise,' he urged posterity, 'and give thanks to God the only inventor,' a piece of advice of which the first part has been more universally taken than the second. Published in France, under the authorship of Jean Nompareil, sieur de Merciston, it did well; and in Germany Kepler, who had first referred to John Napier as 'a Scottish nobleman whose name escapes me' came to think him the great man of the age, and dedicated his next work to him. (The Russians have recently named a mountain on the back side of the moon after him; spelt wrong, but it's the thought that counts.)

'I have not done perfectly as I would, but zealously as I could' he had humbly written. His tank, according to Sir Thomas Urquhart, went as far as a trial in a field of cattle, and was such a success that he had it destroyed, declaring that there were enough 'devices already for the ruin and overthrow of mankind' without his adding to them. Like patriotism, science and mathematics were not enough. 'In vaine' he had once told the King, 'are all earthly conjunctions, unless we be heires together and of one body, and fellow partakers of the promises of God in Christ.' And his father Archie, although voted on to the hunt committee, had declined to take part in Jesuit chasing, that popular blood sport.

It was about now that several younger brothers and uncles, seeing small chance of inheriting, took their share of the Lennox and Napier inheritances and sloped off south over the Border and into Dorset, Somerset, and Bedfordshire. Here they went on the same; quite bright, and moderately eccentric. Richard Napier was a scientist and 'did practise physick; but gave most to the poor that he got by it', according to John Aubrey. 'His knees' this authority continues 'were horny with frequent praying,' and he claimed to be in constant communication with the archangel Raphael; a being whose observations he somehow failed to record. Rather more humdrum was his nephew, Sir Richard, a Fellow of All Souls and one of the founder members of the Royal Society. When Robert Napier, who had had a prosperous venture to Turkey, bought himself Luton Hoo and a baronetcy from James I there were mutterings; for who, the English courtiers demanded, *were* the Napiers? This was the kind of query which nettled King James, for in Scots eyes the English nobility were but the product of every Tom, Dick and Harry unable to hold down a job in 11th-century France, and had largely exterminated each other in the Wars of the Roses; while the Scots had been living on their lands and very adequately defending them from Angle, Dane and Norman since A.D. 700. Who were the Napiers? 'By my sawl,' King James crossly replied, for so did he pronounce his immortal member, 'by my sawl they are all gentlemen these many hundred years.'

In pursuit of this exacting profession Archibald, first Lord Napier, lost all. (There had been a rude popular rhyme all ready for him upon his elevation—'Napier has nae peer, yet a peer is he'.) There was quite a lot of all to lose. Eldest son of logarithms John, he inherited a number of handsome stretches of territory. Parts of Fifeshire had come from the King to the original Donald of the legend, parts of Perthshire from King James II for services rendered by Sir Alexander Napier in 1436 when he rescued the King's widowed mother, Queen Joanna Beaufort, granddaughter of John of Gaunt, out of the hands of the Boyds and Livingstones, and got himself badly wounded in the process. Parts of Dunbartonshire and Stirling came from the Lennox share-out in 1492; and the islands in Loch Lomond, quietly nabbed by the Haldanes of Gleneagles from Archibald (father of logarithms John), whilst he was a fatherless small boy, had been wrested back by this dexterous character and expressly confirmed to him by Mary Queen of Scots on the grounds that beside his hereditary rights his father, grandfather, and great-grandfather had all been killed fighting for her family.

This kind of sweeping loss seemed unlikely in the early 17th century, and Archibald, first Lord Napier, inheriting in 1617, was the necessary establisher, worldly wise, estate improving, listing his clan, circulating birth-brieves, registering the Lennox arms which his family had held since 1100 or so without bothering, Deputy Treasurer of Scotland, pillar of church and state. On he went, on a June day of 1625 in the square tower of Merchiston that was still well outside Edinburgh, slowly enumerating his relatives. Arched eyebrows, beak nose, the long intelligent face above the slashed doublet—'To my entirely beloved kinsmen, Sir Robert Napier of Luton Hoo Knt and Bart., Sir Nathaniel Napier of Middlemarsh Knt and Bart., Thomas Napier of Tintinhull Esq., John and Robert Napier of Puncknowle, James Napier of Baglake in the County of Dorset, Edward Napier of Hollywell . . . kinsmen of my blood and branched from my house, to bear my arms supporters and crests with their due difference as their lawful right and ancient inheritance . . .'; and he committed the family legend to paper for good measure. By the time Archie died, Wishart thought him the wisest head in Scotland, and 'a man of a most innocent life and happy parts; a truly noble gentleman'; but all to no avail. Loyal to the King, Archie died at the age of 73 campaigning with Montrose (whose sister he had married); and the Covenanters, whose document he had refused to sign—'Histories

◉ REGENT'S
UNIVERSITY LONDON

witness what troubles have been raised in all places where Churchmen were great'—scooped the pool. By 1660 the Napiers owned almost nothing but their stone tower of Merchiston and the doublets they stood up in. They also had the heart of Montrose (that talismanic thing) in a steel casket, bequeathed to them by him for 'the unremitting kindness shown to him in all the different turns of his life and fortune'; an admirable possession, but not one that pays the grocery bills.

Archie's son too, young Archie, Master of Napier, had fought alongside Montrose: his big moment coming when with Nat Gordon, one trumpeter, and a single troop of horse, he sounded off outside the walls of Edinburgh and caused that strong city to surrender, and also to release his family, imprisoned in Edinburgh castle. He went into exile with Montrose, and died in Holland of a fever at the age of thirty-four. From Cromwell's 1654 Act of Grace and Pardon, Lord Napier of Merchiston expressly excluded himself—'never embrayce dishonorabill agreyment'. Charles II, restored, was aware of indebtedness and wrote a charming letter to Archie's widow and young son: this, like some other Stewart utterances, rested upon the laurels of its charm. There is a family legend, undocumented, that in return for the loss of half modern Edinburgh and other attractive slices of real estate, the King offered the Napiers a dukedom, which was refused, on the sensible grounds that there is no point in being a duke if the Roundheads have snatched your land, it merely up-grades the hotel bills. (In the event, the Napiers were awarded £3,000, which was never actually paid.) Perhaps that long-usurped earldom of Lennox would not have come amiss; the last Stewart holder having died. But no, it was reserved for King Charles's youngest bastard, dear-loved as Monmouth and equally unsatisfactory, who was made Duke of Lennox as well as Duke of Richmond.

Richmond's granddaughter, Sarah Lennox, had King Charles's thick curling black hair, and more than a dash of King Charles's lambent charm. If you can't beat them, join them, Donny Napier might have thought, among other things, when he married her in 1781; except that he was not much given to thoughts of that kind.

For all her Scots name, Lady Sarah Lennox came from a world far removed from the cold hills and the catechisms of Edinburgh. Brought up in Ireland, pitchforked into the whirl of fashionable

London at the age of fourteen, she was a daughter of the second Duke of Richmond, great granddaughter of Charles II, and thus two more generations from his grandparents Henry of Navarre and Marie de Medici, and of the warm south in general, with its tendency to dark hair and calculation. The marriage of Sarah's parents had been inauspicious in the extreme. Summoned up from Eton to marry an heiress in settlement of his father's gambling debts, seventeen-year-old Charles March had been confronted by Sarah Cadogan, a little thirteen-year-old with a mob cap and a cold in the head. Strictly brought up by her Dutch mother, she was shy and awkward and would not even look at him. 'They are surely not going to marry me to that dowdy?' he had expostulated; but on they went, right through the marriage service and out the other end; sending him away immediately afterwards on the Grand Tour.

Returning home four years later, he postponed facing up to matrimony and went to the Opera on his first night in London. Here he noticed that attention during the longer arias was focused upon a very pretty girl in one of the boxes, and asked his neighbour who she was. Where have you been, his neighbour wondered, not to know the toast of the town, the beautiful Lady March? The comments of Charles March are not on record, but he hastened home and lived happily ever afterwards.

This marriage, made so far from heaven, turned out to be one of the heavenly sort: not even the most envious diarist found a chink in the armour of its joy. The Marches produced 20 children, quite a quantity of whom survived; Sarah Lennox was one of the youngest of them. Charles became Duke of Richmond through his father and Duke of Aubigny in France through his grandmother, Charles II's Louise de Querouaille, history's most successful French ambassadress at the Court of St James, though this was not her official post.

The Richmonds died within a few months of each other, perhaps from exhaustion, and six-year-old Sarah was then brought up in Ireland. She had been, it must be admitted, a bit of a Fauntleroy as a child, breezing up to the not very engaging old King, George II, as he promenaded along the Broad Walk in Kensington and starting a carefree conversation in French. He was charmed, and she became a regular visitor at those sessions when, wholly in the character of the nursery rhyme, the King counted out his money. Once, as a not very funny joke, he seized her up and put her, aged five, into an enormous oriental china vase and clamped on the lid: instead of panicking she could be heard inside singing *Marlbruk s'en va-t-en guerre* in a loud cheerful voice. She was a great one for the childish sally. 'Does Papa *like* hunting, or does he have to?' she wanted to know, looking out at Goodwood upon a horrible day. The sudden break up of home and transference to Ireland ought to have been a shaking experience, but was somehow not.

Her sister, Lady Kildare, was then aged twenty, and her jolly household life alternated between Carton, in Leinster, and Kildare House in Dublin. In this city life was particularly gay and gaudy and non-Hanoverian. The Kildares were happy and prolific and lived in unashamed splendour with nothing pinch-penny about them. Emily Kildare could sometimes be seen 'in sack and diamonds in the afternoon', French horns played at every meal, food and wine were delicious and plentiful and conversation excellent—'Ireland is become the staple of wit' Horace Walpole noticed in 1759. There were so many servants that they constantly fell over each other. Kildare, though morally strict and a leader of the Irish Patriot Party, lived *en prince*; and his wife Emily, though mad about the works of Jean-Jacques Rousseau, did not think of them as precursors of the end of her way of life. A tide of concern rippled through the fun: in 1753 James Fitzgerald, 20th Earl of Kildare, presented an Address of Remonstrance against the iniquities of the Irish Administration which had at least some effect.

Emily Kildare's three little Lennox sisters, Louisa, Sarah, and Cecilia, grew up among her own children; learning their slightly sketchy lessons, learning to ride and drive, to act plays and play guitars, to see the jokes and enjoy the concerts. The influence of Daubigny was still strong enough to make the sisters often speak a vague colloquial French among themselves. They grew up in a world lacking the current English stiffness, flirting light-heartedly with young Irishmen in hospitable Kildare House (now the seat of the Irish government). The fluted columns of its supper-room rang to their laughter, their guitars, their Irish-accented French phrases. Even church on Sunday involved, for Fitzgeralds, a comfortable gallery and a blazing fire. With clockwork regularity Emily Kildare produced another baby every year: her total was nineteen. There was room and warmth for all, and for her three orphan sisters as well. This was the Protestant Ascendancy in its heyday, as yet unteased by guilt; and a family providing as much employment as a small factory.

An easy ride from Carton in Leinster brought the sisters to the woods of Castletown, with whose owner, dark, good-looking Tom Conolly, Louisa Lennox fell in love. Amidst universal acclaim from the elder generation, they were married when Louisa was fifteen. Tom Conolly's new brothers-in-law declared that his jokes were bad, and that he would keep on repeating them: Caroline Fox and Emily feared that he was a silly, toad-eating boy and rather tiresomely concerned about his health—'I hope and believe Louisa won't find it out ever' Caroline wrote, and she never did. But Tom was generous, and much in love with Louisa, who dearly loved him back; and perhaps the general feeling was that with twenty-seven thousand a year and the most beautiful house in Ireland he might be allowed a few bad jokes and an undue preoccupation with his larynx. No one was very grown up. 'I perfectly remember admiring Atty Gore and his brother, chiefly because they were very like greyhounds, which I thought was quite reason enough to be in love with them,' Sarah wrote later.

Tall, shy, and alone, she left Dublin in 1759 to live with Caroline Fox. This eldest sister and her brothers were strangers to Sarah and not all was ease. Richmond, 'so like me in a great many ways and manners', was charming but teasing, and fussed over little niceties of dress and behaviour. George Lennox seemed 'horridly prudish', and his wife, who had been Lady Louisa Kerr, 'directs and gives her advice about everything'; she made a great show of giving in over minor details but 'its plain Lady George will govern my brother. They take aversions without rhyme or reason, they have that odious way of never thinking anything right but what they do themselves ... if my brother gives the least hint he don't like a thing or person, then Lady George takes it up and abuses that same thing or person for an hour. Yet with all these faults I like them vastly, they have a thousand good qualities too. If I am grown pert, you must scold me out of it.' Caroline made a to-do with her children, and 'Ste Fox is a very disagreeable boy and frightfully ugly tho' sensible,' she told Emily. Within a year she was loving them all dearly, and Susan Fox-Strangways, Henry Fox's own niece, aged sixteen and also at Holland House, became a lifelong friend. But why would they try to talk her out of loving Ireland and the Irish, Henry Fox in particular, saying it was only stupidity for an Englishman to *live* on his Irish estates, and much more 'for the good of Ireland' only to visit them rarely? Sarah might be only fourteen, but she knew better—'sure thats not possible.'

Acclimatizing, adapting, yet mocking the feathers and furbelows, the fashions of doing her hair, the footmen grandly handing her into her chair—'On I jogged to St. James's,' she told Emily. For in hoops and curls, teased by Henry Fox and trying not to twitter, she and Susan had been swept off by Caroline to make their curtseys at Court. 'And up I went through three great staring rooms full of men into the Drawing Room . . .'

II

The event was a dire flop. Susan thought King George II 'a neat little old man, honest, upright, and well-meaning', Princess Amelia's manner 'not pleasing and rather gruff', and the Prince of Wales 'at that time a fine pleasing-looking young man, a healthy youthful complexion, a look of happiness and good humour'. The old King was interested to see Sarah again, and found her quite as sweet as he remembered; he attempted to cuddle her and treat her as if she was still a five-year-old. Sarah had blushed and backed away and gone stiff and he had said loudly, Pooh, she is grown quite stupid, into a horrid silence. Lady Yarmouth, the King's old and unlovely German mistress, regarded her with glassy eyes. No Irish laughter, no English kindliness; only the hard, unamused German stares. Sarah had stood scarlet-faced, utterly confounded, until George, Prince of Wales, pitying her plight, had come up and talked to her in kind tones, covering her discomfiture, giving her time to regain her poise. She liked him heartily for it—'very agreeable, and a mighty pretty sort of man. He don't talk nonsense, and pester one with music, but talks like other people.'

George III, as he soon became, had good manners, spoke perfect English and showed signs of having a heart. He was a beautiful dancer; and his smile revealed an advantage far from being usual in Georgian England, a row of perfect teeth. Though his bright blue eyes were slightly goggly, they had an honest open look. Having once begun, he continued to cherish Sarah at her court appearances. But he was fatherless, and much under the thumb of his bossy German mother, daughter of the Margrave of Hesse, and swayed by Lord

Bute. His conversation at these *tête-à-têtes* was general. But what did she and the King talk *about*, Sarah's family demanded? She could never remember, unless something funny had happened. 'He often talks,' she said rather vaguely, 'about the ways and habits of Kings.' Soon Ste and Charles James came back from Eton for the Christmas holidays and they started acting plays and all else was forgotten. The play was *Hermione* and they performed it on Twelfth Night and Charles James afterwards insisted that it was declaiming Hermione that had taught him to be an orator. Sarah played the lead, and Henry Fox, carried away, declared that he had never seen a part so well acted in his life.

At the next Court ball, between the minuets and the quadrilles, the young King took Sarah into the tea room and had his first private conversation with her. It went tremendously badly.

'Tell me about your sister's household,' he began. 'Does Lady Emily or Lord Kildare govern? Either a husband or wife must take the lead.'

'I think any husband who allowed his wife to govern would be very foolish.' There was a pause and Sarah continued 'Everybody says you are governed by your mother.'

'And do you not think parents are the best people to govern?'

'Yes, sometimes. But a German woman is not the best person to govern the King of England.'

King George pressed on. Didn't she think this, agree with that?

'No. It would be telling an untruth.'

'But you would not mind telling a white lie?'

'Yes I would, Sir.'

The music started up again; and perhaps even the King was left with a feeling that Sarah was not exactly cut out for Court life. The Foxes insisted on knowing what had passed, as soon as they were all at home, and this time Sarah actually remembered. Next week they did another play, *Jane Shore*; and Horace Walpole, in the audience, was 'excessively amused . . . at Holland House . . . Lady Sarah was more beautiful than you can conceive . . . acting with so much nature and simplicity . . . her very awkwardness gave an air of truth to the shame of the part. . . . When Lady Sarah was in white, with her hair about her ears, no Magdalen by Correggio was half so lovely and ex-pressive.' Later on, in a more indigestive mood, he pointed out that she had 'no features'. Others said that her eyes were not large, and she herself complained that her nose was too big; but even the daughter

of her enemy, Lord Bute, described her as 'celebrated for her sur-
passing loveliness and her delightful fascination of manner'. Everyone
grants her a vivid, flawless complexion, lasting well into her late
seventies; but we have to take it all on trust, for in her portraits she
looks cosy, but no great shakes.

In February Sarah was fifteen, and on the nineteenth there was yet
another ball at St James's Palace, with glittering chandeliers and
shining floors, velvet coats laced with silver, powdered heads,
diamonds, and sweeping skirts of satin and brocade. The young King
took heart. After a long look at Sarah, he suddenly crossed the room
and made a cautious embarrassed proposal of marriage to her
through her cousin Susan, asking her later what she thought of it.
Teased and irritated by the use of an intermediary, Sarah replied
brusquely that she thought nothing of it: a fascinated Court, who had
already been making up to Sarah in a way that made her laugh,
watched while the young man, with a very red face, moved stiffly
away. Who, at fifteen, is not proud and immersed in their own embarrassment, and insensitive to the pains of a feeling-hearted young
man obliged to do his courting before a great blaze of interested
eyes? 'H.M. is not given to joke,' Henry Fox pointed out, 'and this
would be a very bad joke too. Is it serious? Strange if it is, and a
strange way of going about it.' And particularly from one who had
insisted that what he loved in Sarah was her lack of guile. But his
hands were tied. Already, at his mother's behest, he had given ear to
the list prepared for him of suitable German princesses.

He had made one desperate bid, writing to Bute, begging for a free
hand. 'The truth is the D. of Richmond's sister arrived from Ireland
towards the middle of Novr, I was struck with her first appearance at
St. James, my passion has been increased every time I have since
beheld her; her voice is sweet, she seems sensible, has a thorough
sense of her obligations to her sister Lady Kildare, in short she is
everything I can form to myself lovely. I am daily grown unhappy,
sleep has left me, which never before was interrupted by any reverse
of fortune; . . . I protest before God I never had any improper
thought with regard to her; I don't deny having often flattered
myself with hopes that one day or other you would consent to my
raising her to a throne; thus I mince nothing to you . . . I submit my
happiness to you who are the best of friends.'

Lord Bute minced nothing either. 'With the utmost grief I tell it to
you, the case admits not of the smallest doubt.' Bute was the best of

friends to his own interests: let no one imagine he was going to let Fox in. 'Think, Sir, who you are, what is your birthright, and prepare your mind to hear the voice of truth.' Bute continued humbugging in this vein, bringing the full weight of his dominance on an unhappy young man already enthralled by his heavy dragoon of a mamma. 'I stifled my grief till retired to my chamber where I remained several hours in the depths of despair,' the King sadly recorded. The card indexing of the German princesses meanwhile continued in secrecy. 'You have thoroughly convinced me,' Bute's victim answered, 'of the impropriety of marrying a countrywoman . . . I am born for the happiness or misery of a great nation, and consequently must often act contrary to my passions.'

These brave and unselfish words George III made good. Not even his best friends could think him clever, but he did try hard to do well. With Sarah by his side he might have succeeded better, might have avoided his illness. With an unnecessary sacrifice of personal happiness he gave up hope of her, his second love, and married and faithfully stayed by his stiff little German Princess, Charlotte Sophia of Mecklenburg-Strelitz; 'not in every particular as I could wish', he sadly confided to Bute. Often in after life, in ravings, he called on Sarah's name; people believed that he kept his affection for her, just as she kept a kindness for him. Though declaring, even in moments of worst financial woe, how glad she was not to be Queen, she never would speak against him on this; though she did let slip a regret on hearing of his first bout of madness. She wished she could help him; she had heard that madness sometimes responded to 'steady kindness . . . I own I did almost exclaim, Poor soul, if I was yours I would never leave you an instant, but try and calm your suffering mind.'

From Castletown Louisa cheered her with good reports. Sally was 'the prettyest, genteelest mild obliging sweet Creature ever met with and so civil'. Everyone in London was 'dying for love of you, including Lords Huntingdon and Newbattle and the dukes of Marlborough and Devonshire'. This did not do either. 'Mr. Fox and my sister are always settling every pretty man they see for me to marry,' Sarah complained to Emily. 'I dont like people to have that notion of me. You want to know how I manage my money—very ill indeed; for I have spent it all and owe besides.' Marlborough's proposal 'Mr. Fox told me was a thing he should like vastly, but I doubt its being lucky for me as my sister tells me he is so entirely given up to women that its quite dreadful, his father did the same, and after he was married. But that sort of love would not content me . . .'

Her happy ending was some while away. Nor was she so guileless as the King supposed, being at this time taken up with a rather more dashing and decided suitor than poor George was let to be. This unserious fling provided the beady-eyed court ladies with some powerful ammunition: every move was reported to the King with a heavy stiffening of innuendo. She had met John Newbattle (eventually Lothian) in Kensington Gardens, aided and chaperoned by the George Lennoxes, Lady George Lennox being John New-battle's sister. This young man was described by Henry Fox as 'a vain insignificant puppy, lively and not ugly, who made love to all the girls'; but the key word in this description is probably 'lively'. While his sister and Sarah's brother retired to a discreet distance, he proposed to Sarah in the park, and although his parents forbade the marriage, this rencontre was observed and reported on to the Palace. The parental decision did not prevent Newbattle from overtaking Sarah next day on her way down to Goodwood, riding alongside and being lively all the way down and probably seeming less ugly with every passing mile, and finally getting himself asked to stay by the encouraging Lady George, who also furthered a walk or two on the downs. It may be that off his horse, and staying in the same house, John Newbattle's vain puppyishness began to outweigh his liveliness; and at this point Sarah either went or was sent to stay with Susan and the Ilchesters in Dorset. But the seeds of doubt as to her steadiness had been well sown. Not so did young ladies comport themselves in Mecklenburg-Strelitz.

Sarah's next piece of unsteadiness was to fall off her horse in Maiden Bradley on the way back from Longleat. In fact it was her horse who came down, rolled on her leg, and gave it a painful fracture. She was carried to Mr Henry Hoare's new house at Stourhead, where the Bruton doctor who set her leg reported her as 'the most agreeable and merry patient he had ever met with'. Next day she proceeded to Redlinch 'upon men's shoulders in a very pretty bed made for the purpose, . . . singing most of the way'.

'Broken leg!' exclaimed the London gossips; 'if you can believe that you can believe anything.' In spite of all the witnesses they insisted that she had really only gone to the west to produce an illicit baby by George III, and the son born about now to the wife of Susan Fox-Strangway's brother was swiftly attributed to Sarah.

But the hunt was now truly away: Conollys, Kildares, Foxes and Richmonds, all hurried to the scene to cherish her and offer their advice. The King, they assured her, had trembled with emotion on hearing of her accident; a reaction which compared very favourably with the ruderies of John Newbattle, who had commented that her legs were so bad anyway that a break could hardly spoil them. At the other end Henry Fox hastened to St James's on every occasion to tell the King how patient, brave and sweet-tempered Sarah was being. The King continued to radiate concern and interest and Sarah too began to reflect that he really *was* very nice, and completely un-puppyish. And when Caroline Fox, who had faithfully nursed her, took her back to London at the end of May and the King greeted her with eagerness and warmth, Sarah began seriously to like him. Even Horace Walpole, not, as he said, 'apt to fall in love with Majesty', described the young George as 'the most amiable young man in the world..'

His pen was in action again on the night of the Birthday Ball on June the 4th. 'The Birthday' he thought 'exceeded the splendour of Haroun Alrashid and the Arabian Nights. . . . Do you remember' he asked Lady Ailesbury 'one of those stories where a prince has eight statues of diamonds, which he overlooks, because he fancies he wants a ninth; and to his great surprise the ninth proved to be pure flesh and blood, which he never thought of? Somehow or other Lady Sarah is the ninth statue; and you will allow, has better white and red than if she were made of pearls and rubies.' Even her enemies admitted that she absorbed the King's whole attention: 'their conversation went on till all dancing was over, and everybody sat in suspense, and it approached one in the morning ere he recollected himself and rose to dismiss the assembly.' Susan was jubilant—'I almost thought myself Prime Minister for some time after the first Birthday Ball': she was wonderfully unjealous of her surpassingly beautiful younger cousin, being herself a *jolie-laide* with long blue eyes and an oval face full of spirit, well able to hold her own. They told each other the truth without resentment and her affection for Sarah was a great support throughout these dicey days.

Fixed though he was, the King could not resist a last burst of this pleasing dalliance. 'He had no eyes but for her and hardly talked to anybody else.' And why, demanded the sensible Henry Fox, 'should a young King not show the strongest symptoms of love and desire for the prettyest creature in the world? . . . Her Ladyship, with modesty very natural to her, and yet with looks as unaffected, returned the fondness of his eyes and gallantry of his discourse as much as even he could wish.' Yet the discourse had not been much, in comparison, with 'the *language des yeux*'. Both kept blushing, 'and in this pretty way did these two young lovers entertain one another and the whole ball room for an hour. . . . As he was going, he turned and spoke again and again, as if he could not force himself away from her.'

But on Sunday Fox's hopes were dashed: the King looked crushed and melancholy and spoke spiritlessly to Sarah. It was thought he had had a parental dressing-down. Certainly his mother and sisters watched the King 'impertinently and indecently', Fox thought. 'We were so near that nothing could be said,' Sarah told Susan, 'and they wacht us as a cat does a mouse, but looks and smiles very very gracious'; and every time they met this fond but unmarching commerce of love continued.

It was felt by Sarah's family that she needed a little coaching. Next time the King asked her what she thought of his proposal, she was not just to say 'Nothing', and cause him to stump off. 'I am allowed to mutter a little, provided the words, *astonished, surprised, understand,* and *meaning* are heard' she commented mockingly. She was also encouraged to make hay in a becoming dress in Holland Park; for along Kensington High Street, where the buses now roar and fume, the King was wont to go riding of a fine June morning. 'It makes me sick at my stomach. I shall be as proud as the devil. . . . Pray burn this. Adieu, dear Suke. P.S. I went Thursday but nothing was said; I won't go jiggitting for ever if I hear nothing I can tell him.' Yet as late as June 18th the King, speaking at St James's as loudly as if he did not care who heard him, exclaimed to Sarah with desperate fervour, 'For God's sake remember what I said to Lady Susan before you went to the country. Believe that I have the strongest attachment.' Sarah did not know what to do, say, or think; and the courtiers stepped up their toad-eating in a way she found really ridiculous.

Perhaps the King hoped to wring from Sarah some like admission that might mitigate his fate. 'What he did intend I can't imagine' Fox complained, like many a brother-in-law before and since. On the morning of July 1st the King wistfully told Sarah that he thought the Duchess of Portsmouth (Charles II's mistress) was a very sensible woman and one whose family had added lustre to the English scene. But an honest mother, Sarah Cadogan, and an honest grandmother, Anne Brudenell, had come between Sarah and that Breton adventuress of a great-grandmother; and this statement evoked no reply. This was his only slip. Earlier he had been heard severely brushing off a courtier who had advised him to make an unorthodox pass.

Summoned for that afternoon, the Council was informed that King George III was formally affianced to Princess Charlotte Sophia.

The most surprising thing about this whole episode was the calm and sense displayed at this point by Sarah. 'Does not your chollar rise at hearing this' she asked Susan, 'but you think I daresay that I have been doing some terrible thing to deserve it, for you won't be easily brought to change so totaly your opinion of any person; but I assure you I have not. . . . He always took pains to shew me some prefference by talking twice, and mighty kind speeches and looks; even last Thursday, the day after the orders were come out, the hipocrite had the face to come up and speak to me with all the good humour in the world . . . what business had he to begin again? In short his behaviour is that of a man who has neither *sense, good nature,* nor *honesty.* I shall go Thursdy sennight; I shall take good care to show I am not mortified to anybody, but if it is true that one can vex anybody with a reserved, cold manner, he shall have it I promise him.

'Now as to what I think about myself, excepting this little revenge, I have almost forgiven him; luckily for me I did not love him and only liked him, nor did the title weigh anything with me, so little at least that my disappointment did not affect my spirits above one hour or two.

'I did not cry I assure you, which I believe you will, as I know you were more set upon it than I was. The thing I am most angry at, is looking so like a fool . . . if he is so weak as to be governed by everybody I should have but a bad time of it. Now I charge you, dear Lady Sue, not to mention this to anybody but Ld and Ly Ilchester, and desire them not to speak of it to any mortal, for it will be said we invent storries, and he will hate us all anyway, for one generally hates people that one is in the wrong with and that knows one has acted wrong, particularly if they speak of it, and it might do a great deal of harm to all the rest of the family and do me no good. . . . We are to act a play, and have a little ball; I wish you were here to enjoy them, but they are forwarded for Ste, and to shew that we are not so melancholy quite.'

Family emotion now centred upon the bridesmaid question. Sarah's suitable age, and her rank, would oblige the Royal family to ask her; but of course she must be indignant and affronted and must decline. Kildare was violently against it, his wife for; Caroline Fox told Sarah she would be 'mean and dirty' if she accepted, Henry Fox told her to go by her own feels. Even Susan disapproved. 'Why refuse it and make a great fuss' Sarah asked Susan. 'Those that think at all about it will say perhaps that I want spirit and pride, which is true enough, for I don't dislike it in the least, and I don't like to affect what I don't feel, tho' ever so right. You have the happiness of having a proper pride, which I am not endowed with. I was always of opinion that the less fuss or talk there is about it the better, and to let it drop to the world. But to him and his sisters I was and always will be as high and grave as possible.' Being a bridesmaid was, she pointed out, by far the best way of seeing a royal wedding.

Henry Fox was indignant at the brush-off, but Sarah's resilience soothed him. 'Her mare is lame and her squirrel ill,' he wrote to his brother. 'These two misfortunes do really vex her. The other sat very lightly upon her indeed.' The squirrel and the mare both died, but Fox was pleased to note that Sarah seemed comforted by a hedgehog that she had rescued from the haymakers and brought in to breakfast. But he blamed Bute; and the difficulties of racial integration added to his anger. 'Every man has at some time or other found a Scotchman in his way,' he later complained, 'and everybody has therefore damned the Scotch; and this hatred their excessive nationality has continually inflamed.' But his hopes of a peerage were not dashed; soon he was made Lord Holland, and 'the sudden and great rise in stocks has made me richer than ever I intended or desired to be,' he declared later, though 'obloquy generally attends money so got'. He continued very indignant with the George Lennoxes, whose untimely backing of the Newbattle affair had helped to spike Sarah's guns. Her liking for Newbattle had been 'more a commerce of vanity than of love'; she had simply wanted to prise Lord Newbattle away from Caroline Russell, whose daughter-pushing mother, the Duchess of Bedford, was the aversion of all. This lady soon afterwards secured the Duke of Marlborough for her daughter, by a series of machinations which Fox declared made everybody sick; though perhaps his own machinations over Sarah had not been totally blameless.

He backed her up over the bridesmaid question—'Well, Sal, you are the first vargin in England and you shall take your place inspite of them all and the King shall behold your pretty face and repent.' 'He was ashamed and well he might,' Fox reported after the wedding. 'The Coronation is fixed for Sept 22nd. It will save the lifes or at least prolong the lifes of a great many partriges.' An element of embarrassment continued to hover over the wedding; and at one point Sarah, dressed magnificently in silver-embroidered satin and a high headdress, was obliged to back nervously away, pointing out that she was not the Queen. Lord Westmoreland, a very old and partly blind Jacobite, had at last been persuaded by friends to attend the Court for this Hanoverian celebration. Vaguely aware of her looks and dignity, he went down on his knees before Sarah, the prettiest Stewart of them all. 'He always liked Pretenders,' some wit hastened to point out.

In the undying tradition of writing nonsense when reporting on royalty, one excited and embroidering witness insisted that King George's eyes, during the wedding ceremony, never left the chief bridesmaid's face; but with the best will in the world, this is an impossible feat; unless the bridegroom happens to have eyes in the back of his head.

III

It was felt by all her family that there would be no peace till Sarah was married. With a great effort of will she refused Lord Erroll, 'not without tears at seeing so great a man for an hour upon his knees'; it really would have been much easier to say yes and get him off the floor again. He was known as the mighty Ajax, was fourteenth earl and a great bigwig in Scotland, but somehow too old for his age and pompous with it. 'So resume your good opinion of my resolution,' she told Susan, 'for if I am not encouraged I shall never arrive to perfection.' For distraction from these emotional toils Sarah read through the *Iliad* again and wished very much that she had Susan there to read it with her, bought a new dressed sack, had her hair coiffed by Monsieur L'Estoret *'en perfection'*, played quadrille with the Keppels and Russells and Lord Carlisle, and went to the Birthday in a gown of garter-blue satin with a white and silver body decked with garter-blue trimming, where Lady Northumberland complained to her that the crowd was so great that one could not even *walk* gracefully.

Lord Newbattle was still around; being safely regretful in the middle distance—'I will keep out of her way for fear of loving her . . . I have lived in a kind of Hell to forget her . . . I should have made a damned bad husband.' Sarah sent him soothing messages: she liked to end up friends. Although the mighty Ajax had even wept while making his offer—'we are on civil and friendly terms as if nothing had happened: that I like.' In pursuance of this principle she later visited the King and Queen and was kindly received; admired their fine handsome baby boy, and was ticked off by Caroline Fox for kissing it and by its nurse for calling it a fine child instead of a fine prince. Her Fox nephews were good company but Ste departed to the university, urging Aunt Sarah as his final piece of advice not to go to plays and operas too often and not to refuse a good match when she could get it. Charles James was in a mood; 'as disagreeable about acting this play as he can be,' she told Susan, 'he won't learn his part perfect, won't rehearse, and in short, shews plainly that your not being here is the reason he won't enter into it and be eager, which you know is the only way of going on with comfort.'

Her marriage to Charles Bunbury in the summer of 1762 took them all by surprise. 'Mr. Bunbury is a fortunate man,' Henry Fox considered. 'Not rich enough, but 'tis a match of her own making, and happiness don't depend on riches. Her least qualification is her transcendant beauty.' The bridegroom in fact was not pushed for money, being the son of a well-off baronet with two substantial Suffolk properties. He was handsome and fashionable and a popular character, and also a bit of a fop; but he lived in the country, was even fonder of horses than Sarah was herself, and she felt for him a steady affection that seemed to her like love, so stealthily had it come on.

The usual arrangements creaked on above the heads of those principally involved. All were agreed that so young a couple were bound to overspend their income and that therefore it had better not be too large in the first place. Her elder brother hoped that Sarah's portion of £8,000 would not be asked of him 'in principle' before the

(Seven Years) War was over: the signing of peace would make it possible to get some of his capital out of France. 'The young lady makes it her choice to have no pin money' Henry Fox wrote to Sir William Bunbury. 'As to jointure the D. of Richmond, Lord Cadogan, Lady Caroline and I all think that we must not be content with less than £1,000 a year rent charge.' To Mrs Vesey who asked Sarah to dinner without her affianced, Fox wrote in a more flippant vein:

> Be it known to Mrs. Vesey
> Without my Bun I can't sit easy.

Views on Charles Bunbury varied. He was a member of Dr Johnson's famous literary club, and a fashionable figure on the Turf. Walpole called him 'a chicken orator', and in the House he was mockingly known as the infant Hercules. Reports on his private life were not glowing. It was all a bit of a *Mariage à la Mode*, and Sarah, just turned sixteen, parentless, and dazzled by Bunbury's elegant up-to-dateness, pressed on willingly enough. It was a good match for everybody; Sarah was the grander and Bunbury was the richer. The blaze of family approval, which meant a great deal to her, obscured any lack of warmth elsewhere. 'I think you are so lucky to meet with a person that has such a universal good Character, that I'm delighted that its to be,' Louisa rejoiced. 'Lord Palmerston who knows him very intimately gave him the most aimiable character that could be, you may guess that made me very happy.' Her own hopes of breeding were come to nothing again but she would not be cast down; 'one is never so happy as when one is at home in the country. Sometimes,' she went on, her mind casting back to Bunbury, 'them wild people do turn out very well.'

'You call Mr. B. an old story, not justly for its quite a new one I think,' she had told Susan in December. 'He has what is called followed me constantly whenever I have been in town, I have not put myself in his way . . . his conversation is generally loud and of indifferent subjects, only broad hints now and then that he likes me . . . if he says no more he is a Shabby Dog. . . . He has got a free access into this house by coming to see Ste and talking politics to Mr. Fox. He is worse than Lord Shelburne I think. I have worried you with a tiresome letter about myself. . . . Prince Prettyman might have a little share in a refusal (if I had an offer), yet he had not the least with regard to Ajax, upon my word he had not. . . . In your answer call Mr.

B. the Marquis, for he is so like a Marquis in a French storry book that I doat upon that name for him. . . . Lord Shelburne is here *caccling*, that's no news, but its for want of better. I dread my sister's persisting in the quarrell with Ly George, I only want her to visit in as formal a way as she pleases, but not to give the town such a fine story as they will make of a B. and S. not visiting: its like the Finches family, is it not, and that is so horrid I think one should avoid it if possible,' she concluded sensibly. No more of Mr B., but from Barton, Suffolk, in June, a letter informs Susan that she likes this place vastly: 'they let me go my own way here and when once I do that I am comfortable'; and she is hers sincerely, S. Bunbury. To her sister Emily Sarah wrote a wonderfully un-reassuring postscript. She had not been frightened on her wedding day as Louisa had been, but today, the second of her married life, 'I am ten thousand times more terrified. Hers was shyness at first, which one always gets the better of; but real dislike I am sure is not so easy to get over.'

But get over it she did. By September she was trying to control pangs of jealousy over Bunbury—'I am in a constant fear of making him angry, for though he loves me, yet not one in ten men like to have their wives tagging after them constantly, I can see he don't like it, and I will get the better of it.' She was never going to flirt again. 'Indeed my dearest siss, I torment you with talking of myself; but I am very selfish, and cannot resist the pleasure of telling my thoughts to you, who I love so excessively . . .

'Are not you glad of this charming peace? All the world will go to Paris . . . I shall like it very much . . . but fear very much that I shall get into a routing way; and I have set my heart upon being *settled*.' Did Emily think Lord Kildare would possibly allow the Fitzgerald boys to come away from Eton for a week at Barton? There would be shooting, and all the hunting they liked, and 'it would make me vastly happy indeed. . . . Of course if anything I do disobliges you, you will tell me' she entreated Emily in conclusion of a letter not exactly breathing a satisfied contentment. 'I am making a little plantation here, and I doat upon it of all things,' she told Emily on November 7th. 'I shall grow as great a gardener in time as you I hope.' Emily's husband, James Kildare, would not let the boys off for the week from Eton: he was strict: Sarah understood him. 'I have a different love for Lord Kildare than for Mr. Fox or my brothers, for I look upon him as a father and would not do anything without his approbation. I hope that he will like Mr. Bunbury . . .'

Louisa was glad to hear how well liked Sally was in Suffolk, and by all the Bunbury family, father-in-law, sisters-in-law, etc., 'for I know well enough you can do anything well, when you have a mind, you Creature ... Think of poor Mr. Conolly getting so drunk t'other night that he was sick for two days, the poor soul was drawn into it ... If the Queen takes to pigging every year London will always fill about this time, which I should think very disagreeable and very inconvenient to most people; she should think of that.' She told Sarah, 'the Duke of York says you are the only bride that has kept her good looks', and that the Bunburys together were reported everywhere as 'the prettyest couple imaginable'. 'Everybody says that Dear Sarah is more beautiful than ever this winter,' Louisa told her brother Richmond in February of 1763. 'I am told that the people of Suffolk say she is sufficient of herself to carry any election for Mr. Bunbury; don't say I said so but I hear terrible accounts of his coldness and reservedness. Yet while Sally doats on him his agreeableness to us is of no real consequence ... I own I rejoice at Mr. Fox's being made a peer, for then he will enjoy his health quietly and peacably.' Poor Emily had lost yet another little girl and had accepted this disaster without distraughtness—'You must more than ever admire her Religion, Temper, and Sense ... never the least cross or peevish or fretty.'

Marriage did not at once transform Sarah into a mature and sensible being. Her continued debbishness is not surprising; she was still only seventeen. 'Lord Ossory is an agreeable sensible man and I like him vastly ... I danced with Lord Petre, and he is a nasty toad and I longed to spit in his face ... O Tempora, O Mores! Master Jacky Swale never even thought of you. The agreeable Mr. Shute was so drunk last night that he swore at his partner Mrs. Harland, till she left him and took another. You need not envy me, for my devil of a horse is as lame as a dog, and Mr. B. has been coursing, hunting, and doing every pleasant thing upon earth, and poor me sat fretting and fuming at home with Lady Rosse; in short I am patient Grizzle to the last degree. ... As to politics I have renounced them and their vanities ... I have planted all the trees you bid me and others that I have thought of. I have fished out two cedars as high as a chair and flourishing charmingly; is not that a treasure? ... I hunted twelve miles one day which tired me to such a degree that I was as sick as a dog and at night I could not even touch a sausage ... Mr. Pitt has got the gout and soar throat and a fever, so there's an end of him for some time . . . Lord Granby is better, but he is very unlikely to live, poor soul; you should write a note to Germany to order him to live! . . . Lord Villiers, that little toad, pretends to be seriously in love with me. . . . Newmarket was charming, all the charming men were there. Mr. Meynell lost sums of money on a horse of my brother's beat by the little mare Hermione of Mr. Calvert; its name was Goodwood, and got by Brilliant; but I hear he has made up all his losses again at cards at Euston, where the Duke and all the Newmarket folks are; he, a fat wretch, has won everything on earth; poor dear Mr. Greville has lost . . . poor Lord Rockingham, thrown into convulsions and a fever by a surgeon, has been very near dying. . . . Mr. Bunbury is gone to Woburn and I am called the widow, and Mr. Fox exercises his wit upon the occasion. This cold weather keeps him very meek.

'Pray, are you absorbed in thought, or reading, or what, for you never favour your friends with your news?' But Susan was absorbed in far more serious business.

As Sir Thomas Bertram, of Mansfield Park, in the county of Northamptonshire, so well knew, amateur theatricals put ideas into people's heads. Thanks to the determination of Charles James Fox, the plays at Holland House had gained a professional recruit, Mr William O'Brien, a handsome actor with an impudent attractive Irish face and a great deal more skill and address than all the others put together; and he and Susan Fox-Strangways had fallen in love. The Ilchesters had refused to hear of their marrying—an *actor*! quite beyond the pale—but Susan was a young woman of considerable determination. She was having her portrait painted this spring of 1764, and on the day after her twenty-first birthday, setting out for her sitting, she despatched the footman who was with her to go back for a cap in which she was being painted. Round the corner was Mr O'Brien in a hackney coach; they were married at Covent Garden church and then drove to O'Brien's house at Dunstable, from whence they informed Susan's parents of what they had done.

Rage and consternation amongst Ilchesters, Foxes, Digbys, Devonshires and all places west; and Sarah, suddenly rather more grown up, spent the next few years mediating between the parents and their erring daughter.

Henry Fox and his older brother Stephen Ilchester reacted very differently to the elopement. Having himself made a clandestine marriage with Caroline Lennox—the Richmonds would have none of him—Henry was in no position to be starchy. Lord Ilchester's objections were very strong, but probably more moral than snobbish or financial: Susan had lied to him when she pleaded for a final farewell interview with O'Brien and then used it to plan the elopement. This, maybe, was the unforgivable act; for Ilchester was not a savage parent.

There was a moment in 1770 when his eldest son, Lord Stavordale, losing £12,000 on the roll of a single dice, had commented What a lucky thing I was not playing for high stakes, and even for this he had not been cut off with a shilling. Nor does the story of the Ilchester oak show Lord Ilchester up in an implacable light. Quartered with the army at Limerick, young Lord Stavordale had taken to meeting Elizabeth O'Grady, a pretty local girl, under its branches on the summer evenings. Her father, a poor but respected squireen, had felt there was no future in this romance and written to Lord Ilchester to tell him that his son was in danger of contracting an unsuitable alliance. A timely military command had whisked the young man back to London, and a month or so later O'Grady received a letter from a Colonel Mulholland who was visiting Limerick and who said that he knew Lord Ilchester well and wished to come in person to convey his lordship's most obliged compliments and thanks to Mr O'Grady. The hospitable squireen pressed him to stay for a week, at the end of which Colonel Mulholland said You have a sweet pretty daughter, but she seems inexplicably sad for one so young and lovely.

O'Grady pooh-poohed the suggestion; but his visitor went on pressing the point until the Irishman finally was cornered into admitting that his daughter had had an unhappy love affair, from which, as she was so young, he hoped shortly to see her recover. After a further few days of reverting to the subject Mulholland drew forth the information that the bar to the marriage was parental.

How, he wanted to know, could anyone possibly object to such a daughter-in-law? O'Grady, doubtless pausing as all Irish gentry did to point out that his family went slap back to Brian Boru, the High King of Ireland who had died fighting the invader at Clontarf in the year 1014, admitted frankly that his daughter had no portion; and at length, over port in the evening, that her young man's father was Lord Ilchester, so rich and grand that he would not for a moment consider such an alliance for his eldest son.

I am certain, said Captain Mulholland, that my friend Lord Ilchester would be very far from objecting.

O'Grady shook his head sadly. He could see nothing but sorrow, argument, refusal, and a heart still further bruised. How could the greatest friend speak for another man in such a case?

Colonel Mulholland could keep it up no longer. 'I am Lord Ilchester,' he announced with superb aplomb, 'and I welcome with pleasure so charming and good a wife for my son.' And Stavordale and Elizabeth O'Grady were married and lived happily ever afterwards.

There must have been something rudely flash and untrustworthy in his eyes about poor William O'Brien.

It took Lord Ilchester five years to arrive at financial forgiveness, under strong persuasion from his wife and from Henry Fox, now Lord Holland, who characteristically kept the wolf from the O'Brien door by giving Susan £400 a year and by finding her husband a job in New York: it was thought better to put the Atlantic between him and Papa for a while. O'Brien was a good actor, and his public also were enraged. Why should this chubby darling be swept from them and set to grow flax on the banks of the Hudson river?

This event, which rent a happy family in half, showed Sarah at her best. She had already given signs of a warm and imaginative heart, at the death two years before of 'my poor friend Car Hamilton, . . . One finds all one's love awaken at the danger of a person one loves. I don't think she ever knew how much I did love her, and I cannot help reproaching myself for not loving her more. . . . Your sweet letter is enough to make me love you more if possible than I do at present, for it shews your goodness of heart and friendship for me to the last degree . . . about my poor Caroline . . . I have one comfort which Louisa has not, and that is so true, sincere, and amiable a friend as you are . . . a partial friend, that I can trust with my faults.' She had warned Susan against her elopement, as a friend will; aware of the danger and not themselves enjoying the love. After the plunge, Susan underwent a miserable reaction; and it is in consoling her that Sarah, now nineteen, comes of age.

'The seeing of you always puts me in spirits; they are quite sunk to think I cannot go to you the minute you want me. When I think of you, and think of you in distress, it quite distracts me.

'I, that have thought so much about you, can foresee some prospect of content, if not of perfect happiness, then sure you must see more than even me, or you would not have taken such a step.

'. . . I don't know what reason and prudence might make me think, but affection and love for you pleads most in my heart, and I must hear you are as well and content as it is possible to be in your case. That you will have melancholy thoughts at times I do not doubt, I should not love you if you had not; but sure that love that pleaded so strong against your duty may make you happy now; it must, my dear Ly Susan, and I am sure it will, at least I judge by myself; I think Mr. Bunbury's love and attention would make me happy whatever happened to me. It won't prevent me feeling miserable at times as I now experience, but yet I think from what I feel myself you may expect great happiness; don't my dear, give way to your low spirits, not only your but your husband's happiness depends so much on that, that you must get the better of yourself, and if you are inclined to be chearfull never think it wrong in your situation, for as I told you, your whole business is to please him.

'As to your distress in changing house, be above the fear of that trouble; it only appears bad to you because you're melancholy, don't make a misfortune of what is really none, let things take their chance . . .

'I know I seem to talk nonsense, but I stand to my text; when my spirits are good all situations are equal to me with a person I love, and the more I have to employ my attention and time, the better my spirits are; besides you are not *nice*, and you have sense enough to find amusement in anything, at least you *could*, and its very hard if it should fail you now. . . . I am certain half my faults arise from being too much at my ease, I must be in pursuit of something, and so must you, I know. It is equal to me what it is; I had rather it was something in which I might oblige Mr. Bunbury, but when that is not the case tis ten to one I shall do wrong. You cannot want occasions of pleasing Mr. O'Brien. . . .

'Can you, my love, think that I would give you up, or that Mr. B. loves me so little as not to feel the distress you are in; indeed you mistake us both; I cannot see you yet, for I think your poor mother and father want me more than you can, and I really am so miserable I don't know what I say or do; all I know is I cannot do anything that will add to their misery now. . . . I am so delighted to hear you are better; God bless you, dear soul, think that I love you the more you want my love; Adieu, my sweet dear. . . .'

After all these admirable sentiments she was unable to resist a frivolous postscript at the end of the month. 'I was at Court and

P.W.' (Prince William, afterwards Duke of Gloucester) 'did not enquire after you but he looked very dismal.'

Louisa's views on mortality and morals floated over. She reported that Susan had told her that Sarah was behaving like an angel to her in this *crise*. 'I don't know whether for the sake of one's friends Death would not be more welcome, for then one is secure of their happiness . . . you know my opinion of them kind of things is not the common one, but I do think that marrying the person you like is so much the first thing to be considered that everything else ought to give way to that . . . you should comfort her as much as possible by trying to pursuade her she has not acted wrong; for as the thinking herself bad cannot unmarry her, and the feeling guilty to a Person of her quick sense and feeling might throw her into a melancholy that would make her ever after miserable, it is absolutely necessary that she should be comforted as much as possible,' Louisa concluded, handsomely anticipating the findings of Freud. How sad that she could not persuade Tom to have an actor to stay! 'I wish so he was an Ensign or any other Profession but what he is.'

The cruelty of the London gossips was not to be taken into account; malice was an infectious disease that people inevitably caught in London. 'I always hated London and shall now more than ever, the greatest punishment would be to make me spend my life there . . . in the country we can be happy together and not at the mercy of infernal wretches. I don't think I can ever be good in London, and certainly not be what I call charitable, which is having a good opinion of people; one's ear grows so accustomed to hear people abused, that one grows not to mind doing the same. . . . If Susan can once reconcile herself to the having disobliged her Father and Mother there is nothing else to make her unhappy, for with her good sense she may set herself above feeling little worldly mortifications, which in fact are not mortifications and are only made so by people's vanity.'

They were growing up, out of feckless girlhood and into the actualities of life. Even mild Louisa suffered from slight mamma-in-law trouble—'Lady Anne Conolly is a very good kind of woman but I don't doat upon spending my days with her.' And Tom, though Louisa recounts nothing of this, was losing ever more out of his thought-to-be bottomless coffers in gambling. Auntliness, if not motherhood, was settling in on them. Even beautiful Sarah was known to the young Fitzgeralds as Aunt Bum, except for 'pretty little Edward', who charmingly referred to her as Sasarah.

Things were criss-cross. Sir William Bunbury had died in June and Charles had been in prolonged low spirits. They were rich, and childless, and Charles became bored with extreme ease, and for all his good nature, was neglectful; and except during the flat-racing season, hurried away to London to gamble and to take a rather sketchy part in politics. Lord Holland's recent part in politics had been more than doubtful; he had been described by the newspapers as a wolf and a hyena and was made ill by it. Ste was very much in love with Miss Greville and it was not prospering. The O'Briens were discovered to have left behind debts of over £2,000 and Lady Ilchester (who had been the rich Miss Strangways) was secretly and sadly paying them off herself in order not still further to enrage Lord Ilchester. It was difficult, Sarah complained to Susan, to go on defending them from charges of extravagance when Mr O'Brien had had his portrait painted before leaving England and had had the bill sent to Lord Holland. She reported him 'much displeased at your accounts, swords, guns etc. for Mr O'Brien, debts of £2080-15s.-4d. For God's sake my dear dear soul, don't give room for their anger any more.' She had been told not to mention Susan's name to Lord Holland, 'but I am certain we shall easily work on his good nature to forgive you, you know him too well to doubt his goodness: when you compare him to any other uncle upon earth you'll find the balance so much in his favour.' Susan's mother, too, was being 'sweet and amiable' about the debts. But Susan dourly reported that New York was vile and its inhabitants without exception vulgar.

Sarah bent herself to cheer, to amuse, to encourage. 'I long to know how Mr. O'Brien and his flax go on; has he got the instruments to work it yet? I beg my compts to him. . . . I have begun my gown, its vastly pretty and I love it vastly, the stripes go on like lightening, but the flowers are a little tedious. . . . The race at Euston was the prettiest thing I ever saw; I doated upon it, for I rid on my beautiful Weazle, who was gentle enough to let me gallop backwards and forwards, so I saw the whole course. Mr. Bunbury is quite a determined horse racer. . . .'

This was really the crux. How many marriages, in England and Ireland have been eroded, down the centuries, by the horse? Bunbury's concentration was to some effect: he won the first Derby with his horse Diomede in 1780. But by that time he had lost Sarah.

*

'I do not like your letters the less for their silliness,' Sarah assured Susan; rattling on likewise with any nonsense that might lift the gloom of exiled Susan, stranded on Long Island.

'Ld Carlisle has been here from Cambridge, he is grown very tall and is really the most agreeable young man I ever saw. . . . The Duke and Dss of Grafton are absolutely parted; he allows her £3,000 a year, the reason of their parting is only that their tempers don't suit, all this looks as if they would soon be friends again.' The Duke of Gordon had been ill for weeks and was thought to be working up for his father's madness. 'The Princess of Brunswick is brought to bed of a bratt, and they say she has not been taken care of, and that the Prince is not good to her, but I don't believe a word of it, do you? The Duke of York has £3,000 a year added to his income which makes £15,000 a year, he is in great spirits and has begun giving balls; and the Duke of Gloucester is following his steps and has supped at Ly Harringtons and trots about like anything. The Duke of York's house is furnished with the furniture out of Hampton Court. . . . I don't wish Sir Francis Delaval ill tho' I own I can't help feeling my bile rise at the thoughts of him; I forgive him *as a Christian*, but I own I hate the sight of him. . . . The Opera is in great fashion. . . . The Duke of Gloucester is desperately in love with Lady Dowager Waldegrave; its a falling off I think from your little cunning face to her insensibility. Lady Tavistock is breeding and very sick and there is a sad fuss kept with it; the D. of B. ordered Russel Street to be new paved because it was dangerous for her. . . .' (The end-product of this particular tizzy was John Russell, great-grandfather of Bertrand ditto.)

'Sir Charles Coote is come to England and is finer than ever; he was desired by the Queen to dance a minuet at Court, because she heard he danced so well, so he set off, and twisted and twirl'd about most prodigiously. . . . Ld Shelburne is to be married to Ly Sophia Carteret, it has been about this 12 months but is only now declared: its a very proper match I think don't you? . . . Do behave well my dear Netty, its the surest way to move the hearts of the people you depend upon. Charles' (Charles James Fox, now 16) 'is violently in love with the Duchess of Hamilton, think of his riding out to see her, you know how he hates it. He is all humbleness and respect and never leaves her. I am vastly glad to see him improve so much. . . . Mrs Fitz Roy tells me she has heard of you from the Delaneys, and that you are vastly liked. . . .'

Not all was frolic: the extreme precariousness of 18th-century life saw to that. 'I fear poor dear Lord Holland is breaking very fast; the idea of his death is what I cannot use myself to in the least. . . . My poor sister Kildare is losing one more of her little girls I fear; she is ready to lie in too. . . . Ly Digby is dead; she came to town a fortnight ago with child.' And soon Lord Tavistock had fallen off his horse and broken his neck and his poor wife's 'quiet composed way will make her suffer much longer than almost anybody'.

The financial row banged on boringly. 'I can write of nothing but these vile accounts now, for I hear of nothing else; perhaps nobody will name them to you and then you'll think I make it worse than 'tis, but indeed I do not. . . . I send you your mother's answer to my letter as I think it kind and sensible beyond what I can express or conceive; indeed she is charming . . . I do not mean that you are ungrateful, for I own you are not, but you grumble at everything you can and the great fault you have and that which Lord Holland is more angry at, is that you will not use the uncommon understanding that you have. . . .' Susan replied with a crisp telling-off of Sarah's frivolity. 'Believe me,' Sarah agreed 'I have thought it, and am as much displeased at my giddiness as anybody can be, . . . for I have thought very seriously lately, and don't see why I should behave like a *silly vain fool* when I am not one. . . . I do firmly intend to be more exact in my behaviour.' She had just met Lord Newbattle again and not so much as flicked an eyelash at him. 'We shook hands and promised always to take one another's part if we were abused upon any subject, but to have little or no conversation together. My sister Holland told Louisa that she had observed me and Lord N. and that it was impossible to behave better than I did, so you see I am very pert upon this good behaviour of mine and its so pleasant to feel one does right that I never intend to feel otherwise again.'

This resolution was faintly dented by a visit to Paris with Lady Holland in the spring.

They set off in April 1765, Lady Holland, Ste, Charles James, Louisa Conolly, Sarah, and the kind of timeless family friend that is called Tatty, and whose improbable name upon this occasion was Mr Clotworthy Upton. Sarah had never been abroad since the days when she had bowled across France over the Loire to Aubigny in her father's coach, with a train of sixty servants and fifty-two horses, as a little girl of five. 'I am so taken up with everything I see that I hardly know where I am. The town is beautifull, and the people so genteel, that its a real amusement to drive about the streets; I have seen no beauties yet. . . . The houses are dirty and cold, but yet I own I like the stile of them infinitely.

'The Opera is the most ridiculous music you can imagine; 'tis most like to Mrs. Clive when she immitates an Italian singer, than to anything I know, but the dances and the scenery is beyond anything I ever saw. The actors have all been quarrelling and Mlle Clairon talks of going into a convent.' Garrick had had an enormous success in the Paris theatre; they had met him at Calais on his way home. In May 'we were at L'Ile D'Adam, a place of the Prince de Conty's, its very pretty and an agreeable house. He is the most agreeable man that ever was, he is about 47. He is like my father's picture but handsomer; in short he is delightful. Louisa and I both doat upon him, for their is no sort of attention that he did not shew us, and indeed he is the same to all his company. . . . There are very few handsome women at Paris: the Dss de la Vallière, who is 52, is the handsomest woman I saw. Her face is now as beautiful as an angel and really looks only 25; her person is bad, but she hides that with a cloak. The Pss of Monaco is reckoned a great beauty, at home she would only be a very pretty woman. The Pss of Chimay is my favourite.'

'I like Paris of all things,' Louisa Conolly, married six years and now twenty-one, informed Lord Holland, who had been too unwell to come. 'Sarah and I are delighted at the people's being so kind to us; I would not have come with anybody but my sister Holland for the world, for they do doat upon her so much that everything that belongs to her they like.' The Hertfords too had been very civil; their house was beautiful, 'quite a pallace'. 'I must tell you that Sally learns to dance and to be graceful from a famous dancing master here, who desired her to leave off biting her lips before that she attempted to do anything, for he said she could have no grace with that abominable trick; however I think he will spoil her, for she walks with such an air, that you would not know her to be the mean wretch that she is at other times! She and I went to St. Cyr the other day, and one of the nuns told us that if we would kneel and pray to the relicts (sic) of a saint that was there, we should have children, for that the Dauphine had never had any children till she had; so that you may be sure that we immediately began our prayer: if we succeed we will send the Dss of Richmond there.' For the good-

CAROLINE
m. Henry Fox, afterwards 1st Lord Holland

EMILY
m. (1) James Fitzgerald, 20th Earl of Kildare,
afterwards 1st Duke of Leinster, (2) Mr William
Ogilvie

LOUISA
m. Thomas Conolly of Castletown

Victoria and Albert Museum, Crown Copyright

SARAH
m. (1) Sir Charles Bunbury, Bt. (2) Colonel
the Hon. George Napier

natured Duchess of Richmond, like Louisa and Sarah, was childless, and obliged to fall back on cherishing her husband's little illegits and taking them to the sea for their healths.

'Ste is reading a play,' Sarah informed Lord Holland in this same letter, 'and I cannot write very much, but I must tell you that Ste and I are grown very thick. Charles is as mad as a dog at it, and really takes it very ill of me . . .

'Oh, bye the bye, I suppose my sister has told you how well we were received at Marly, and how we luckily saw the King and the Royal family, but she has not told you . . . he embraced me twice, and that one of the Seigneurs said, "*En verité, c'est trop, Sire*". "*Je ne sais si c'est trop, mais je sais que ça me plait,*" says the King. Is it not charming? Now don't go and repeat this nonsense to everybody I beg.'

It was of course very charming to be kissed by Louis XV, once because she was a duke's daughter and therefore entitled to it, and twice because he liked it. And she could not help warming to the French, because they so liked her. Was there perhaps a brighter life to be lived than a long haul in Suffolk with a man who genuinely preferred horses? England was in the throes of a political crisis and she and Louisa came home on June 2nd into the midst of it, 'the Bedfords most prodigious glumpy, the K. still sulky'. 'The fidget they are in is not smoke you may immagine.' The summer wore on anti-climactically. Bunbury owed his seat in the Commons to Bedford influence which was awkward for Sarah as she believed it was this faction that had ousted her dear Henry Holland. One of the Bedford contingent, Weymouth, was now appointed Lord Lieutenant of Ireland with Bunbury as his Secretary: the anticipated delights of this move were dashed when Kildare announced that Weymouth was so unpopular in Ireland that the Fitzgerald family could have no intimacy with the Bunburys, 'which will intirely destroy my pleasure there'. She was at Newmarket 'to see the sweetest little horse run that ever was; his name is Gimcrack, he is delightful', when the adminis-tration fell, whereby Bunbury lost this prospective £4,000 a year job. 'Ld Rockingham, the D. of Grafton, and Genl Conway kissed hand the day Gimcrack ran. I must say I was more anxious about the horse than about the Ministry . . .' Sarah concluded flippantly.

How was Susan? 'I reproach myself with my neglect very often but I never mend; I believe I shall go on doing so all my life in all those things where my intollerable indolence is concerned. . . . I own that for a time I was provoked at your manner of taking everything, and by hearing all your affairs talked over so much I worked myself up to be quite out of humour. . . . I trust my dear Netty that you'll forgive me, for you know me too well to expect me to be always reasonable; I recollect that I wrote to you in a monstrous passion once. When I am angry I am more absurd than anybody, for I write and say every nonsensical thing that enters my head. But I need not make myself uneasy about it, for I feel I love you too much to make it possible you can doubt it. I am in very low spirits just now, which puts all this in my head.' She had sent Susan French china, green and pink lutestrings, trimmings for dresses, reams of news about the latest fashions in words—'boar is a fashionable expression for tiresome people'—in clothes and hair-dos—'I am sorry for our English taste . . . among the common run of people here such figures as one sees at public places are not to be described'—but she wanted to send her something bigger, a real present. 'The thing I would choose for *myself* would be a very good horse; if the expense of keeping it is not an objection I think it a very good thing, but pray tell me your choice sincerely.' Susan opted for a chaise instead.

With their affection, their tiffs, and their presents, 'I intirely agree with Mr. O'Brien that it is like lovers. Indeed I cannot enough thank you for your eagerness to make it up, and I am very well content never to name it again.' Susan had still been angry when Sarah went to Redlinch in September to plead her cause with the Ilchesters, and on to Melbury—'how beautiful, all the orange trees and myrtles are delightful'—but had not got much forrarder with the male members of the family. It was nonspeaks on the subject of Susan; with father and brothers, and even sisters, till Sarah broached the subject, but Lady Ilchester was kind as ever. 'I wished very sincerely for eloquence to persuade what I had so much at heart, but it was in vain. . . . Income . . . was the only power or tie by which she could direct your way of life.

' "But, Madam," sd I, "must she always be dependent?"

' "Yes," sd she, "upon her mother; *that* is no very great misfortune. . . . If she will, she may be very well contented." '

Altogether, it had been a frustrating summer, and ended in grave sadness with the death of the Kildares' eldest son. 'It was impossible to know him and not to love him. His fever, which lasted three weeks, had prepared us all for the event, but indeed it was shocking to see him dying, as I did, for I scarce left him,' and she went with

Emily Kildare to Ireland for six weeks to comfort her and the surviving Fitzgeralds.

The silences about Charles Bunbury are almost deafening: increasingly Sarah's heart turns to her own family, though the rare references to her husband are uniformly loyal. 'I am grown to love Ste excessively, in my journey to Paris I grew to know him better, and I love him dearly now. I find he is vastly liked in general. Miss Greville's match with him is quite off, why I don't know; but he never proposed tho' he liked her. I think he takes to Ly Mary Fitzpatrick most; I wish it might succeed, for he will make any woman happy if his figure can be got over, and I do love sweet dear little Ly Mary: how happy I should be to have it in my power to make a stronger friendship with her . . . Ly Harrington wanted to get Ste for Ly Bell, but it would not do. I own I wonder at it, for 'tis not possible to see any woman more beautiful, . . . her face very expressive and lively. . . . Mr. Crew is a fine catch for any Miss, he is very rich and is a very good kind of man, but he is so prodigiously afraid of being married to, that he won't speak to a Miss.'

For the first time in her life Sarah began to be ill. She was at Barton with a fever for six weeks—no Charles Bunbury to soothe and comfort—and was concerned about Susan in the American troubles. 'I am like the vulgars, and fancy everything is savage but at New York . . . I feel quite frightened about these rebellions. Sure my dearest Netty, you won't be such a goose as not to do as you are bid, and run any risk to keep up your character of courage. I don't to this minute understand anything about the cause of it all; I am so far from a politician that I never should have asked if you had not been there, and when I did, I was not the wiser for it . . . the fever, tho' not dangerous, made me so low that I could not have wrote a word.'

Louisa, concerned, poured forth good advice to the young sister she was not able to come and see. If husbands, in 1766, did not wish to cross the Irish sea, wives could not do so either. 'Low spirits', Louisa insisted, 'come from the body's not being well . . . fix that in your mind and don't torment yourself with thinking you have done this thing or t'other thing wrong and foolishly . . . if you can't ride, take a good resolution to go out airing . . . at this time of year the King's Road grows pleasant when the spring is coming on, and the nosegays one gets give a chearful feel . . . pray my dear Sally where is the head would not be turned with the particular partial reception that you met with?' Two months of distraction and fun did *not* add up to a lifetime of selfishness. 'For God's sake do take care of yourself,' she urged poor London-bound Sal. 'This preaching sounds like an old nurse but I live in such dread of having you ill. We are delighted at Ste Fox's match.' The Duchess of Bedford had had the imperial nerve to call Sarah 'insincere, of all the absurd foolish things, she must be an absolute driveller,' and even Louisa's kind heart hardened.

Tom Conolly had survived a bad hunting accident and 'I feel so overcome with God's goodness to me that I can never have done thinking of the subject and have such pleasure in opening my heart to you,' she told Sarah. 'I always feel anxious about you when you are in town, for fear of your charming spirits getting the better of your strength.'

'How do your poor dear bowells do after it all?' Sarah countered sympathetically.

Sarah was 'troubled to find that the right of taxing America is thought so certain that it was not even put to the vote . . . of course it will make a riot. . . . The very little I know of politics is that Mr. Pitt is given up even by his friend the D. of Grafton, who owns that he is totally impracticable and that it is impossible for anybody to deal with him. . . . By way of news, Mr. Rousseau is all the talk, and all I can hear of him is that he wears a pellice and fur cap, that he was at the play and desired to be placed so that he might not see the King, which as Mrs. Greville says is "a *'pauvreté* worthy a philosopher". His dressing particularly I think is very silly. . . . He sees few people, and is to go and live at a farm in Wales where he shall see nothing but mountains and wild goats. *Autre pauvreté.*'

Poorness seemed to be about. 'Poor Ste is come to such an excess of deafness that I can't bear it, for I do love him so very much that it goes to my heart to see him so.' Charles James was once again hopelessly in love, 'poor soul, he's in a piteous taking', and Henry Holland 'so low that you can seldom get him to speak, and so touchy and peevish that the least contradiction hurts him from exerting himself so much . . . 'tis very natural that sickness should alter people's temper, yet I cannot bear to say it to anybody but you.' She herself had been 'sick, is it not ridiculous? . . . I am very well, only grown thin and as Lord Holland says, very like halfpenny ale. As to my phiz, it is grown to look older, I have less colour, and my nose has grown long, so you may guess I am not much improved. . . . I am passed the age of a girl, it is time for me to check my vanity . . . you see 'tis still vanity that carries me on.' For it was certainly not love.

Love, however, had raised its sweet head elsewhere. 'Miss Greville is to be married to Mr. Crew . . . I am sure you will be glad, for you liked her I know, and he is a very aimable man, and there is no harm in his having £10,000 a year you know. . . . Lady Harrington is as mad as a dog at Mr. Crew, because she chose he should marry Ly Bell, who is very handsome still but not married yet.' And Ste and Lady Mary Fitzpatrick were now 'the happiest of mortals . . . she is so free from all art and affection . . . that her character fully answers the greatest partiallity you may take for her from her manner. . . . Her voice goes to one's heart and leaves a sort of tenderness in it . . . my dearest Netty gains a friend by her in this family'; for Mary Fitzpatrick, in addition to every other grace, had been kind and generous in her views on Susan.

Rumblings from America went on. 'My brother is just awake, and bids me tell you that the repeal of the Act is passed in the House of Commons, and will be a very near thing in the H. of Lds very soon; he is viollent *for it*.' But many besides the duke of Richmond were not awake at all and the sad drama of obstinacy and stupidity continued to unfold, but did not prevent Sarah from sending Susan's chaise off to New York. 'You must know that there is now a rage in London for grey equipages, and Mr. Beauclerk came out in the most *fringant* equipage, all grey and silver, that ever was seen; now I was such a niny that I order'd the chaise to be so too, not considering that there is no flat space to make any pattern upon, and that the high varnish was the great beauty of it; so when it came home it was quite different from what I meant, and I was very mad and was going to send it back, but I considered that it was of as much use to you as if it was green, and that I should perhaps make you lose the season for it, so I let it e'en go, and ask you a thousand pardons for my conceit.'

William O'Brien, scraped willy-nilly off the boards and more or less transported to the U.S., had declined to grow flax and had resolutely opted out of all the jobs laboriously collected for him by the Hollands, Richmonds, Bunburys, and that industrious helper, Mr Clotworthy Upton. But like many another anti-establishment figure, he had blossomed into an admirably affectionate and faithful husband. It was not he but Susan who complained, remained low-spirited, refused to retrench. And what, Lady Ilchester asked, writing to Sarah to urge her once more to advise Susan, would happen when Henry Holland, so shaky a life, died, and his £400 a year died with him? Sarah tried again. 'I am vastly sorry to hear you are so much out of spirits . . . I had resolved never to say anything more to you by way of advice, because I know from experience how tiresome it grows and that it ends in one's hating the person that gives it, or in its losing all its weight . . . I wish you would write to me, and tell me why you intend to build if you intend to come away? . . . My dear soul, I do not wonder at your mellancholy letters, but do, if you can, be as little so as possible; being chearfull is not only one's interest and pleasure, but its a right thing and one's duty toward God, who never meant to make us miserable; if we make ourselves so, we frustrate His intentions.

'Compare your life with the greatest part of the world: you lived a perfect, happy, contented life till 20, you then married the man you loved and chose from the rest of mankind. . . . Have you not friends trying to make your income certain and independent and much greater than you could have expected, and have you not a certain and supreeme happiness in your good luck with Mr. O'Brien? You could not *know* his caracter; you trusted to chance; from his youth, spirits and situation he was *more* than likely to be inconstant; obliging him to leave his country was almost a certain way to make him grow cross, this you had reason to expect. He has proved to be sensible, good-tempered, aimable, constant, and the best husband in the world, is not this luck?

'Believe me good husbands are not so common, at least I see none like my own and your description of yours, from which I rekon we are the 2 luckiest women breathing and that we do not deserve it if we are not thankful for such a blessing every day of our lives. . . . I should be a monster of ingratitude if I ever made a single complaint . . . Lord what a long letter and I intended to say but very little. I'm very much tempted to burn this as I have done by many and many a letter that I have written to you, but tomorrow I set out for London and in 2 days for Paris and shall not find time to write if this don't go so I'll trust to you to forgive it. I will get some flower roots and the flower pots which you wanted.'

Susan took some while to forgive all this good advice, there was no letter from her for more than a year. But Sarah was preaching as much to herself in all these adjurements to content, in all this praise of what she called 'aimable' husbands. She had from early on unconsciously betrayed the shallow base of her happiness with Charles Bunbury. 'Pray now who the d-l would not be happy' she had asked, a year after marriage, 'with a pretty place, a good house, good horses, greyhounds etc. for hunting, so near Newmarket, what company we please in ye house, and £2,000 a year to spend? Add to this that I have a settled comfortable feel that I am doing so right, that all my friends love me and are with me as much as possible, . . . where is the wretch that would not be happy?' And she had raised silver pheasants and planted shrubs and bred spaniels and tried hard to make do without children. Somehow it was hollow. A kind of smart half-amused boredom set in. 'This devil of a frost hinders me, and so Mr. B. and I sit grumbling and scolding and growling; he because he can't course, and I because I can't hunt, and that I fear twill kill my dear cedars.' Later the realism is increased—'Charles, thank God is infinitely better, and indeed I think quite well, only I dare not say so, for he loves to be thought ill.' Life seemed clamped into this ordinary, dull mould; the set-piece of a prosperous, weary, cold-war marriage.

She was too live, too clever, too passionate, too much of a good thing altogether for a man who liked life to be a jolly potter with half-hearted politics, horses, dogs, and cards. Amiable Bunbury must have felt quite exhausted. 'Ste says that he would not marry either Louisa or I, for that one of us is always in the right and that he can't bear that in his wife; don't you think that must be me?' she had asked Henry Holland from Paris. And to Susan, 'you don't know perhaps that I am reckoned to govern Sir Charles; I really think it is true, but I use very little art about it, for the moment I want anything I tell him of it, and he is so very good and spoils me so much that he seldom refuses, so that it comes to the same thing as being henpecked Ld Holland tells him, only that it is *fort flatteur* for me. . . .'

Bursting with life and vitality, with affection and interests, full-blooded Sarah was altogether too much for smooth and elegant Mr Bunbury. And when, this winter of 1766–67, they set off for Paris after a long 'nervous fever' of Sarah's, the poor fellow was perhaps relieved that they were accompanied by a third, the tall and young Lord Carlisle, who had signed on in the capacity of hopeless adorer. It would allow Bunbury a chance to float off and buy horses.

IV

Life has now to be seen through other eyes, for Susan lost all Sarah's letters between 1768 and '75, and there are but a few written in '67 and '68. The other eyes were blind, in the case of Madame du Deffand, and extremely unreliable, in the case of the Duc de Lauzun. In defence of this hero it must be said that his journal was printed after his death and that there is no sign that he intended publication; it was simply a private gloat. As a recorder, he is not always truthful, owing to his inability ever to write down anything unflattering to himself. Never could Sarah have uttered such long and flowery speeches as he attributes to her, nor held such extravagant sentiments, but there are bits in the diary about her which read remarkably true to life—notably her habit of insisting on sitting down to a square meal just when he wanted to make a tremendous emotional scene. He had a way of falling into a dead swoon whenever the pace was hotting up; perhaps Sarah felt she must get some hot food down before having to set to work with the restoratives. He records every one of his swoons with faithful accuracy, for a trembling sensibility was then coming into fashion. Other witnesses have discredited de Lauzun on other matters, but he must sometimes have been telling the truth, richly embroidered though it is.

His seduction of Sarah—if indeed he did seduce her—reads true to form. He was a smart young man, and an old hand. Finding her surrounded in Paris by the duc de Chartres, Carlisle, and about eighteen other regular subscribers, he decided to try a different line. Disposing swiftly of two current mistresses, he opened the campaign by saying within her hearing at a Paris party 'She is not bad, but I do not see anything in her to turn a man's head. If she spoke good French and came from Limoges no-one would give her a thought.' But like Fitzwilliam Darcy he lived to unsay these words, although it is possible that Sarah, like Elizabeth Bennet, did at least have her attention caught.

'Do not waste your time on me. Do not speak of love unless you wish me to bar my door to you' Sarah is supposed to have said.

Lauzun, surprised, thought this was just the English form, and pressed on with his courtship undaunted. He tried all the tricks of the trade for some weeks and eventually won through to a declaration of love from Sarah by appearing in a state of distracted grief, with a chalk white face and a long and plausible tale of woe; and this too reads true, for sympathy with distress was Sarah's Achilles heel, and de Lauzun was skilled enough to throw himself into the part of the stag at bay.

Madame du Deffand told George Selwyn that Sarah's success in Paris was prodigious—'all our youth and fashion have had their heads turned by her. Although she is not considered outstandingly beautiful all the principals have taken her up and emulate her.' She thought Sarah sweet, lively, and polite, but believed that she received all this eager courtship more for the look of the thing than from genuine inclination—'I think she has sufficient intelligence to find our young gallants rather stupid'. Madame added that she feared Sarah was a coquette, and this was a damning indictment. In Paris the thing for a radiant young married beauty like Sarah was to take a lover discreetly and hang on to him until either she was ditched or else equally discreetly found a better, instead of all this harmless flirting with twenty young men at once which got no one anywhere and simply depressed the market.

Difficulties of Anglo-French communication obtruded between Sarah and Lauzun. When he pressed the point she explained to him slowly and carefully that there was a different ethic across the Channel. Though the French ladies took lovers as they took a glass of champagne, for the English it was a different thing. It was a shattering step which meant the loss of a whole way of life, of honest reputation, of a quiet mind and innocent sleep. In France also there was little danger in taking a lover, in England much. This, she added, does not always restrain us, but as we choose our own husbands it is less permissible in us to stop loving them, and the crime of deceiving them is never forgiven us.

All this reads not unlike one of Sarah's talks to Susan, and de Lauzun was amazed, regarding Sarah with the incredulous tolerance that most of the civilized French reserve for the surprising moral antics of the English. 'I do not wish to have a lover,' she had said in an extremely casual and unserious manner. 'Imagine whether I can have a French lover, who is as bad as ten others by the scandal he creates and the trouble he causes. And you especially, Monsieur le

Duc! You do me too much honour!' Thus Lauzun, in the afterglow of imagination. All the same, this unexpected mixture of rebuff and friendliness continued to intrigue him. He was on guard at Versailles, but he got leave of absence from his colonel; and when in early February the Bunbury coach bowled out of Paris with Charles Bunbury and Sarah up, de Lauzun bowled too. At a dark and dirty inn at Pont-Sainte-Maxime he was not best pleased to find himself obliged to share a bedroom with Lord Carlisle.

Madame du Deffand had continued to like Bunbury for his admirable good manners but was shocked that de Lauzun saw Sarah three times a day. 'No young woman of our world could behave as she does without being much talked about. However, the note among people here is rather one of astonishment than Scandal. She pleases, has naiveté, a caressing manner, is likeable.' 'Although she loves me warmly she grants me nothing' Lauzun mourned to his journal. Madame du Deffand thought he was being used as a stalking horse. 'I am pursuaded that Lady Sarah loves Lord Carlisle, and that idea makes me pardon many things in her conduct that I have found neither sensible nor in good taste without this motive' she told Horace Walpole.

In London the tale was taken up by Lady Mary Coke. This character, born a Campbell, had married a son of the Leicesters and parted from him after two years, to spend the rest of her life expounding upon human frailty with a moral tone as high as the cliffs of Dover, and whisking round from house to house in the hopes of catching out one of her friends in the act of producing an illicit baby. She met de Lauzun in London while he was paying his respects to the French ambassador; he had just handed Sarah into her chair and did the same for Lady Mary. It did him no good. 'Courtesy signifies nothing in a Frenchman,' she pointed out crisply. 'He has no advantage in his person which does not in the least convey the idea of his being of one of the most considerable families in France, and heir to one of the greatest fortunes. Lord Dillon told me he was sure he would not have less than fifty thousand pounds a year English. He married lately the heiress of the Duc de Boufflers, a young lady of sixteen years of age and in all respects amiable; but his attachment to my Lady Sarah seems as if he were insensible to her merit.'

De Lauzun, doubtless not uninvited, pursued the Bunburys to Barton in Suffolk, and here, by his account, Sir Charles shortly left them alone for some weeks. 'The time that I spent at Barton was certainly the happiest of my life' Lauzun declared at the end of it, though the right true end of love was not arrived at all at once, even in these propitious circumstances. When Sarah finally seemed about to give in 'she appeared so offended and distressed when I took a few liberties that I did not persist. This charming torment continued for several nights. I had ceased to hope for consummation, when, clasping me on one occasion with the liveliest ardour, she gratified all my desires. . . .' Sarah was just twenty-one, and having been publicly jilted by the best parti in Europe would perhaps have been more than human if she could have resisted de Lauzun, the pin-up of all Paris. De Lauzun is a proved liar, and the human race is so notoriously improbable that one cannot judge by probabilities. But the flat-racing season had not yet begun, steeple-chasing was scarcely yet invented, and in general very rich grand French dukes do not spend six weeks in Suffolk in midwinter just to admire the scenery. As against this is a letter which Sarah subsequently wrote.

Sarah now appears to take de Lauzun seriously, as if thinking the whole thing was a life arrangement. Why not, she suggested by his account, go off to the West Indies where she had relations who would befriend them? (What relations? they come into the story nowhere else.) Leave Paris forever? De Lauzun evidently had great difficulty in retaining consciousness at such a suggestion, and Sarah rather unsympathetically rode away from him. The West Indies were simply not in his scheme of things; and at this moment Sir Charles opportunely developed stomach trouble and had to be taken to Bath, and Sarah, with, according to de Lauzun, many extravagant protestations of undying affection, now gave him his congé. De Lauzun's reactions were predictable: he fainted dead away.

Life in England was too much for him altogether, and after swooning once or twice again in his attempts not to be brushed off, he fades from the picture, hurrying back to France in plenty of time for the Revolution, in which, in fact, he escaped demolition. Poor Sir Charles's stomach became much worse under the general strain of life and his doctors told him to go to Spa in France—'I hope it will agree with him which will comfort me for my trouble, but I own I am wore to death with routing. My spirits are vastly lowered since you saw me, I long much to stay here a whole long summer' Sarah told Susan in May from Barton; 'though I say it that should not say it, this place is very much improved since I came, there is not much alteration in the look of the whole, but a great deal in com-

fort. . . . Sir Charles has been very lucky at Newt and won with all
his horses, which delights him as you may guess. . . . I hear Ly Mary
Fox is with child; I'm not sure tis true, I hope it is tho' for it would
make Ste so very happy. . . . You cannot think how French I'm
grown, for I liked being one of the very few English women taken
notice of at Paris, it flatters one's vanity, and of course one thinks the
people very *sensible* that like one. Its a little troublesome here tho',
for I'm obliged to see them more here than I wish, and London
abounds in French.'

'I beg you will not forget to send me word whether you build your
house or no, and to give me a plan of it. I wrote you a long letter
about it last autumn, but you never sent me any answer, you monkey.
Bye the bye, I have no right to scold, for I wrote to my sister H. from
Calais to say I was going to sail in very stormy weather, and then
forgot to write to her from England, but took it for granted she must
be sure I was safe; you may guess how Lord Holland *gave it to me*
for my giddiness.' But of other giddiness Henry Holland seems
unaware, and he lived very much in the world.

Through the summer months the Bunburys were at Spa and cheerful
enough, it seems—'you need never ask a soul to eat, but dine at two
or three o'clock in peace. You may walk out in the street or in the
promenade close by all the morning, buy your own greens and fruit,
read the papers at the booksellers, go a shopping, or make parties
for the evening. After dinner you go on foot to the rooms, play ball,
or walk, make your own party and walk home (or in a chair if sick).'
Hours were early because the cure began at six in the morning; the
fountain was two miles from the village and the horses who took one
were *pénible* unless one had brought an English saddle with one. Sir
Charles Bunbury's stomach mended and he cheered up. 'I am in love
with Madame de Tomatis,' he wrote to George Selwyn.

George Selwyn was one of those rum characters that are thrown
up by all advanced civilisations and who make one have second
thoughts about advanced civilisations. He was a genuine necro-
philiac, his greatest pleasure was to watch a public execution. Short of
physical dissolution, he would turn to someone dying of love, hurrying from victim to tyrant and back again, feeding misery with
enough scraps of hope to keep it alive, and then injecting an occasional lethal dose of innuendo to increase the torture. It was his

delight to manipulate other people's lives, and he would go miles to see a really good corpse. But he liked the card room, dances, gossip; was excellent company, and strayed from time to time into a good natured action. A dying friend most beautifully summed up his character. 'Should Mr. Selwyn call, show him up at once. If I am alive I shall enjoy seeing him; and if I am dead he will enjoy seeing me.'

He now took a hand in the Sarah-Carlisle business. Sarah had forbidden this young man to write to her; but Selwyn merrily sent messages of a slightly distorted nature which further demented poor Carlisle, struggling vainly to be free; and at the same time he kept in constant touch with Sarah, danced with her at Almacks, and spread all the rumours which his fertile imagination could suggest. She became known as a fast woman; and how much flame there is below all this smoke it is now impossible to tell. No one (except perhaps Lady Mary Coke) could take seriously the words of *Town and Country Magazine*, that loathsome publication which is the chief evidence against her. Sarah herself, long before her trouble, always stoutly refused to believe London lies—'till I have better proof than the reports of this vile town I never will believe anything'; and she had insisted, when Lady Caroline Hervey married Vernon and was accused of carrying on with a lot of other actors, that the rumours were a pack of lies. 'This vile, scandalous, ill-natured world' she had apostrophized it, long before it turned its attention to her. 'This sounds viollent, but I'm in a rage just now with the world, for I hear every day such a pack of lies that it provokes me.'

The only concrete evidence against her was the discovery of her name, accompanied by that of the actor Powell, scratched on the glass window of a house of assignation; and this looks bad, were it not for the changeless instinct of the human race to identify itself with the more glamorous by scrawling their names up in public places. Sarah greatly admired Garrick, and expressed sympathy for the ages unborn who would never see him act; and Powell had taken his place whilst he was abroad on tour. In her only reference to him in her letters Sarah records that 'Mr. Powel, Holland, and Mr. Yates scream at one another like screech owls, and holloa their parts without any feeling or sense', a comment which does not seem to breathe ungovernable passion.

Whatever went on or did not go on, the rumours of it reached Susan across the Atlantic; and now it was her turn to scold Sarah, for that old shortcoming—giddiness. Sarah replied to her at length. Either she is telling the truth or she is an unconscionable humbug. She seems free of self-deception, but the pressures of the age drove many an honest person into humbug.

Susan had broken the silence of more than a year. 'After having long long waited for a letter, my dear Netty, I was more than recompensed for the delay by the charming, chearfull, pleasant letter I received a week ago,' Sarah told her.

'I will answer it exactly, my dear Netty, and must therefore begin with those same stories you say you have heard of me. You begin with that, and I must begin with thanking you for your kind, sensible, and gentle way of advising me; I am very conscious that the less a woman is talked of the better in general, and in particular upon such subjects. I will not say it is my misfortune to have met with people envious of my happiness, and try to excuse myself by blaming others; no, I will own the truth, I have had the vanity to love general admiration and the folly to own it . . . I have too often proved that my vanity got the better of my resolutions.'

Perhaps, like a debtor, she is owning up to the small debts and keeping the large ones hid? 'It would be much too long an argument to talk and justify myself (which I can do) of various things I have been blamed for, but be assured, my dear Netty, that my morals are not spoilt by the French; they are so totally different from my caracter and from what I was brought up to think right, that it would be having a very mean oppinion of me indeed if you thought 3 months could undo all that nature and custom had taught me. That I have in every action of my life kept up to the very good education I have had, is, I fear, too much for me to say, I believe it was scarce possible (tho' I have seen an example of it in Louisa, but she is an angel and I'm a weak, unsteady, thoughtless, vain creature), but still I do assure you it is not possible with a good heart to change so totally.' This rings true; and she wanted very much 'to make Sir Charles happy, to keep the affection and esteem of my relations and friends, to be treated with regard in the world', in that order; and in all these, specially the first, had succeeded beyond her hopes. 'I have not at present any guess of what or how you have heard of me. I know what might be the foundation of many stories, but they must have been improved, I fancy before they could reach so far. . . .

'I feel as if I have returned your very kind and affectionate advice (for indeed it is not a scold), with crossness, so must add more about it to assure you, my dear Netty, that I take it kindly of you', which was why she had entered into 'a sort of justification of myself . . . I have got a cross peevish way of answering advice, and that may have appeared in my letter, tho' believe me it is not in my heart. . . . 'Lord H. and my sister are gone to the South of France. I'm going to Ly Mary, who is near lying in; she is frightened at the thoughts of it, poor soul. . . . I have seen nothing of your familly this summer, having been at Spa. . . . Sir Charles has bought you a lottery ticket, but only on the condition that you will accept of it. The number is 58–800.' It is not a letter ringing with guilt or with justification.

By next February she was still hard at the job quest for William O'Brien—'Mr. Upton and I agreed it was not worth asking for anything under £500 a year, as its throwing away one's interest'—but a fresh drama was rehearsing itself and about the truth of this there is no manner of doubt. In her cheerful, mocking, affectionate way she had been fond enough of Charles Bunbury, spoiltness, boredom and all; had truly tried to cherish him and keep him happy. But now passion, like a whirlwind, appeared in her life. It lifted her right over the trees and into the next field, dropping her there with a resounding thump. Her fling with William Gordon is her first fully authenticated one, and it made enough noise for six. Perhaps she thought, if she had time to think anything, that she might as well be hung for a sheep as a lamb.

Lord William Gordon was impetuous and handsome, with dark red hair and a romantic pale face. His manner was alternately high-spirited or darkly brooding. He might have been accused of taking a leaf out of another Gordon's book, if Byron himself had not still been twenty years away from being born. William was the kind of character who would now have worn his hair very long: as everyone else then had very long hair this form of protest was not possible; he accordingly cut his very short. After King George III (too young), Lord Erroll (too elderly-mannered), Lord Carlisle (too lovelorn), and the general French admiration (not nearly lovelorn enough); after Bunbury (too bored), and de Lauzun (too excited), William Gordon seemed to Sarah dazzlingly live and real; an exact contemporary; generous, casual, wild, and madly attractive; one who would gang his own rebellious gait, which happened now also to be hers.

They met some time this winter of 1767–68. It is not known when, or how soon Sarah succumbed; but after six sterile years with Charles Bunbury she was instantly with child by William Gordon. This brought her up with a round turn: where children were concerned she was very far from being irresponsible. Unless they were the children of princes or very rich dukes, life for those born outside wedlock in this epoch was a prolonged martyrdom: (it seems to be the fate of such luckless infants to be born during times of living it up, and to mature during times of living it down.) Sarah went back to Barton and Charles Bunbury accepted the situation, out of kindness, indifference, or, as people afterwards thought, because he was glad enough to be thought capable of fatherhood and had had enough of club room jokes. Maybe he hoped Sarah would be more happy and settled with a baby. It was due in December. Later, Bunbury made a sworn deposition that he had not slept with Sarah since January.

A slight note of sadness creeps into Sarah's letters; her love for William warring with her deep love of home. They were going to Spa again for Bunbury's health—'journeys have taught me only to prize my dear old Barton and home the more . . . the trees do grow so fast that it does one's heart good to see them. Our library is almost finished, and is a charming comfortable room.' There were the horses, ever-loved; and the peacocks, silver pheasants, and other birds so tame that they came to be fed. The loved habitat, the friendly familiar faces, were seen and longed for as a drowning man looks on a native shore; but she turned to tease Susan all the same. 'I saw a gentleman that went with you to Quebec and that gave me a very exact and comfortable account of you. I hear you're very fat, but look very well. I'm sure your pretty little sly face is not altered; what would I give to see it.'

As for her own looks 'my phiz is grown rather course and older as you may think, and my nose grows longer, as you used to swear you saw it grow', she told Susan in May. 'I hardly ever ride now, but walk or drive about in a cabriolet.' Contrary to rule, she was very well, instead of being continuously off-colour as she had been these last two years. In June she was writing a letter in the third person from Henry Holland to Susan—'Ld Holland does not desire to vex Ly Susan, and finds he can't write without offending her. . . . For he is as sure that I shan't offend you,' Sarah continued delightedly springing out of the third person and into a more natural method of converse, 'as he is, that if he writ, he should. . . . Pray let me once more remind you of what he has done . . . Ld H. has been not only good to you but most astonishingly kind and generous . . . I have never named your mentioning being in debt to anyone, for I don't see the good of it, if it will make them angry. . . . My sister sends her love to you, and joins with me in wishing you would take yr £2000. Adieu, pray answer me soon, and do not write in a passion with me. . . . The patent is just come for the place for Mr. O'Brien; it is called, I think Secretary-Marshall-General for the Island of Bermuda. Adieu once more, my dear Netty, don't be angry with me, and be assured I love you.' But perhaps Susan was angry; and tore up all her letters for the next seven years.

From Ireland the ever un-jealous Louisa, ignorant of the baby's origin, rejoiced in its coming. 'It is absolutely impossible for you to guess my sweet Sally at the pleasure I feel in thinking of your situation.' Here was the steadying event they had all hoped for. 'I shall be so happy to hear when you feel the little Brat.' She hoped it might be lively. 'I do admire lively people extremely, my brothers are vastly pleasant, my Brother Richmond to be sure I do doat upon.' 'My sister Holland tells me you propose suckling your little Infant, I rejoice at that.' 'You are a most provoking little Toad' Louisa adjured Sarah in September, 'two letters to Emily and not a word of your being quick . . . Don't fret yourself with the fear of not suckling as that would be the most likely thing to drive away your milk.'

Six weeks after the baby was born (and acknowledged by the kindly indifferent Charles Bunbury and respectably christened in the chapel of Holland House with Lord Holland as godfather), William Gordon resigned his commission and Sarah left home, eloping with him to Knole, ruled over at this period by the wicked Duke of Dorset, delighted to encourage and shelter any form of goings-on. Here she was pursued by a horrified party from London: with tears and reproaches Caroline and Louisa persuaded her back to Holland House. Worse was to come for here, Lady Mary Coke had it upon the most excellent authority, Sarah had further staggered Louisa Conolly by her determination not to marry William Gordon 'for that he has not a good temper'. Which made it all the worse when she left home with him again, setting up house in Berwickshire, at Carolside, near Erlstone, a square white house lent them by one of the Homes. 'So wild a declaration and so devoid of shame or principles I have seldom heard from a lady whose birth and education must have instructed her with sentiments far different' Lady Mary Coke declared; and she could hardly get in and out of her carriage quickly enough as she whizzed round London being first with the news. In Paris Madame du Deffand had come under the influence of Jean-Jacques Rousseau—'he would prove that Lady Sarah's morals and her conduct are substantially in accord with the Golden Age, that the sentiments of her husband and her relatives are quite natural, and that she is a perfect model of sincerity and good faith'.

Temporarily indifferent to all this brou-ha-ha, William and Sarah wandered by the banks of the river Leader, along a path which they named the Lover's Walk. Romantic in advance of the Romantic Movement, they planted two thorn trees, so close together that their branches must inevitably entwine. Their relations wrote forcefully to them by every post, pointing out their folly, their wickedness, their inadequate finances. So little do times change, that a London acquaintance, begging admission to the house because of a rainstorm and hospitably received, was able to confirm the rumour and sell the story to the newspapers. The scandal was printed excitedly in all the London sheets: 'Lord W.G. and Lady S.B. . . .' Lord Bute may have congratulated himself upon his prescience.

The summer weather in Berwickshire, normally one of the drier counties, remained grimly wet; and a reaction set in. There was absolutely nothing to do; and if there is a thing the Scots and the English cannot be without it is something to do. In April Sir Charles Bunbury applied to the Ecclesiastical Court for a partial divorce and separation—'Lady Sarah Bunbury, being wholly unmindful of her conjugal vow, did contract and carry on a lewd and adulterous conversation with Lord William Gordon,' the lawyers gloatingly wrote. In Berwickshire, as the months passed, the conversation grew a thought more desultory.

Sarah became contrite and melancholy: William began to regret his regiment. Day by day the hills wept, and William's uncertain temper came into its own. Bunbury might or might not complete the divorce by an immensely expensive Act of Parliament; in any case it would take about eight years to effect. Sarah's sad elder sisters and brothers told their dear Sally that everyone in the family was quite ill on account of her goings on: Caroline was poorly, Lord Holland had had a relapse, Richmond had boils, Sir Charles Bunbury had shut himself up in shame at Barton. From the far north the Gordons weighed in gloomily to the effect that they would in no circumstances increase William's allowance of £500 a year: both duke and duchess were firmly of the opinion that Sarah would not be a good wife for William. Lady Mary Coke had it for a fact that Sarah was spending money 'like a drunken sailor', and *Town and Country Magazine* whipped up its circulation with talk of 'Messalina and Gordianus'. From this lush time Sarah's brothers and sisters were excepted. Even George, once thought prudish, forebore to reproach. Richmond and Emily mourned to each other: Louisa echoed the general distress, but 'tis amazing the pleasure some people have in making things worse. Would not any of us', she asked in May, 'run with open arms to the unfortunate Sarah and forgive her from our hearts? Consider what goodness of heart she has left . . . we must trust vastly to that . . . At present passion is so strong that reason does not operate, nor even Religion. Hope, which we can never be destitute of, must encourage us.'

More rain fell, the baby teethed and had rashes: it seemed likely that the divorce, even if forthcoming, would take half a lifetime to effect. William became still more moody and excitable; finally he rode away. In September he was reported to have set out for Rome on foot, 'with cropped hair and a knapsack on his back', accompanied only by a very large dog.

Sarah was less extreme. In any case she had the baby. It had had the good sense to be a girl; thus avoiding any accusations of jiggery-pokery about Sir Charles Bunbury's baronetcy. Sarah went to Goodwood with it, and here her brother Richmond gave her a home. To avoid embarrassment for his friends, who naturally could not be expected to sit down to a meal with such wickedness, he installed her in a small farm house in the park, and later built a little house for her. In these disgraced days he was always kind to her, not being a hypocrite, and having a mistress or two of his own. When, after eight years, her divorce was achieved, she went sometimes to stay in a retired way with her ever-faithful sisters, Caroline at Holland House, and Louisa Conolly in Ireland, or with kind cosy Aunt Albemarle at Stoke—'What's an old aunt fit for,' she would ask Sarah, 'but to make those she loves comfortable?' Lady Mary Coke found Sarah playing cribbage one day at Holland House with her sister Caroline and Charles James, and simply did not know where to look. Greatly daring, she accepted an invitation to sit down, and even played two rubbers in company with this monster of vice.

Nor did the hounding press let go. It was in that dangerous state when its freedom was scarcely trammelled by a very sketchy law of libel. *Town and Country* happily printed an imaginary letter purporting to come from Sarah in which she begged Bunbury in moving terms to forgive her and take her back. On February 15th, 1774, the *Morning Post* printed a bald assertion that Lady Sarah Bunbury was with child by her nephew, Charles James Fox. Not until two years later was Cosmo Gordon, author of this and equally scurrilous lies, found out; and even then, all that happened was that the other members of his regimental mess refused to speak to him. Henry Holland died three months after the publication of this particular squib, and his wife Caroline followed him three months later. Even Lady Mary Coke admitted that Sarah 'behaved with great affection to her ill sister'. Poor Ste lived only three months more to enjoy Holland House and plant more trees; and five years later his little wife Mary also died leaving two little children—'Good God! What an ending to all that once happy family' Sarah mourned. 'It tears one's heart to think of it.'

All was reconciliation and joy between Sarah and Louisa, who longed to 'mumble' Sally's child. 'I am so perfectly happy and contented about the essentials of your mind and conduct.' It was over; the lost sheep was back in the fold and they could talk about more festive matters. The little Fitzgeralds were acting a play, and 'Eddy was really inchanting; one was ready to eat him up.' This doomed darling had already enslaved his aunt Louisa—'almost too perfect a little being, having no fault but too much warmth of temper,' but even that was generally directed against himself. She tried not to be what she called 'partial', a grave crime in an aunt, but much as she loved them all, Edward had been too much for her scruples. 'Eddy's love for me is quite astonishing, not at all like a child's but that of a steady Friend, and I do assure you I depend upon it as much as if he was grown up.'

And as if forewarned of Ireland's fate, of Eddy's fate in Ireland's cause, she ended on a note of sadness. 'It is not possible to live in this country without perpetually feeling distress on account of the greatest number of its inhabitants which are poor . . . the most part without exagerration have a bare subsistence.'

In Sussex de Lauzun had already put in a solitary appearance. He got into Sarah's house by pretending to be a footman with a message from Holland House, and went upstairs and found Sarah giving supper to her little girl Louisa, who was considerably alarmed at this sudden incursion. He found Sarah 'wearing a simple blue dress . . . more beautiful and more seductive than ever before'. Her hair had been simply dressed, and un-powdered: they had had a two hour conversation and then de Lauzun had come away. Probably true enough; but de Lauzun could never resist extracting a full dramatic dividend. According to him Sarah had begged him to take charge of her child—'if she should lose me she would have no other chance of having a protector except yourself.' This is patent nonsense: Sarah had shoals of faithful sisters and cousins who were all falling over each other to be given charge of the poor little Holland orphans: never would she have bequeathed her daughter to a scatty Frenchman not her father and liable to pass clean out at the first breath of contrariness. It is characteristic of de Lauzun's odd mingling of fact and fiction.

This twenty-two-year-old girl who had kicked over the traces had now to pay the penalty for it in eleven years of virtuous solitude, a third of all the years she had lived. Castletown was a refuge, 'even Mr. Conolly seems to like my being here, and shows me so much kindness that I hope it is not disagreeable to him, and I'm sure it makes Louisa happy for she scarce passes a day without telling me that having me with her is one of the greatest pleasures she has; there is something so pleasant in being so sincerely loved and welcome.' Louisa too had long since come to terms with social obligations: she could not do with all the calling and the leaving of cards, and compromised by suddenly asking everyone in sight to dinner; and at Christmas time Castletown rang and glittered with a series of truly splendid parties. At other times people floated in and out with the minimum of formality, so that those who did not want to speak to Sarah did not have to make a conspicuous thing of it. She was sad to note that among these was Emily's charming mother-in-law, old Lady Kildare: Sarah respected her principles and understood it, but hoped in time to win her round to forgiveness.

For the King too there had been a painful moment. He was due to come down to the House to give his assent to the Act of Parliament— necessary to a divorce in the 1770s—in which it was publicly declared that the woman he had loved was an adulteress; but a face-saving formula was found. Henry VIII had not been asked to declare *Le Roy le Veult*, when he divorced Katherine of Aragon, so George III was let off an ordeal which his pride and his kind heart would have disliked; for in England as long as anything can be found to have happened before, everyone is perfectly happy about its happening again. Sarah was now Sarah Lennox again. Once the darling of Holland House, the ninth jewel of King George, and the rage of Paris, she was now a charming lonely skeleton kept more or less in the family cupboard. She could sometimes be seen in the distance taking her little girl for walks across the park, or to bathe in the sea at what she described as 'a little puddling bathing place of my brother's by the sea', a graceful figure bending over the rock pools, solitary in a world that would not 'countenance my fault'.

Upon this scene arrived the familiar Napier figure, tall, unlucky, handsome, and totally penniless. Nothing was missing—the hawk nose, the arched eyebrows, the wry humour, the indifference to public opinion, the extravagant sense of honour. George Napier also had the incurable Napier habit of always being a younger son; being sixth out of the ten sons of Francis, 6th Lord Napier. Generally considered to be one of the most active men in the army, and also one of the handsomest in an epoch when this advantage was freely canvassed, he was so strong that he could bend thick iron bars with his bare hands. He was a friend of Sarah's younger brother Lord George Lennox, and had fought in his regiment, the 25th, in Corsica, where he met and married Elizabeth Pollock, daughter of another soldier and 'as poor as himself'. Quartered in the neighbourhood, they came to dinner at Stoke, where Sarah was staying on a visit to her kind old aunt, Lady Albemarle. She had heard of Donny, for so was George called in his family, and expected to be disappointed; but was not. Colonel Napier, six-foot-two, in a red coat, ruffles and a Tom Jones hair-do, fully answered his repute.

Sarah had been feeling low. The divorce was going on, with a great flourish of newsprint. 'I cannot but feel extremely sensible to the unpleasant renewal of this affair, and altho' I never look at the newspapers yet I suppose others do. . . . Being alone is not pleasant and yet I hate to see anybody, even the servants, whom I know studdy the newspapers, and I supose make their remarks upon me as I sit at dinner.' She soothed her ruffled spirits by a visit with little Louisa to Lady Albemarle, who was the kind of aunt at whose house you could arrive at midnight without putting her out or dimming the warmth of her welcome, 'and you who know the regularity of old ladies and the great fuss they make with little things will judge if she is not most delightful'. And here, sitting at the dinner table in the spring sunshine, was her fate.

Donny's parlour trick, she had heard, was the squashing flat of pewter mugs with his hands, but fortunately it did not come to parlour tricks. Could anyone so handsome and tough possibly also be intelligent? Yes, it appeared, Colonel Napier could. Either now, or later during the remaining weeks his regiment stayed in the neighbourhood, she learned that he was a scientist and a geologist, was widely read in several languages, and familiar with 'ancient and modern history'. He also had what Sarah later described as 'a friendly mind'. Educated he might well be, for he and his nine brothers, in their battered tower of Merchiston, had been taught by David Hume, the historian and scientist. He and his wife soon left for America, where the colonists were making trouble, sympathised with by a great many of the English, including Donny himself. There was no time for further conversation about ancient or modern history; and in America terrible trouble awaited Colonel Napier, though not of colonist making.

There is no evidence that Sarah thought of him at this time as anything but an intelligent and charming man happily married to someone else. Donny was twenty-five, and full of the joys of spring: he was probably not less affected by Sarah than most other men with whom she came in touch. At any rate the thought and feeling of both of them now existed in each other's minds. Sarah was thirty-one now, gentler than of old, but no less caressing and fair.

Over the American war Sarah really and for full five years parted company with her kindly thoughts of King George III. The resistance of the colonists was 'neither treason nor rebellion, but perfectly justifiable in every possible political and moral sense' her brother Richmond insisted in the Lords, and she was every inch with him. Her letters ring with indignation—'this horror of civil war'—'so vile and fruitless a service where he (Harry Fox) may be killed and cannot get any honour'. The O'Briens were now back in England and naturally pro-colonist—'you are viollent for your American friends' Sarah protested all the same. 'I hope they are good sort of people but I don't love Presbetiryans and I love the English soldiers.'

'I've heard the news of the action near Boston' she wrote in July of 1775. 'Oh Lord! how it makes ones blood run cold to think of *any* action, much more such a bloody one as that, and among one's own people almost.' Were not the colonists themselves being hasty, egged on by Charles Lee? 'However good the motives of liberty may be, they should not be hurried on, nor fought at the expense of innocent lives, when it could be obtained without fighting' Sarah pontificated sensibly. 'Now if they free themselves of our King they will only fall by the ears together and quarrell among themselves and be just as unhappy . . . I don't believe the King is so great a tyrant as my cousin Charles Lee would be were he king himself, for he loves his own way as well as anybody; in short I think there is no deciding who is precisely wrong and who is precisely right. Those who cause most lives to be lost are the worst. . . .

'The Bostonians' Sarah declared sweepingly 'are quarrelsome, discontented, hipocritical, enthusiastical, lying . . . not likely to make a good set of people in general; and yet I hate the King should conquer too, because he sits there at his ease at Windsor and fancies he has nothing to do but to *order* to conquer such a place as America —so insolent it will provoke me beyond all patience, and were it not for the blood, every drop of which I think of full as much consequence as the King's, I should wish him to have a compleat mortification in having Ireland whisk'd away from him whilst his troops are sailing, and so have him obliged to give up America and look like a fool without Ireland; he uses poor dear Ireland so ill already that he don't deserve to keep it.'

'So vile a war' she anathematized it next year. It was now being fought just where Susan had lived—'I understand your horror perfectly well, and feel all goose skin at the very idea of it, it makes me creep all over. Only think of the horrible attempt of burning the town, think of the poor sick in it . . . !I am sure I can thank God very sincerely I am not Queen, my head would have been off probably. But if I had loved and liked him, and not had interest enough to prevent this war, I should certainly go mad to think a person I loved was the cause of such a shameful war.'

'Only think' she exclaimed in 1777, 'of the horrors of employing the Indians and allowing them to fight in their own way! I am not much pleased with my friend Sir Wm. Howe either, for tho' a most humane man himself he has not contrived to keep strict discipline in his army, and I hear of horrible cruelties among them, from too good authority to doubt. Oh what a dreadful thing it is!' Why must the authorities drag in the German Hessian troops to fight in America? If there was a thing really calculated to get the colonists' temper up that was it. The war got stupider every day; it was pointless suffering, and all between relations. 'Poor America, was there ever such a brute as Genl Burgoyne. . . . Though an American in my heart as to the *cause*,' she wrote in August '78, 'I cannot bear my poor country-men should suffer, who are to the full as innocent as the Americans. I hope and trust Harry Fox is well by not being named.'

It was almost a relief when the French chipped in: nobody minded fighting them, having been doing just this on and off for six hundred years. Things in this dismal war looked up; on his way to defeating the French in the West Indies Rodney beat the Spanish ships off Cape St Vincent and relieved Gibraltar. 'Tis a delightful thing and I am glad Adl Rodney had the good luck of being able to show his merit, for he is a great friend of our dear Admiral and therefore has merit: indeed he is much loved by all who know him.' 'Our Admiral' was Keppel, Sarah's first cousin: he had had an inconclusive meeting with the French fleet and had had his masts blown to bits by them, which had enabled their ships to get safely away into Brest. He was court-martialled largely on account of a party political row, to the distress of his mother, poor old Lady Albemarle, 'whose spirits are terribly hurt'. But he was acquitted; and she looked ten years younger. Keppel became a national darling and baptised a pub on the Hard at Portsmouth; the sailors cheered him wildly, the sea-officers who were offering to resign their commissions if Keppel were censured stopped offering, and 'all the fine ladies, Ly Betty Compton, and the Dss of Rutland, wear his hair in lockets'.

The war in America had brought Donny Napier worse wounds than an outraged moral sense. In 1775 he had exchanged into the 80th, raised a company, and been ordered to America, where he served under Clinton; offering, when Major André was caught and hanged, to take his place as a spy in uniform, which Clinton had refused to let him do. Whilst Donny was besieging Charlestown his wife and small children fell desperately ill with yellow fever in New York; and when he came back to join them only one of his family, a hollow-eyed wan little girl called Louisa, was still alive. He himself became so dangerously ill with the fever that Clinton, despairing of his recovery, sold his commission while he was *in extremis*, using the money to pay off medical expenses and hoping to save something out of the wreck for the surviving child. Donny was carried un-conscious and near death on to a homebound transport.

Flying in the face of all responsible medical opinion, he recovered; to find himself out of the army and without hope of being able to buy his commission back. He came ashore in England as plain Mr Napier, a widower with no prospects, precious little money, and a solitary thin little girl.

His love, his son, all the hopes of his promising military career, lay buried in America. He could not take off for those newly found Antipodes, Australia and New Zealand: the pale, shocked, bereft face of three-year-old Louisa stood between him and this possibility. He had been bred in war since he was twelve; he loved the army and knew no other trade. There was nothing for it but in misery, solitude and ill-health to start all over again.

V

No moans were forthcoming at the time, but when it was all over, Sarah admitted to Susan that her life in Sussex had been very lonely. She had no carriage and therefore no means of getting to see her friends; and found that her friends did not often come to see her. Her family alone remained staunch and unswerving; she depended wholly upon them. Lady George, her younger brother's wife, was less warm: if Sarah had only married her brother John Newbattle (now Lord Lothian and an immensely respectable married man) in the first place, the whole kerfuffle and scandal need never have happened. But to Sarah's immense delight, her brother Charles Richmond was building a house for her: they spent happy hours together over the plans. 'A *home*, a *pretty* home, and one given to me by the best of brothers. . . . It is in his park just a mile from Goodwood in a valley open to the south, with a little prospect, and the hills round it planted, which make fine sheltered dry walks and rides, and from them there is a noble prospect; in short, it is *exactly* what I like, and you know that a paradise can't please one more than *just what one likes*', she rejoiced to Susan.

Through '77 and '78 Halnaker was slowly building. 'You cannot imagine how pretty my house is, I hope to get into it next summer,'

Sarah wrote in August, 'and have laid out occupation for myself for many years, as I am determined to furnish it by slow degrees, for the sake of my pocket as well as my amusement; my brother puts chimney pieces and ceilings for me, and I shall live very comfortably in it for a year or two with bare plastered walls, and do the bed-chambers neat and comfortable first, and so on till its all done. My house consists of a large staircase of 20 by 16, a housekeeper's room on one side, a pantry on the other with a passage to the offices, which are out of the house; and then to the front I have a drawing-room of 28 by 18, and a dining room 18 square. Above stairs are 2 bed-chambers of 18 square and a little dressing room, and two smaller bed chambers at the back for servants.

'You see that nothing can be more compact. Besides this there is a little green-house by way of pavilion to answer the offices and a little colonade of 4 columns of each side to join them to the house, so that its both pretty and convenient. I am only afraid I shall ruin myself in furnishing it, for nothing ugly should be put into so pretty a house, and to split the difference I mean to have everything *plain*, which is never *ugly* nor *dear*.'

Richmond's wife, too, was invariably kind; taking Sarah up to London to see the dentist—'my teeth are woeful'—and Louisa up for a month to have dancing lessons. Sarah greatly admired her good-nature and her 'practical philosophy'. When Richmond went to France the newspapers all announced that it was to become a Roman Catholic and 'to talk in the French Parlement', though in fact it was to visit his French Duchy of D'Aubigny and his French mistress, whom Sarah knew and thought very charming and suitable and much better than his previous one, 'a little dab of a miss 20 years younger than himself and he allows it was very ridiculous'. The 'prodigiously philosophical Dss' accompanied her husband; and when the Sussex militia—'my dear brother has made himself excessively ill by his hard work training and talking to the men, which has strained his stomach'—were ordered to Exeter, the Duchess went too.

' "Well" said she, "if I must I must, now let me see what's the good I can find in it? First of all, thank God, the Bishop of Exceter, my good cousin, is in Heaven and won't plague us with his dignity nor his tiresome wit; then I can see Mount Edgecomb which I never should have seen otherwise, and I shall have my own friends for society, and when I'm tired of them I'll read a thousand books I can't find time to read at home." ' Sarah greatly took to this calm philosophy, but could never quite arrive at it herself.

The Fox-Strangways row rumbled on interminably and was perhaps a useful counter-irritant for Sarah, who never drew breath until she got them all settled: it took her eighteen years and reams of paper. By the simple process of never answering any letters William O'Brien had managed to refuse all jobs found for him in Bermuda, Jamaica, America and places west, and had arrived back in England with Susan, to be greeted with a certain reserve; which Susan deeply resented. Sarah assured her that she would never be happy until 'thoroughly reconciled to all your family', and that she had better pack in all this highty-tighty. Lord Holland died; Lord Ilchester died; and still the battle grumbled on; 'you may please your mother, why not do it?' Sarah besought Susan. 'She loves cards, you should make a point to have a party for her, and whoever she likes are those to choose. I long to hear how you go on.'

Not very well, as it happened; and Sarah pleaded on. 'Your family . . . have the worldly and unconquerable prejudice of being hurt at your situation [of marriage to an actor]. They therefore very unreasonably expect more meekness from you than belongs to your character and they meet with a hauteur that would be condemnable in the Empress of the world. . . . To be high-handed is the most tiresome of all good or bad qualities; it never gives the owner any satisfaction; it always makes quarrells and never mends them. I'm no judge whether it holds good *dans le grand monde*, but I'm quite entirely certain it don't hold good *en famille*. . . . Your manner in general had almost convinced your brother you did not love him. . . . No matter how it began, the matter is to end it.'

Prickly Susan objected. 'I still fear they may think it interested motives alone that makes me try to be well with a rich sister. . . . My brothers and sisters are very unlike yours. I wish there was a Ly Louisa among us to keep us all from *freezing* as we do when together . . .'. Sarah urged her to look at Emily Kildare, now duchess of Leinster and a well-known tower of common sense. The good effects of her 'meekness' had been immense—'I assure you my sister *gains* friends instead of losing any by her manner.'

William O'Brien smiled on while the tide of battle rolled to and fro over his head. They had perched near Salisbury, in a village where Ste and Mary Fox had a house, Winterslow: when they died and Winterslow was burnt down, the O'Briens were given Stinsford by

Lady Ilchester, a charming manor house in Dorset, and presently a sinecure was found for William in Dorchester, which brought him in a neat income and involved the minimum of trouble. He acquired two very pretty red and white spaniel dogs and some rough shooting, and lived happily upon his wife's relations into an advanced old age with a still unwrinkled brow.

He and Susan had been right to elope. Well did his perennial exuberance and robust absence of conscience sort with Susan's moody intelligence, her pride and her redeeming sense of humour, her courage and her affection. They had no children, but they also had remarkably few rubs: and happily did William, reft early from the boards and now transmogrified into a country gentleman, stride his fields with his new guns and his new dogs, his still cherubic face shining with good country living, while his wife's friend Sarah banged industriously on, determined they should all make it up.

'I will tell you fairly that as far as I can judge it is not upon the old score that they are shy of you, but upon finding that you give yourself what seems to them *airs*, and I know of old that nobody but a very very few unprejudiced persons can put up with that. . . . You toss up your head, a *great crime* in many people's eyes, for it denotes contempt, and you have a directing way. . . .' To young Lady Stavordale Sarah insisted that Susan did this to everybody, partly because in her extreme youth Henry Holland had praised her for it. And 'it's her manner of speaking, she has no thought of governing, its her *way*, in short.' Sarah and Susan were now past having tiffs— 'To do you justice you never let the want of any advantage deprive you of fun,' Sarah admitted to Susan. 'Why is Ly Holland thought to be out of the way of her friends at Winterslow? It is not further from town than Chatsworth, and yet the finest ladies find time to go there.' Not until 1780 was peace between Melbury and Stinsford signed.

Sarah's nephew Charles James was another not to be deprived of fun. He had grown up wild and saucy, swanking about Paris in red heels and fancy waistcoats and writing Italian verse of all things. He was always at Newmarket, or Almacks, where the lowest stake was £50: he had lost £40,000 before anyone could turn round, and poor old Henry Holland, ill and sad, had had to pay it. Horace Walpole did not help by calling him 'the first figure in all places—the hero in Parliament, at the gaming table, and at Newmarket', Charles James was far too much inclined to think that himself without having it underlined. But on his father's death, so shortly followed by Ste's, he had turned over a new leaf and was devotedly kind to Ste's little orphaned boy; and he had really become serious over politics, making his name in the most surprising way by opposition speeches during the American war, which he had denounced with real fire and expertise. He was all set for stardom and any minute now would start being known as the Man of the People. Sarah remained devoted, and thought his speeches were almost always splendid. It seemed rum, at 37, to have one's nephew Secretary of State.

'I am very grave and dignified' Sarah reported from Ireland in 1775; but it wasn't really her strong suit. 'When lovely woman stoops to folly, And finds too late that men betray, What charm can soothe her melancholy, What art can wash her tears away?' Goldsmith had recently asked, and come up with death as the only answer; but Sarah had a better one—let her turn to homes and gardens. Making them pleasant was, she thought the most innocent of all ways of spending money, the most absorbing of amusements. Anybody, Sarah considered, could be happy in Sussex with 3 or 4 acres, and country beauty and amusements, even though it was a bit of a political and social desert and not on the way to anywhere. 'I am now up to the ears in blankets, beds, curtains, grates, fenders, chairs, tables etc., and I wonder I did not inform you that the price of blankets is fallen because of the American War, which I never approved of till now. . . .' Harry Fox was back on leave from America, 'a good portly figure but not a bit too fat to be active, stirring, an excellent walker. He breathes short like poor Ste, which vexes one for fear of its being from the same cause, but his looks, his manner are all delightfull, he has the true good military air, . . . he is not handsome by way of beauty but . . . has all his two brothers' pleasant ways of ease, good humour, fun, and quickness of remarks, without having wit and brilliancy. All his accounts of the service are told with such modesty and propriety that its charming; as to his opinions, I dare not venture to give them for fear I should misquote his ideas by any mistakes, but this I'm certain of, that he adores the Howes, he thinks America *cannot* be conquered, and laughs at the folly of supposing it; he is tired of that sort of war, but longs to pursue all sorts. . . .'

Harry was delighted to find a house where he was fêted and admired; his return had been forlorn. Holland House was no more home to him, being now the property of his four-year-old nephew,

Ste's son and third Lord Holland, whose pretty mother was at present dying of consumption in her twenties. Death was as rife as ever: the expectation of life in these times must have been about thirty-five years. Susan's young sister Lucy Digby was dying of cancer, and poor Emily Leinster was in process of losing yet another child, Gerald Fitzgerald, missing at sea. (She still had the flower of the flock, darling Edward, and would have him for a few more years.) Susan thought that the danger of French invasion in Sussex was so great that she begged Sarah to bring Louisa and take shelter with her in Dorset, but Sarah thought she would stay put and help her neighbours, none of whom could speak a word of the language if the French *did* come.

She was busy teaching her daughter, and reading up at nights to keep ahead. Louisa Bunbury, surprisingly, as both her parents were reasonably intelligent and had smashing looks, had turned out neither pretty nor clever; but Sarah, though admitting to feeling mortified, was resolved that Louisa should be allowed to be herself— 'I will not be like Lord Chesterfield, fretting and wishing for what is not in *the nature of the beast.*' Louisa had an angelic temper and liked cards: one must build on that. 'I should have the vapours all day if I played an hour at cards; my aversion to them is insurmountable, but my daughter makes up for it.' She let her go about with the Richmonds and other friends rather younger than she would have liked; but in Louisa's circumstances it was a good thing; if people got really used to her as a child they were less likely to be beastly to her about her equivocal birth when she grew up. Sarah was not going to make the poor child go about handicapped by such a discredited mother; nor make use of her 'innocence and pleasing ways' to get herself asked around 'as I see many mothers do. . . . I have the greatest dislike to letting her be like Fanny Wriothesly was, at everybody's service, . . . I will never appear with her in public myself and she shall never appear but with those very few near relations whose protection is so very advantageous to her. I hope you think this is a good plan, my dear Ly Susan, for your opinion is one I hold very very high, both from your uncommon understanding and great knowledge of the world. . . .'

Louisa grew steadily more attractive, in spite of her big mouth, small eyes, and nondescript features; evidently she had charm, and 'luckily I am no admirer of prodigys . . . a very moderate share of tallents make people to the full as happy as others.' 'If I can moderate her excessive giddiness and make her apply enough to learn all the necessary things . . . I shall be satisfied.' And Louisa was much liked: even the bossy Duchess of Bedford had been nice to her—'I am quite doved with her old Grace'—and so had the kind Bunbury relations.

While Louisa was away Sarah switched to dogs. 'I desire my compts to Mr. O'Brien and tell him he could not apply to a better person than me in the dog way, for in the first place I shall be delighted to give him a dog, and 2ndly, I pique myself on understanding them; but in order to suit him exactly I must ask several questions which I have enclosed. My brother has a very pretty breed, but its of the old Holland House Ranger breed, and inherrit all his crossness and pomp, which some people don't like; now I do. There is another breed which is all good temper and gentlness. My brothers have also famous pointers which I can get some of. I have some very pretty spaniels . . . I am mighty glad Mr. O'Brien takes to some country sport. . . .'

The next to blot her copybook, though in a milder way, had been Emily Leinster. She was over, in the spring of 1774—'you will find me the same after twenty years, full of a thousand faults, only much increased, and having no one merit but an affectionate heart towards those that love me,' Sarah assured her. By the end of the year Emily had married William Ogilvie; rather too soon, it was felt, after James Leinster's death; but the marriage had been precipitated by mad Lord Bellamont, married to Emily's daughter Emilia, who had told all and sundry that his mother-in-law was up to no good with her sons' tutor.

Richmond 'could not disguise his being sorry, but should keep that to ourselves'. He had fears about their happiness, 'because in the common order of things any inequality between husband and wife generally tended to make them less happy.' There was besides what Sarah called 'my brother's abominable strong prejudice against the Scotch in general.' Once again Sarah swung into action as peacemaker over this precipitate match. 'I allow that if you sit and think of all the reasons against it, you may find a thousand; but is she not worth our getting over all those sort of nonsensical notions for her sake?' 'I assure you I mean to do so in time, but at first, I own, among ourselves, I can't use myself to it in a moment,' Richmond had not unreasonably replied.

'My brother has wrote down, I understand, a great deal of good advice to you,' Sarah told Emily; 'and though I propose to be such a fool as to tell him that advice after twenty-five is absurd,' yet he would surely send it. 'Its his foible—and I do not blame him for examining every subject as he does and sifting it to the bottom'; yet he could not help, being so petted and admired, having a little undue vanity. People would go on so about his 'consequence': imperceptibly he took the idea. 'In short he is spoilt a good deal.'

Emily must understand this and be the calm and patient one. 'If you take fire (as I have known my sweet sister do, and her pretty face colour up at the most distant and slight hint that could be meant as blaming those she loves) you will find your brothers and sisters [in-law] the sons and daughters of Adam, and the family fault of vanity and self-opinion will be marked . . . I really believe they will feel this as little as any people; but I believe its human nature . . . I am not the least afraid but that they will all shew you the greatest kindness; and I am also sure they will never allow you to be blamed in their presence.' If Emily would only accept the first repercussions with good nature, all would soon be well.

Richmond sensibly did not send his four pages of advice to his elder sister, and 'Mr. Ogilvie's merits will surmount it all' Sarah rejoiced. 'I comfort myself with the surprise they will be in when they see he is not what I am convinced in their imaginations they figure to themselves.' Louisa reported happily upon William Ogilvie; but as her brother Richmond pointed out, Louisa was but too prone to like everybody. But he came round. 'To do my dear brother justice, I must say that contrary to most people, he is very apt to change from wrong, but never from right.' It was funny that Emily had told Ogilvie that Sarah was pretty, when he was going to see 'a thin, pale, long-nosed, hollow-eyed, coarse-featured woman' Sarah continued gloomily; 'added to my poking figure and negligence of dress.' He would have a shock. Had Emily heard that Louisa had again taken thirty-six hours to cross the Irish Sea—'Dear Soul! I long to hear how her poor dear bowels do after it.' And the election? 'If they lose it Conolly will have the happiness of having something more to growl and splutter and swear at. But he finds something that answers that purpose every day . . .'

Time passed, and it had moments of being melancholy, and especially in post fever depression. 'I am not a philosopher, for I am

frightened at being sick and fancy I shall never recover, and now I
am well I do a thousand foolish things, . . . sitting out in the dew with
my aunt Albemarle, because I would fancy that at 32 one can do just
as one does at 73, but I find its a mistake.' (Aunt Albemarle, born
Anne Lennox, had had fifteen children, eight boys and seven girls;
Gus Keppel, the admiral, was her second son.) 'I am not young
enough for anybody, I think, for I really feel myself growing old in a
thousand things.' She was determined not to let herself sink into the
sins of old age, crossness and discontent. 'You and I shall never go
again all bonneted up and hooded up in publick and giggle and laugh
at the ridiculous people we see, but I won't promise but that we shall
laugh at them at home and have the more comfort, . . . and enjoy our
fun in a quiet way' she told Susan.

She need not have worried. Like Aunt Albemarle, she had one of
the secrets of eternal youth, an abiding interest in the human race,
in other people, their lives, their characters, their doings. How was
Susan's mother? 'Does she enjoy her former amusements at Melbury
in improving the place? Has she made anything more of the pretty
wood with the water in it, which in itself was so beautiful? Does she
love cards as well as she did? Has she many neighbours who can
easily come and make her party?' And what was going to happen to
the Damers' servants, turned off with fourteen months' wages owing?

The young too were a permanent source of pleasure. George
Lennox's three girls were 'all as different in their characters as it is in
nature to be. Louisa is middle-sized, elegant to the greatest degree
in her form and rather plump; she has a true Lennox complexion,
rough and shewy, her hair is fair, her eyes little and lively, her nose
is like her mother's, which is pretty, and her mouth and countenance
like my sister Leinster's, full of ten thousand graces; her teeth good
but not superlatively fine. Her sense quick, strong and steady; her
character is reserved and prudent but so very complaisant that its
hard to discover she has a choice, and yet she has her prejudices and
is firm in them. She likes the world as one does a play, for the amusement of the moment, but her turn is a jolly country life with society,
where walking, working, and a flower garden are her chief amusements; she don't love reading, calls everybody *wise* or affected that
is in the least learned; she is herself free from the least tincture of
affection or of vanity, not seeming to know how pretty she is. She is
feminine to the greatest degree, laughs most heartily at a dirty joke,
but never makes one. . . .

'Emily is a fine tall, large woman with a Lennox complexion, but red or auburn hair; her features course, her mouth ugly, and yet her teeth excessive white; her countenance very pleasing and all goodness like her character, which is more like my sister Louisa's than anybody I know. . . . Georgina is rather little and strong made; her countenance is reckoned very like mine, for she has little eyes, no eyebrows, a long nose, even teeth, and the merriest of faces; but all her livelyness comes from her mother's side. She has all her witt, all her power of satyre, and all her goodnature too, so that if she is not led to give way to the tempting vanity of displaying it she will be delightfull, but you know by experience the dangers attending on witt, and dear little Georgina will I fear experience them. . . .' (Dear little Georgina fell in love with Edward Fitzgerald and he with her. Parental discouragement followed; and he went exploring in Canada, to give the parents time to come round. Far from it; in his absence they married Georgina to Lord Bathurst, thus unknowingly saving her from a sad and early widowhood and launching Edward on his marriage with wild, beautiful, and revolutionary Pamela Seymour.)

The reverse side of being interested in people is a passion for gossip. 'If I was not afraid of running into the spirit of scandal I would tell you all the chit-chat that comes round to me, but I have a constant monitor that tells me for ever "Would you like to have all your faults the topick of conversation?" ' The constant monitor knocked off sometimes for elevenses; and Sarah reported to Susan that Georgiana the beautiful and sweet new young Duchess of Devonshire 'who has no fault but delicate health in my mind, dines at 7, summer as well as winter, goes to bed at 3, and lies in bed till 4: she has hysteric fits in a morning and dances in the evening: she bathes, rides, dances, for ten days, and lies in bed the next ten, indeed I can't forgive her, or rather her husband, the fault of ruining her health, tho' I think she may wear ten thousand figarees in her dress without the smallest blame.' Nor could she resist a comment on Lord Sandwich, who had lately hit the headlines with a resounding clang. This grand tall man with a chalk white face, eleven years Civil Lord of the Admiralty, had brought up a young mistress, Miss Reay, in the way she should go, at Hinchinbrooke near Huntingdon; but she had taken up with a parson called Hackman and gone away for two years to live with him. Remorse ensued and she returned to the fold at Hinchinbrooke; whereupon Parson Hackman, driven mad by jealousy, shot her dead one evening as she left the opera house in London, thereby exposing

the whole picnic to the cold public gaze. Sarah was sorry for absolutely everybody. 'Don't you pity that poor devil Ld Sandwich
just now, and the poor girl too, and I think the poor man too; tho' I
think it quite right he should be hanged I pity him monstrously.'

Nor could she resist giving Susan a blow by blow account of Lord
Egremont's passage of arms with the Duchess of Gloucester, whose
daughter he had gone through the movements of wanting to marry.
'Lord Egremont has long professed to like Ly Maria Waldegrave but
never could bring himself to propose in form. During this time the
Duchess of Gloucester abused him continually in the most publick
places, which did not encourage him to have any dealings with her,
but however love, or whatever you please to call it, got the better,
and he did propose; he wanted to be married in a moment, but Ly
Maria being a ward of Chancery it was impossible. . . . The Dss of G.
was pleased with all but the *man*, to whom she had taken an aversion;
there goes a story that she required £6,000 a year jointure for Ly
Maria.

'Now whether it is her behaviour that is the cause, or that other
people have got round him, or . . . only his dread of not making a
good husband, but he took the resolution of going to Ly Maria and
telling her . . . he felt himself unequal to making her happy, but if she
chose it he would marry her. She very properly resigned all claim to
his word, and did it "like an angel, and without a reproach"; this is
his own words. He accuses himself of being mad, says he has used her
cruelly, but that its less cruel to leave her free than to neglect her
happiness when she is his wife. He speaks of her in the highest terms,
this he did to my brother, so I can vouch for the truth of it, and I am
glad I can, for it takes off a little of the shamefullness of his conduct. . . .

'You may guess the riot this event has created of rage and joy in
different parties; I pity the poor girl most sincerely. I forgot to say
that all the *forms* of Royalty so terrified Ld Egremont as soon as he
was looked upon as of the family, that some say *they* drove him to be
off. . . .' Poor Lord Egremont, badly bruised, left the lists of marriage
for ever: Maria, more resilient, married Lord Euston four years later.

'I have been running on about these people as if you cared about
them, which I daresay you do not, for whenever one is but an inch
out of the great circle one becomes a looker-on, and in doing so one
acquires an excess of indifference about it all, which one can as easily
lose the moment one returns among them again. . . . I can send the

dogs before you go, as I wish them to be under your protection when they arrive, and not be neglected by servants.'

Her child, her dogs, house, garden, gossip; aunts, nieces, other people's mothers, other people's lives—all very well at sixty, but Sarah was in the full bloom and ardour of her early thirties. An autumn light fell again on the downs; birds in the new plantations sang fit to burst at yet another empty spring. Summer and corn cocks, winter and snow-drifts, night and day for eleven years: the lonely, even, passing of life's prime.

A meeting with Charles Bunbury, which Sarah had long wanted but never expected, effected a kind of release—'I never felt satisfied not to have received his pardon. . . . The first day I saw him I was too much overcome to have the least conversation with him, but his extreme delicacy in avoiding to give the least hint about my conduct, and the ingenious manner in which he contrived to give me comfort by talking about Ly Derby's conduct just as I would wish him to talk about mine, did at last restore my spirits in some degree, and when he came the next day to see me I had a very long conversation with him, during which without naming my faults or the word forgiveness, he contrived to convince me he looked upon me as his friend and one whose friendship he was pleased with. I cannot describe to you how light my heart has felt since this meeting . . . the very friendly manner in which he treated me gives me the most comfortable feel, and to add to my satisfaction he has shewn all sorts of kindness to my dear little Louisa, whom he told me he liked vastly, and has invited to come to him whenever she is in town. I had the very great satisfaction of seeing him in good health and spirits.' She had gone off into a fit of crying at his kindness; he had laughed at her and 'we parted the best of friends in the world, but it is very true that every mark of his forgiveness is like a dagger to my heart'. She rejoiced later 'at the manner in which Louisa is received, and cannot say half how much I admire Sir Charles and his family for not letting my faults influence the reception of an innocent person'.

William Gordon, on the other hand, appeared quite to have forgotten his child and was pursuing an heiress with intermittent success, and having the best of three rounds with her guardians. The old spoil-sports were preventing his girl from pressing a pre-marital £10,000 into his palm. He had become increasingly a show-off; but is last seen in a more human light weeping for joy at the acquittal of his younger brother (poor deluded Lord George, as Sarah called him) in his trial for high treason after the No Popery riots.

Sarah felt freed and light-hearted; and Charles Bunbury, after all the hoo-ha and the immensely expensive divorce, now expressed a wish to marry her again. They had both grown wiser, and perhaps easier. The Sarah who had jaunted off and left him was not the same Sarah who could write as she did this autumn of the Garricks. 'Poor Mrs. Garrick, to nurse him when he was sick and admire him when he was well has been the whole and sole occupation and business of her life; her loss is one of the very greatest a human creature can feel: I looked upon him as more than the first genius in his line of life, as a generous and humane man whose failings were wonderfully slight when compared to the temptations he has to fail.' And there had not been much wrong with Bunbury except that he had never learnt at his father's knee that when you have a very pretty wife of twenty-one with whom you only sleep every second Tuesday in the month it is not a good idea to leave her alone in the house for weeks on end with an amorous French duke. But Sarah had not the heart to marry anyone so obviously blissful as a bachelor; so well, and jolly and unworried. 'I hope I shall never be idiot enough to marry *avec toutes mes années et tous mes défauts*; but if ever I do you may consider me as mad, and that I've met with a man as mad as myself.'

The necessary lunatic was at hand. Donny Napier was in Ireland, intermittently employed and trying to recruit a company so as to get a captain's commission again, when he met Sarah anew. From the first time of seeing her he had been quite unable to imagine why no one had married her as soon as she was divorced and free. Now that he himself was widowed and free, he wasted no time. He was twenty-nine, and had never suffered from indecision.

'You would hardly believe' Sarah wrote to Susan when all was settled a few weeks later 'that a man who has had reason to know the distress of poverty and the inconvenience of marriage should choose to put himself in the same situation again, and you will think still worse of his sense for the choice he has made of me, for most undoubtedly all things considered there is in all marriage 1,000 to one they will turn out ill, and in mine 10,000 to one against us; but no one argument that has been urged to Mr. Napier has had the least effect upon his determined purpose. He says he has known me long enough to judge of my character, that he has a peculiar turn of mind which prevents him being mortified about my character. . . . My disposition, such as it is, suits his, and if I love him he has not the least doubt of our being happy. . . . He laughs at every objection that is started. He knows I *do* love him, and he says that loving me to the degree he does, he is quite sure never to repent marrying me, . . . it is not a new thought; he was always exactly of the same opinion with respect to the world as he is now; in short nothing can be more firm, or if you please to call it so, obstinate, than he is in thinking that I can make him happy. . . .' Calmly she argued with Susan the pros and cons. 'The only advantage upon earth I have over you is that I can bend my disposition to anything that is necessary, which you cannot. I admire your tough, oaklike mind; but I avail myself of my own weakness and at least take this good of it, since I have suffered by the bad of such a bending, pliant turn of mind.'

Susan thought she was entirely mad, and did not hesitate to say so. Give up pretty Halnaker, and the kindness and protection of the Richmonds, to go off with a homeless soldier who hadn't even the wherewithal to buy back his commission? She replied disparagingly, and in the tones of one who had never left home herself to go off with an Irish actor with no visible means of support. 'I hardly believed myself awake when I read your letter. I perceive by it that you are extremely in love, and of course everything will appear to you in a very delusive point of view; that is all I wish you to beware of. . . .

'It is the very nature of passion to deceive,' she pointed out sternly. A sentiment felt for the first time one naturally thought could never alter; 'an illusion any second passion must destroy. . . . As to Lady Albemarle's opinion I don't think its of much consequence, and if it did not so well agree with yours at present I don't believe you would,' she added shrewdly.

And had Sarah considered her image? 'There was a propriety in your retreat, and a dignity annexed to the idea of one great passion, tho' unfortunately placed, that gratified yr friends and silenced yr enemies.' And then, money! 'Tho' Capt. N. may be used to live on a small income and economise, he will not like it a bit the better. . . . I am sorry, if you will marry, that it is a man of small fortune. Poverty . . . is an additional and never-ceasing little plague that goes on tormenting one incessantly, and neither time nor habit, that lessens every other ill, has the least effect on this.' There was, she pointed out in mild terms, no fool like an old fool. 'What does the Dss say to you? Does she laugh at you and say its all mighty foolish?

'My dear Ly S.,' Susan went on, softening slightly, 'it is my most sincere and ardent wish that you may be as happy as the lot of humanity will allow. . . . I am now at Melbury with my mother, and surrounded with oaks, but I assure you I have nothing of the oaklike disposition you imagine. I am become quite a willow and very often a weeping one, for my spirits are but low.' William O'Brien was in London, having suddenly decided to try his hand at being a barrister —'I can't form any scheme for this law situation that affords me any pleasure.'

Sarah, as she had realised, was very much in love: she played this down to Susan and plugged the calm reasonable attitude, continuing undeflected on her course. 'I do not wonder that my marriage should appear imprudent to you, not only because in fact it is imprudent in a worldly light, but also because everything in this world may be seen in two very different lights. . . .' But had Susan allowed for 'the pleasure of being so sincerely loved', and for 'the hopes of that pleasantest of all societies, which a married person only can enjoy?' Of course her brother Richmond had said Why change when you are well off, and there had been the whole question of her daughter Louisa's future to be considered. The Richmonds and Bunburys were endlessly kind to her—would they continue so to be if her mother jaunted off with a penniless soldier seven years her junior? And what would the Napiers say? They were bound to think it 'undoubtedly a very bad match for him in every light'.

The Napiers took it calmly. They did not share the flap about money by which the Stewart Lennoxes were so sadly hamstrung, and held the eccentric view that a sensible man of twenty-nine who has been married before is liable to know what he is about, and that in any case there is no future in trying to stop him. 'Mr. Napier says I have but one fault which is delay, but that it is so great a fault that it puts him out of all temper.' He could not see the sense in trying to placate relations by a humbugging delay until they came round to the idea—'he is very little acquainted with the world' Sarah thought, and ended her letter by telling Susan 'be convinced that my not following your advice don't make me the less obliged to you for it'. Sustained only by Louisa and Tom Conolly, Emily Leinster and Aunt Albemarle, and amidst otherwise universal headshakings, they were married on August 27th, 1781, at Goodwood parish church;

and a week later Sarah told Susan that if she couldn't be happy with such a husband there must be something radically wrong with her.

Donny Napier was admired as a soldier and much liked as a man; but as husband to an extravagant and sociable woman he seemed marvellously unqualified. They had expensive tastes and wealthy friends, indifferent health, little money and ten children—one of the perfect recipes for human misery. In addition to which Donny entirely declined to embark on the career of toad-eating which alone could remedy their situation. Their joy survived all ups and downs.

'Till I was past 36,' Sarah wrote two years later, 'I find I never knew what *real happiness* was, which from my marriage with Mr. Napier till now is much greater than I had any idea of as existing in human life.'

Part II

Summer in Kildare

VI

However much they loved justice and mercy, the minds of persons dwelling in previous centuries were unclouded by the vain dream that chance could become equal or that life could be made fair. They wasted little time, sleep or energy in mourning over bad luck, but got on with life. In the game of snakes and ladders Donny Napier had trodden on the head of a snake, and for all his intelligence, skill and courage, gone whizzing down from his colonelcy to the square one of unemployment; and was probably due to stooge around in the army doing odd jobs for years, never retrieving the lost time. Against a proud man who refused to toady his way up again the dice were heavily loaded. The system of buying commissions was idiotic, but it was an insurance policy against the danger of military take-over, and rule by persons like Franco, Goering, Nasser *et al* (the British people having had a bellyful of this from Cromwell) the premium on it paid by granting commissions only to people with a stake in the land and hence an interest in the preservation of legal government. It was a maddening necessity that soldiers accepted, like rotten biscuits, until the arrangements got better and the danger receded.

Sarah too had blotted her copybook in a permissive world, not so much by sinning as by sinning openly; but she knew it for her own fault and did not blame anyone else during her long penance. Better eschew the hard luck tale: the experience of the ages having told that a chip on the shoulder is the heaviest load that can be carried through life. 'Without honour life's a burden,' George assured his sons; and against self-pity the face of honour was set like a stone.

Both Donny and Sarah were at one as to laying hold on all the personal happiness available; but she did not go along with his whole philosophy. Surely families must get themselves on? If her great-grandmother Louise had taken Donny's line her descendants would all still be milking cows in Brittany instead of swanning round the Sussex downs laying out race-courses and having their horses painted by Stubbs. Other ideas had been bred into Donny in a youth in those bleak northern hills whence he hailed; he was firm in them; no amount of coaxing seemed able to beguile him out of them. What a bore! His father, that stern Scots lord, had had ten sons, loved them, given them a first-class education, launched them, and let them sink or swim. Sons could earn, Donny thought: there was no need to save up and buy rotten boroughs for them. He seemed to think daughters could get by with religious faith, long eye-lashes, and fifty pounds a year.

Sarah had her times of missing the world well lost for love; even with Donny life was not without its rubs. She seemed always to be awaiting yet another baby in small hot lodgings, with the usual 'uncomfortable feels', and the good jobs going the way of everyone but Donny. Would nothing make him suck up to people and remedy this situation? (It seems rude to refer to George Napier as Donny when Sarah herself never spoke of him but as Mr Napier, or Colonel Napier, as his case might be; but it is the only way to sort him out from his son George.) It felt all wrong when Stanhope got two jobs from Charles James Fox and Donny nothing beyond the £300 a year brought in from his task as superintendent at Woolwich Arsenal; for 'Mr. Napier has the *rage du service* beyond imagination' Sarah would complain when he was away bothering about something military but unremunerative.

She had not lost her lively partisan interest in the great world, and a return to London after her marriage had been delightful. Whatever was felt about hushing Sarah up was not shared by Donny. No one so gay and charming must be secluded. 'I have been at the Play; the divine Mrs. Siddons drew me there, and fully answered my expectations. . . . I have not yet been to an opera, but I have to several assemblies, where I went on purpose to show that it was not my husband's wish that I should shut myself up, but on the contrary.' All her old friends, bar the Duchess of Bedford, had received her warmly. To give a party herself was impossible, because of the ever-hounding press, but she followed her own family's fortunes with her usual mixture of passion and mockery, of which the last was increasingly to predominate.

Charles Lennox, son of Sarah's brother George, had been hit by a tennis ball at Portsmouth and was in danger; which seems odd. At

Goodwood her other brother had been 'bit by a general, for Mr. Conway has made him fortification mad'. She thought it foolish; being instructed perhaps by Donny. 'I am afraid his witts are in mortar, or he had much better sharpen them more for the keen tricks they are to encounter. Security is dangerous to generals in the field . . .' and would be as dangerous to Richmond in politics. At Goodwood also was the diarist George Selwyn, interested to see Sarah after all this while: like everyone else he remarked on the great improvement which happiness had given her looks. He thought Donny Napier a fine figure of a man but found his face uninteresting and rather cross—'*rébarbative*'—and turned at once to the more congenial task of wondering whether Miss Bunbury was more like the Gordons or more like the Lennoxes. Selwyn was of a sort to rebarb the faces of characters even more generally tolerant than Donny, who looked to the diarist a poor subject for manipulation and whose physical splendour was depressing. He was six foot two and looked immensely strong, though he admitted that when he met Catherine the Great's enormous lover Count Orloff at a dinner party, he could stand upright under Orloff's outstretched arm, and thought it would need two of himself to take on the vast Russian.

Another connoisseur too, was able to admire Sarah in this 1781 autumn of returned happiness. The nineteen-year-old Prince of Wales, afterwards the Prince Regent and George IV, heard that she was staying with Donny's uncle and aunt, General and Lady Cecilia Johnston, whom he knew; and insisted on coming to meet her. He was not disappointed. 'She should have been there' he told the assembled company, pointing at Windsor, when Sarah had departed; and adding that he absolutely understood his father's feelings.

As so often towards the end of a war, influenza raged in the spring of 1782. 'So general an illness has never been known here in the memory of man,' Sarah wrote from a London that had finally banished its bubonic plague but a hundred years before. 'I have never heard for certain that it was fatal to anybody, but its horrid troublesome.' In July Lord Rockingham, the Prime Minister, died suddenly. Would Charles Richmond get the job? Sarah passionately hoped he would, for not only did she love him for himself and admire his liberal principles, but with Richmond in office Donny would surely get his commission back.

Though as to graft, he was as hopeless as Donny. He had been Master of the Ordnance when her husband was at Woolwich, and had entirely refused to provide the many available perquisites which Donny would have been as firm in refusing. Richmond had always been extreme: Lady Holland's family would not allow him to bring up Ste's little boy as he had begged to do when he was orphaned, because he was 'a rebellious man'. He had even advocated embracing the Irish—'not an union of legislature but an union of hearts, hands, of affections and interests'. He had brought in a bill a couple of years back for annual Parliaments, manhood suffrage, and equal electoral districts, which was rejected, needless to say, without a division. He was too far out for Prime Minister, except in the eyes of his younger sister, taking up his cause with verve.

For the King had plumped for Shelburne. Richmond thought it 'a very unwise measure to put so hated a man as Ld Shelburne at the head', but 'desires no more than to have good measures pursued and while Lord S. does that its sufficient,' Sarah recorded. 'C. Fox flew out into a violent passion and resigned . . . my br has been these 3 days negotiating between Lord Shelburne and the angry parties to settle matters, he has talked his voice quite away and sunk his spirits and health and nothing is yet fixed.' 'Shall I thwart Shelburne out of dislike to the man?' Richmond demanded. 'As to Charles,' Sarah continued, 'my br takes his part with the King, tells him that Charles has been ill-used and must have allowances made for his anger. . . . He has talked, and been patient, and tried every persuasion to inspire them [the ministers] with true love of their country, but poor dear Charles is so surrounded with flatterers that tempt him to think that he alone can overset the whole fabric, that its in vain to talk. . . .'

Sarah, although already eight months gone with child, threw herself delightedly into the whole Whig business. 'I saw old Ld George Cavendish this morning, and find that it is not Charles alone that is violent; all the Cavendishes, all the Rockinghams all agree and lament my brother's being *imposed upon*. . . . Thank God my brother is allowed by all to have acted a most upright disinterested part; if it turns out well or ill is another question.' All very agitating, but if only Lord Howe could meet and beat the French fleet no one would mind anything. Charles James Fox, coalescing with North whom he had long abused, was quickly bounced out of office: fed up, he went off with Perdita Robinson, the actress, and was said to be practically living at Sadler's Wells with her. 'The pains he takes to marr the genius that Providence gave him! . . . He is all day figuring away with her. I long to tell him he does it to show that he is superior to

Henry Fox, 1st Lord Holland

Sir Charles Bunbury

Susan Fox-Strangways

William O'Brien

Alcibiades, for *his* courtezan forsook him when he was unfortunate, and Mrs Robinson takes *him* up'; but Sarah resisted thus teasing her nephew, and instead made him godfather to her son.

All savage breasts were soothed by the news that Admiral Rodney had met and beaten de Grasse, the French admiral, in a sea-fight off the Saints, a group of islands in the West Indies. During his comfortable open imprisonment, de Grasse was accorded in England the popular enthusiasm due to one who had obligingly been captured in his own flag-ship during an otherwise unsuccessful war. 'The Comte de Grasse is here, *fort fêté* by gentlefolk and mob too, for they doat on him for being big, and their vanity increases by every inch of his size I believe. He is mighty well pleased with their huzzas, but is going to take his tryal at Paris, where I fear he won't come off so well, poor man.' 'I cannot submitt my faith implicitly to the forecast of either my brother or nephew,' Sarah admitted in August, 'each being liable to err in judgment; I have at least the pleasure to think both . . . follow their ideas of right.' Donny seemed to have 'pleasing, odd, friends', and to be insufficiently worked up about ministerial changes. He seemed not particularly Whig or Tory, but a monarchist, and passionately against all forms of oppression.

Six weeks overdue and a fine healthy boy, Charles James Napier was born at the end of this August of 1782. 'I am perfectly recovered, all to being a little weak and nervous, *au reste, je suis enchantée de mon fils.*' And Louisa, most luckily, was delighted with the baby, 'wondering how I can be so little taken up with it, which you see entirely precludes all idea of jealousy, a passion which happily for her she is not disposed to have, but which you know people are but too apt to create in young minds where it would never come of itself.' By March of 1783 Donny had got round Sarah and re-entered the army as an ensign, which must have been boring after being a colonel, but perhaps more interesting than inspecting gunpowder, whose manufacture at Woolwich he had managed to improve: ('Mr. Napier is by nature a very active person in what he undertakes.'). Soon Sarah had got round the C. in C., General Conway (or so it was thought), and Donny was commissioned a Captain in the 100th Regiment. 'I wish him back in the Guards' Sarah mourned, 'for while a man belongs to *young Regts* he is always at the mercy of the whims of Ministers, and in the Guards a man is never ordered out but on *real service*. . . . A company in the Guards is the utmost of our ambition, and particularly suited to Mr N. who happens to have 4 or

5 of his oldest friends collected in the First Regt. of Guards. . . .
Mr. N. is not unreasonable and is so averse to an improper promotion that he would be happy to be assured of a company in 3 or 4
years.' She had 'a great mind to be in a rage' with Charles Fox when
he got jobs for others, specially as 'not an officer in the army would
grudge Mr. N. a reward for his services'. But 'Charles has good
qualities enough to atone for a thousand faults, and I have no right
to expect from him an attention which no one relation of his ever
yet acquired. I am determined not to grow unreasonable.' Both
Ogilvie and the Conollys regarded the army as an unlucky addiction,
a dangerous and ultimately lethal drug from which Donny must be
gently but firmly weaned. 'I wish very much something was settled
about him,' Louisa Conolly grieved to Ogilvie in July of 1783, 'for
I see that they will have millions of children—and yet he is so army
mad, that I think one should run a great risk of making him uncomfortable by desiring him to give it up, which makes one look to
that line for serving him in, and yet the difficulties are without number.' Which would be worse, the withdrawal symptoms or the money
difficulties?

'Dear Sally, how it does grieve me to have her so very frequently
disappointed in what her heart is so naturally set upon; the advancement of Mr. Napier,' Louisa told Emily in December. 'But I am
troubled at his gout in the stomach, tis so very dangerous; and if
anything should happen to him, she would be distracted . . . The dear
creature certainly never had but one fault, and thank God, that has
now ceased; so what can one wish for more now?' Richmond and
George Lennox were, Louisa thought, depriving themselves of a
great happiness in keeping away from Sarah because they had not
liked her marriage. Oh these Scotsmen! Here was another one of
them taking off a pretty Lennox sister. All very well to meet them
about the place, but how would you like your sister . . . ?

'What say you to polliticks? I believe that chaos was quite a joke
to present times,' Sarah asked Susan. Her brother puzzled her.
' "What does very well between you and me won't do in politicks."
. . . I see he is a little come off of his friend Lord Shelburne, but still he
approves of him in general tho' not in detail.' She turned with relief
to family news. 'My Louisa is just as you left her, only a little taller,
and very happily weaned without the least mortification of the vile
habit she had acquired at Richmond House of supposing it quite
necessary for a girl of her age to go to publick places at least once a

week.' She had had a most interesting conversation with Mr O'Brien, who had been to dinner. Charles Fox was now comforting himself with Mrs Armistead, and 'I have no gossip to tell you but that the P. of Wales is desperately in love with Ly Melbourne, and when she don't sit next to him at supper he is not commonly civil to his neighbours. . . .'

Into the drama of Burke's and Charles Fox's Bill for the better government of India Sarah entered with passion, and this time Donny was wholly with her—'tis the cause of humanity' he said. Passing the Commons, and the Lords without a division on its first reading, it had been thrown out partly on the King's instigation in order to unseat Fox and make place for Pitt; and here partisan Sarah did not allow old affection to trammel her indignation. They had even tried to bring in the old Duke of Montrose (a Napier kinsman and therefore sacred in Sarah's eyes) against the Bill—'but the old soul nobly resisted and said he was too old to turn fool or knave, having as yet deserved neither of those epithets during a long life. But poor pitiful changelings who tremble at the King's name were soon found' Sarah declared scornfully, in disgust with these men of straw who had gone back on a bright future for India, and on her darling Charles James into the bargain. 'Oh how I grieve that my dear brother was among them! It quite breaks my heart! What a head! To be misled by boys, Flatterers and knaves! A head capable of every good, which the best of hearts would dictate to him if he would but *let his own sense and heart guide him!*'

And a few years later Sarah had drifted politically away from Richmond, that charming and handsome brother whom the toughness of life and the shock engendered by the French Revolution were turning less liberal every year. Walpole, a keen fan, thought him 'intrepid and tender, inflexible and humane beyond example', but the more candid Burke pointed out to him that 'your grace dissipates your mind into too great a variety of minute pursuits, all of which, from the natural vehemence of your temper, you follow with almost equal passion'. From this pleasing weathercock of a brother Sarah turned increasingly away to sail on the even keel of Donny's judgment, and especially when Richmond, in argument in the Lords, reproached Lord Thurlow, the Lord Chancellor, with his low birth; (to which Thurlow spiritedly replied that but for an accident his grace would not be amongst those present in this august gathering). In the nineties Sarah was really shocked with her brother for getting his very young nephew a colonelcy over the heads of older and better officers—'such a *jobb*', as she truly pointed out; though in 1783 she had thought him almost too liberal—'I won't name my brother's politics to you,' she had told Susan, 'because I really do not understand them, but in my poor opinion he wants to spin sentiment, which does mighty well in *love* but not in *politicks*.' 'He will be so very right that he will be very wrong,' she added with the realistic sigh of down-to-earth characters with starry-eyed relations; but frivolity broke in, and to her relief 'My 2 brothers and all the Lennoxes are gone a frisk for a month to Paris to pay their respects to the King: the Dss would not go.'

This was to be the last Paris frisk for many a bloody day. Six years later the surge and thunder of the Revolution sounded doom on many an English ear, and Fox with his 'oversetting the fabric' ideas was discredited in the House; though even his enemies admitted that his remaining forty followers would all hang for him, such was the grace of his eloquence and the delight of his company, not to mention the excellence of his ideas. 'I am more hurt than surprised at his abominable neglect of Lord Ilchester, and yet I am certain he loves him as much as ever: but these wretches who surround Charles quite undo him in a thousand instances,' Sarah sadly thought. To all his family's content, he was now sobering up a little: clearly Mrs Armistead was a good thing in his life. 'His finances are Somewhat better than ever,' Sarah rather guardedly reported. 'He does not game now but in horse racing; which is such a passion of his (for he loves the animal and the calculation) that I doubt he will ever give it up.'

'The horrors of Paris exceed all immagination,' Sarah wrote in 1792, 'but don't fancy there is the least danger of the like in either England or Ireland. In the former all spirit is gone, and an Englishman and passive obedience are synonymous terms; in Ireland there is great spirit left, and it wholly depends on Government to turn it to a proper channel . . . but the Govt. does very foolishly in trying to raise up quarrels between the Catholics and Protestants for the purpose of an *excuse* for an union that will ruin Ireland, for the nasty Presbetereans will run away with the bone.' And from near Dublin, where they had bought a house, the Napiers surveyed the darkening Irish scene.

Family life had not all this while stood still. After Charles in 1782 came Emily in 1783 and George Thomas in 1784, all within eleven

months of each other; and the rate of production would have continued had not Sarah 'had the bêtise to be frightened of the bad
Cheshire roads and to miscarry the very first night of my arrival here:
was there ever such a stupid thing?' This was September of 1784, and
she was off again in a flash: William was born next year. Hard
pounding, in an epoch without anaesthetics or antiseptics: the dis-
comfort was no less than now and the pain and danger infinitely
worse, but at least in Sarah's walk of life there were other hands to
pluck those soggy yelling dear-loved bundles from their cradles in the
black winter dawns, and Sarah, though mocking herself for her
excessive fertility, makes no complaint of the rate of progress.

But her sister Louisa, whom she loved more than anyone in the
world bar Donny, made no progress at all. Wife of kindly nervous
Tom Conolly and mistress of the beautiful immensities of Castletown, she was now forty-one and childless after twenty-six years of
married life. Might she be allowed to adopt one of Sal's children, as
it was now perfectly clear that her young sister, married to a zestful
young man whom she adored, was all set to pup once a year till the
change of life came to her rescue? And could it be Emily, a daughter
to rejoice Louisa's heart now, and comfort her old age later? Emily
had 'turned out quite beautiful': after long discussion and with a
powerful wrench the Napiers agreed. It gave Sarah a tightening of
the heart; 'but when I consider *who* it is to, I consider it a duty to my
child quite incumbent on me.' Emily, large-eyed and nearly two, was
borne away to reign over the glories of Castletown by Louisa
Conolly, 'that self-same unalterable dearest of sisters, who is ever and
forever the same in affection and tenderness', she at the passing of
whose Protestant funeral even the Catholic Irish were to kneel
weeping by the road (one of them so far anticipating opinion as to
say that if the priests said she would not go to Heaven the priests
were talking cock).

Sarah had plenty to distract her. In 1784 the 100th Regiment was
disbanded, and the Napiers had moved into Stretton, an Inigo
Jones house of the Conollys' near Wolverhampton. 'We are all
on the march, infantry and all'; but it was infantry with a father on
half-pay, and for such London was far too expensive. Stretton was
damp but everybody seemed at first to thrive and the neighbours
were charming, specially the Crewes: Mrs Crewe had been pretty
Mary Greville and Sarah, still firmly repudiating cards, spent a happy
visit gossiping of old times with her. Luckily 'Mr. Crewe and Mr. N.

took excessively to each other and sat up talking and playing at chess till 2 or 3 o'clock in a morning . . . as young Mrs Crewe says, there are so many men in these days who are ennuyé to death if they are not exactly in their own set and at their own amusements, that a man who likes anything is quite a treasure in the country. . . .' And Susan's troubles once more provided a distraction from country quiet. Poor William O'Brien had badly upset his stomach by trying to be a barrister: he had had to give up, and Susan was off to Spa with him; where Sarah assured her there was no need to take grand clothes as Queen Marie Antoinette had been there last year and she and her ladies had worn only 'white linen levettes and nightgowns all day long and a chip straw hat with ribbons'.

But in spite of Donny's refusal to be bored in Staffordshire it was turning out disastrous. Louisa Bunbury had developed chest trouble, which had refused to respond to a diet of bark and milk, and she became seriously ill. 'I am wholly taken up, with Mr. Napier's help (who has been more kind and tender on the occasion than I can express) in watching her every hour.' Louisa urged them to come to Castletown for the softer air of Ireland, but the move was in vain, for Louisa Bunbury died of consumption; the fall of a sparrow just seventeen, not beautiful, not clever, not even thought of by her natural father, simply a merry character with a large mouth and the usual complement of hopes and dreams who had been the centre of Sarah's life for eleven years, the point of endeavour, the object of all plans. This function of redemption once fulfilled, she seems to bow gracefully out. Ill since April, she died in December a week after yet another little half brother, William Francis Patrick Napier, was born.

Sarah was used enough since infancy to the untimely deaths of parents, brother, sisters, nephews, nieces, cousins, friends; but this tragedy struck home. 'She made me see every pleasure in its brightest colours. . . . It is not reason, it is not what is left (happy as it makes me). . . . No, my dear Lady Susan, tis religion alone that can soften such a loss: her death carried up my thoughts to that Heaven where I know she is. . . . I owe it to the way of thinking of my husband and sister, that in the first emotions of distress they turned my mind to see the truth, from them I have derived the way of thinking which alone could procure me peace. . . .'

The winter seemed very long, all the children were ill with different diseases: they planned to go back in the spring to Stretton, to live there with 'great oeconnomy' and hope for a better job to augment the half-pay which was all Donny could hope for in peacetime. She and Louisa spent the winter making and decorating the Print Room at Castletown, but by May Sarah still had moments of feeling 'as if all nature was darkened before my eyes, and I had no further business on this earth'. All this while she had been delighted to note how the Conollys had come to love Donny and enjoy his company for himself. 'Mr. Conolly in particular has formed the strictest friendship with him, and I'm much mistaken in their characters if it ever changes.' Despite political differences, it never did.

A year later the scene is brighter. Events, in the shape of another expectation, had overtaken them and they were still at Castletown, from whence they felt they must move soon whatever Tom and Louisa said. 'Emmy is just recovered of a feverish cold, and my eldest boy Charles beginning to pick up a stronger share of health . . . Castletown goes on as usual, always the receptacle for society, comfort, and friendship, and very often for innumerable personages, some old, some young, some agreeable, and some very intollerable. . . . Christmas was very full and very sociable . . . quiet at one end of the long gallery and dancing at the other. . . . We have enjoyed our quiet time which is owing to the bustle of Parliament. Now we have the world telling the news once a week, and we are rid of them soon. . . .

'The Irish politicks are vastly too intricate for a *volume* to describe, much less a letter . . . God knows how it will end, but to an impartial looker-on it appears as if the best people were often made the instruments of harm.

'I hear that in England all goes on piano piano, but still it does creep on towards the opening the eyes of the world to many things they hitherto saw darkly and falsely. . . .

'As for ourselves, our march is fixed on by *us* to begin on the first of May towards Stretton with our tribe, but the Conollys object, and all I can obtain is that if I will do them the favor to produce another puppy in the month of July, they will swear not to ask us to stay longer than Septr, for without this promise I must absolutely fly while I can move. I am afraid of growing like the bitch in the fable, and if you were to see my noisy sturdy boys you would really comprehend the likeness, for even Castletown can scarcely suffice to their spirits and riots.' By June 'the Conollys could not miss of carrying their point in persuading me to lie in here, and my full intention is to decamp in August, but they seem so positive we shall not that it is not easy to swear against their intentions'. The puppy turned out to be Richard. 'She wished for a little girl, and so did I for her, as my conscience forever reproaches me, for having got possession of her only little girl,' Louisa mourned. 'She won't hear of taking her back, which out of principle I offer, though it would grieve me beyond the power of describing to part with my little angel, whom I do love a very great deal too much.'

A scheme was afoot for the Napiers to take or buy a house just outside Celbridge village—'Sarah and I you may imagine are vastly eager about it, but we dare not yet set our hearts upon it. Mr. Napier's own thought it was originally, and he seems to like it vastly. Mr. Conolly also thinks it is the very best possible thing for Mr. Napier, and the most likely thing to draw him off, by degrees, from the Army,' for poor Donny was still feeling the pull of that unfortunate addiction.

'I really flatter myself', Louisa went on delightedly, 'that it is a prudent scheme for them, irrespective of the very great pleasure I shall have in it. And then it is not parting her and Emmy, which will be a great relief to my mind. Mr. Napier is to the full as much pleased as she is with the house and place, and amuses himself with making his fences and ditches good, and planting rose trees . . .'

But he had moments of appalling despair, Sarah confided to Emily, when he felt that he was wasting his life, his skill, his energies; when he told Sarah that she alone made his life tolerable to him. By next day he would recover; ashamed of being insufficiently grateful to God for the blessings of his life.

They loved both Conollys, and only to Emily was a note of mockery for Tom's hypochondria ever allowed to creep in—'what he terms want of appetite—viz two plates of soup, three pork steaks, half a chicken, and a tart. Dearest Louisa is deaf; but why she should be blind I cannot guess.'

There was no escaping from Louisa's determined family love, or from the pull of Emily, and the Napiers settled into the square, grey, three-storeyed house just outside the village of Celbridge after the birth of a fifth son, Henry, and just before the birth of Caroline. Celbridge House, always referred to by Sarah as 'my pretty little house', was of a size which no one with an income of under ten thousand would now think of taking on, though Sarah remained blissfully convinced that she was pigging it. 'I rejoice I was never Queen,' she wrote in a postscript to Susan in 1789, 'and so I shall to my life's end, for at the various events in it I have regularly catechized myself upon that very point, and I always preferred my own situation. . . . I am now much happier than I deserve to be.'

She was sorry to miss English friends, and the Sussex countryside. Though mountains and rivers were pleasing in Ireland, 'the country is ugly, poor, neglected, bare of trees; the roads are between mudd walls, no fields to ride in and desperate hedges and ditches to cross if one goes out of the road, so that riding seems to me impossible for a woman, walking out of the grounds still worse, and hunting, coursing and following shooters quite impracticable.' Ireland was far away from 'furious Foxites', the ins and outs of Charles Lennox's duel with the Duke of York—'I hope it is not St. Leger who orriginally said the offensive words for he is a great friend of Mr. Napier's which would add to the misfortune of the whole affair'—and the old King's recovery: 'I rejoice to think he is relieved from misery . . . all mad people are the better for the kindness of their friends, when they see them often.'

The only worry was that Donny was not well, he had never been so robust since his yellow fever; they thought of a trip to Tenerife 'where I hear the climate cures the most desperate complaints', but came down to earth with an '8 days' sail, Mr. N. at once finding the good effects of the sea' on 'the wisest, cheapest, easiest march', by sea to Bristol. Here little George fell very ill of a putrid fever, but at Hot Wells he and Donny both recovered, though 'Mr. N. will not allow me to treat him as an invalid'; and Sarah saw both brothers, Richmond 'good-humoured and gracious, he is grown old and consequently family affection recovers her power in his heart': both had come specially to see her, and George was equally gracious, 'and thats pleasant tho' I shall probably never see them for ages.' Annoyingly, they just missed 'Mr. Napier's sister returned from India,' where Montrose's heart, still in its filigree case, had had a number of adventures, including saving her from a French shot on the deck of their ship.

Lady Ilchester was dying and a reconciled Susan was nursing her mother, accompanied by William O'Brien: 'his acquiessence in it is a still greater proof of his honourable mind, which I always thought and am now perfectly convinced of,' Sarah applauded. 'After all the lamentations about you, the very event has put it in your power to return all your mother's adoration of you tenfold, for had you married Lord Lansdown for example, I beg to know if he would have given up ten *days* to such a life, or allowed you to do so. . . . In short, all is for the best in this world and we may always turn our errors to virtues,' Sarah concluded in her best poker-work vein.

William Ogilvie had made his first speech in the Irish Parliament in 1787, approved of in general by his new family. But Donny, as so often, saw further. 'The only point Mr. Napier differs from him is in the possibility of Ireland's receiving good ultimately if England is hurt; although it very evidently is the case at first. But Mr. Napier says its like making separate interests between husband and wife, convenient and pleasant enough perhaps for the present, but hurtful in the end.'

By February of 1790 Sarah was forty-five, awaiting her eighth but not yet her final child in Celbridge House, set just beyond the end of the village street, a furlong back and above it, and facing south east towards the blue hills of Wicklow. 'I am not brought to bed but mean to be so before the end of the week' she told Susan on the 15th. 'I have had a long tedious illness from a jolt or a cold or something, that made me keep my room six weeks, so that in all I shall have the satisfaction of being a poor helpless unwieldy prisoner for three months before I can rout about to my satisfaction, which is the most barbarous of things to me this year, as I am just settled in my new, dear, comfortable, pretty little house, and have 40 things to do every day, which I now do by proxy, and you know how terrible it is to *describe* where a rose tree is to be, or a shelf in the house, and all those little finishings that require *l'oeuil du maitre.*'

After the pleasures of retailing these rubs to Susan's receptive ears, Sarah continued in less melancholy vein.

'But to say truth my very pretty little flock of brats surrounding our fireside would make me an ungratefull creature to complain. I have 5 boys . . . I hope to have another girl to comfort me in my old age, when my boys are gone to school. I am perfectly well now of my complaint and in remarkable good spirits for *me* (so near my time which is apt to lower me), but in short, the delightful prospects of a *home*, pleasant in its self, well situated, the hopes of bringing our living within our income, and yet to be comfortable, the good health of our children, our own *tollerable* health inspite of this detestable climate (the only draw back to our satisfaction), the friendly affec-tionate joy shewn by the Conollys at every mark we give of pleasure here, the pains and care they take to lessen every common difficulty that occurs, all together spreads a gleam of sunshine on us that has its full effect on Mr. Napier's spirits and mine. . . .'

The dream of peace and family life was threatened on all hands. Ireland itself was heaving like a volcano, and the European war clouds were piling up. The Austrian Emperor was smarting over his guillotined sister; nor were other potentates more inclined to let the French Revolution get on with itself. They were foolish enough to attack France; and soon the answering revolutionary armies were boiling over the borders of their own lush land: for a moment the glamour of democratic freedom dazzled the eyes of at least the young, and blinded them to the drawbacks of marauding armies and ravaged lands. Like Charles James Fox, Donny and Sarah deplored the incessant wars with France—but if France was going to bang on into the Netherlands, if France was going to occupy all Europe?

'I am very very uncomfortably situated about it,' Sarah gloomed, 'for my love for my husband, my large family, my age, and my dear home (so long sought after) necessarilly make me dread it, and yet I am quite persuaded by Mr. Napier's arguments that having no Friends or interest with Ministry, it is his *duty* to work for the main-tenance of his children, and what line can he pursue with so much advantage as that in which he was bred, which he understands, which he likes, and of course is best suited to, and in which he has worked his way for 26 years?

'To resign it at the eve of war is neither consonant to his principles or his interest, for it is his only chance of promotion, and if it please God to approve of his steady attachment to those principles he was bred in, as I think it must, I will hope he will be enabled to sell out at the end of the war, and so reap the reward of his good intentions in securing *something* for his children, which is *all* his ambition.

'It seems to me very cruel and at the same time very odd, that Ministers generally promote both in army and navy men who are *fine*, or rich, or contemptuous about their duty, in preferrence to those who really love it. Sure its most useful to employ those who love the business! And yet I have the most vexatious examples of the contrary in the Napier family, for my brother-in-law Captain Patrick Napier left us and our comfortable home, for fear he should be out of the way in case he had the least chance of being employed at sea; but yet he says he is sure he shall not till all good ships are employed,

and nothing but wrecks left, one of which he may possibly get, if
war takes place.'

By 1794 war had come, and Donny and Sarah turned their backs
on the mild comfort and security they had achieved—'we can feed,
clothe, and keep (at a common school in the village) our boys, and
tho' we can neither have carriage, dress, company, or many luxuries,
yet we for ourselves could desire no more. But when we consider my
age and our 9 children who are left totally destitute at our death
(mine particularly). . . .' Even if Donny side-stepped the cannon balls,
Sarah's five hundred a year went back to the Richmonds at her death,
and fifty years was a long span for the eighteenth century—('Poor
Ly Westmoreland's death has shocked us all very much! Ten days
only from full health, youth, and prosperity!') Louisa Conolly was an
angel; but who with an elderly nervous husband would take on five
rumbustious little boys?

Mr N. was adamant. 'He rekons it his duty to seek service . . . and
having acquiesced I will never forsake him as long as it is in my power
to be of comfort or use to him, nor indolently stay at home when he is
going through fatigues and dangers. . . . Lord Moira is very much his
friend, so I build hopes that 26 years' service and persevering zeal will
now meet with its reward from a *respectable* officer such as Lord
Moira is, if he is lucky enough to be under his command. . . .'

As to the country, Sarah shared Charles Fox's view. 'We should
have flourished by peace and we shall be ruined by war, and come
back to where we began with the loss of millions of men and money;
but its an officer's duty to fight the enemy when war is *begun*.'
Braced by this thought, she began to pack, but was unable to resist
sending Emily a mild quip at the sister and brother-in-law whom they
both loved—'Conolly is pretty well, but he terrifies Louisa with his
croaking. And when she wakes, she expects Robespierre or Danton
to guillotine her before night.'

Early in 1794 Donny was appointed deputy Quarter Master
General to the army Moira was to command in Holland. 'I have
reason to rejoice in his health now, it being so much mended; my
own also, and I must finish by telling you that Louisa Napier, aged
17 (when misses are likely to be tempted by peace, plenty, and
pleasure), has been *pressed* by the affectionate kind Conollys to live
at Castletown in our absence, but has declared, if it is practicable to
take her without adding to our cares, she prefers going with her
father and me to any part of the world: have we not reason to love

such a dear firm character, whose affection supersedes all considerations?'

There is a moment at the beginning of a war when life suddenly seems clear-cut and simplified, fears and jealousies are forgot and people integrate: would we could feel a like impulse at some surge of peace. Now that the French were ravaging the Netherlands and the war was fairly launched, Sarah responded cheerfully to its trumpet; leaving the youngest six children to the care of Susan Frost, 'my faithful maid who has lived with me 26 years', the local doctor, and Louisa Conolly up the drive at Castletown, to follow 'the best and most attached husband that ever woman was blessed with' and 'march to any of the four quarters of the globe chance may direct'. The quarter actually directed by chance turned out, prosaically, to be Southampton. 'I go like a poor captain's wife, as I ought to do, in a chaise and pair, three of us (no maid) and one man on horseback.' Fifty years old, and with failing sight, Sarah had no intention of ceasing to enjoy life. Bowling through the midlands with the farewells over, her spirits rose. 'I hope to look at all my friends, which is a great pleasure after nine years.' With her sat Donny's daughter Louisa, all seventeen-year-old anticipation; and their eldest son, Charles James, large-eyed, burning, and already gazetted an ensign in the 33rd though small for his eleven years, and devouring the scene with untarnished interest and a gaze already shrewd.

The destination, once arrived at, was a thought damping. They were stuck in Southampton lodgings: Sarah had had visions of a pretty little house at Cowes, sea-bathing when summer ripened, walks along the cliffs of the Island. It was all very different. 'By degrees the army increases, various are the occupations of Major Napier, and constant and unremitting is his attention; ceremony don't belong to his character, and poverty makes us confine ourselves to a cheap lodging with 3 small bedrooms and *one parlour*, into which are introduced about 20, 30 or more people of various denominations from 8 in the morning till 11 at night. The Commander in Chief *et sa troupe dorée*, Commanding officers of Regts of Artillery, sergeants, clerks, waggoners, *all* march in at *all* hours on *business*. To this is to be added, *les dames de la ville*, now and then the wives of officers, officers themselves sometimes on duty, sometimes as visitors, half a dozen very young men who belong to the department call in; and run in and out like children for a hat or paper forgot' Sarah went on, half complaining and half madly enjoying the bustle and life of it all.

The Free French were already with us, exactly as known 150 years later—'The Toulonnese people, 600 of which inlist into some French Corps here, many more sailors paid on board the transports, an endless list of officers who come in dozens *pour faire leurs homages a mon General*, and begging to know who is to pay them, and when he bows and says not him, they bow and go on with ten thousand demands, the Artillery officers in particular, who have discovered that the field pieces in England are no use, and want Major Napier to send to Bruges for some French ones taken by the D. of Y. If you can suppose anything more troublesome than a Frenchman it is a *recruit. . . .*'

If Donny would only take time off to go to Ireland and recruit a hundred men he would get back his long lost colonelcy; but as usual 'he *will not* prefer his own business to his public duty', so Sarah was busy recruiting herself—'I have no place to be in but this coffee-room of his, and am forced to be civil to one set, while he writes and talks with the other, whom he very often marches into our bedroom without the least ceremony.' Yet if Susan and her husband could stick it, 'be assured I could not receive a more delightful addition to the pleasure I have in the glympse I get of friends here. . . . I have litterally nothing to say but military chat and that is too diffuse for a letter; politics still more so, and family chat is for being together. . . .

'Lord Howe's victory fills us all with joy now.' Here was a real ray of light and hope, amongst the unpromising news from Flanders. The Glorious First of June, that battle which sounds like a blaze of buttercups and was in fact a four days' running fight conducted in shifting fogs, driving rain, a strong head-wind in which the flagship Queen Charlotte split her jib, and on the final Sunday a long slow heavy Atlantic swell, seemed at the time very smashing and successful with its captured and dismasted French ships of the line; though in fact the bulk of the grainships full of American wheat got through to Brest and saved the Revolution from being starved out. It was also smashing in another and strangely old-fashioned galleonesque way— the Culloden, a 74, had a hundred panes of glass shattered. Michael Seymour, a twenty-four-year-old lieutenant in the Marlborough, also had his right arm shattered, and the French—what was war coming to—actually fired on frigates, previously considered exempt, like ambulance drivers. All the same—'Patrick Napier my poor brother-in-law is moaping himself to death at Ulverstone in Lancashire in despair for want of a ship, I have not heard from him since the great

1st of June by which I suspect he is quite broken-hearted at not having been there.' Louisa reported from Ireland that Susan Frost was complaining of William's wickedness; but this seemed, in Louisa's view, to boil down to nothing worse than his 'climbing great walls, and losing all his things'. But Louisa felt sure William would do well in life, with his 'beauty and quickness'. As ever, she was trying not to have favourites, but 'George is a most delightful boy and I fear I am growing partial to him.'

In the hot little Southampton lodgings, surrounded by a squash of other soldiers of all sorts and sizes, Donny was in vivid spirits, happy and lively again as the redcoat boy she had met so long ago at Stoke. Among the throng Sarah had noticed a charming-looking man, slightly grizzled and with a humorous face, and had wanted to talk to him, but in the way sat Paget, later to become a noted home-breaker and cavalry leader. 'A bright-eyed, white-toothed animal of a boy was vautré in the chair near me with a careless saucy look. I eyed him with a glance; Thinks I "Thats a London beau of the first order of incivility I am sure." But Donny says he is a fine boy and very civil and not *fine*. But Donny never finds out finery—he talks them out of it before they have time to be fine . . .'

Left behind when Donny went with the army to Flanders in the 'heat, dust, bad smells, and noise of Southampton', Sarah felt sadly flat. 'Major Napier writes in astonishment at the strange confusion that pervades in everything there, both political and military, so you may guess it is bad when he is astonished, who had a tollerable guess at it before. . . .' Donny's passage at least had been jolly: en route he had had dinner with Captain Tom Pakenham and wife, recovering from fever on the Isle of Wight—'Mrs. Pakenham writes me word Major Napier passed a most comfortable evening en trio with Mr. P. and her, talked over all the war, and was in good spirits as far as related to this army.' He sailed early next morning in Lord Darnley's yacht as far as Deal, whence he crossed to Ostend in the packet.

'I leave you to guess the balance of my mind,' Sarah told Susan, 'for an action has or will take place. I shall add no more, for I am hitherto tollerably firm and not apprehensive from nerves, tho' very much so from reason, and I really think we are such strange beings that nervous feels are less conquerable than reasonable fears. I fear

I should lose this *équilibre* of hopes and fears were I to write long to you, my dearest Ly Susan, for I must not be of the *larmoyante* set just now: I have too much at stake not to put on a false courage at least in lieu of real.'

Donny landed at Ostend with the few thousand troops under Lord Moira who had been sent to reinforce the Duke of York, still hot from marching his men to the top of the hill and marching them down again. Moira's force was at once confronted by a seasoned army of sixty thousand men under the French revolutionary General Piche-gru, and by that totally new phenomenon—a nation in arms. England had been playing her old hopeful game of Let's Pretend. Let's Pretend that if you hate war heartily enough it can't happen. If we turn our backs on Philip of Spain, Louis XIV, Napoleon, Wilhelm II, Hitler, who knows? They may vanish. Oh dear, they haven't: it's too bad of them: send out the armed forces, no matter if there are only seventeen of them, with no trained officers, rotten ships, no food, six rifles, or seven fighter aircraft. Let Donny Napier languish on half-pay in Leinster, let Patrick Napier mope himself to death in Lancashire for want of a ship, let the seamen arrive at the verge of mutiny for lack of food or pay, let the soldiers be crowded on board their troopships for many weeks so that they die in their hundreds of a virulent fever while Whitehall dithers. Only, whatever you do, don't spend money on being actually ready, on forestalling the early disasters: soldiers and sailors are cheap and expendable and money isn't. French armies had overrun the Netherlands, the Dutch were entreating help, and in the House Pitt was declaring that the general security of Europe had never been so threatened as by 'the system of ambition and aggran-dizement which the French had discovered'—as if such a thing had never been discovered before—but no one in authority had for one moment stopped being Whigs and Tories and done some homework and foreseen.

The convalescent soldiers had been revived in this instance only by the 7,000 bottles of beer supplied to them daily by Lord Moira out of his own pocket. 'He is a plain-dealing man of honour, sense, spirit and perseverance,' Sarah thought; and he was going to need them all. Faced with the sixty thousand Frenchmen, he could either re-embark at once or risk joining the Duke, which he did by a month of forced marches across the front of the French. 'My military knowledge does not extend to the view of any use in delaying the loss of Ostend, if Ghent is gone, for its only use was to send in provisions,

ammunitions, and men from England to the fortified towns,' Sarah
guessed from Southampton. There was a night on the long march
when the exhausted soldiers refused to move further and lay where
they had fallen, till an Irishman, roaring with laughter, rose and
shouted at them 'Boys! didn't the lord give us bottled porter when
we were sick at Netley, and hasn't he the right to take it out of us
now in sweat?' On they went; but to read of this campaign is to share
Donny's 'astonishment at the strange confusion that pervades in
everything'. The British were muddling, but not muddling through.
Their reinforcement was as ever too little and too late, and the
French soon had them and the Belgians and the Dutch on the run.
It was splash splash and into the sea again, this time via Germany; to
the mocking sound of the Marseillaise: but there are always a few
bright boys who can learn, and it could be said that in this and a
similar Flemish fiasco ten years earlier, two intelligent young soldiers,
John Moore and Arthur Wellesley, had at least learned how not to
conduct a campaign.

'I trust in God they are making an honourable retreat' Sarah hoped,
'because he would be so miserable about a shabby one.' 'My only
comfort' she went on to Susan, 'in his absence (besides knowing that
he is in pursuit of what he has called his duty for 28 years) is the
occupation of promoting his advancement . . .' and she was busily
recruiting. 'Pray ask any military body in your neighbourhood if
there is any chance of recruiting men of five feet four inches or over,
for 10 guineas and as much under as possible?' With Donny safely
bogged in Flanders, the old boy network swung into action, for
Mr Morse of the War Office had been at school with Lord Ilchester
and obligingly produced a hundred men out of his waistcoat pocket.
'We shall be a long time prowling about like wolves for our prey,'
Sarah thought, 'for after all, it is a sad sad business to enlist, but one
of those evils for which there is no remedy. . . .' 'Think of my bad
luck about recruits' she exclaimed to Susan, having failed to snap
up a bargain. 'If I had seen an officer one fortnight sooner who is
here, he would have sold me 20 at eleven guineas per man. Now they
are gone. My Dublin stock too, which was 40, is reduced to 26 . . .
Mr. Napier croaks sadly' (at affairs in Flanders) 'I hope he is not
right.'

'But my spirits rise in proportion as I look back to early days,
which promised me a more flattering hope.' Better the squashy noisy
lodgings, and the anxiety and the reluctant recruits having to be

bought in for £10 apiece out of a slim income, than being Queen to a King whose ideas and politics seemed increasingly wide of the mark, or at any rate increasingly unlike hers and Donny's.

For Sarah had been got. She would play along now for life with his notions; astonished though she was that Donny should be so set on the army—'a line of life he is so ardently attached to that no disappointments can conquer it. He has made me prosolyte to his sentiments, and tho' it must be in perpetual sacrifice of my own peace and happiness, I am convinced that a true military man (of whom I see very few) will never bring about any point of pecuniary advantage to himself or his family, but in that line to which they have devoted all their abilities.'

There was no arguing with him. 'If Major Napier's active turn of mind, studdy, quickness and perseverance had been used in any other line, he *must* have acquired a sufficiency for our family large as it is; but his passion for the army has decided that our 5 sons are to serve their country, and to take their chance like him for fortune. I confess the perspective is *dark* to me,' poor Sarah continued, 'for as I fear none of them will equal him in tallents, . . . I have little hope that they will even *earn their bread*, much less gain a sufficiency, and if my happiness was not so secured to me by family attachments to him and my children I should with the deepest melancholy dwell on our sad prospects.' Great-granddaughter of the worldly and money-minded Charles II, and of Louise de Quérouaille, who had slept her way industriously up to be his mistress *en titre*, not scorning even such unlikely stepping stones as the Archbishop of Cyprus on her way, Sarah had been dragged kicking and screaming, or more accurately, laughing and grumbling, into the Napier fold.

VII

In 1798 Spain and Holland, under the thumb of Napoleon, were at war with England, the Austrians had surrendered to him, the Poles were submerged, the Prussians sitting on the fence, and Russia in the grip of a mad Czar. The Irish, sizzling for some while, finally rebelled against the British government. In 1798 the French sacked Rome, emptied the papal coffers, seized Venice and shipped off the bronze horses from St Mark and in the full release of revolutionary fervour swept through Switzerland and Italy raping more women in less time than anyone since Attila the Hun; they threatened America; and landed in Egypt en route for the Indies. It was fire and sword as far as the eye could reach and further. In 1798 the British, moved by the desire to push the French out of India, stormed Seringapatam and went on under the brothers Wellesley to assume power over all India save Rajputana, Punjab and Sind; a proceeding described by the British Government in a masterpiece of understatement as 'a vexatious and painful interruption of tranquillity'. 'Everything that lives is holy' Blake cried out about now, as people sometimes do when the destruction of life is at its height; and Wordsworth, walking up from the Wye valley by ruined Tintern Abbey in the summer of this year told his sister in impromptu but unfading lines 'All which we behold is full of blessing', as if the affirmation were forced out of him into an air vibrating with pain and in the pangs of a terrible birth. In the midst of all untowardness Coleridge this spring finished committing to paper his great mystic vision of damnation and grace, uttering into a haze of smoke and blood its final conclusion

> He prayeth best who loveth best
> All things both great and small;
> For the dear God who loveth us,
> He made and loveth all—

and no one, needless to say, took a blind bit of notice.

In England life proceeded much as usual. Taking a break from her recruiting sergeant activities, Sarah 'spent the day with my sister Leinster at Boyle Farm' (Thames Ditton), 'which is now the seat of beauty, luxury and ingenuity', where was Charles Fox, 'who like me was all enchantment with the place', and from whom Sarah, flushed with gratitude over Susan's good offices with Mr Morse of the War Office, endeavoured to extract a job for William O'Brien in Ireland. Charles Fox, with tears in his eyes, had expressed himself willing, he was fond of both O'Briens and thought Fitzwilliam might oblige him. 'To specify what you want is the best way,' Sarah advised.

The Napiers were back in Ireland themselves by October. Moira had been recalled from Flanders, and Donny with him; Sarah's recruiting efforts were brushed aside and he was given command of the Derry Regiment. 'Its having been so long sighted after makes it more precious than it is in reality,' Sarah felt; 'for us its a new raised regiment, the half pay is only eight shillings a day, which don't do more than feed eight children, and we have nine and ourselves to feed, clothe, educate. . . .' She was going 'to follow Mr. N. to Derry 100 miles northward, where I shall stay till the Regt is ordered on service, and then what I shall do next is doubtfull, sufficient to the day is the evil thereof. . . .' Nothing at the moment was happening about Mr O'Brien—'alas, friendship, good nature and natural interest for ever fail in political business. . . . Do not open your heart to hope, expect nothing, and if it comes well and good.'

What came next in Ireland was far from well or good, and a hateful task soon went with Donny's colonelcy. Both Napiers were convinced that the Irish were being driven into rebellion by the extraordinary stupidity with which they were governed; but they would, Sarah thought, never break out into violence unless 'really wickedly treated', in which case they would join up with what she described with great disgust as 'Levelers and Presbeterians'. Leinster, Conolly, and Donny Napier all supported Catholic emancipation, as did many others; but the poor old King had been persuaded by its opponents that to grant it would be to break his coronation oath. In the Lords, Moira described the Irish administration as 'the most absurd as well as the most disgusting tyranny that any nation ever groaned under'. Portland had promised reforms, and Lord Fitzwilliam was on his way to carry them out as Lord Lieutenant. Meanwhile the British regiments in Ireland organised themselves to repel a possible French invasion.

There had been alarms six years before, when the French first declared war on England, and kind Mrs Crewe had urged Sarah to bring all her children over to the safety of Cheshire till the danger was over. But Sarah had been brought up Irish, and was unable seriously to imagine anyone hurting her. Panic-stricken letters came from friends in England just as they were all preparing for a rollicking dance at Castletown, after a very merry Christmas—'its all a bugbear', she assured them. 'I am not afraid of Catholicks but very much of the mob in all places' she added sensibly. 'I abhor 300 and odd of the French murderers, and pity the rest who are slaves to such tyrants. I pity the deluded multitude, and I wish them success at home, but ruin if they go *one step* out of France. I think our King's war very wrong and very foolish, but still I wish it success. As for Ireland, I know for certain that if the Govt gives the Catholicks their just rights, and make a reform of boroughs, pensions, and places, all will go happily, smoothly, loyaly, and well; and as certainly I know that the tricks played every day by Govt to sow division and avoid acting honestly will bring on a *strong* inclination to join the French if they land. This is the crisis to save Ireland, and alas! I see no steps taken but to ruin it.'

Even before the insurrection of 1798 the English soldiers in Ireland had, Sarah thought, 'perpetrated horrible outrages with impunity'. They were looked on with loathing and fear. On a June day when the troubles had hardly begun the five Napier boys were making hay in a roadside field with the Irish, when some passing soldiers asked them a question. George, then eight, was so rash as to talk back at them. Being 'idly answered' by this small boy, two soldiers drew their bayonets and climbed the bank into the field, announcing their intention of killing him. The terrified Irish haymakers, with good cause, fled; but Richard's and Henry's legs were too short for flight, and the five little boys drew together in fear amongst the tumbled hay, squaring up behind ten-year-old Charles as the two men scanned the scene to make sure there were no witnesses.

By the mercy of Providence, at this moment Donny appeared. 'His eyes rapidly caught the scene, and leaping like a panther rather than a man he was quickly upon the soldiers, swaying a six-foot quarter staff which he generally carried and used in surveying.' The two soldiers leapt back into the road where they stood at bay with fixed bayonets: Donny with his staff was after them like a flash. Rallying his four little brothers, Charles rushed them over the bank to support their father; but there was no need. Long after, William remembered how they had seen one soldier rolling on the ground and the other in their father's grasp. Propelling him towards the village with one hand and beating him over the head with the flat of his own bayonet as a persuasion against warring with children, Donny delivered him to his sergeant.

A childhood spent in the middle of a civil war matured the boys with bitter speed. Men working in the fields were shot at random by the militia: midnight raids and cruel murders were made in reprisal. The wanton cruelty of these irregular soldiers and the sectarian passions of the magistrates filled Donny with towering rage. The Irish administration were a set of **** *****s, and he had no hesitation in telling them so to their faces. It was not surprising, and greatly to his credit, that he made enemies and died a poor man, for the Irish administration of this epoch was all of graft and greed. His five small boys drank in his rage and ardour: Charles and William, in particular, grew up as passionate reformers, but their childhood taught them also that civil war and rebellion were the worst of all methods, and that armed revolution immediately gets out of the hands of the idealists who promote it. (The Young Liberals are eliminated in the first ten days and what takes over is the brothers Kray.) The greatest victims are the poor on whose behalf the effort is made: forty years later after oceans of innocent blood have flowed and a priceless heritage of beauty and culture destroyed, the poor are not even marginally better off than they would have been by a bloodless process of lawful change. All this the world well knows, yet none knows well to shun the heaven of self-righteous demagogery and banner-waving that leads men to this hell.

In Celbridge the bodies of the dead or dying being carried in were now a daily sight, and the infuriated authorities wanted to burn the village to the ground; a proceeding which Donny twice prevented. (Civilians, as Charles was to note again later in life when dealing with the Chartist troubles, are often far more bloodthirsty than soldiers.) But Charles could not help, sometimes, being fourteen, from rejoicing in the excitement of it all. One night, when his parents were away, a marauding party of a hundred men besieged Celbridge House; and Susan Frost, his mother's maid, held it all night with the aid only of one very old manservant called Laughlin Moore and the children. It was Indians and Cowboys in good earnest, except that they were still known as Greeks and Trojans. Quite other feelings seared Charles's susceptible heart when on his way to school one morning he came upon the body of an eighty-year-old woman, lying in the village gutter in a great swamp of her own blood, the murdered mother of a man supposed an informer. The death of this one old woman probably saved the lives of thousands of others, whom Charles, in later life, would be at pains to succour.

Amongst the blazing ricks and the pikes and the searches for arms, the Napier children were growing up. Emily, Caroline and Cecilia are all described as being pretty and sweet, but the knockout looks were reserved for the boys. George and William, with hair of a Charles II blackness, and Henry, with crisp fair hair and immense blue eyes, were handsome, bold and stalwart. Richard was scholarly and intellectual, but as nobody mentions his looks they were probably only so-so. But Charles, for all his limp and his shortsightedness and his small stature, had the star quality. His face was not much more than pleasing and his eyes fine: his truly redoubtable nose was largish even in childhood and in its final form is still on view in bronze at the corner of Trafalgar Square where it is almost enough to hold up the traffic. Nothing about him was usual, least of all his childhood. Like King George VI, he was the victim of a barbarous nurse. Apart from dropping him and breaking his leg, she once nearly murdered him, and underfed him to a degree that stunted his growth. 'I am not one who knows how to nurse and fuss over a little child' Sarah had light-heartedly said, leaving him in her charge when he was a baby, and Charles had to be rescued by Susan Frost from Suffolk, who had been his mother's maid since her Bunbury days. This stalwart loving character restored him to happiness, and Sarah took on as soon as he was on his legs.

Compassion woke early in Charles; the sad cawing of a rook sent him into desperate tears as a two-year-old—'Whatta matter poor bird whatta matter?' Courage struggled with great sensitivity: he was one of those high-strung heroes who as a small boy can cut their flesh to the bone in an accident and endure the pain in silence. His attitude to birds also hardened. When he was ten he was fishing the river one day, when a half-tamed eagle of great size and ferocity landed on his shoulders and tore from his hands the fish he had just caught. Undeterred, he caught another fish, and was seen holding it up, daring the eagle with one hand and menacing it with his rod with the other. Donny's stern financial principles were early instilled. Sheridan, who knew his father, met and talked to Charles as a nine-year-old and eventually offered him a tip, which was refused with thanks. The cynical Sheridan was taken aback by this—'Your boy is a fine fellow but very wonderful' (by which he meant extraordinary). Wonder in one form or another Charles was to excite for most of his life.

Commissioned in the army at eleven, he went with his father to the camp at Netley near Southampton, being sent back to school in Celbridge when the regiment was transferred abroad. Celbridge village school was a Catholic one; to it Charles and George and William went daily, learning nothing very much but the three Rs, and a lifelong sympathy with the underdog. Financially they never had it good; there was no question of sending any of them to a public school, nor even to the select Protestant establishment a few miles away. Unaware of deprivation, the five boys ran races and leapt stone walls with the little paddies, and led cavalry charges down the village street at Celbridge mounted on lean Irish hogs. Perhaps because of his infant disquiets, Charles's spirits veered like the wind. He would roll with laughter at mild family jokes, or, unjustly beaten by a master, shut himself into the boothole and weep for hours with shame and rage. But when the troubles broke out, it was Charles who un-hesitatingly took charge, and was allowed by all the others at his school, including the much older and stronger captain of games, to have charge. Although a Protestant, a foreigner, slightly lame, and small for his age, he raised and led a force of volunteers, all Catholics, in support of the law and order of an existing regime which was repressively anti-Catholic. He also induced all their parents to supply them with drums, uniforms, and well-hardened wooden fusils. When William led a mutiny of two against his authority, this rebel was court-martialled and sentenced to be drummed out of the corps. Charles allowed the punishment to be carried out, but at home sought by every means to restore Wiliam's morale, and gave him all his most cherished possessions. In the end, William's courage bought his reinstatement by common consent; and Charles, mounted on his cherished grey pony, led his united army on a route march past the smart Protestant school in the next village, compelling them to keep eyes front and not respond to the jeers and catcalls of the rival establishment. Staunchly Anglican in belief, Donny had taught his sons to be equally staunchly non-sectarian in behaviour. Religious feelings ran very deeply, but this did not prevent some of the most vigorous fighters for Irish independence from being Protestants. It was an odious struggle, in which Donny and Sarah often felt they were on the wrong side; but then the rebels were so idiotic with their ideas of asking in the French—as if that ever did anyone any good. 'Becoming an independant people is not practicable without the French whose alliance is sure to be usurpation, despotism and com-pleat poverty if the invasion succeeded' Sarah pointed out.

The incident of the hayfield may have been kept from Sarah; she makes no mention of it. In the midst of it all, she found time to urge Susan to be nice to the Prince of Wales, who had taken Mr Sturt's house in Dorset—'I warn you not to let yourself be deceived by false rumours to think so ill of him as the world does, . . . Like all other men he has his faults, but his perfections outballance them; I know what I say, and you love justice, so don't be led away by prejudice. How is Mr. O'Brien? Whats his present politics? Firm, I will ansr, for it is his old text. Give him my love and remember us all as affectionately as we do you. Col. Napier won't give up his argument to you of course, but it does not lessen his regard you know.' In England it had been a pleasure to hear Donny and Susan arguing politics, especially after listening to Mary Crewe doing the same thing.

'I could not help observing that exclusive of your superior sense, which of itself must make you a better companion, the life of a fine London lady produces but very flimsy materials for society *out* of it, whereas your life produces an agreeable society to *any*body. However I love and like Mrs. Crewe, and I was pleased to see that this same namby-pamby life has in no degree altered her character, she is the same honourable generous-minded creature. . . .' But her conversation with a sensible man! 'Although she is grown to see that Mr. Crewe's dry laconic sense is worth all her sentimental ideas . . . *her own folks* are the set best known by the name of *alarmists*, and with them she is all bustle, and joy, and grievance, and anxiety, and indifference too about politics, of which she talks *incessantly*, never listening to an answer, and in her arguments with Mr. N. I could not help being struck with the comparison to yours and his. She pretending not to care, to *have* no opinion, and eternally arguing without grounds and never listening; you professing to care, having a clear opinion, supporting it ably, listening and giving up to matters of fact all with the best temper, so as to make the argument instructive and entertaining . . . the difference good sense makes as people advance in years!'

By 1796 England was going through the movements of granting some Irish reform. A moderate Viceroy was on the way, enjoined by the Duke of Portland to effect a greater measure of Catholic Emancipation. 'No mortal here yet knows (tho' the 9th of October and Ld Fitzwilliam expected the 28th) on what system he is to govern here! . . . It creates an odd scene, and the toad-eaters of the Castle don't know how to look, whether to laugh or cry.' How would Fitzwilliam manage? 'To reform all these flagrant abuses which so immediately prevent the securing peace in Ireland . . . must raise the hornets' nest, viz. the Beresfords etc.

'Query! Can Lord Fitzw. withstand such an attack?

'Certainly not, if he is not strongly supported in the English ministry.

'Will the D. of P. support him?
'Yes.
'Can he?
'No, is my answer, for Mr. Pitt will in an underhand way en-
courage the very people that are turned out, who will upset Ld.
Fitzwilliam, and all things coming back to their own channell, poor
Ireland *pays* for all these political commotions. . . . If Ld. F. *will* and
can reform, then every real well-wisher of this country will support
him?' But could he? Would the old guard and its old prejudices be
too strong?

As ever in Ireland, politics bedevilled the religion, and religion
bedevilled the politics. As ever, it was not a hard and fast division.
Most of the Irish rebel leaders were Protestants, and many of the
Catholics were for loyalty to England, on the 'always keep a hold of
nurse for fear of meeting something worse' principle. 'Wherever the
officers attend the Regts are excellent' Sarah noted, 'and many divide
on the Sunday mornings on the Parade, one set to Church, one to
Mass, and one to the Meeting House, and *never* does one syllable of
religion arise to cause the least dispute'. In the long run, as so often,
money was the real issue. Would the British government fork out or
wouldn't it? Mr Beresford, of the Ireland Revenue Board, was in
London, complaining alarmingly to Pitt.

The situation of the British government was not just now particularly jolly. Terrified of sedition, they suspended Habeas Corpus
between the years 1795 and 1801, and were rapidly and splendidly
populating Australia by transporting thither all those with independent ideas. Most of the British army was in the West Indies where
40,000 of them died of disease in three years; (these islands which to
us flash like jewels, to our forbears loomed like so many Belsens of
almost certain death). True that Nelson and Jervis had beaten the
Spanish fleet off Cape St Vincent, but the sailors had subsequently
mutinied owing to their lack of pay and their stinking conditions,
and the Bank of England had suspended cash payments, while a
French fleet was at large in the Atlantic and said to be making for
Ireland. The naval mutineers, basically loyal, packed it in on a slight
concession and inflicted a resounding defeat on the Dutch off Camperdown and the Bank of England smartly recovered its morale, and
started lending to resistance moves on the groaning continent. But
not to those in groaning Ireland.

'We are in the further limmits of the land at Londonderry, where

Mr. Napier is slaving himself as usual in forming the Regt' Sarah reported gloomily on the eve of Christmas 1794. Nothing had happened over Mr O'Brien's job—'I do not see plain how sinecure jobs are obtained' Sarah admitted, 'as our line you know has hitherto been to obtain but little and work hard for that little, yet most difficult have we found it. . . . P.S. If the French are serious in meaning to exterminate us, I trust they will now find our *infants* (you know what infants are colonels now) as brave as their soldiers now are. It is self deffence carries them through, and so it will us.' 'Mr. Napier has in his own head formed the defence of this island so compleatly that it grieves me to think it will be done quite otherwise, if it should unfortunately be in question' she told Susan in September of 1796.

Apart from an early excursion in the Mediterranean it had been Donny's lot always to fight in wars that were unjust, or stupid, or ill-conducted, or all three; in America, Flanders, and now Ireland. His was the perpetual dilemma of the signed-on man, the thinking soldier or sailor. What b.fs, what unspeakable b.fs, the representatives of the sovereign people often were; but if everybody in the armed forces started forming political judgments on insufficient evidence and then acting upon them, where would you be? Cohesion was the only hope for a pint-sized offshore island so often threatened by enormous continental hordes. Greece, that nation of passionate individualists, had done the other thing and had now lain for three centuries under the absolute rule of Turkey, and any dictator could and shortly did walk right into and over proud and splintered Spain. Even the rule of Addington, even Liverpool's administration was better than that. Like some of those attacking Suez in 1956, Donny sucked his teeth and went on attacking. All else was chaos come again. King and country, however daft: he and his fellows had signed on the dotted line and were brought up not to go back on their word.

The tragic drama unrolled with the kind of ruthless logic that pursues long stupidity in high places. Reforming Fitzwilliam arrived; seemed to be going too fast, offering too much; panicked the home government, already shaken by Beresford's reports. Fitzwilliam's recall sent Sarah into a frenzy; and probably Donny too, since their views on Ireland were shared. 'A Lord-Lt that I *really* loved and highly respected, and with whom our friends joined, tho' he derived his power from Pitt. . . . The D. of P. had *positively settled* that the Roman

Catholicks were to be *on the same footing as the Protestants in Ireland in everything* long ago and *said* . . . Ld Fitzwilliam had full powers, the time and manner were alone left to him.' Fitzwilliam had proceeded as he thought right and 'The D. of P. never wrote to approve or disapprove and kept Ld F. in constant difficulties for want of an answer for 3 months. . . . Then came the vote for the money . . . a formal recall from the D. of P. and showers of letters to Lord F. to arraign his conduct. . . . The *Hibernian* will tell you the truth as to the serious, solemn, decent and sad multitude of all ranks that followed him to the waterside.' Well might they be sad; they were attending the requiem of Anglo-Irish friendship before a sleep of two hundred years. Not treating with the moderate Grattan involved the army and the administration in being joined by the fanatically low-church and partisan Orangemen, to the permanent detriment of Anglo-Irish relations. Sarah mistrusted both sets of rulers.

'I think the *new ones* and the *old devils* are like hackney coachmen set to drive manèged horses, they looked frightened and are doubtfull which is the best chance to save their necks, whipping or coaxing. God send they may be wise enough to try the last, and all will go smoothly, for it matters not *who* does the good if its done for *Ireland*' Sarah concluded in a passion of underlinings.

There was a party in the Council that was refusing to allow Catholics in the newly-raised Yeomanry, which was, Sarah thought 'declaring war to them at once'. 'The great weight of Monarchists are holding out their hands in prayer to the independent part of Ireland to come quickly and save them from the dire necessity of turning Republican, with whom they are in treaty, if they do not directly obtain full emancipation and full reform. The die once cast it is too plain to see that they will not *refuse* French help if offered, which *now* I am convinced they would do with honest indignation. . . .' 'What are we all to do if the invasion is made as there is great reason to suppose? While the troops are busy the rabble will plunder every house; thats a clear case, and by no means a pleasant perspective. I wonder how it will all end, for by Christmas time something decisive must happen I think. . . . However I shall stay and guard my garrison with my five boys, Charles at the head, who has just got a new horse, and I daresay thinks himself and his horse equal to Alexander and Bucephalus.' George, on the other hand, seemed to his mother like 'an infant Hotspur'.

The fever increased: the clamp of authority tightened. 'Cellbridge as yet holds out, though five houses are now burning. . . . I feel most prodigiously sunk with all the surrounding distress, but I am determined to exert myself, for the little use I can be of' Louisa Conolly decided on May 21st of 1798. 'Our footman and 12 Castletown servants and workmen have been taken up as house-breakers and United Irishmen,' Sarah wrote ten days later. 'From the nearness of the connection one has with servants we have heard all the ideas, all the complaints on both sides, and both are mad, both are guilty . . . the oppressors, the provoked to wrong, the revengefull, the cunning, and the seduced! These last indeed claim our pity, for human nature is weak, and their wives and children are real objects. . . . Our man was an idle silly English boy whom we scarce knew . . . poor wretch, we are bound to see he has a fair tryal, which alas is the fate of few in these terrible times.' Many rebels had, she thought, 'taken a fashionable oath from drunkenness; they are to be pitied'.

'Plan something, and plan in time' Sarah demanded desperately of her brother Richmond, who must have still some influence. 'I am sure there are many people willing, and a few able, to try to put it into force, but here all is a chaos of self-interest, spite, distrust, and no plan whatever. Yet a plan might be made use of to strike all parties with its merits. The trial at least would be made, and if it failed, your mind would receive comfort from having attempted the salvation of a whole people by trying to avert a civil war. By a plan I mean you to point out what should be done and undone, and who should do it. I know that a very sensible plan of this sort was written and sent to the prince; but it is too vague.' It was Tom Conolly's plan, and only to her family would Sarah confess her doubts of Tom. 'I so well know its author, that one day he is be-chancellored, another be-Ponsonby'd, another persuaded to believe every thing by a third party, and so on; from such vacillation what plan can be attended to?'

First, it was essential that the kick of dismissal be given to several individuals in the government, who were 'too well Pitted', i.e., set against Catholic emancipation; but 'here we have nobody fit to give the kick though plenty fit to take it'. Why would not the Prince press the urgency of Ireland's case upon Pitt? Surely he had enough authority for that?

'What are we to do?' Sarah asked, not unreasonably, 'are we to fight for a cause the head of which won't support itself?' But to

England, deeply involved in war with France, the cries of stricken Ireland sounded in vain.

Civil commotion notwithstanding, Sarah had no intention of losing touch. 'I desire that at your leisure you will send me a correct list of the young ones,' (Susan's nephews and nieces), 'that I may know by what names to follow them in the world and hear what becomes of them; for though they grow out of my memory, they do not out of the sort of interest I always feel for the children of my friends. . . . My affections follow the generations as they arise.'

Her affections were to be rudely wounded. Emily Kildare, who had been Emily Leinster since her husband was made Duke of Leinster in 1766 ('dukes abbound', Sarah had mockingly commented) had an innumerable flock; almost as prolific as Sarah, and starting much earlier, she had had George, Charles, William, Henry, Robert, Edward, Gerald (lost at sea), and Olivia, Sophia, Isabella, Charlotte, Emilia, Lucy, and four others, besides two non-survivors. Upon James Leinster's death Emily had still twelve children at home out of her nineteen, and felt lost in the face of all the decisions; she presently married William Ogilvie, the kind and sensible Scot who had been the boys' tutor for seven years. Her marriage to this much-liked man was welcomed by all except one rather highty-tighty daughter, Lady Emilia. 'You hurt our rank,' Louisa Conolly told him, 'but that is all you do,' and the advantages, she added, were many. Emily made the best of both worlds, continuing to call herself Duchess of Leinster and acquiring much help and comfort and three more little girls from William Ogilvie. Carton and Leinster House in Dublin now belonged to her eldest surviving son, and she and William Ogilvie were living in London the better to educate the children, when the bitter blow fell.

All her children were dear; but the flower of the flock was handsome, wayward Edward. 'He is the child of her heart, and the idol of his family' wrote Elizabeth Vassall, a shrewd contemporary observer who afterwards became Lady Holland, wife of Ste's son. Edward was very much a young man of his times. The French Revolution, like the thoughts of Chairman Mao, either excited or repelled contemporary youth. Lord Edward Fitzgerald was one whom it fatally excited, leaving him immortal in all Irish hearts.

Family worry was concentrated on dear Edward, for he was the leader of the Irish patriots. In 1798 this much-loved nephew of Sarah's was thirty-five, a handsome charmer, with black waving locks, thick black brows, and those widely canvassed Irish eyes, blue as the sky, and set in a great smudge of curving dark lashes. He had a cleft chin and a full curving mouth, from which issued a number of unpopular theories. As a boy he had fought with distinction in the American War and after an exploration in Canada had resigned his title and been turned out of the British army for this republican gesture. He had entered the Irish Parliament, from which he soon resigned in despair of getting anything done in the way of real reform. Though wild, impractical, and a Protestant, he had the kind of compelling character to unite the mass of Irishmen behind him; but he was too great a darling of innumerable powerful relations to conceive that fatal ill to himself or his friends could come from communication with the French. He had married Pamela Seymour, alleged daughter of the Bourbon prince 'Philippe Egalité' and of Madame de Genlis. She shared his ideas, alternately fascinated and terrified by his activities; so pretty and sweet that 'she cannot be vile Egalité's child, its impossible' Sarah thought.

Sarah gave Edward a firm auntly talking-to about his folly in *thinking* of promoting a French landing; but her words, listened to with his usual grace and good manners, fell on unheeding ears; for England, that great bossy bullying governess, has always stood between Ireland and any recognition of the harsh realities of European life. For Edward Fitzgerald had been doomed ever since in his desk had been found the fatal papers proving he had indeed been in communication with the French. How little England knew of what really went on in Ireland to bring a darling son to this! thought Sarah. How could Emily ever recover? Sarah herself was so overcome with misery that she could hardly write even to Susan, except to justify Edward, with her usual warm family partiality, against English calumny. 'I can hardly think,' Miss Vassall, a friend of the family wrote, 'steeled as hearts have become, that his brother's request to see him can be denied, but bad times make bad men, and one can't answer for one's best friend.' And when Edward died, 'He had the facility of attaching men of all ranks to his person; his loss has brought forth more genuine unfeigned tears of sorrow than would perhaps the death of 50 other individuals. . . .' The Fitzgeralds, Anglo-Norman in origin, had been in Ireland since the 1100s, and Edward was fully identified with the Irish in their sufferings and their aspirations, though dangerously unaware of what a French revolutionary army of occupation would be like. In March of 1798 the blow fell. A warrant was issued for his arrest, and a reward of £1,000 was offered for his apprehension. A Bill of Attainder was to be brought against him. His young wife was at this time expecting her third child, and Tom Conolly, fearing to touch the pitch of rebellion and be defiled, refused to shelter her in his house. Donny Napier, risking his hard-won job, urged her to come at once to them at Celbridge and stay as long as she liked.

On May 19th Edward was betrayed and his hiding place in Dublin discovered to the Castle authorities. The house in Thomas Street was surrounded, and Edward, startled out of a deep sleep by a rush of armed men into his room, had fired at one and stabbed another, fortunately in neither case fatally. Wounded himself in the shoulder, he had been carried off to Dublin's Newgate prison. Donny had hastened to Dublin to do what he could, and had come up against a blank wall of refusal. He could not see Edward and find out the truth about his alleged treason. Nothing, he told Edward's stepfather William Ogilvie in a letter, could save the young man from the scaffold but a petition to the King, which Donny urged Ogilvie to prepare at speed. The Castle authorities would chop him as quickly as they dared.

On June 3rd Tom Pakenham's wife Louisa, who was Tom Conolly's niece, sent word to Castletown from Dublin that Edward was very ill from his shoulder wound and in high fever, and urged Louisa Conolly to come at once if she wanted to see her nephew alive. So well known was Louisa's goodness that she alone might be allowed in to see Edward Fitzgerald where he lay now in extremis.

Louisa Conolly had tried with desperate energy to brush aside all official red tape and see her seriously wounded nephew; but Camden, Lord-Lieutenant, had refused her also, although Louisa, grande dame as she was and respected throughout Ireland for her goodness, had gone down on her knees to him. Emily had suggested application to Lord Clare, the detested Lord Chancellor; more generous, he had hurried away from dinner with his napkin still in his hand, to convoy Louisa, and Edward's brother Henry Fitzgerald, past the turnkeys of Dublin Castle and into the narrow cell where Edward lay.

While he was a little at ease from pain, she asked him what book he would like read to him: the alternatives were Shakespeare and the Bible. This blue-eyed, rash, and gentle revolutionary who so alarmed

Celbridge: 'my pretty little house'

Castletown: 'my noisy sturdy boys, even Castletown can scarce suffice to their spirits and riots'

Tom Conolly

Edward Fitzgerald

the British government, replied ' "Shakespeare speaks truth and is charming: but come, read me the death of our Saviour." He listened to it frequently with strong emotions, but they appeared pleasant. He never complained of pain or of any sort of inconvenience, was sweet-tempered to the last moment; in short he lived and died the most benevolent of mankind.' (But he had, in fact, gone out of his mind for some hours on hearing the shots with which four of his captured followers had been executed, their death had been such torment to him.) 'His inhuman persecutors' Sarah continued passionately, 'would blacken his memory after having brought on his death by depriving him of every comfort of mind that they could rob him of, but his soul was not in their power, thank God!'

Emily Napier had been deeply struck by Louisa's emotion. 'When she came back to her carriage she said with a violence of feeling the more remarkable from its contrast with the sedate and tranquil dignity of her character, "I who never before kneeled to aught but my God, grovelled at that man's feet in vain." After it was all over, Louisa wrote to William Ogilvie with as much consolation as could be gleaned for Edward's mother Emily Leinster, who had not been in time to see him.

'Thanks to the great God! Our visit was timed to the moment that the wretched situation allowed of. His mind had been agitated for two days, and the feeling was enough gone not to be overcome by the sight of his brother and me. We had the consolation of seeing and feeling that it was a pleasure to him. I first approached his bed; he looked at me, knew me, kissed me, and said (what never will depart from my ears) "It is heaven to me to see you!" . . . though I saw death in his dear face at the time. He said nothing that marked surprise at Henry's being in Ireland, but expressed joy at hearing it, and said, "Where is he, dear fellow?" Henry then took my place, and the two brothers frequently embraced each other, to the melting a heart of stone; and yet God enabled Henry and myself to remain quite composed. . . . Edward's senses were much lulled and he did not feel his situation to be what it was, but thank God they were alive enough to receive pleasure from seeing his brother and me.

'When we left him, we told him, that as he appeared inclined to sleep, we would wish him a good night and return in the morning. He said "Do, do," but did not express any uneasiness at our leaving him. We accordingly tore ourselves away . . . the last convulsions soon came on, and ended at two o'clock, so that we were within two hours and a half before the sad close of a life we prized so dearly. He sometimes said "I knew it must come to this and we must all go"; and then rambled a little about militia and numbers; but upon my saying to him "It agitates you to talk upon such subjects," he said, "Well, I won't."

'I hear that he frequently composed his dear mind with prayer, was very devout. In short, my dear Mr. Ogilvie, we have every reason to think that his mind was made up to his situation, and can look to his present happy state with thanks for his release. Such a heart and such a mind may meet his God! The friends that he was entangled with pushed his destruction forward, screening themselves behind his valuable character.' Louisa arranged Edward's funeral as she hoped he would have wanted it to be; and miserably, they all returned to Castletown.

'Affliction would have sunk us here,' Sarah told Susan, 'had not so great an object as rebellion and civil war at our doors roused us. It is extremely dreadful, but, thank God, has not yet materially hurt any of us; for by Mr. Conolly being at home, my sister has been able to do infinite good. Col. Napier has also been able to *keep off* the enemy by great activity, and Mr. Conolly by influence to avoid many horrible things, so that we have, as I may say, stemmed the torrent till Ld. Cornwallis's arrival, whose pacific intentions leave room to hope for peace and quietness.' To her brother Richmond she wrote slightly differently on June 27th—'My husband gains strength in proportion to fatigue and thinness, I think. I hope it will not essentially hurt him; he made me come here with my children, to clear our house for action, as it is the first to fall on, if they come this way; and we expect them every day. My dear Sister is as usual much the better for the constant employment of doing good, and much has she now to exert her talent on. Mr. Conolly is at home well-guarded, and wishing to do good, but knows not how.' 'Our house is a perfect garrison,' Louisa told William Ogilvie in July, 'eighteen soldiers sleep in our saloon and we are all blocked up and shut up except by the hall door and one door to the kitchen yard, and are frequently all ordered into the house upon the alarm being given of rebels near . . . many are daily coming in begging protection . . . I find that many are forced into rebellion and of course are grievously to be pitied.'

The family were all shattered by Edward's death. 'I own to you that I do not grow better,' Louisa Conolly wrote to William Ogilvie six weeks after it. 'The complicated scene of distress that involves our family is perpetually before my eyes, and that of my dearest sister whom I love so much better than myself, grieves my heart.' 'Suffering as we all do from various causes' she told him ten days later, 'it becomes extremely difficult to steer the little bark of reason, justice, and humanity that yet remains among us, through the ocean of fear, mistrust, treachery, cruelty, and revenge.' In its loss and shock, the ranks of the Lennox family closed. Helped thither by Louisa, Lady Edward and her three little children were on their way to Goodwood with a train of sympathetic Fitzgeralds. 'Don't let my sister fancy that it will be crowding or distressing me' the duke of Richmond gallantly wrote. 'Far otherwise, I assure you: it will give me real pleasure to be of any use to you all on so melancholy an occasion.'

'Edward was born with the most romantic benevolent heart' Sarah declared on July 20th, 1798, in a letter headed 'Castletown, where I was forced to come for fear of our house being burnt.' 'His imagination carried him beyond the bounds of practical philanthropy, and the times led too plainly to the strong desire of freeing his fellow-creatures from the *real* and *manifest* cruelties and oppressions of the Govt of Ireland . . . we all agree to his wife's opinion and confidence in his honor, justice, and humanity . . . if he had met with as fair dealings as his own he would have lived to be as thoroughly known and consequently admired as he deserved to be by all good and honest men—men now blinded by the mysterious jigglings of a wretched set, who have availed themselves of the strong engine of fear. But yet wickedness cannot *always* thrive, and truth will force itself into light. To time and God I trust!'

In their extreme shock even Sarah and Louisa, although they clung together, grated just a bit; the little bark of reason and humanity wobbling in the storm of sorrow. When Donny had first come to them with the news of Edward's capture, they had both had such violent hysterics that even calm Donny had feared the tragedy might be a triple one. And Sarah had grieved Louisa by her open rejoicings over some Kildare rebels who had been released from Naas. Now Louisa was to grieve Sarah by her resolute forgiveness of people whom Sarah thought of as Edward's murderers. But maybe Louisa, less partisan, remembered that Edward had been offered a free exit if he would leave the country; one could not altogether blame the government that he had refused to leave his United Irishmen.

'I should feel myself the meanest unworthy relation to a large and much loved family could I stoop to hide the hatred and contempt I feel towards their oppressors. Yet I blame nobody who acts otherwise, because they have not the same sensations. But everybody ought to speak as they feel' Sarah told her brother. 'I have felt great relief from the absence of almost all Ministerial persons from Castletown for 6 months.' Lord Castlereagh was her chief object of scorn: she believed him the prime mover in the Bill of Attainder against Edward Fitzgerald; but to Louisa in her kindness Castlereagh would always remain on the side of the angels because he had married Tom Conolly's niece, the charming and much-liked Lady Amelia Hobart.

'I have seen Lord Castlereagh but once,' Sarah continued, writing as if through clenched teeth, 'the rest of that sett but seldom, and always studdied my conversation so prudently as to impress them with the dread of my entering into any interesting subject, lest they should hear truths from me that they are conscious that they ought not to have deserved. This makes our meetings far from pleasant, but it saves me from what I wish to avoid, paining my dear sister Louisa's feelings.

'Don't imagine she is not nearly as much au fait as me; but she excuses, doubts, pardons, and forces herself to show no sign of displeasure, because she has as usual transferred a wrong thing into unkindness only to her, and therefore she has an opportunity of exerting her self-denial and Christian forgiveness in the Highest Degree, by calling it all want of kindness to her; she hopes to forget as easily as she forgives and she succeeds in both.' Indignant as she was, Sarah had a faint feeling that Louisa might, ideally, be right. But anger in the human heart is so much more fun, more satisfying, more native, than forgiveness. People oughtn't to be like Louisa, like Donny; it sets too high a standard!

All the same—'How wrong therefore would it be for me to counteract her religious exertions by showing plainly I don't blame it only as unkind to her, but as unfeeling in itself. One must therefore be content to touch their sensibility by a reserve which they cannot mistake, and indeed I try to make my two daughters follow my example and refrain from going one step further, particularly Emily whose duty calls on her to make one affection fight the other, so as to do right by both. But it is with the utmost difficulty I have persuaded both my affectionate warm-hearted girls to preserve the least appearance of forgiveness when they have such strong anger. They profess themselves Lady Edward's friends, and as such they profess to hate all her oppressors, and those who approve it.' What was the sense or humanity in confiscating all Edward's money and leaving his widow and babies penniless: how forgive this? If any storm of revenge rocked the bark of human reason, surely such treatment did.

'I cannot but love them most affectionately' Sarah went on in defence of her daughter and Donny's 'for the sentiment and boldness to support their just attachment. The only thing I fear is their letting my sister see that their anger falls upon what she loves and believes quite guiltless. For she herself is as warm as possible in the cause when she thinks it is deserved, as for example—

'The Speaker one supposes a chief agent, and to Miss Charlotte Burgh, Louisa let out all her anger in ten times stronger words than I ever used. We all congratulated her on having thus publicly said: "The greatest comfort I have in Castletown is that I may chuse my society and never let those set their foot in it who have leagued against the Duke of Leinster's family to persecute it by false Witnesses for the sake of money, and who are watching in hopes to criminate him to get his estate by the same false unlawful means they have robbed the widow and the orphan. When such men as Reynolds are to be believed as Angels of Truth, I am sure my word would go for nothing, though I can prove him a lyar, and therefore I have done with Dublin society."

'Charlotte Burgh was thunderstruck, and we all hoped Louisa's animated resentment would do honour to the whole family, when behold she repents of having spoken truth, has called herself to task for violence and unchristian sentiments, . . . and she redoubles her kindness to those she fears she was unjust to by being angry. When Religion conquers reason it becomes enthusiasm.' (Enthusiasm in Georgian times was a dirty word; having the pejorative force of communism, colonialism, racialism, extreme sentimentality, or any other of those emotive sounds at which reason departs and passion takes hold.)

'Dear angel, she is so attached to the system of Humility, that the world may trample on her without her perceiving it. For every now and then her natural noble spirit rises in its natural beauty and she assumes the advantages which superior goodness and proper independent pride has assigned to its possessor for the purpose of keeping bad people in order—but enthusiasm ruins all—except her private worth, nothing can tarnish that.'

In private life Louisa was perfect, without flaw; but when it came to great events? Surely one must stand up for freedom and justice: could countries be run purely on a system of Christian forgiveness? And should Christians forgive the unrepented wrong inflicted on the innocent? Long long ago Sarah had said to unhappy runaway Susan, 'think that I love you more, the more you need my love'; which was all right in human relationships, but could the body politic survive in a rough world on such terms? 'Our next connections' she told her brother Richmond later 'would do very well as kings with viceroys over them, for thats their foible.' Was there a shaft of jealousy here, of Tom's misused power, for Donny's little used intelligence? But whatever her foibles, to stop loving Louisa was not possible. She could even be right. To encourage people to make remembrance of past wrongs a national hobby might be to do them grave disservice.

To the huge relief of many besides the Napiers, Camden was now replaced as Lord-Lieutenant of Ireland by Cornwallis; he of whom Napoleon said that a dozen men so honest would redeem a whole nation. Though unsuccessful in the American War, he was able to repress the ferocity of what William Napier called 'the domineering Orange faction', but six months later Sarah was still feeling the shock and strain of it all; Donny's absence and danger, the enmity, the night raids, the abiding fear that all was being mishandled. 'The government' she had written in 1797 'urges on a civil war with all their power', and in March of 1799 she confessed 'I hate writing, my dearest Ly Susan, when the least *attempt* at collecting one's thoughts brings a thousand vexatious ideas so rapidly in one's mind, that *selfishness* (that first ruler of the human breast) leads one to fly to daily dissipation to avoid remembering *truth* . . . all that the best philosophy can teach is to enjoy the present moments free from the pangs of conscious guilt. We have never in word, thought, or deed, contributed to the misfortunes of this ill-fated country, and sympathising in the distress of others is our only misfortune individually. As to the weight of taxes etc, I may truly say they bear nine-fold on us, with our nine children, but you give them chearfully to support a war, which *we think was wicked*, is absurd, and will be ruin . . . I cannot be so ungrateful to the Supreme Being as to repine at *such* things, when He has blessed me with the greatest happiness human nature permits—my own beloved family! All healthy, aimable, affectionate etc, in short everything that can render my latter days content and thankful. Your kind letter has roused me from an indifference I begin to feel for all out of the circle of my family. Your affectionate and anxious enquiries made me recolect what dangers I was surrounded by that could alarm you. I see none. . . .'

Susan could now really reassure herself about their personal safety. 'I have not the least cause to fear in this neighbourhood,' Sarah told her, 'beyond the general and great cause in common with the British Empire, viz, the fear that Ireland will soon be lost to the Crown, for which I do most sincerely grieve. Like you I cannot help loving the King, for old acquaintance sake. You know I never could be made angry with him [she had forgotten the war with America] . . . nothing shall ever make me accuse him of the faults of others. My husband you know is a decided royalist and a supporter of monarchy, consequently a decided anti-Democrat and anti-Republican. . . . Ld. Cornwallis sent for Colonel Napier to offer him the place of Comptroller of Army accounts.' This task Donny had at first declined; it would interfere with his army job, he hated the thought of a desk after 30 years of soldiering; he wanted no favour through friends—'however dear they are to him it militates against his system to bind others by favors done him'. Above all, 'he had such an abhorrence of the character and conduct of the Irish Administration he dreaded the appearance of having any connection whatever with such a set of ——s, which he, who you know is pretty plain-spoken, made no secret of calling them. . . .

'All these reasons Ld. Cornwallis overset at once. He took both his hands, and said, "Napier, we are old friends, old soldiers, and understand each other. . . . No soul ever recommended you, not even our friend Conolly. I want a person of trust, of abilities, of firmness and of integrity to fill this place, which I laid my hands on instantly for *you*. Don't refuse me, I shall be miserable if you do." It had been unanswerable. 'He hates it, but will work like a slave. . . . The only comfort of this place is that we can treat all *dirty Ministers* with the most sovereign contempt. . . .'

The die once cast, Donny would be 'perseveringly uncomfortable to himself rather than flinch when he engages'. The problem of Ireland was gargantuan. 'Lord Cornwallis sees all the evils and endeavours to remedy them, but he must first give honesty, humanity, and sense to the country gentlemen, magistrates and colonels of Militia of the Kingdom of Ireland, and thats no easy task.' Her spirits, as ever, rose with the very act of writing to Susan and she shrugged off the Irish miseries and turned to gossip. 'Your account of Colonel Digby's family is very pleasant, he was always the best of beings, and I am rejoiced he is happy and comfortable; will you remember me to him as an old but not changeable friend. I love Mrs. Crewe very much, and like her company, but her politics worry me like those of other people. . . . I must tell you of a pleasant event in our family, after so many the contrary. Sir Charles Ross, beau, brave, noble, *d'un caractère distingué*, in short, quite up to any description in a romance, having also (what in a romance goes for nothing but in common life is not indifferent) a fortune of £8,000 a year, fell in love with Ly Mary Fitzgerald at Bristol, where she was attending her sick mother, treasured up his love in his heart to ponder well, came over to Ireland as General on the Staff, listened to all the torrent of lies told about the family, had decernment enough to divide exactly lies from truth, waited for her return to make his proposals, was accepted, and they are going to be married.'

By autumn a November sadness has set in. 'I think with melancholy that perhaps my dear children are born in unfortunate times. Sometimes I flatter myself that those very bad times work up as many dormant good passions as bad ones, and hope my children may possess them, and *earn* their future happiness by virtues, even tho' (like gold) it is tried by fire. And as no signs of peace are to be seen, I must make up my mind to war, and having a husband and five sons all likely to be employed, I must not allow myself any other ideas, but those of life being a passage in which there is much bustle, and to be happy if those I love get through it well.'

In 1801 in a final burst of jiggery-pokery the Union of Britain and Ireland in one Parliament was pushed and bribed through the Irish House, largely on a promise of Catholic Emancipation which was then not fulfilled; and the fires of an enormous hatred and suspicion were stoked up. But to Charles and George, to William, Richard, Henry, and their schoolfellows, at least the green fields around Celbridge were free to race and chase in without risk of extermination by either side in this ferocious all-out fight. Even so cruel a war had had its lighter side. Charles, aged fourteen, but still very small, was leading his company of boys on a night patrol in the early days, when the moon suddenly came out and surprised him in confrontation with a platoon of his father's men. He was seized up undignifiedly into the arms of its hugest Irish sergeant, uproariously mocking and kissing him. A well known rebel sharp-shooter admitted to Donny after the troubles were over that he had many and many a time had the chance of a good shot at him but had never had the heart to take it. Thirteen-year-old Ensign Napier, the colonel's little boy, was always so close beside him as to make it too dangerous a shot.

VIII

At what point does some dream of life come to possess the young, some noble myth enslave them, that can redeem or destroy? For *some* dream will come: they are left vacuums at our peril. Upon the Napiers life imposed a violent stamp. Born in a violent age and reared in a place where violence was rife, fed on alarms and excursions, on wars and rumours of wars (but perhaps no more than the 1939-45 generation were), the Napier children were growing up. The amount of literature on which to loose the infant imagination was not at this time very considerable, but what there was was great. They grew up with the Bible—not a notably pacifist document in its early stages—with Moses and Joshua and Gideon, with the *Iliad* and *Odyssey* and with North's translation of Plutarch's lives. There was also Malory's *Morte D'Arthur*, and Froissart, equally insistent that 'Prowess is so noble a virtue that one must never pass over it too briefly, for it is the mother stuff and light of noble men'. Both their local uncles, Mr Conolly and the Duke of Leinster, had fine libraries in which the children were allowed a free run (Louisa by now really thought of them all as hers); and in these two great houses there was a constant coming and going of well-informed, educated and amusing people, so that the young Napiers did at least scramble into slightly more education than was afforded by the village school, though not much of it was of a nature to soothe their savage breasts. What performed this essential function was an uninhibited flow of parental love.

The long evenings fell over Celbridge House, over the damp, the cold, the small corner of warmth by the blazing fire, the candles spaced about the darkness, the stiff-backed chairs, few and elegant, the listening little boys stretched out on the carpetless floor; drinking in Hector and Achilles, Alexander and Darius, Douglas and Percy. They lay and listened in the firelight in a degree of comfort not so far removed from the times of which they heard as our degree is far removed from theirs. 'And now I dare say, said Sir Ector, thou Sir Launcelot, there thou liest, that thou were never matched of earthly knight's hand. And thou were the courteoust knight that ever bare shield. And thou were the truest friend to thy lover that ever bestrad horse. And thou were the truest lover of a sinful man that ever loved woman. And thou were the kindest man that ever struck with sword. And thou were the goodliest person that ever came among press of knights. And thou was the meekest man and the gentlest that ever ate in hall among ladies. And thou were the sternest knight to thy mortal foe that ever put spear in the rest. Then there was weeping and dolour out of measure.' It was the stark and age-old cult of Western Europe still holding sway; addressed to adults, praising adult life. A far cry from Peter Pan, from staying as a boy; it was a legend unprettified by Alice, by Benjamin Bunny, by Winnie the Pooh, by the dream that children, left alone, are unadulterated darlings.

Charles enjoyed an intermittent passion for his lesson book, George less, and William none. This future historian, whose rolling periods were to be an inspiration to Winston Churchill amongst many others, started life as a resolute dullard. Richard was quieter than his brothers; really studious and clearly going to be clever; and Henry, blue-eyed and philosophical, looked set to sail through life, but in fact did not; for him it was to be one long battle against contrary winds. Emily was Conolly-based, and Caroline and Cecilia were pretty and biddable and too young to start worrying about. Donny was not a great worrier over his children's future: but a note of slight disappointment and impatience slips into Sarah's tone when talking of Donny's Louisa, her step-daughter; the note of an irresistible woman faintly irked by a quite resistible child. Louisa had been very much diverted by Susan's messages, 'but she is Napier still. . . . She keeps sad company for success, for her two present maiden friends are Ly Mary and Ly Emily Fitzgerald, so that she has no chance but a cast off beau, for they are both rather pretty, I may say almost handsome, very very agreeable, lively, charming girls, full of tallents, and at the same time so natural, merry, and equally civil, that they gain all hearts.' Still, she loved them all; delighting particularly in the company of the five boys, lively and diverting, coming in with news from the outside world, village tales, and splendid histoires learnt from their many Irish cronies. (Among others present in the neighbourhood there was a young man with a beak nose mooning about, called Arthur Wellesley, of whom no one entertained a very high opinion, except Donny. 'Those who think lightly of that lad are unwise; he has in him the makings of a great general.' But then Donny often had these eccentric views.)

For her own Louisa, child of her brief passion for William Gordon, Sarah never ceased to mourn. The other apple of her eye was Charles, her luckless eldest son; noble in a strange unchildish way, intractable, and always able to make her laugh. What would become of him? He bore a charmed life, and yet was so accident prone that never a year was to pass in his long life without some minor disaster to health or limb. Conscience drove him like a powerful electric current permanently switched on; yet he was irrepressibly funny, bubbling with invention and nonsense. 'An exuberant humour rioting like a merry devil in a nun always possessed him, and in adverse circumstances most strongly,' William wrote, and Leslie, one of Charles's ensigns, later told his brother that 'all the time I was ill he used to sit with me for hours and make me laugh whether I would or no.' When interested or enraged, his eyes, huge and black behind his glasses, blazed in a manner that really alarmed people; nor did they ever know at all what he would say or do next. The conventional started by fearing him slightly mad, and all but the most incurably pompous ended by succumbing to his charm and dynamism. In time the cynical Greeks would think him in some way holy; and to the Indians he also seemed possessed by a spirit, though whether holy or hellish was another thing. Which would win, his blue devils or his irrepressible mirth? Either way, he would take some hard knocks. And his health was lamentable. 'Charles is always a poor, pale-faced, thin, dismal-looking wight, like a little old man with a cough.'

George was the answering-back little boy whose quip in the hayfield had nearly put paid to all the little Napiers when they were barely into breeches. A cheerful, buoyant, hot-tempered character, whatever devils tormented him were red rather than blue. But so successfully did his mother impress upon him that he must never go to bed at night without making up a quarrel, that at 44, in a private memoir written for his children, he was able to boast that he had never lost a friend by his temper, or lacked one at need. His inclination was for the sea, and he was entered on the books of *Invincible*, Captain Thomas Pakenham. The sea, however, did not incline itself to him; before joining a ship he opted out of a life of seasickness and decided to enter the Church—'there is no situation in which one can prove more useful to mankind or more sure of being acceptable to God,' he thought, looking back. Here a weakness at Latin proved the stumbling-block: George decided he liked 'fighting, a red coat, and a sword'. Lord Cornwallis got him a cornetcy on January 1st, 1800, and 'No boy of fifteen ever felt greater delight than I did on reading in the Gazette "George Thomas Napier, gent. to be cornet in the 24th Light Dragoons".' His uncle and godfather, Tom Conolly, bought him one of his horses (and eventually left him a little money in his will). George was away.

Stampeded by Cornet Napier, the Dublin tailor finished his uniform in record time; but the crown of it all was the helmet. When Sarah put it on his excited head, with its motto Death or Glory, her eyes filled with tears: George was not less moved himself. He made an inward vow that Death or Glory should be his watchword. Unfortunately there was not much of either about at Dublin Barracks, where he joined his regiment next day. All the same—'you will easily imagine what a happy fellow I was to be my own master at fifteen, with a fine uniform, a couple of horses, a servant, and fifty pounds in my pocket, the first, last, and only money I ever received from my parents, who had not the means to give me any more.'

Not surprisingly George, when released into the rollicking atmosphere of vice-regal Dublin, learnt nothing (apart from increasing his knowledge of horses), except 'to drink and enter every kind of debauchery'. 'As to gaming,' he told his sons 'I warn you against it as the most dreadful of all vices; it corrupts the heart, debases the mind, destroys the temper, and ruins the prospects.' It was covetousness, that degrading thing, run wild. After six months of all this George was plucked out of the Dragoons by his father Donny and sent as lieutenant to a line regiment at Limerick, on the other side of Ireland. Here he consoled himself for the loss of his horses by the fact that Limerick, then as ever, was full of the prettiest girls in the world. He and Charles shot snipe together, and kept each other's secrets; and long afterwards Charles remembered the girls of Limerick as being the prettiest and the wickedest in the world. They were almost the only good things he could remember of Limerick;

and it is a period of his life upon which George, writing his memoir for his sons in the height of the Victorian epoch, does not dwell. George was long legged and handsome, stalwart and yet full of dash. 'He was a bolder rider than I was,' Charles insisted, 'and when his blood was up all the devils in hell would not stop him in a hunt or a battle.'

At school George had been, by his own description, a dunce. Perhaps he was daunted by the fiery perceptive intelligence of his older brother. He was certainly not insensitive. We cannot cheer ourselves with the illusion that our forbears endured what they had to endure in the way of wounds, childbirth and unanaesthetised operations with the aid of stronger nervous systems than we now have. Their surviving letters belie it. 'Naturally of the most tender disposition and feeling, George has gone through such scenes as he cannot bear the recollection of at all,' Sarah would report after Corunna. But he had great resilience and fine physique; was recognisably sanguine. When he joined General John Moore at Chatham, that officer, surveying this six-foot eighteen-year-old with dark hair and very bright black eyes, had after 'a very kind welcome' looked him up and down with a quizzical expression George could not quite understand. Finally Moore had laughed and said 'Oh! You will do. I see you are a good cut of a light infantryman. Come and dine with me.' George loved his brothers but went his own way and thought his own thoughts, cutting fewer mental capers and making fewer enemies than they did, giving them money when he was flush and accepting from them when he was pushed, fighting fewer causes, loving simpler girls. Long before he saw George, Moore had defined his idea of what he wanted. 'As we are light infantrymen he must be active and tolerably good looking . . . I wish them to be gentlemen's sons, with tolerable education and with looks and make that will do for soldiers.' Small fortune did not matter; what did was 'a mind bent on being a soldier', and this George indeed had. He was on Donny's even keel, with Donny's single-mindedness.

William was the legendary third son of song and story; with looks, charm, brains and courage. His best friend was an Irish poacher with whom as a small boy he went on many an exciting night expedition before being caught and hauled before his father. Begged off a beating by beautiful young Lady Londonderry, whose husband's woods were involved, he noted perhaps for the first time the effect of his bright eyes upon Ly L. and the effect of Ly L's bright eyes upon

Papa. Loathing his book, William at fourteen was quite unable to spell and wrote atrocious English. He grew up very athletic and agile, with long legs, flashing eyes, and a wide-awake ferocious intelligence which he started quite suddenly to apply to the printed page. But never did he even begin to learn to spell.

Basically agin the government, William was also capable of taking a stern poacher-turned-gamekeeper line, and getting away with the kind of letter he wrote at the age of 17 to his friend Charles MacLeod from Castletown in July 1803—'I am very sorry that you have got into a kind of company from wich I have so lately escaped that is to say Jockys gamesters and idlers, that you have your own sett apart from the other oficers of the Accademy and that you have got a supercilious hauty manner to all the others, now consider the consequences of it . . . your prommotion ruined for ever and for what? to be laughed at not only by the sensible men of the army but even by the very people you keep company with. . . .' Charles Mac-Leod remained William's greatest friend until his death at the siege of Badajoz ten years later.

William could easily have been spoiled by his superabundance of charm and attraction, or thwarted into a lethal bitterness by ineffectual rebellion: he was never anywhere near an easy character. He made bad enemies in later life when permanently tormented by a bullet lodged too near his spine for removal. Like Charles, he was an occasional prey to devils: his were unquestionably black. He would lam into anyone inflicting cruelty, with such force that he was lucky never to have actually murdered: he could nurse revenge for an injured brother like the fiercest Highland Chief: yet to a mad armed boy threatening suicide, and death to anyone who tried to stop him, he was all patient calm and sensible reassurance. On balance he was a loved and honoured man, though a passionate and partisan one. 'His immensely high animal spirits when young seemed to render him quite wild, but this was only in appearance,' a friend wrote, and Sarah too warned people of William's 'giddiness' when he was going to stay with them. 'But,' Shaw Kennedy went on, 'he had so completely the control over himself that in my 55 years' acquaintance with him I have never known of him anything but purity, and the most high-minded and honourable bearing in all that he has said or done.' He lacked deviousness, or indeed tact, and had very little notion of getting himself on; living by his own wild northern lights.

All agree that William's looks when young were dazzling; black-haired and very slightly fiendish he had that touch of fire and brimstone that makes havoc among the girls. He was equally slain by them. Among the Irish he was able to recruit freely when it came to raising a company, because he was so recognizably one of them, and induced them to sign on by winning bets that he could run faster and jump higher than any of them. At 14 he was an ensign in the Royal Irish Artillery, but exchanged into the 62nd, after which the Duke of Richmond, whose godson and favourite among the boys he was, bought him a commission in the Blues, a regiment he did not long adorn, leaving to join his brothers in learning his job under Sir John Moore at Shorncliffe.

Richard, who came next, was the bookish boy. Gentle and sympathetic, he was always the one who had to break terrible news, to write the letters when anyone died, to tend the deathbed when anyone was dying. He got a first in mathematics at Oxford and became a Fellow of All Souls, but was the only one of the five brothers who failed to make the Dictionary of National Biography. No mystery here; his eyes, like his mother's, went wrong.

Henry, youngest son, was calmer, and lonelier away from home, and looked quite different with his waving fair hair and large mild blue eyes. He was very ready to be amused and his compassion took a less violent form. He was agile and philosophical and bent on going into the Navy, where presently he found himself. Once away from his overwhelming older brothers he showed well able to fend for himself in love, argument or war. He too was extremely strong, and had not been at sea very long before he saved the life of a drowning sailor by a strange but effective method. (It seems odd that so short a while ago there was no knowledge of life-saving, and that seamen and fishermen rarely learned to swim, seeming to prefer to drown swiftly.) Spilled into mid-ocean a mile from his ship Henry brought his sailor up from depth in a clutching panic. With difficulty Henry threw him off, and alternately pushing him from the back with his feet and pulling him upright by the shoulders, proceeded by this strenuous method to bring him alive to the ship. In the East Indies Henry distinguished himself only by hanging between life and death with fever for a record number of days; but alas it left him so depleted by permanent internal weaknesses that it marred his career. Nobody could say that the brothers were physically lucky: even George with his robust frame ended up short of an arm. On the other hand they were very lucky to make old bones at all.

None of the brothers went to a public school and all openly admitted to the pangs of love. 'My heart is a *cinder*' Charles would complain, and 'I am in love *eternally*' George echoes. William once jumped over two cows side by side in the street of Ballina when dared to try it by the belle of the neighbourhood, but she had pushed her luck and he forgot her, excited and attracted by the ash-blonde oddness of Lady Hester Stanhope. Celbridge House was known in the neighbourhood as the Eagle's Nest, owing to the beaks of its inhabitants, and their habit of soaring out unexpectedly on forays.

'Such are our father's sons,' Charles wrote, long after, thinking of them all in their various jobs as generals, 'but none of us is his equal. I have never seen his equal, but possibly sons are not good judges. However, we all resolved not to disgrace him, and were he alive, he would be satisfied.' Their parents do not seem to have imposed any fierce standards; and Sarah at least had no extravagant hopes. In 1804 she sent Susan O'Brien one of her periodical reviews of the family situation, couched this time in her more customary vein of cheerfulness, though Donny was overworked and far from well, and the boys all away. Henry was going to sea, 'by his own positive desire'. The eldest three were all away learning soldiering, and Richard 'Studdying for the Church. I do and shall miss them sadly, but, thank God, they have good principles, good hearts, good constitutions, and good friends. As to their good sense, time alone must prove if I am partial in thinking that they don't absolutely *want* it, though I by no means brag of genius or shining abilities among them.'

Louisa Conolly, that pillar of stability, had been swept out of Ireland for the while. Local devastation in Leinster had been terrible during the troubles; Dunboyne had been burnt to the ground; and poor Tom Conolly had distressed everyone by succumbing to the 'agitations and schisms of Ireland' and going to Devonshire with a nervous breakdown, and Louisa had of course gone with him. 'He with 27 thousand a year, an angel for a wife, many real friends, very tollerable health, a lovely place, many attached servants, power to keep the neighbourhood quiet (if he knew how), his own Regt quartered here to help him, is hourly in a sort of despair wishing himself dead, hurting his health, raving of dangers that don't exist, saying he is harrassed to death because he has not got a friend on earth. In short his nerves are gone' Sarah thought. 'I cannot be selfish enough to wish them to stay as I'm convinced peace of mind will ensue . . . from a different scene: . . . they are thinking of some place in Devonshire for his asthmatic complaint. Ireland will have lost its greatest charm for me when they are gone.'

She felt low altogether. Donny's new job was a dead loss—'nothing but his friendship to Ld Cornwallis makes him keep it . . . Col. N.'s place is *called* by the Ministers I hear, 14 hundred, 3 thousand, 12 thousand, and even 30 thousand, because each man speaks as his conscience would admit of in private perquisites and bribes. But to him it is exactly £600 salary; but as a proof that ministerial wicked-ness has infected me, I write to you on gilt paper for the first time these 20 years' Sarah mocked. Urged by Cornwallis to help him 'to clean out the Augean stable' of the Irish administration, Donny had, as a first act, abolished all fees; thus reducing the £20,000 per annum that his predecessor had enjoyed to £600 a year of bare salary. Poor Sarah felt a thought melancholy sometimes yoked to such firm ideals. Nine children! could he not, for once, do as others did?

What with his integrity in a far from honest world, his good looks and good courage, his loving heart and his intellectual interests, his even keel and what Sarah called his 'friendly mind', Donny Napier seems a little too perfect; and it is a relief to find that he could, in the happier times before the troubles, lapse merrily from grace. 'At eleven in walks Mr. Napier, drunk as an owl,' Sarah had reported to Emily a few years earlier, 'with two colonels I had never seen, and Edward Fitzgerald, as drunk as his good uncle.' Donny had insisted on their all being fed, be it only with bread and cheese; the footman was ill, the cook was in bed, there was nothing much in the pantry or larder, and Edward Fitzgerald, still in his twenties, ate for four. The two colonels were speechless; at three in the morning Donny was still making a night of it and woke her up to say that there was a pirate ship approaching the house (which was twelve miles inland), and he and the others roused all the children by firing pistols from the terrace at this imaginary vessel. Next day, not surprisingly, Donny com-plained of gout in the stomach, and was twitted by Sarah on his owlishness.

The new century found Sarah not at her most serene; they were in lodgings in Dublin, 32 Kildare Street, a corner house, not over clean, and providing 'a worse dinner than anywhere in Dublin, where everybody but us think dinner an important affair, likely to remain here all summer and winter too, for ought I know. My poor husband works hard at his office from the moment he is up till 5, then gets half an hour's ride. He *was* very ill from this life, he is better, but detests it equally now, sees no good that will accrue from it to the country, and certain evil to him, without emolument worth taking; but he consoles himself with the proper pride of having acquitted himself with honor of the trust reposed on him by Lord Cornwallis.

'Virtue is its own reward in this case, I fear; not by Ld. C's fault, for his friendship meant it to be of use, but it won't turn out so. I have been ill, having lived retired, and hate Dublin; . . . Ireland is getting into tranquillity and industry, and those who are so happy as to have no office may enjoy their roses and honeysuckle, mine blow in vain for me. I only go out of a Sunday like a *cit*, alas!' Was it for this they had left charming Celbridge?

Once moved into a house at Sackville Street, morale recovered. Susan had had an operation for cancer, and withheld news of her pain and danger until it was successfully over,—'you are one of the few living patterns of the firmness one ought to set before the eyes of one's children' Sarah told her, 'for what can be better than to bear God's will with manly, humble, resigned, and patient fortitude?'—and now, fully recovered, she was writing to Sarah in good spirits. Once again, after the pattern of their childhood, Susan was the sustainer, the elder, the good example to Sarah's giddiness. 'How kind you are . . . to give me the comfortable idea of your philosophical happiness, which you do not allow any weakness of mind to interrupt! . . .' The unseen monitor took another tea-break and she was off at once on a happy gossip with Susan who alone had shared it all, remembered everything that she remembered. Susan's niece had married Mr Frampton of Moreton—'it secures you a comfort the more, and I wish you ten thousand. Family connections alone give them in old age, when the heart clings to relationship with redoubled tenderness. I feel a *little* mortified that Mrs. Frampton remembers me only *at a ball*, for my admiration of *her* made an impression on me which no time has erased . . . I heard of all her merits, and saw all her sweet manners and beautiful face. She was like the Dss of Marlboro' in her improved state; for you may remember the great difference between the bouncing Ly Car Russell and the gentle Duchess of M., . . . who to me has always been pleasing from the moment she *secured the duke*. . . .

'My dear Ly Susan, is anything *new* under the sun? Don't we see the same nonsense repeated every day, at least in the trifling world, and I think in the real great world one may say the same. Is not Caesar returned in the shape of Buonaparte? The same genius, the same promptitude to concert, to execute great plans! One is lost in guesses of what is to follow, so I never think about it. . . .

'My eldest son Charles is aide-de-camp to Sir James Duff at Limerick; the General is an old friend of ours, and has shewn it by sending for this boy (unseen). You may guess the fidgets I am in to have him succeed . . . he is delighted with their kindness. . . . My 4 other sons are at home learning from masters to be ready when occasion offers to go into the army. Louisa and Emily Napier are at Castletown, and my 2 little girls with me; we have got a large house, and are as comfortable as we can be in Dublin, but its a hateful place' country-bred Sarah insisted. But though 'Col. Napier is fixed in his office of Comptroller of Army Accounts much against his will', it had been fun at Christmas to meet among others at Castletown, Mark Kerr, the son of her first and unserious love, John Newbattle. 'Ld Mark is playfulness itself; *just* his father at 17, without the *wit* or the *devil* about him. It diverts my sister and me to see the sons married men at Castletown, where their father was just such a boy. Ly Mark is beautiful, sickly, and interesting.' Donny was well and she was well, and even all the children were well; her heart was up again. In autumn her mood was as gay. 'I am this very week like Prince Prettiman [their girlhood name for George III] between love and duty, for my 3 eldest boys have left home to go to quarters, and I am so glad they are promoted, and so sorry to part with them': and in the spring she was sending Susan '12 yards of sarsenet, which is the prettiest wear possible and fit for summer . . . I assure you a poplin is not *wearable* in these days, when to look *lank* and like *Patsy Jenkins* is the *ton*,' and she sent Susan a paragraph about the sleeves as if they were both young girls instead of stately matrons in their late fifties. 'Colonel Napier's compts to you, *you abominable Pittite*. He won't abate one inch of his attacks on his bad Governt, tho' to his astonishment he found himself a sort of Pittite malgré lui, for he is a violent *Catholic* man.' For Pitt, for all his good efforts in Europe, had left the Catholics still disenfranchised.

William was having a close-up of this villainous figure: had put his head right in the lion's den: was expecting any minute now to have it bitten off. Eighteen years old, he had been taken by his friend Charles Stanhope to stay with Stanhope's uncle, Mr William Pitt, in his house at Putney. 'Arriving rather late, the great man was at dinner when I entered the room; he immediately rose, and giving me both hands, welcomed me with such a gentle good nature that I instantly felt—not at ease, for I was not at that time much troubled with what is called *mauvaise honte*, but—that I had a friend before me with whom I might instantly become familiar to any extent within the bounds of good breeding.'

William hardly knew which to be more interested in, wicked Mr Pitt, or fascinating Lady Hester, who was quite unlike anyone else he had ever seen, pale, and mannish in an exotic kind of way, amusing and devil-may-care.

'Lady Hester Stanhope also treated me with the most winning kindness. All this produced a strange sensation; for I came determined to hold fast by my patriotism though in presence of a wicked minister, however polite or condescending he might be found.' He had meant to sell his life dearly; were there no takers?

'Brought up amidst Whigs, and used to hear Mr. Pitt abused with all the virulence of Whigs, I looked upon him as an enemy of all good government; and my father, though not a Whig, had always condemned his war against France as an iniquitous and pernicious measure. Thus primed with fierce recollections and patriotic resolves, I endeavoured to sustain my mind's hatred against the minister, but in vain; all feelings sunk, except those of surprise and gratification, at finding such a gentle, good-natured, agreeable, and entertaining companion. I say "companion" deliberately and with a right. . . .'

To William's amazement, the Prime Minister delighted above all in pillow fights, and in what he called 'practical fun'. Pitt's nephews, assisted by William, were holding him down on the floor and blacking his face with a burnt cork, when they were interrupted by an announcement that Lords Castlereagh and Liverpool had arrived on state business. The Prime Minister had kept these great men waiting for twenty minutes, treated them with coldness and gravity, and insisted, the minute they had gone, on continuing the pillow fight. Prime Minister at twenty-three, he had really had no time to be young.

William brooded the contrast between his first cousin, Charles James, and this great rival. 'I had often been in Mr. Fox's company. . . . His manners were totally different from Mr. Pitt's, always agreeable, gentle, kind, and good-natured, but not attractive to

young people, inasmuch as he did not seem to take much interest in
them, and rather to bear with them than like them; at least, such was
the impression he made on me. Whereas Mr. Pitt's manner was that
of joyous hilarity and delight at being able to unbend his mind, as it
were, when he could do it safely; he was very attractive.' All very
unsettling and illuminating for a fiery eighteen-year-old who liked to
believe that black was black and white was white. Could Pitt have
been right about Union with Ireland? In the desperate all-out war
with Bonaparte, did it matter more to secure England's rear, or to
right Ireland's wrongs? Pitt died too soon: 'it was his sinister destiny
to be judged by the petty fragment of a large policy he did not live to
carry out' thought Rosebery, his defender.

Mr Fox, that charming volatile rival to Pitt, was causing concern
to his family. Once more the other members of Brooks's had paid his
gambling debts, but he was hopelessly in the red again: it didn't
really do, for someone about to become Prime Minister at any
minute. There were conclaves: finally the family clubbed together,
paid off the debts, gambling and otherwise, and made an annuity of
£3,000 a year for him. The effect was electric: he never touched
another card, stayed out of the red, and married Elizabeth Armistead,
a delightful plain woman who had been his mistress for years. Relief,
relief, in every Holland, Richmond, Fox, and Napier breast. Some
friends were for the marriage; and some violently against. Sarah took
all her family visiting, to show how for she was.

Louisa Conolly, and her husband Tom, still slowly unwinding
from his civil war experiences, had been staying at Wentworth in
Yorkshire, which had once belonged to the great Earl of Strafford,
been inherited by the Rockinghams, and left by Rockingham to his
son-in-law Lord Fitzwilliam. 'Charles Fox's marriage was just then
sur le tapis, and Ld Fitzwilliam said to my sister that all things considered he was glad of it, for that it would be much less disadvantage
to Charles to be seen with his wife than his mistress. I am so glad
Lord F. does not take *à travers* about it, for as my most ardent wish
is for dear Charles to be happy, whatever contributes most to that, I
wish; and as he loves Lord Fitzwilliam, it will please him to know he
is not among those that fly out on the subject.' What mattered much
more was that Harry had taken it so well—'the conduct of his
brother Harry had been so kind that I love Mrs. Fox and Harry even
more than I did, and that is saying much. I know it would have made
Charles *miserable* had Harry been unkind, and all the "*clinquant*" of

Paris would never have made up to him . . . he has a heart that retains his ancient affections very strongly.'

The Conollys had taken Louisa, Emily, and George to stay in Yorkshire with them. 'All are enchanted . . . happy were they to make this northern tour, where they have seen what neither London nor Dublin have, *true old English solemn grandeur*, magnificent castles, parks, trees, plate, and hospitable establishments, all display'd at stated times, and perfect quiet in the interim. How infinitely more *sensible* is that style than the eternal *guingette* of everybody's house near a town.' She was pleased her children should have a sight of this ordered leisured peace before it departed for ever (though it may have appealed rather more to Tom Conolly's shattered nerves than it did to Louisa, George, and Emily in their teens and twenties), for 'my heart cannot yet use itself to those most necessary delapidations of time and generations'.

Clouds were gathering. 'The great and sad feature of this year has been miserable anxiety about my dear husband's health. Even before January he was far from well owing to the wretched office he worked in, like the black hole of Calcutta; it produced continual illness.' He had been very ill again through the summer, with fever and delirium at times: she had been 'between hope and fear till June, when I was promised that warm weather would compleat the cure, instead of which cold weather came and he grew worse . . . much better suddenly, then ill again in August, when to my joy and gratefull heart's content all September began the perfect and entire cure!'

She seized on every gleam of sun. Though 'we are immovable I believe in this odious town . . . since Col. Napier has got a large, good, airy office, my heart is at rest. My son Charles is at Shornclif, near Folkston, with the Rifle Corps; cold enough for winter poor soul; the rest are at home. . . . My nephew Leinster, who felt very much the loss of an old friend, is at Carton surrounded by a numerous fine family enjoying himself very much. . . .' 'As to matters of importance such as war and peace, civil war, etc', she told Susan in January, as 1803 swung into its ominous stride, 'I am too well broke in not to be a philosopher: I enjoy the *present*, and wait till sorrows come to fret about them.'

The anniversary of the King's wedding next year found her equally serene; and she had slipped into the cosy middle-aged practice of making slightly more of an old romance than the facts justified. For if the young George III, with his affection and kindness and his slightly prominent blue eyes, had made her a direct, loving, first-hand proposal when she was a girl, would she in fact have turned him down? What she had rejected was not the young man himself but the whole palaver; the feeling that an ordinary but not unpromising affection was being made the tool of powerful men acting without regard for the happiness or well-being of either of the people really involved; the feeling of being pushed and manipulated in an ordained direction before she was ready to move anywhere. Why could they not be left alone, to get on with it or not get on with it as feeling dictated? Female freedom had moved a cautious step forward in one generation: it would not have been easy to make Sarah marry in settlement of a gambling debt, although in fact her mother's arranged marriage had worked out far better than her own free-will first marriage did.

Sitting in the September sunshine at Clifton where she and Donny had come so that he might take the waters, she covered the paper with the writing which already she could barely see. Susan had known it all—she would add and subtract as she thought, and still remain an entranced listener.

'P.S. I am one that will keep the King's marriage day with un-feigned joy and gratitude that I am not in Her Majesty's place. It was the happiest day for me, in as I like to attend my dear sick husband better than a King. I like my sons better than the Royal sons, thinking them better animals and more likely to give me comfort in my old age. . . . It is pleasant to have lived to be satisfied of the great advantage of a lot which in those days I might have deemed un-lucky. . . . Ideas of 15 and 60 one cannot well assimilate, but mine began at 14, for if you remember I was not near 15 . . . and ought to have been in the nursery . . . when my poor head began to be turned by adulation in consequence of my suposed favour . . . I always consider the King as an old friend that has been in the wrong, but does one love one's friends less for being in the wrong even towards oneself? I *don't*, and I would not value the friendship of those who measure their friendship by my deservings. God help *me*, if all my friends thought thus.'

Mildly pontifical, content with her lot despite the uncertainties of Donny's health and her own increasing blindness, she was laying up a necessary capital of happiness for the heavy expenses that lay ahead.

IX

At Limerick as the old century ended and the new one began Charles was see-sawing through the pains of adolescence; for ever in and out of love and battling with his accident proneness and his sixteen-year-old sexual drives. The Shannon flowed swiftly through the city, mild airs blew in from the west, and not far to the north and south the unchannelled Atlantic beat on a rocky shore. Among green and bouldered fields dwelt the poor in windowless cabins; smoked like so many herrings but intermittently happy around their peat fires, not yet aroused to anger by thousands of years of unconsidered apartheid. The town itself was unimpressive. 'I remember nothing good at Limerick' he wrote years later 'but the pigs and the gloves; and nothing pleasant but the women, who were quite delightful and as wicked as they were pretty....' A stern Scots strain in him warred with his mother's light-heartedness: Methodism was the latest thing, should he become a Methodist? But a pretty girl quickly put paid to his impressment with Methodism—'a rascal half pursuaded me to be a Methodist; but he seduced his maid, she seduced me, and so betrayed the secret....' Perhaps Methodism was no help after all.

His mother, needless to say, was concerned about him; and equally needless to say, her concern was for the wrong reasons. 'I hear there never was such a set as now inhabit Limerick' she told Susan, brushing aside all remembrance of her own gay youth; 'the women all beautifull, impudent, gay and idle; the men rich, selfish, gourmands and bloodthirsty.' She keened with Susan over the temptations of the world and the perils of young men exposed to it. 'How well written is all you say about your young nephew. How truly I feel it who have 5 sons *proportionately* exposed to the dangers of the world, but certainly exempt from *flattery* as they have nothing to bestow, tho' nothing is so precarious as the character of a *rich young lord* in London! What a miracle if he escapes!' Set so much as a foot beyond Hounslow Heath or Mill Hill and certain doom awaited; as it yet does.

But Charles's ills at this moment were physical. Out shooting with George, he had broken his leg with such a loud crack that his brother heard it from two fields away. The break was so bad that the doctors

152

threatened amputation. To one so young and unboundedly active as
Charles a life of dot and go one seemed a fate worse than death. The
germ of suicide, that occupational disease of adolescence, assaulted
him. He sent the maid out for some laudanum.

'Luckily the doctors found me better, and so saved me from a
contemptible action.' They then proceeded to set his leg crookedly;
and he rose to his feet to find them pointed north and south. He
asked for twenty-four hours to decide whether to have the leg broken
and set again (there were, of course, no anaesthetics). 'All that day
and night were Miss Massey's pretty eyes before mine, but not soft
and tale-telling, not saying *Pig will you marry me*, but scornfully
squinting at my game leg. The per contra was two ill-looking doctors
torturing me. . . . However my dear Miss Massey's eyes carried the
day, and just as I had decided, she and Miss Vandeleur came in the
dusk, wrapped up in men's great-coats, to call on me: this was just
like the pluck of a pretty Irish girl; I would have broken all my
bones for her. . . . Be quick, quoth I, as the doctors entered, make the
most of my courage while it lasts. It took all day, and part of the
next . . . I fainted several times.' George, fifteen and very worried, was
sworn to keep the secret from his parents while the danger lasted.

But Charles is next heard of riding the 90 miles from Limerick to
Dublin in a day, his legs as good as new. 'You need not dear father
tell this to Mama or anyone else, but the doctors say my escape was
miraculous.' General Duff wrote to Donny advising him to apply for
leave for Charles as he was still unfit for duty: 'I am sure you will
never consent to do anything of the sort' this affronted seventeen-
year-old objected, 'which you must think, and which you may be
certain I think, would be disgraceful and unbecoming the character
of a British soldier . . . I have just heard that a new expedition is
talked of in England, I must contrive to go.'

Scots blood was strong in him and he was hasty whenever his pride
was touched: a thistly dignity upon points of honour plagued him all
his life. He had hardly been at Southampton a fortnight before he
and another young man were with difficulty talked out of fighting a
duel over an unimportant difference of opinion—'it is hateful to
think how near foolish passion was in involving me in a desperate
duel.' He was a crack shot and a fine swordsman and would probably
have killed the arguer, and tormented himself ever afterwards with
guilt and shame. No expedition materialized; and England, after
Ireland, seemed to Charles to be all talk and no do. There were ideas

in plenty; and republican murmurs wafted over from France.
Charles found himself on the other side, but not wholly in sympathy
with those who shared his views. ' "The Loyal", such was the phrase,
like the cavaliers of old, adopted obscenity, drinking, oaths and long
hair as badges of their politics.' (These youthful tokens of faith
stayed with him, bar the drinking: he remained foul-mouthed and in
old age had hair like a mountain lion.) He called his horse Ça ira
after that catchy, French revolutionary tune: there was a go-
aheadness about revolution! There was not nearly enough to bite on,
in the sleepy south of England, and the Peace of Amiens made it seem
unlikely that there ever would be. 'As to remaining an English full-
pay lieutenant for ten or twelve years, not for the universe! . . . How
the "old lieutenant" sticks in my gizzard. Rather let me command
the Esquimaux than be a Subaltern of forty years old. Colonel
Stewart says I ought to insist on the Prince of Wales giving me a
company, or fighting me for taking the liberty of calling me Charles.
Marry come up, my dirty cousin!'

Excitement and gloom chased each other in his heart. 'I am a
determined rake, in love with four misses at once. Yet would to
heaven I could get home. Make George and William say how tall
they are. . . . Nobody but myself ever had such a feel for home; my
heart jumps when thinking of you all together and merry in the old
way. This wishing for home makes me gad about in a wild way, for
melancholy seizes me when alone in a cold barrack room.' He must
sell his horse, 'the dearest little wicked black devil you ever saw, and
so pretty'. Could his mother, if his father agreed and wouldn't be
troubled by it, get hold of the £100 still due to him for forage? He
wanted it desperately for his friend Cameron, to save him from the
Jews, who would ruin him. 'He is such a fellow, that unless sadly
pushed, he would not borrow, even from me.' A month later Charles
is 'most wickedly in love with the second Miss Gage. Her eyes are
beautiful. She is to me the most charming creature ever beheld. I
think of nothing else and hate any company where she is not.' He had
organised his commanding officer into going three times to Firle and
taking him along just to see her. 'Colonel Stewart asked me to-day
if that old uncle the duke would not purchase me a company? My
reply was—could not tell, because I never asked him. . . . Most of our
generals are more obliged to the Duke of York than to the Deity for
their military talents.'

At Christmas time he was beset with what he called 'Blue devils'.

Fine enough to dance with Miss Gage at the Lewes Balls and to make her laugh and to speak volumes with his large lustrous eyes, but that was as far as it could go, for a penniless son with eight brothers and sisters and the whole of his way to make in the world, in a profession he was beginning to hate. 'What a curse to have a turn of mind similar to mine! Misery to oneself, and teazing to others, unless disguised, which can only be with those not really loved. Great exertion or perfect tranquillity is necessary to me, who have not that superior intellect which can regulate itself.' A day or two later things were worse. 'The expense of London is dreadful, it absorbs all my pay, and here I cannot go such a blackguard figure as in Dublin . . . to live in dread of tradesmen and abominate the sight of a bill is a life not to be borne. We are going to Guildford, where there is, I hear, a fine new gaol: that to me is significant.' The bloody establishment, spending money on shutting people up, instead of redressing their wrongs! 'Last night I sat up till two o'clock, writing on the old subject of grievances, and lashing myself into a fury with everything. Abusing the army, pulling off my breeches, cursing creditors, and putting out the candle all in a minute, I jumped into bed and lay there blaspheming, praying and perspiring for two hours, when sleep came. . . .'

Three days later he got his company; but it brought him no change of mood. 'At one time' he wrote on December the 29th 'my hope was that a company would cure me of my aversion to the army, though nothing could make me like it; but the first feeling is not to be conquered, or surely being a captain at twenty-one would create in a warm imagination ideas of future honours, of hopes and wishes to rise to the head of my profession, and all the deuce knows what, which such reveries lead to. But not one thought of pleasure or happiness from promotion could be forced up. . . .'

This sadness, as his brother William later pointed out, was not 'a result of youthful perturbation at finding the world different from his childish conceptions, it was of his nature, and adhered to him through life.' It was, we would now think, a result of his tormented babyhood. The passage with which this melancholy letter continues, gives the impression of a born writer held by an iron will and a deep family-solidarity-cum-patriotism to a profession that went dearly against his grain. 'How different are George's feelings: he will be in Paradise though up to his ears in mud at Hythe. How happy he is to be thus contented with present pleasures, and sanguine as to the future! To me military life is like dancing up a long room with a mirror at the end, against which we cut our faces, and so the deception ends. It is thus gaily men follow their trade of blood, thinking it glitters, but to me it appears without brightness or reflection: a dirty red! And for the future? Aye, the future! What is it? Under a long feather and cocked hat, trembling, though supported by hessian boots, gold-headed cane and long sword, I see the wizened face of a general grinning over the parapet of a fine frill, and telling extraordinary lies, while his claret, if he can afford claret, is going down the throats of his wondering or quizzing aides-de-camp. Such is the difference between the hero of the present time, and the idea formed of one from reading Plutarch! Yet people wonder why I don't like the army.'

By February his weathercock spirits are up again. 'Resolution has worked a miracle: my low spirits are thrown off in a great degree, not quite, but I am now as eager to carry all by storm as I was ready to desert five days ago. Not that my opinion, or dislike, is changed, but that no man can make a figure in anything who does not go hand and heart to work . . . I am now anxious to return to Chatham, having no uniform here, and coloured clothes with soldiers smell so militia-like, it makes me ashamed to look a Coldstreamer in the face.' He had bought a new horse, which always had an instantaneous effect upon his spirits; getting him cheap from a guardsman who could not manage him—'more of an Arabian than a racer, with a beautiful curved neck, and fiery as the devil, yet without vice; he run away because he knew his rider, but has found me his master . . . Ça ira was to him as the great devil is to the little one.' (Ça ira, aptly named, had nearly killed both himself and Charles.) 'Being, dear mother, in all the horrors of a new coat and cocked-up hat I cannot write much' he told her from Chatham; 'I fag at French, eager to learn, as most of the officers speak it, and it is hateful to be a dunce.' Their drill, though, was not up to much: 'even the major is unlearned, the adjutant superbly so.'

In April came a tragedy that brought on another bout of introspection that left Charles physically ill. His great friend Cameron died of a putrid fever: what shook Charles most deeply was that after the first few days of misery he could not feel anything. Why if Cameron must die, could he not have died in battle, in the imminently awaited invasion? 'But a little thought taught me that God was the best judge. When a thing cannot be helped my mind becomes strong to bear it; but if unhappiness can be helped it becomes unbearable.' All the same, his mind could not leave it. 'The shock is passed mother, and having a conviction that he is happier than we are, the grief is less. To think of him is a pleasure, and my curiosity is great to know where he is gone, what happens to us. Whenever expecting to be sent into the next world, my feelings have been the same as when expecting any great pleasure: the feeling is strange. . . . Does Cameron know what we are about, what I think of him? Is the little he saw of us here forgotten? Perhaps he has not a conception that for us there is a world he has quitted. . . . How odd that we should be so attached to life. My feelings are incomprehensible. I cannot pity Cameron, being sure he is in regions of bliss, far beyond what we can conceive; but my own dislike to die puzzles me. Run away in the beginning of an action I would not . . . it is more the feeling of being mangled that would affect me: dislike to being maimed is greater than to being killed. . . .'

He was not to get through the experience so easily. Shock had him in its grip. 'Ten days ago Cameron died, and this day I have been talking and laughing in the mess like a happy being. The next moment a dose of laudanum, that would make me forget everything, tempts me to rest my brain, which is often confused in a way difficult to describe, thinking of five-hundred things at once. I go to bed wishing for sleep, or anything to lose that feeling, and next morning rise merry! . . . Would that this were the effect of resolution and reason. It is not. I do not feel grief. I am a table, a stone, there is no feeling. Yet I cannot read or study, my mind will not rest on anything which keeps me in-doors. Nicolay has desired me to drill the regiment for him; that I like, and we are throwing up field works also, and that I like. . . . Company is my great want, yet I don't like my company at mess, though in great spirits all the time. Would I were with you! I am just in a plight to fall in love, merely from wanting the company of somebody who can be loved.'

He could bear death, but not separation. And why would everybody go on at him about his dead friend? Condolences upon Cameron's death from other friends annoyed him, so did his picture sent by an aunt—'so great is my dislike to anything that puts me in mind of him. . . .' 'Do not write any more on this subject' he besought his mother, 'pity is hateful!' At this point, perhaps because he looked so ill, the doctors took charge, and ordered him very hot baths. 'My dearest father, I am reduced by pain to such weakness as only to lie on a couch,' he wrote next week 'and am absolutely like a skeleton. My long nose, pale face, and black beard makes me worse looking than Lord Ruthven when he murdered Rizzio.' Five days later he was back in action, writing politics to his father about Pitt and Fox.

Apart from intelligence, resolution, and physical courage, he could hardly have seemed less suited for a soldier, prostrated as he was by the death of one friend, longing to drug himself out of thought, haunted and paralysed by a sensibility taking the dangerous form of a state of non-feeling. Yet, as William said, 'the profession of arms, first adopted in his father's conscientious views, was to him a patriotic object at the time, and moreover was his only means of existence: hence with this double stimulus he set the strength of his brain against the softness of his heart, and bravely accepted a fate which doomed him to a life-long struggle.' For Donny was dying; and the ending of his father's life would soon seal Charles into the army. To his sons he had been not only an admired dependable father but in George's words, 'the truest and warmest of friends'. His truth and warmth had launched Charles on his profession: and weakness or disinclination had now to vanish before pressing need, for Charles and for every other trained man.

Thomas Creevey, that busy Whig M.P., visiting Shorncliffe in September of 1803, found Sir John Moore's officers 'so modest, so civil, so alert'. Not a puppy among them, not a trace of pertness: he was much impressed.

'Are the French coming?' he asked the General. Moore spoke with some contempt of their invasion plans. Bonaparte was doing harm by threatening invasion; he thought him not mad enough to try it. What, Creevey wanted to know, would happen if invasion did come?

'The invasion would, I am confident, end in our glory and in his disgrace.'

Creevey supposed that Moore had great confidence in his own troops? The General thoughtfully told him that he relied on his own brigade to meet the enemy in the water, before ever they set foot on land, and to give a good account of themselves. And after that, Creevey persisted? Upon what did he rely?

'Upon the people of England' Moore superbly replied; and he asked some local volunteers, who had drifted to the scene, what they

would do if the French landed, and was told he would be supported
—'We'd rather fight it than drive it!'

Brave words, with unconquered Boney only twenty-one miles
away. At Boulogne, across the Channel which seemed to the English
on clear days extremely narrow, Napoleon and his Grande Armée
stood poised for the leap; trained veterans, well-armed, well-equipped,
and with all the dynamic of revolution in their hearts. Subduers of
half Europe, they were only waiting for their navy to draw off the
British fleet and leave them twenty-four hours for a clear passage to
the island, there, they believed, to go through the raw levies of the
militia (which the extreme haziness, optimism, and kindliness of the
English always leaves them with at moments of dire crisis) like hot
knives through butter. Apart from great-grandad's army, there were
40,000 trained troops as well as a front line: could they have put up
enough of a fight against those superb unbeaten legions of hundreds
of thousands? George Napier, talking it all over long afterwards
with Marshal Soult who had been at Boulogne with Napoleon, asked
him if the Emperor had really meant to invade? Soult was sure that
he had. Would he have succeeded? *Ah, monsieur, c'est une autre
affaire*, Soult had said, concluding the conversation. George himself
'from all I have since known and seen of the French troops' felt sure
Napoleon '*never* could have reached London'; besides the trained
40,000 there were 50,000 reservists and 'large bodies of armed
peasantry, all breathing defiance and rage'. But the danger had been
enough to settle Charles, at any rate for the time.

'Two spiritual fountains constantly played within Charles Napier's
breast,' thought William, writing long after, 'the one sparkling to the
light of glory the other flowing full towards the tranquillity of
private life. He could not repress his inward sense of genius and
natural right to command; nor could he stifle the yearnings of gentle
affection.' The last, William thought, would have won, 'if his country
had not been plunged in such a terrible war. Duty impelled him, and
that duty must be done was as much his motto as the Duke of
Wellington's; how many times did that phrase burst from the lips of
poor soldiers in the Peninsula when called to face danger, endure
fatigue, and suffer privations from which nature shrunk!' There was
also, though William does not mention this, the haunting image of
Donny. A live father can be talked to, argued with, rebelled against:
the tyranny of the admired dead father is absolute. Larger than life,
and very much larger than Charles, the handsome figure of Colonel

George Napier, brave, intelligent, and never given scope for his powers, strode through the imagination of his son. There is no more powerful push to ambition than the admired dead father to whom the world has not done justice; and in our own day Winston Churchill and Louis Mountbatten are witness to it. Something long due, some meed of fame and recognition, must be wrung from the world to lay those charmed and disregarded ghosts.

Bonaparte aside, Charles's resolution 'to meet and sustain all evils' was now to be severely tried. 'Take my watch, Sarah, I have done with time' Donny told her, dying after a brief illness in October of 1804.

The sun was slowly setting upon Sarah's generation: references to ailments came thick and fast. Brother Richmond is 'terribly gouty', brother George Lennox 'has got St. Vitus's dance to such an excess as to preclude all exercise', and another luckless relation 'poor Ly Charles Fitzroy' is about 'to have her leg cut off for a swelling'. Even William O'Brien's ebullience is dimmed and the doctors and his wife have put him on the water wagon, which Sarah doubts is 'a safe extreme to adopt at such a late time of life. A little good wine I should think was wholesome' she pleads for him. 'The poor King continues ill, a public calamity from its consequences, and . . . the private misfortunes of the Royal family go to one's heart. Great people suffer sorrow doubly, poor folks, they are not made to it, it comes with violence and drives them to indifference or despair.' Sarah perked up at 'Lord Nelson, keeping up the true old tar,' at the Nile battle, and on a more private note, at O'Brien's Dorchester sinecure—'how comfortable this will make you, dearest Ly Susan!'—although they both knew that 'money is a good thing to have, but friendship and regard will ever fill our hearts with ten times more pleasure', still it was very satisfactory all the same.

She herself from time to time has 'errisipellas' and 'tedious confinements with bile and gout in my stomach': only Sir Charles Bunbury, happily restored to bachelordom, is still going like a bomb. Winning the first Derby, he narrowly misses the kind of immortality acquired by 'our friend, Mr. St. Leger': he and Lord Derby toss up for who shall have the great race named after him and Derby wins. The name of Bunbury has to wait till the end of the nineteenth century; when it is made immortally funny by Oscar Wilde.

Poor Tom Conolly had never recovered the standing which his support of the Act of Union had undermined: for all his generosity and his hospitality he was not now a popular man, despite Louisa, despite her foundations (with Tom's money) of an industrial school in Celbridge for the boys, and for the girls, a factory for making chip-straw hats, whose sales she promoted amongst her interminable ranges of relations. Sarah could still not resist the odd jibe at helpless Tom, though never in public; but Donny had gone on being steadfastly fond of him. On April 27th of 1803 Tom Conolly died at Castletown. 'This once happy house is now the mansion of deep and solid woe' Donny recorded on May 1st. 'I am just returned from committing to the grave all that remains of an honest man. I speak from thirty four years experience, during which long period I never knew a human being whose enemies were more transient and whose friendships were more permanent.' But in that, as people sometimes do in obituaries, he more described himself.

Louisa was stricken. For forty-five years she had laughed at Tom's bad jokes, taken his imaginary ailments seriously, and loved and cherished him almost into respectability. Now she was alone, consoled by Emily, and soon redoubling those efforts of kindness and compassion to all within her reach which had long been the core of her life. To her Napier nephews she seemed 'like a pillar that will not break'. If Sarah was one of life's enhancers, Louisa was one of life's upholders. They would all soon have need of her.

By July of 1804 'Col. Napier's health has caused miserable anxiety for nearly 3 years', in August he has a relapse 'and suffers extreme weakness being sadly reduced by pain. . . . I am so giddy with calomel and sickness I can hardly hold a pen.' Flashes of hope and pleasure still come to Sarah; from her nursing place of Hot Wells, Bristol, she has seen '3 brothers, a sister, a train of Foxes and Lennoxes, besides having brought about the collection of 5 *boys here*'; but by the end of August she admits to Susan at last 'the truth is my dearest friend there is a sword, a most sharp one, hanging over my future happiness.' Once again in September, she seizes on the last straw of hope, Donny is just a bit better, 'my spirits at this moment are quite unwisely good because I ought not to be too sangwine, but his evident recovery and . . . an assurance that unless some unforeseen accident happens all will go on smooth this winter has so relieved my spirits.'

Susan had been wonderfully kind to William on his way to join the 43rd; 'for all his giddy ways he is not unmindfull of kindness', and Louisa 'my best part' had come back from nursing someone else in London. While there is life there is hope; and to no one more than to Sarah.

By September the 25th the alternations between hope and fear are too much, and an announcement that Sarah has 'St. Anthony's fire in my face and head', though Donny has 'infinitely less suffering', is followed by an incoherent 'In mercy my dear Madam come to your friend, my adored parent will soon be no more' addressed from Louisa to Susan O'Brien. 'I have less feeling from age than my poor Louisa, worn out with watching and grief' Sarah adds soberly to her stepdaughter's note, out of 'that fictitious calmness that precedes despair'. The sword had fallen. 'One week's fever has destroyed twenty-three years' happiness.'

Overwork in the stuffy Irish office had finished what yellow fever at Charlestown had begun, and left Donny wide open to the tubercle bacillus which in these days brought nearly certain death. He had been 'so efficient a person that people of all denominations come to him with their wants, their complaints, their doubts, and whether it belonged or not, he never failed to exert himself in forwarding every useful thing': such people often die in their early fifties. 'From his great comeliness and talent as an officer he had been much noticed by George the Third,' William recorded; yet somehow nothing had come off, and the abilities which everybody knew to be excellent had never found full scope. He was one of the few who had added to his stature as a soldier in the American war; he had introduced carronades into the Navy, and when controller of Woolwich laboratory had experimented with and improved on the composition of English gunpowder and rockets, and written reports on his findings that were translated into several languages: perhaps he should have been a scientific Napier and not a fighting one. And yet he had followed his bent; no one had pressured him in, unless perhaps the times in which he lived. It had all ended in giving himself consumption totting up army pay in a stuffy little office in Dublin: and in the world of time to which he now said goodbye with no overt regrets, there could have been much more. Like some great kindly Man Friday on a friendless shore, we know him best by his footmarks.

A far-seeing man, he had hated to fight the Americans, and to lose them to his country; but his sojourn in their land had made him guess their coming greatness. What he deplored was their misguided republicanism. He longed to have a hand in another young country, Australia, and to save its people from this unfortunate American weakness. What happens to republics? They get carried away by glamour and fooled by advertisement, enslaved by dictators, enthralled by aged generals; why not save themselves by having hereditary referees without political ambitions to blow the whistle when arms begin to be twisted and broken glass to fly?

All but the rarest live within the ethic of their age. And in this Donny was not rare; he loved glory, wanted much to serve his country, believed that here true glory lay. In all known time that had come before him, in all the myths and civilisations on which his had been built, the fighters had been the heroes. At his back were all the high-piled sureties of religion and history. Even Christ had not told soldiers to stop fighting, but only to be contented with their pay. 'Prowess is the mother stuff and light of noble men'—nothing had yet arisen to dowse this fiery dream.

A man must love his family, his clan, his country; only so in time might he graduate into loving the world. And in Donny's youth Britain alone of great powers had any form of freedom or of popular say in public affairs: she felt herself the glory of the world. Men were in love with the idea of England, as they might now be in love with the idea of Chairman Mao, as an ideal of human betterment. The nations not so blest as we, the British sang, and meant it. The men who fought in Nelson's ships, in Wellington's armies, ill-conditioned, ill-fed, ill-paid though they were, fought for something more than drink and spoils; for a life which, narrow as it was, was still a great deal better than anyone else's. Not everyone could write Gray's Elegy, some should take Quebec, or it must in its turn, must in its turn, to tyrants fall. The paths of glory lead but to the grave; but where, by all that's holy, did other footways end?

Donny did not pressure his sons into the army except by what he was, as admiring sons of coal-miners were tempted down the mine. Only a weakness in Latin kept George out of the Church; Richard was encouraged to make this his career; Henry liked the sea and that was it. Was Donny the disappointed man projecting his dreams upon defenceless young? Of course: there is some of that in all of us, in every dealing between old and young; in every priest preaching, teacher teaching, ruler ruling; in every father yelling at his son. And when we abdicate, opt out in an irresponsible wish not to have to pronounce on the appalling intricacies of right and wrong, what proxy rushes in? Not the innocence, freshness and idealism of youth, but a tyranny untempered by any sense of variousness or mercy, by any knowledge of life's subtle forces or its hard immutable facts. To reject a hard-won heritage of civilisation for its imperfections is to despise humanity itself, is a snobbery as blind and vicious as any that we know.

And so Donny did not hold his sons back from the army, though the causes he himself had fought had almost all been false or failing. There had to be some clever men in the army, or we should never survive: their sufferings therein might be proportionate with their intelligence; that was in the hands of God, or as it was beginning to be called, the luck of the draw. At least the myth that mastered Donny's sons was not a selfish or ignoble one.

Donny had had 'a person and countenance very commanding'; and it had commanded him a lot of love. 'I never saw his equal' Charles recorded, at the end of a long life that had included Sir John Moore and the Duke of Wellington. 'I loved him with an unbounded affection and respect,' George wrote, 'and in my heart his memory and the principles he inculcated will never fade.' But it was William who, in his biography of his brother Charles, written in his seventies when he had become slightly carried away by the roll of his own sentences, composed the epitaph on Colonel George Napier.

'Although a soldier, always ready for service on the principle of protecting his country, he regarded war as a dire evil: what he yearned for was power to establish a new people on his own views of legislation; and often he longed to govern Australia, then a mere receptacle for thieves, foreseeing that it might become a great state. When the vileness of the population was objected, he answered that Rome sprung from such a source, and it was an advantage, because benevolent despotism could be exercised without imputation of tyranny. His view was to raise a great community, founded on sound monarchic principles, as a counterpoise in the world to the great advancing American republic. His principles were indeed immovably monarchical: yet he was so vehement against the cruel oppression of the times, that many persons supposed him to be at heart a democrat, Lord Edward [Fitzgerald] amongst others:- whereas he held democracy to be an ever-seething cauldron in which the scum continually rose to the surface; and he rejected with abhorrence the republican creed which presents assassination as the greatest of virtues. What he opposed and denounced was oppression, coming from any quarter. Gentle as the dews of spring he was to the poor and helpless, but rough and dangerous as the storms of winter to the dishonourable and unjust: and with overpowering force of body and mind he could impose his will: God had made him for command.

'Kingly rule he judged the best, but he was no king worshipper; he never undervalued men's right of freedom in thought and action, consistent with the public welfare: nor did the headlong progress of republics towards greatness escape his observation. But restricted sovereignty he thought absolutely necessary for keeping the foaming turbulence of democracy within just bounds, while leaving unimpeded the natural flow of energy and genius towards prosperity. His son Charles adopted his views, and both of them, with a practical paradox, while rejecting as a golden dream the notion that nations can ever become great and yet remain simple and virtuous, strove with indomitable energy in their vocations to make that dream a reality!'

X

'Were you here I should feel more safe from the chaos that presents itself to my brain at moments' Sarah had told Susan from Hot Springs at Bristol during the last days of Donny's life; and Susan came. But when her husband died Sarah found that what she had named 'that fictitious calmness that precedes despair' was not in fact fictitious. 'It was not *me*, a total change ensued; naturally subject to tears, to horrors, to nervous sensations, all disappeared, and my loss seemed only like an awful warning from heaven to lose no time in fulfilling the trust reposed in me.' 'Your sympathising heart seemed to give me all its pity' she thanked Susan, such a lifeline during the time when she had felt 'in prison' with 'those sensations which I ever supposed were felt by the Royal family of France in the Temple.' And people had been movingly, whole-heartedly kind; Donny's sister Mrs Johnston, Louisa Conolly and Emily Leinster all hastening to her; Charles Fox coming later; Lord Dorchester busying himself about her pension; and particularly the Bathursts, lending her

Cirencester House to recover in; 'the mind cannot resist the sensations of gratitude in grief, whatever it may do in prosperity . . . insensibly the gloom began to clear.' The Almighty was in charge: 'why lose one of the present precious moments when one could do some good in the world?'

'Such sentiments preserve me from much additional pain; they have prevented my dear children from falling into that sort of despair that belongs to youthful sorrow, and it gives them strength of mind to meet adversity with firmness. Alas! adversity is their lot; there is no deceiving oneself a moment on this sad truth, and the sooner we bring ourselves to meet all its evils with firm resolve the better.' In the event adversity was tempered by a pension, a payment that came not of right but of grace; fairly earned by Donny Napier and applied for in the orthodox manner with nil success, but arrived at in actual fact by what Sarah would have called 'a Jobb', a kind of comical bullying of Pitt, then Prime Minister, by his niece Lady Hester Stanhope. This eccentric charmer had a softness for that dazzling young redcoat, William Napier, and on the way home from a party in the early hours of a London morning she perceived that there was still a light on in the Treasury and whipped uncle Pitt in to sign the necessary documents.

But there had been a long year's delay; money had intruded into Sarah's peace; the Celbridge tenant had gone bankrupt and could not pay the rent, and although 'I have no right to complain, for nobody need starve with £500 per ann.', this would die with her. She had six children unprovided for, and though the three eldest were launched in the army she could do nothing to assist, and two of them had been ordered to Ireland to recruit. This had cost them 'near £200, which young men cannot easily save out of their pay you know'. Sometimes it was difficult not to feel '*le beau temps en est passé*, all now appears to me in life a doubtful dream'. Debts, money worries, anxieties; and now suddenly came news that Emily's son was gone too: out of her seven sons, he was the fourth to die. 'A new misfortune: the poor Duke of Leinster is no more! Six days fever carried him off at Carton, once the scene of youthful joy, now the scene of desolation! What havock does Death make in a circle where I enjoyed all happiness. Death comes remorseless on, and sinks them in the tomb!' There could not but be spasms of miserable gloom; and the perpetual ache of an unhealed wound which any new grief quickened into pain.

Debts, she was bound to admit, had piled up during Donny's illness, 'debts which the situation obliged us to create, and which my want of good management allowed to increase to near double what they were'. She longed to pay them all off at once. 'If it proves possible to manage it without selling Celbridge (at least till some good offer is made for it), is it not much more just I should be pinched, even in my small income, in order to give my children a future chance? . . . My dear sister, who is the most accurate calculator, says that if I live with my 6 children within my annuity of £500 I may in some years hope to clear it; but still you see my children are left destitute at my death, and in the mean time cannot be educated as they ought to be. . . . My generous sister is you know excessively cramped in her own circumstances for several years, and is in fact as poor as me, to speak comparatively of her situation and mine; but she gives me the little she can afford with such a warmth of heart. . . .' Tom Conolly was dead, and Castletown was let for the time being to Admiral Pakenham. To see about Celbridge House 'we must be at Castletown, where I shall feel the unpleasant sensation of knowing that it is not my dear Mr. Conolly I live with, but Adl. Pakenham, a very sincere friend, but still only a friend. . . .' In the end Sarah sold horses and furniture and mortgaged Celbridge and its seventy acres to pay off the debt, having failed in an application to 'my brother Richmond as the person who I felt myself most entitled to ask a favour of, conceiving him both able and willing to assist me'. She had asked for a loan, in order not to have to sell Celbridge off for a nothing to the first comer, but brother Richmond had suddenly turned into a John Dashwood and refused a loan, 'taking 2 sheets of paper to prove he cannot afford it'. Charles and George had both come out strongly against such an application, but Sarah's love for her own family blinded her to its weaknesses.

Twenty-two-year-old Charles was relieved at this outcome: he became at this juncture very proud and Scots, full of dignity and independence. His father's death effected a gradual but salutary scaring away of the worst of Charles's blue devils. He was determined, if possible, not to be helped by anybody. 'I am more anxious we should merit your friendship than profit by it,' he wrote rather brusquely to Lord Moira in answer to an offer of help. 'I will not further intrude on your time, but trust you are convinced how sensible we all are of your extreme kindness. Your obliging offer to lend me money if necessary, I thank you for, but I am not in need of it.'

'I am glad' he told his mother sternly 'the Duke of Richmond has refused a loan to you. I do not like borrowing at all; it is much better to sell Cellbridge than to be obliged to any human being. My beautiful horse is gone to be sold for what he will fetch: the money will clear me of all debt. I cannot exist while owing money, it makes me more melancholy than anything. . . .' Becoming less starchy, he was glad she had found a good home for that first and adored charger, his little old grey mare.

Sarah must have remonstrated; and Charles at once eased her off his own high horse. 'Dearest Mother don't let my whims prevent your asking or doing anything you wish. Do all you like and think best.' Talking to her about accounts without laughing would, he told her, be as easy as flying. She was off to Ireland to settle her affairs, meaning to cross with Louisa by the February full moon (an orb which regulated life in the eighteenth century rather more than it does now). 'It's a business that haunts me; I would fain defer and defer. . . .' 'I think Sussex will be my *point de réunion* for a year or two, after which bringing my girls nearer London will answer better, but how all this is to be arranged God alone can tell, for my old and infirm brothers and sisters, the uncertainty of my 3 sons' quarters, my own age, health, and circumstances are a compound of ifs,' Sarah considered early in the year of Trafalgar. On the way to Ireland a bout of sadness came on again, 'for here I first see a table full of those among whom I miss one more forcibly than in London, where none knew and loved him as those here.' But it gave her 'a mournful satisfaction', and the rest of the party were 'all going to see Castles and Colleges etc., in our road which diverts my girls very much and Isabella Fitzgerald'. And Castletown restored her, 'I am paying every day and my spirits wonderfully *comforted*, for I can find no other word to express it. The quiet of this place, which I love, its majestic trees and solitude soothe me; my angelic sister's character strikes me more forcibly here than elsewhere, and raises me above my own weak nature sometimes.' 'I am happy to tell you', Louisa wrote to Emily Leinster on 14th May, 'that I think our dear Sarah's mind is making a progress towards composure and arrangement.' There was all the business of the house-letting, going on slowly ('as I think all business does'), and Sarah 'must go through some forms of chancery to make the title good; so that these delays are, of course, a little teasing, but perhaps the exertion and occupation of it do her good,' Louisa concluded cosily; still, as ever, considering herself in the role

of Sarah's mamma. The weeks did their work, 'the affection of those
with me, the hope of meeting those away, the grandeur of nature,
the simple pleasures of grass, trees, water, fine weather' in their
course, made 'my spirits just as good as ever they will be, chequered
by pleasure, and pain from reflection. . . .' Slowly, painfully, her
bruised heart was recovering.

Her battle for a pension continued with a total lack of effect—'I
do not mean to abate one step of my pride when I claim a just
reward.' Why should Donny's daughters go hungry when he had
served his country all his life? Friendship was beside the point:
Donny had been described in the Annual Register, not a biased
publication, as 'a brave soldier, an upright servant of the public, and
a truly amiable character in all the relations of life'. But he could be
as brave, upright and amiable as he liked without stirring the
Administration or the Treasury out of their indifference.

Neither Caroline nor Cecilia was robust; what could happen to
them when Sarah died if they had failed to marry? All her friends
urged her to write to the King, a source of pensions; but this she
could not quite bring herself to do. 'I will *not sue* . . . I cannot bring
myself to ask a favour of any human being except as the just reward
of faithful services; in that light alone, and on this ground alone will
I ever write a line or speak a word to obtain what is necessary for my
children, only because of their father's high character . . . a man to
whom difficulties were only the incitement to exert every virtue, and
on whom adversity and prosperity equally found the mind prepared
to act up to every principle of honour, justice, integrity and humanity
. . . I will not use underhand favor. . . .'

Brave words; but as the months went by and the weekly bills rolled
in, the long deferring of hope chiselled away at Sarah's pride and
forthrightness. 'Courts are not the soil where family affection and
cordiality flourishes, and I pity Kings for being robbed of that
blessing by their situation; for they have all the tender feelings of the
heart as warm as their subjects.' Could not the matter be brought up
by someone else who could touch these tender feelings into action
for a family in distress and well-deserving? 'In the present sore
moment poor Mr. Pitt is not to be blamed if he forgets to arrange my
business,' Sarah conceded, for he had, after all, the battles of
Austerlitz and Trafalgar banging on around him. As to Pittites and
Foxites, 'I sometimes laugh in my sleeve at their brags, but I cannot
enter the least into eagerness about either side's success, it is quite

les ombres Chinoises to me'. More months passed, and still nothing happened. Supposing, Sarah asked Susan, rather tremblingly, supposing Lady Ilchester were to say something, only in passing of course, to the King about her blindness? 'But then one never supposes right when one's interest is in question, so I make over the decision to your better judgement.' Lord Hawkesbury, noble fellow, had urged Pitt to defer the pension till Sarah grew tired of applying and gave up: she owed its eventual payment (£300 for herself and £600 between the four girls) entirely to Hester Stanhope and to William's bright eyes. What became of luckless families whose sons were not friends of the Prime Minister's niece?

The health of her youngest was a further anxiety. Cecilia was really not well; the specialists had advised sea bathing, which would be possible from Dublin. Henry, her youngest son, had been taken under the naval wing of Lord Mark Kerr; the only catch about Lord Mark Kerr was that he had not yet got a ship. Richard, fourth son, being coached by a Mr Jones near Bridport, 'an excellent character, and quite master of Greek and Latin' and comfortably within the range of the O'Brien's kindness, was at odds with his clergyman tutor over 'principles and religion . . . Under the specious pretext of opposing what they call French philosophy, [he] lets himself go to all manner of sentiments which I shall certainly not fall into,' Richard complained; and it would lead to fruitless quarrels. A 'violent' clergyman, switching off Latin and Greek and trying to indoctrinate him in anti-revolutionary principles was more than he could stomach. He was eighteen; old enough to have principles of his own. Was it simply homesickness, Sarah wondered in a letter to Susan? Before he left Ireland she had felt that 'however heroic he speaks now he will feel the first parting from his family most keenly'. Was it just personal dislike of Mr Jones? If so he must be polite to Mr Jones and put up with it—'a soldier and sailor both feel these distresses and know it is for many a year they must submit, and they do. Therefore Richard must have submitted too for *one* year to what all mankind is sure to meet with in the course of life, and *well off* is poor Richard if he never finds a worse evil.' Would it be spoiling Richard to remove him? (What would Donny have said? What would Donny have thought right?) Was it just that she dearly wanted him back herself? There was a good parson near Castletown, to whom he could go daily, but 'your judgement is worth ten of mine', she told Susan. Richard went back to Ireland, set himself a stern schedule of work, and abided by it. 'If his mind is fortified in its excellent dispositions before he goes to Oxford, where he must be his own master, I conceive myself to have done my duty by him more strongly than in any way.' But Richard, deflected either by his dislike of Mr Jones of Bridport or by his own mathematical successes at Oxford (where he got a first), later abandoned his career in the Church and became a barrister.

'I am extremely mizierable at having made my father uneassy,' fifteen-year-old William had written from the Royal Irish Artillery Depot at Cork in 1801, and his spelling, like Sarah's, never really came under control. (Fortunately his wife could spell, and transcribed his books correctly.) 'Charles is a lazy theef, unatural villein, and George a damned rascall,' he contributed a year or two later. But when his father died next year he made a real effort. 'I cannot say to you anything more about my father than you know already, for I feel many things that I cannot express. I can only offer up my prayers to Heaven, and put my trust in that Being he has so often told me never decieves.' William was feeling disgruntled: he did not care for his company. 'How I envy George! he looks round him and sees every officer truly a brother.' Or perhaps it was a mood, a part of his sorrow: on the company he certainly made no impression of disgruntlement but only of being rather different. At Shorncliffe his brother officers noted that he would stop whatever rag was going on when the newspaper arrived and would absorb himself in it; questioned about its contents he would happily repeat whole articles verbatim, a practice which soon caused them to stop asking. His memory was prodigious; he knew the whole of Pope's *Iliad* and *Odyssey* and many other long poems by heart: he had a kind of throw-away facility that made Shaw Kennedy think him 'the man of the greatest genius I have ever known or communicated with personally'. Others commented on his black hair, blue-grey eyes, and 'extraordinary grace and activity', and Major Hopkins on his 'naturally polished, pleasing, gay manners, his fine and noble figure, beautiful features and intelligent countenance'. He was restless, unsettled, a puzzling figure to many. Though always reading and drawing, 'he joined the soldiers in all their sports, leaping, running, and swimming', and although he was a superb billiard player, he gave it up because he thought it took up too much time. He further astonished his messmates by expressing himself proud to be considered an Irishman.

William had lately, on Sir John Moore's request, exchanged out of the Blues into the 43rd, glad enough to leave the glamorous uniform and the fourteen shillings a day of the Blues for the hard work and the six and sixpence plus the privilege of learning his job under the great Moore at Shorncliffe. The relief of finding someone who knew what it was all about! George also had gravitated to Shorncliffe, having exchanged into the 52nd. Moore offered him a company in the regiment; he was about to refuse it when a great friend, Frederick Bentinck, offered to lend him the necessary £950. It took George twelve years' saving out of his pay to settle the debt and interest; Bentinck, rich and generous, meanwhile urging him not to bother. George was early made aware of the hard facts of cash: he and the two brothers Rowan upon first joining the 52nd ran themselves in debt and left the mess and lived in rooms for three months on bread and milk in order to get straight. All the same, money did not seem greatly to trouble them; it was communal within the family; the brothers were forever sending each other ten pounds; whenever they had any to spare they spread it around.

The studious Charles had got himself into the Staff Corps by his application to mathematics, military drawing, the principles of fortification and engineering; he too was training at Shorncliffe. 'Here' wrote William, many years later, 'Moore so fashioned the 43rd, 52nd, and Rifle Regiments, that afterwards, as the Light Division, under Wellington, they were found to be soldiers unsurpassable.' Here the lucky Napiers had found an admirable father-substitute; Moore treated all his young officers with paternal goodness. To Sarah he wrote telling her that if she had a dozen sons she could not do him or Colonel Mackenzie, a greater kindness than sending them to the 52nd—'there is but one sentiment about them'.

Charles had already started to argue, as the best way of staying sane in the army. Colonel Stewart, his extremely keen commanding officer, had left orders that all Martello towers on the beach should be visited day and night by the subaltern on duty, and was angry to find that this had not been done.

'Impossible,' Charles said.

'That word is not in the military dictionary, sir!'

'But in arithmetic, Colonel, it is—to walk forty-five miles along a beach mid-leg deep in shingle.'

Sarah had feared that all three boys would be going off to India, so far and feverish; but Sir John Moore, handsome, reassuring, and upright in his red coat, had come to see her in London and told her they were going no further than Sicily. It was gratifying that the boys were doing so well, but all the same, ought she not, now that they had no father, to send them an improving book? Off went *Mason on Self Knowledge*, and would Charles promise to like it? No he would not, and William also thought it 'as stupid as need be and not useful'; they had passed it on to George—'We will stick to conscience.' Charles was in a Mum-teasing mood: he and William were going off to fight Napoleon in Russia: it seemed the only way to get at him. Would she send them some fur-lined breeches? 'You say that my aunt Connolly having recovered her spirits is proof that prayers are of use: it is only proof that reason and resolution made her comprehend that low spirits were weak and foolish when indulged. How can we suppose the decrees of Providence are to be altered by the whims of mortals? Thanksgiving should be our prayers, and they should be silent ones, for there can be no good in telling aloud to mortals how thankful we are for the gifts of the Creator: our enjoyment of them is the way to be thankful. The *Spectator* gives far more pleasing ideas of futurity than old Mason, without making us believe we are the greatest sinners, as he does; and Addison was a good Christian.' She was not to be alarmed about the country; they were safe since Trafalgar; even if the French managed to land forty-thousand 'our country is not to be conquered by Frenchmen'. All the same, if they did come it would do some good. 'Take away Lord Huntley and a few other young men, and what a set of nobles we have: They should all be sailors or soldiers now. In truth our princes are the only great people who set a good example; and though one cannot say much for their talent, they fight, and bestir themselves, instead of staying in London . . . I have no low spirits now, that is all given up.'

Pitt was dying; and what Charles feared would be a futile expedition was in mind for the continent. 'It is madness to expect success from a small army equipped, and its movements arranged, by ministers who do not know what the operations of war are, and will not ask advice from those who do.' 'Keep up dearest mother,' he wrote in April. 'You will be very low leaving Castletown; who would not in your place. . . . Put away every melancholy thought, employ every minute in arrangements, and think only of meeting your sons in England.' Of course she would often go back there with Aunt Louisa; it was far from a forever farewell to Castletown and Celbridge. 'Enough of preaching, and as Napoleon says to the pope, God have you in his holy keeping, and blow you over with a westerly wind.' By 1806 Celbridge was sold, all debts paid, and Sarah in rooms whose address she described as 'Sloane Terrace, near London'. And she was reconciled to her brother Richmond, which was a relief, as she loved him and he had been so kind to her in her earlier hard times of disgrace. Charles was much at Goodwood, making maps with him and arranging sites for gun emplacements: together they were seriously planning the defence of Sussex; Charles at last being able to get his military ideas across to someone able for carrying them out.

By May of 1806 Sarah was established in 21 Hans Place, and although the sitting rooms were no more than 15 × 13 and their wallpaper a bright yellow that troubled her eyes, it was 'a little, quiet, clean, airy place', she assured friends who proposed driving there to see her 'from London'. 'I began with the Napier chronicle to put you *au fait* of us' she told Susan, 'and now by way of a laconic ansr to your politics I will write all my eye will permit. . . . I saw C. Fox [now Prime Minister] he came on Sunday to see me, and happy was I to *see* that his dropsy and water on the chest and the Lord knows what of his liver etc., etc., is all fabricated. He is *very very* anxious and very much worried, but sleeps well if he can get to bed by 12; if not, he lies awake and *thinks*, and owns that it *wears* him. He is also billious with heat and worry and he chose to *frisk* to B. House* in silk stockings out of respect, and so got a pain in his bowells and was ill, but all is gone now he says. . . .

'I spoke to C. Fox in general terms about my sons, and he took up the first thing to be done most good-humouredly; its a naval transaction and he entered into it. I then spoke of my nephew Mr. Johnston in India and he also entered into *that*, but I did not feel courage to ask a decided favour for my sons . . . C. Fox is so thoroughly occupied with the essential business of England, viz. with Buonaparte,' Sarah rather belatedly recalled. 'I had rather be disappointed S.N. than the cormorant Mrs. Bouverie, and I love C.

---

* Buckingham Palace.

the better for being duped to the end of the chapter. . . . Let Charles be as full of faults as you please,' she assured the Pittite Susan, 'and I grant you he has plenty, still it was the hand of Providence that placed him at the helm of a sinking State, and he is *trying* to save it without the least shadow of interested motives.'

As to gossip—'Ly Crewe seems *oppressed* by her new dignity. . . . Genl Moore told me the Sicilians were he believed well inclined to us, and if so their country was impregnable, but he seemed to think the Court of Naples would hamper him . . . also to hope more than saving Sicily might be done.' For the Lennoxes—'the sad damp of bad health pervades through the whole society. My brother is immovable in his *rising pallace*, to show which he hobbles about whenever he can move.'

As to the London news, it was, Sarah thought 'all a tourbillion that I do not understand, tho' it's all on the old system of a constant pursuit of interest or pleasure, only in new ways; but also as usual, you meet with jewels among the rubbish very frequently. . . . A very little of the world will serve both Louisa and Emily, and I assure you my sister Louisa and I are forced to drive them into the world; but we think a little of it is just right.' Cecilia was better, 'her feverishness is lessened and her looks mended. . . . Our situation here is the admiration of all my friends; for strange as it seems scarce any of them ever saw Hans Place, and it is so cool, so quiet, so retired, they all say I ought to give them a breakfast in our little garden,' and so she would, but for the hounding press, which she dreaded to start up again, '*one line in the papers* about me would cost my heart many a pang. There are people who never comprehend these feels, so I say nothing and do nothing.' She was back to herself making practical plans and enjoying jokes. 'Henry is to have unexpectedly 3 months holidays'; she was going with him to Goodwood 'to keep him to some learning', and Charles was hoping for his majority. The activities of her numerous family kept her alive and interested. 'Charles waits daily for orders to sail to the Cape of Good Hope. George is now sailing to Sicily from Plymouth with the 52nd. William is recruiting in Ireland, Richard reading with a clergyman, Henry now at St Hellens in the *Spencer*, a 74, ready to sail for America [on Whitelocke's ill-fated expedition to Buenos Aires], Louisa with her friend Ly Mark Kerr, Emily and Caroline well and Cecilia mending . . . so you see my thoughts have a wide field in the globe to stray in. Yours, my dear friend,' she assured Susan 'still more than ever dear when old friends drop off and lessen that first loved circle. . . .'

Spring of 1807 found Sarah cheerful in spite of 'a most charming cataract which Phipps is to rid me of when I am quite blind, so I wait with patience and no confidence'. A great comfort, she told Susan, had been her reconciliation with 'the D. of R., my dear brother [now 71 and widowered] who became dear to me as I saw myself more beloved and useful to him. It softened the past pains, and led me to enjoy the present pleasure of devoting to his age, infirmities, and returning love, that sacrifice of anger it has cost me so much to make. I have been repaid, amply repaid by passing the last four months of his life almost entirely with him.' And, would Susan believe it, 'my sister Louisa has got an Opera-box! To our great amusement, but like herself in all things she says its her duty to the young ones. She goes everywhere consequently this spring, will establish Louisa and Emily Napier *sur un bon ton* in the world, and hereafter they may take more or less of the world at their choice. The K. and Q. have by a mere chance seen extracts of my sister's and Emily's letters from Goodwood after my poor brother's death, and it at once opened to them the angelic mind of my sister, and in consequence the Queen shewed both her and Emily such marked favour, that I quite love the Queen ever since for doing my beloved sister *justice*.'

By 1807 the British army, still for the most part massed on the south coast, although Moore was keeping the French out of Sicily, was becoming frantic. Napoleon bestrode the continent; yet the papers were full of praises for the Russian, Austrian and Prussian troops, and 'in southern England' William reported, 'the military were treated as enemies if they were not called so.' No one took the faintest notice of the news from India, Wellesley's victory at Assaye had failed to impinge in any way upon the British public. 'Lord Moira and Moore are the only generals the army confide in,' Charles wrote, 'with others they trust to their own courage.' William agreed. 'Such was the indomitable fierceness of the troops,' he wrote of the Peninsular men, 'that they recked little of reputations, boasting that they would fight any general through any blunders.' George was in Sicily, but Charles and William felt doomed to nothing better than a discreditable seat in the dress circle. 'Buonaparte's defeat at Pultusk is dwindling to a kind of drawn battle,' Charles told his mother on February 6th, 'which is probably drawing and quartering for the poor Russians.' On the other hand, 'don't you admire the Cossacks' mode of tying French prisoners by their hair to their saddle bows? It is so delicate and careful, so just and Christianlike.' 'One campaign would make me *asy*, and suit my notions, viz. go fight.' It seemed a dead-lock of a war, tending neither to peace nor fighting. Even the Navy felt damped at the general immobility and the post-Trafalgar flatness —if such a victory did not bring peace, what could? 'This horrid gloomy din of war' Captain Codrington mourned in February of 1806 from Castejena, longing for a new government to bring its cessation. It was that glum moment in a war when everyone knows things have to be worse before they can be better, and yet nothing starts rolling towards the much desired conclusion.

Charles was obliged to fall back on history—'Tell Richard Xenophon has become a great favourite with me, the Ten Thousand were great *raps*'—and on love. He was captivated by the beautiful Mrs Barwell—'between her and Miss Trowbridge, who is a surprising mixture of beauty, good nature, and fun, the devil is not more flaming than myself: I go about all fire.' By May he was in Guernsey, where he became a freemason, was 'adopted by the prettiest little terrier ever seen', took his mare Molly calling with him (she lived to be 35), and reported favourably on Miss X, who had the best legs in the island, and on the two excessively entertaining Miss Carters. He had plenty to do and his low spirits, he told Sarah, were a thing of the past. Even the politicians had pulled themselves together at last, and were taking steps to put the army on a better footing. He liked Castlereagh's new plan of volunteering from the militia, and Wind-ham's plan for keeping it up—'the two plans will in time make a fine army'.

But would it be used in time? Or would Napoleon, stravaguing unchecked over all Europe, be left unopposed until no power on earth could dislodge him? 'We have the most plaguy disagreeable government in the world,' William stormed from his barracks at Colchester, 'reports fly as thick as the generals' skulls.' Russia had made peace at Tilsit and Napoleon now had the whole of Europe, bar Britain, completely under his thumb. He whistled, and they came; and although in many cases they paid the piper, he arranged the dances, and most surely called the tune. Clever as he was, he must be brooding some lethal plan to eliminate the islanders. Trafalgar would not for ever discourage him. What were we going to do about it? Sit and wait? Let ourselves be gobbled up along with the rest of the continent? Mama might go on about opera-boxes, but William's smoky eyes flashed fire, and failed entirely to focus on the Essex belles.

In the event he and Henry were the first to go to war; Henry in the innocence and high spirits of a seventeen-year-old midshipman; William, once launched, looking on it with a clear cool eye. The summer of 1807 sent them on the Copenhagen expedition, described by their brother Charles in his journal of the period as 'a villainous job'. He did not know that a secret plan, made between Napoleon and the Czar at Tilsit to seize the Danish fleet and use it for the invasion of England, had reached the government. To William, on the spot, it seemed that 'our operations were a compound of stupidity, vanity, and villainy'; the commanders, he reported, 'had what they call a gallant action, but which I call a murder of some poor runaways who did not intend to resist'. The pursuit of the enemy found William under the command of a German general, an experience which shook him; as the general freely plundered, and shot any civilian who would not give information. 'His brigade major had in my hearing two days before ordered Major Macleod to shoot all the peasants he met with; but he pronounced it pheasants.' Macleod had thus been able faithfully to promise to obey this order; English mockingness not for the last time confronting German seriousness. William had seen the general next day 'in his uniform, groping in a common sewer for money, and I ordered a soldier of my own, named Peter Hayes, whom the general had called to aid him, to quit such an infamous work and behave like a soldier'. After a pause for rape, the general had himself run a ladder against the local church to enable his men to break the windows and get in and rob it.

William could stick no more. 'I did, at the risk of my commission, tell General . . . my opinion of his conduct when he was encouraging my men to plunder.' He asked to be allowed to take his company back to Wellesley and his own regiment. He was given 400 prisoners to convoy, some dangerously packed loose gunpowder and captured arms, and some Danish women, described as prisoners of war, but William let them free in the first village. Accustomed to steeple-chasing, he guided his three day march by the steeples of the flat country of Denmark; the relief of getting back to his own people was very great. There was some subsequent outcry about the German general's goings-on—'outrages which his own Germans perpetrated under his eyes and with his approbation, nay more, with his personal assistance': the general unhesitatingly attributed the whole to William's company of the 43rd, who had been ready enough to join in, given half a chance. 'British soldiers fight well, but are the greatest scoundrels possible' William frankly commented. Henry had had a less involved time, engaged in a boat attack against the Danish sea batteries at the siege of Copenhagen. He had been delighted by the reply of a giant Irish sailor of known bravery in his boat's crew, who under the hail of thick shot had ducked low and impeded the oars. 'For shame, hold up your head!' Henry had told him. 'Faith and I will, sor, when there's room for it.'

Charles was impressed by his brother William's account of the Danish campaign—'his wish to succeed is not so great as his wish to save. How closely every turn of the head and mind follow religion in spite of worldly concerns, in an uncorrupted heart. . . . Is it [the Copenhagen expedition] an unjust action for the general good? Who can say that such a precedent is pardonable? When once the line of justice is past there is no shame left. England has been unjust! What power will now blush to be so also? By this measure we countenance every action of Buonaparte . . . I cease to regret staying behind, the sword of invasion is not pleasant to draw . . . everyone now says, Poor Danes. A soldier cannot fight an enemy he pities with proper spirit.' (All the same the yells of righteous indignation from Boney had their funny side.) 'I am bothered with Sir Neddy Knatchbull and other squires here who object hugely to their game being shot.' (Charles knew very well that his soldiers were poaching it.) 'I condole with them with the face of a Quaker when a trooper swears in his presence . . . good Sir Neddy really behaves very well.' Back at Hythe there was a beautiful Miss Robb, 'middle-sized, very finely shaped', but far more devastating was a very pretty widow, only 22, niece to the paymaster. 'A widow I am bent on, and she is as pretty a thing as a man could wish to see.'

In 1808 Napoleon made what William, looking back from many years later, considered his fatal error. Spain and Portugal rose against the Emperor's take-over, and he swept south to Madrid to instal his brother as King, leaving his right flank exposed. The British Government decided to support Spain and Portugal, a decision greatly welcomed by the British troops, who were bored so stiff with endless drill, savage punishments, local unpopularity, and the spectacle of Napoleon's unstoppable success on the continent, that they had given themselves ophthalmia by putting lime in their eyes, and gone blind in great numbers in order to get out of the army. Stone cold barracks had also given them pneumonia—'they are dying fast' Charles reported. Six weeks later—'The barrack office have at last sent down fresh bedding for the soldiers; now that so many are dead, and the mild weather makes it of little consequence to the living.'

The Spanish armies were scattered and ill-led, yet it had been a spontaneous rising, and Napoleon was slaughtering the patriots. 'We are bound to help them, poor people,' Charles thought. 'I would rather see England sink with them than refuse her aid in so noble a cause . . . that we shall make some blunder is my opinion, we always do. . . . We have but one chance, which is to annihilate the French army in Spain before succour can cross the Pyrenees; but this requires a rapidity of action we never exert, although we have the power.' The government would haver and dither once again, and send too little, and send too late, and finally involve themselves and the country in infinitely greater loss, expense, and misery than if they had been quick off the mark.

A family sorrow arrested his thoughts: in August of this year seventeen-year-old Cecilia died, despite her summer by the sea. She was the youngest of the family, pretty and sweet and, though nothing special in the way of intellect or personality, was dearly loved. 'That resignation which you ever saw in my mother has not been less on the present occasion,' Richard told Susan O'Brien when thanking her for her kindness. 'She has fixed herself in dear Cecilia's room, which affords her a melancholy pleasure it would be cruel to deprive her of.' But Charles, in the confident self-righteousness of his youth, would have none of this. He felt thankful that William was with his mother; and he wrote to him with the kind of bracing advice he could not have sent direct. Sarah must steel herself: what sorrows might not lie ahead, with the war slowly mounting to its climax and four of her sons involved? Above all, let her not sink into a forlorn inactivity. 'Why should we give up all duties, and the feeling and enjoying the good given *is* a great duty, just because God takes away one gift? Such reasoning would, if several should be taken away, lead to her becoming entirely miserable: it would lead to despair. Often do I hear her, and others, say people are resigned. What, in God's name do they call resignation? It is not in their power to save, so they must bear: but if giving way to grief, or giving up a single duty, or altering in any respect save for improvement, is adopted, then I know not what their resignation means, for to let misfortune turn us into automatons is not real resignation. . . . Aunt Conolly is like a pillar that we know will not break—may God leave her long amongst us!' Could not Caroline regularly read to their mother for an hour every evening without interruption, so that she might be happy at night? And at other times, Caroline herself, being young, would have many other occupations to cheer her. Activity, Charles considered, was the sovereign remedy for practically everything: certainly for his own ills—'a too easy chair is the rack for me.' In sorrow he longed for 'interesting pursuits, duty or danger, or the care of others whom I love, something equal to rousing me up.'

Rousingly enough, Charles's regiment was now posted to South Africa, but this was the last thing he wanted; to be sent away to a peaceful backwater when the major drama was being played out in Europe.

Sarah at least was over the worst of her misery and her shocked stillness. Writing in answer to Harriet Skeffington's enquiries at the end of September in 1808, Louisa Conolly reported that her sister's health was 'Thank God as good as usual again, and her mind is made up, as it ought to be, feeling the sorrow is all her own, and that her lovely Child is removed to happiness'. 'She turns', Louisa continued firmly, 'to the Blessings she has left, with gratitude, and desire to make them happy; so that time I trust will have its usual effect of softening keen sorrow into tender regrets.' It was harder for Sarah than for many—'from her blindness which precludes outward objects from dissipating thought and at the same time deprives her of the resources of occupation, one knows that her poor heart must the longer prey upon her inward grief.'

No one was troubled by Doubt. 'God is able to support her, and from her trust in his mercy I see that it is given to her, and she is really as forward in her amendment as I could reasonably expect,' Louisa told her friend. 'You may be sure that I could not bring myself to leave her. . . . Poor Caroline who was the cradle companion of her dear sister (who was but 12 months younger than herself) has been miserably afflicted, and I am sure could not have been roused from her dejection but from the idea of assisting her mother, whom she has devoted herself to.' They had been lent a house at Wimbledon for a few weeks where she had brought Sarah, 'and it has done us all good, by affording us the society of my sister Leinster, in great comfort, good air, quiet, and walks for the girls and me.'

They were much occupied by thoughts of 'our three Dear Boys; Charles, George, and William Napier, who are all three gone on the Expeditions. Charles (the major) is gone to join the 1st Battalion of the 50th in Portugal, where the 1st Major (a Mr. Hill) died of his wounds. George (a capt) is in Sir John Moore's Regt, 52nd, and *where* they are now we know not, but suppose them on their march to Spain. William (a Capt) of the 43rd is sail'd in the Expedition from Falmouth, going (as tis say'd) to Italy. . . .' (William was actually in front of Vimiero, visiting outposts in the dark pinewoods and noticed by Rifleman Harris as being particularly earnest in his warning 'Be alert sentry, for I expect the enemy upon us tonight.' He had looked Rifleman Harris in the eye most emphatically and he had been right.)

'Consequently (as you may suppose) we are most anxious to hear the development of the Convention in Portugal,' Louisa continued, 'one feels so sure that Sir Arthur had a good reason for putting his name to it, that with respect to him, one *rests* upon that opinion; and the two others may make it appear that they were right also, but until it appears what their motives were for such a transaction, one cannot help regretting Junot being let off so easily after such victories as Sir Arthur had obtained over him—nothing authentic has transpired yet to the public, which consequently has left the Door open to grand complaints, which are poured forth according to the complexion of the Parties who make them, but it is easy to observe a very general discontent, and that is always a vexatious thing.'

The British public continued to feel vexed at the Convention, whereby Junot and twenty-six thousand French troops, after being soundly beaten, were politely transported back by the British fleet to Rochefort in France, bearing with them a vast booty of Portuguese private property—'Britannia sickens, Cintra! at thy name' Byron exclaimed, for once not exaggerating. Others contributed rather ruder and less shapely verses about Sir Hew and Sir Harry—

> Sing cock a doodle, doodle doodle,
> Doodle doodle doo!

'I shall always spell it Hewmiliation in future' said one mocking wit. But Charles at least was immune to vexation: a totally unexpected piece of luck had come his way. Held up at Southampton on his way to South Africa by weeks of contrary winds, he had made such friends among the 50th regiment that they had urged him to exchange into it; and even, miraculously, effected the business without a heavy cash payment. Fair stood the wind for Spain; and for the British army's longed-for wipe at Napoleon, and it whistled Charles's blue devils away with it. He was twenty-five now, head of the family; its supplier of courage and morale, if not of cash. If Richard and Caroline would keep his mother company, Charles would guarantee, whatever the circumstance or the distance, to continue to make her laugh.

'I am this day 60 . . . but I chuse not to look back, for retrospect don't suit me,' Sarah announced stoutly. 'I will hope for the future to learn all the calm resignation and contented way of fulfilling one's duties which alone can make one's winter of life pass off in peace.' 'I have made up my mind to my 3 eldest sons going with Genl Sir John Moore, because—what is their object in life?—*fame*, and where can they learn to deserve it better than in such a moment? A good cause, a good commander, and a good climate at an early age when zeal is warm in their hearts and gilds every horror of war, leaving them only the duties of it to fulfill, which they *long for*! Happy age! Would it not be grievous to oppose their ardour by cold fears and anxieties, which in spite of their spirit they would feel for *me* if they saw me too low. Thus far my mind is at rest. . . .'

It had been a searing four years: Donny, the central pillar of her life, had gone and Cecilia had gone; and her sons were now sailing into danger. But this is the natural habitat of young men in their early twenties and if life does not provide it they go and invent it for themselves (on the roads or elsewhere). They were grown up, and fixed in their jobs, and had at least passed adolescence and stopped smouldering at their parents like so many volcanoes.

Part III

Full of Promise

'My mind is in the anomalous condition of hating war and loving its discipline, which has been an incalculable contribution to the sentiment of duty. The devotion of the soldier . . . (the sign for him of hard duty) is the type of all higher devotedness and is full of promise to other and better generations.'

George Eliot

Part 10

Full of Promise

XI

On the morning of January the 3rd, 1809 Charles sat under a tree
near Lugo after a piercing cold night, eating breakfast in the icy
dawn with his friend and fellow captain Charles Stanhope amongst
the winter hills of northern Spain. George, stalwart and cheerful as
ever in spite of the increasingly short commons, rode by them in a
great hurry. He was Sir John Moore's galloper, and very military and
affairé; teasingly they held up their iron cooking pot of stew, from
which arose a delicious hot steam and an even more delicious smell.
Hungry George would be unable to stop, as they well knew. 'Dainty
dog, can't eat Irish stew,' they mocked him as he rode on, and their
laughter followed him as he cantered along a boulder-strewn hillside.
Next door to Charles were camped the impervious Guards; characteristically they had neatly pipe-clayed their belts and hung them up
on trees to dry, undiscouraged by the fact that the British army was
half-starved and in full retreat and that nobody knew if they would
any of them live to see another nightfall. Chased by a Napoleonic
army several times their number they were on the run for the deep
blue sea; as rearguard they had turned round to keep the bridge
across the Minho river and to tread hard on the toes of Marshal
Soult's spear-heading dragoons.

All that day the rearguard regiments waited, while the rest of the
army filed away over the bitter hills, but it was dusk before Soult
attacked them and was driven off.

'Well, Sir John, after we have beaten them, you will take us on in
pursuit of them a few days, won't you?' Colonel Graham asked.

'No. I have had enough of Galicia.'

'Oh! but just a few days after them—you must take us.'

No comment from the sensible Sir John Moore. The north wind
whistled down the Minho valley, bringing with it stinging showers of

sleet. The long mountain steeps loomed ahead. He would be lucky to get even half of England's only army out of Spain, and he knew it.

William had been some while in Galicia already. After a 'confounded kick-up' in the Bay of Biscay, he had landed at Corunna with Sir David Baird's contingent. 'The Spans here are like Connaught men, as like as sixpence is to a shilling,' was almost his first comment. And although no bands had played 'See the Conquering Hero Comes' on their arrival but on the contrary the Spanish Junta had at first refused to let them land, once ashore it was 'every night at balls, where I danced the waltz, which is their chief dance'. The social welcome surprised him: 'the women are delighted if we dance with them, and the men equally so . . . the religious processions are magnificent and beautiful, and the nuns, old, ugly, and loquacious to a degree.' Amongst those present in Corunna were the Hollands. Stephen Fox's orphaned son, Henry Richard, had in a moment of madness, married a divorced heiress from Jamaica, pretty and clever enough, but Oh! how she threw her weight about. Fanatically pro-Spanish, she had dragged her husband to Corunna in mid-winter for the fun of it: she complained that the English were cold and that Moore was sulking. From these relations William kept well away.

After a night of waltzing, of languishing black eyes and slow Spanish smiles, William bent himself to work, for if duties were not 'executed in a superior manner, the Napier heart will not be satisfied with itself'. His high spirits, whether real or assumed for Sarah's benefit, spilled over the page. The French would never eat him, he was too tough for such epicures. The Spaniards had been hospitable; and while waltzing with the Spanish girls at balls he had learnt quite a bit of Spanish. 'The men are poor frippery apprentice-looking people, but the women have all beautiful black eyes and generally good figures,' and their men-folk were not nearly so jealous as they were reputed. The romantic scenery of the Galician mountains delighted him.

Would his mother send him some toothbrushes and tooth powder —'pray send a large assortment'—for the girls of Lugo and Villa-franca? They had given him introductions all over the place, and toothbrushes were what they most craved as presents. He liked the Spanish upper classes, although the men were proud and dirty; in other walks of life the people seemed in William's twenty-two-year-old intolerant eyes to be cruel, cheating, and crafty; and their treatment of animals made him long to exterminate them. They were up to every villainy, and their only virtue to Protestant William was their inclination to throw off the priesthood that domineered over them at every step of the way. Visiting convents and monasteries he and his friends had found the nuns were nonstop talkers, and the monks dirty, good-natured, and the fattest characters in the whole of lean and undernourished Spain.

William was favourably impressed by Black Bob, in command of the Light Division. His reputation was fiery and headstrong, but he had the essential qualification. 'I like our General Craufurd much; he is very attentive to the men.' Everything he had heard of the Spanish armies was wildly un-reassuring: a very few weeks in the country convinced William that 'if the British troops don't save Spain the Spaniards can't'.

General Moore's view of these allies was neither so arrogant nor so young. They were, he informed his troops when about to enter Spain from Portugal in the autumn of 1808, brave and high-spirited people, warm in their temper and easily offended, but 'a grave, orderly people, extremely sober'. (He emphasized this point: for the reverse side of all that Georgian elegance and craftsmanship was that everyone, rich, poor, and middling, were almost permanently sozzled.) He hoped the British army would cherish Spanish goodwill, and 'not shock by their intemperance a people worthy of their attachments'. The British government had informed him that the Spaniards had large armies in the field which they would immediately bring to Moore's support; but no one knew better than the General that the British government were from time to time misinformed by their agents and prone to wishful thinking. In the interests of a political bonus, they were ready to send off the British army to buy a pig in a poke, trusting to its guts to fight a way out of the purchase, and to its generals to pay the price in the way of accepting the blame if it all went wrong.

George had had an enjoyable spell in 1807 with Sir John Moore's army in Sicily, a country he thought perfectly beautiful, if its inhabitants wouldn't make such a mess of it. In the time of the Greeks, Carthaginians and Romans, it had been famous for the quantity of corn and oil it produced—'always two crops of the finest wheat every year; and if the country was well-governed now it would be extremely rich and happy; but from its abominable laws, and the great privileges and consequent oppression by the nobles, it is a dirty, miserable, impoverished island with a large population of poor in a wretched state of idleness, misery, and ignorance' George concluded severely. The tunny-fishing was beautiful, and well-organized; not so the farming. (The inability of the locals to farm properly was a source of continuous anguish to the English in the days when they strode over the globe. A little draining here, a little water conservation there, the merest touch of a dam, 'Pray allow us, sir. . . .' 'They are starving in a larder!' they would cry with horror. The Chinese alone seemed to have the idea; and when the English got to China [apart from organising a proper harbour] they stopped colonising, not so much because there were three hundred million Chinese as because there seemed no need for agricultural improvement; though they were glumly aware that even the Chinese were quite unable to control their tigrish rivers).

In Sicily George was sent by Moore to round up some suspected French spies infiltrated amongst the local peasants, and went off delightedly dressed up as one with a red handkerchief round his black head. His dark eyes were flashing enough; but it is questionable how many peasants were actually deceived by this regular cut of an infantryman, six-foot tall and speaking no Italian; maybe he acted the dumb giant and left the chat to the locals. Moore had become a lasting influence, with his 'discipline carried on without severity; the officers attached to the men, and the men to the officers'. Charming, clever, and amusing through his sternness, Moore fell in love in the softening airs of Sicily with his C. in C.'s daughter, the young and intelligent Caroline Fox (daughter of Harry); but thinking it wrong for forty-five to propose to seventeen, he bided his time and never said so, waiting for her to grow up. After Spain, he hoped—but for Moore there was no after Spain.

In Stockholm next year it had been Sir John Moore's turn to dress up as a peasant. His army had been sent to Sweden to help King Gustavus against the Russians, now on Napoleon's side after their latest defeat at his hands. But the Swedish king turned out to be eccentric to the point of derangement. Gustavus IV, King of Sweden since the age of fourteen, had never been exactly calculable. His refusal at the last moment, upon religious grounds, to marry Princess Alexandra of Russia had caused that young lady's mother, Catherine the Great, to drop dead in an apoplexy. And although Colonel Colborne fell so much in love with a Swedish blonde that he thought he might go home a married man, Moore could get no sense out of the King, who finally put Moore under guard for refusing to hand the British army over, lock, stock and barrel, to his sole direction. His compatriots were unaware of this and Admiral Sir James Saumarez, who was giving a ball on board *Victory* at Gothenburg for the Swedish ladies, was startled by the arrival of an extremely handsome but unsuitably dressed gate-crasher. 'All the officers looked astonished,' George reported, 'and wondered who the devil the impudent fellow was, when I looked at him and instantly recognised the general. He laughed. . . .' Moore laughed rather less when blaming the government for sending men and ships on 'this wild goose chase': he had never been popular with the Ministry and such comments made him less so: only the old king was firm in knowledge of his excellence. Unencumbered by party affiliations 'old George III was immovable upon that point, and said no man but Moore should have the command of the army'.

And so in the train of this well-believed-in man, to the Peninsula the Napier brothers came, raw and keen and innocent. In the aftermath of Cintra, George was deeply shocked by seeing a French officer shoot an insolent soldier—'no man should be entrusted with absolute power: human nature is not proof against the sweets of it'; and Charles on his arrival later was equally horrified by the Algerian slaves in Lisbon. He had always hated slavery; and being briefly in the absolute power of French privates after Corunna made him loathe it still more. But though already illegal in England, it was not to be finally abolished in the British Empire for another twenty-five years, nor for another sixty in America; and it lingered on far longer among the Arab slave traders of east Africa and their Asian customers. Eighteenth-century Britain was no paradise for the underprivileged, but abroad was incomparably bloodier. Like many of their countrymen before and since, the young Napiers had lived in a kind of hopeful haze about what went on in other countries: arriving on the continent they were halted dead in their tracks by man's inhumanity to man and his still more glaring inhumanity to beasts.

Spirits rose as the army set forth from Portugal towards Spain in the October sunlight of 1808. 'A more glorious set of fellows were never seen,' George thought. The only thing the army lacked, he considered, was experience. (But as Moore knew, and George did not, it also lacked numbers.) For the war in Spain was about to take on a more lethal emphasis. High in the Pyrenees the Spanish vedettes and irregulars looked down this autumn from their heights upon an endless stream of French troops pouring into their country to swell the numbers already there into 300,000 men. Week after week through the narrow defiles the men and horses tramped, the guns and wagons rolled; till suddenly the river of invasion turned black with a new menace. For several days the route was darkened by the bear-skins of the Imperial Guard. And in the midst of them, between the spears and pennons of the Polish lancers, and the glint of the steel-cuirassed cavalry catching the sun, came postilions in the green and gold of the imperial livery. It was the coach of the little fellow in the grey redingote: Boney himself had come to settle the Spanish matter once and for all. His eight great army corps spread like a tide into central Spain. Of all this the British, in Salamanca, knew nothing certain.

A still feudal Spain could lay on some agreeable experiences for those born at the luckier end of the scale, and after a very rough passage over the mountains, Charles and George were enjoying dinner in the Palacio di San Boal at Salamanca on a November evening. Sir John Moore, who kept a good table though he was abstemious himself, presided (the palace had been put at his disposal by its hospitable owner). The meal was excellent and the table was lit with magnificent candelabra and waited upon by the Marqués de Cerralbo's innumerable manservants, and every one was in excellent spirits, advancing into Spain under the command of a general whom they admired and with every hope of meeting Napoleon, rumoured to be in Spain in person. 'If he beats us' one of the young officers pointed out, 'we shall be like the rest of the world. If we beat him we shall be like ourselves alone.' The weather was still fine, the Spanish officials gracious and welcoming; and under Moore's organisation the difficult march over almost non-existent roads had gone amazingly well. But the hush seemed almost unholy: who lurked behind those hills? Spain went on its immemorial way, unlike a country at war, and the Spanish armies were invisible and inaudible and sent no communications whatever.

There was the rub, and Sir John Moore was aware of how far he was sticking his neck out in this daring attempt to cut Boney's home line or at least to deflect him away into a corner of Spain while the scattered Spaniards gathered themselves after his crushing campaign.

But where were the vast armies the Spaniards had promised him? He felt that the British army, of whom there were only 14,000, was 'exposed to defeat, without the possibility of doing good', and he addressed the Spanish Junta at Salamanca in firm language. 'No people ever obtained independence without sacrifices. English aid, though I hope it may prove an excellent accessory, will not do without Spanish union and determination.' The Spanish had risen against Napoleon with enormous courage; but their passionate jealousy prevented cohesion: of what use the English concentration of their small force in mid-Spain if the main Spanish armies were held clamped at each side of the country while the huge Grande Armée of France streamed little opposed down the middle? Halted in this tawny and hospitable city and aware of grave peril, Moore awaited accurate news. Hookham Frere, H.M.'s minister in Madrid, supplied all the military advice Moore did not need and none of the political information he so much did. Could or would the Spaniards resist Napoleon before Madrid? If they did not, Moore would only put his neck in the noose by going there to be encircled and cut off by vastly superior French numbers. Two aged Spanish generals tottered to Salamanca to assure Moore that their colleague was valiantly defending the Somosierra passes north of Madrid, shortly before more up to date news from Graham confirmed the fact that the colleague's army had been scattered and was in full flight well south of the city, where he himself—suspected of treachery—had been murdered by his soldiers, cut in four pieces, and nailed to a tree.

Further un-reassuring tales were coming in from officers of the British army who had actually seen some of the Spanish troops: they reported them to be in rags and miserably armed, but individually fearless, and excellent guerillas if trained and supplied with weapons. But their hopes of holding up regular French infantry were nil. The Spanish forces still in the field, bold enough but with muskets that seldom or never went off, were commanded almost entirely by generals whose prime object was never to co-operate with anyone, much less the British: they were being steadily mopped up by the relentlessly advancing French. From Galicia, thirty-three-year-old General Paget, no defeatist, told Moore 'We do not discover any enthusiasm anywhere. . . . There is no Spanish army; and there is no salvation for the Spanish nation—take my word for it.' Yet 'Madrid still holds out,' Moore wrote to Hester Stanhope on December 5th; 'this is the first instance of enthusiasm shown. There is a chance that the example may be followed and the people be roused . . . I mean to proceed bridle in hand, for, if the bubble bursts and Madrid falls, we shall have to run for it.' Hardly had he written this before Madrid did indeed fall. The British government had been foxed. The promised Spanish legions had melted like snow, and a sensible general could only retire in good order on Portugal and hope to come again in better force.

In Salamanca the British soldiers were becoming increasingly amazed by the odd passivity of the Spanish. At home the Scots, Welsh and Englishmen, and, come to that, Surrey and Sussex, had their differences; but in moments of outside danger the ranks closed like treacle. The Spaniards seemed inexplicable, lounging about all day in cloaks and sombreros in the streets, with apathetic and un-shaven faces, while over the next mountain a savage invader was despoiling their land. Jealousy between town and town was beyond belief: no one in these idle winter days could have foreseen the avenging passion which would one day lick at Spanish hearts till they would sweep at the invaders like a universal forest fire. 'The people here,' one young officer reported, 'have the cool effrontery to look upon the English troops as exotic animals who have come to engage in a private fight with the French, and now that they are here all that the fine Spanish gentlemen have to do is to look on with their hands in their pockets. They do not regard us in the least as allies who are prepared to shed their blood for Spain; they simply look upon us as heretics. In our billets it is as much as we can do to get a glass of water.' The Inquisition had done its work all too well. (Napoleon in Madrid had at least immediately abolished that institution.)

Yet Moore was a shrewd observer and had come to admire the Spanish people. At terrible personal risk they were hiding British scouts and bringing him in stolen French dispatches. If they could dispose of all their medieval generals and fight in their own way! When it came to the moment of decision he thought again about immediate retreat. A change in the central Spanish Junta after the fall of Madrid gave him reasonable hope of a stiffer resistance, and General Romanos was still in the field and prepared to co-operate. While there was the slimmest chance of rallying Spanish zeal and effectiveness he would stay. 'We have no business here, but being here it would never do to abandon the Spaniards without a struggle.' On the fine morning of December 13th, 1808 the British army marched north out of Salamanca, on whose citizens they had made a good impression by their good order and good humour. They were in fine heart, advancing where they had feared to retreat. Their wagons creaked behind them along the bouldered Spanish road: in the delectable sunshine a camp follower with a three-day-old baby stepped out as proudly as any. Moore was going to head an attack on Soult; and what he called his 'family', his admiring and loyal staff, were particularly delighted at his decision. Light lay golden on the hills, and the hopeful face of George Napier glowed above a well-brushed red coat.

At Sahagún there was snow and thick fog, and an accumulation of unhopeful news, though Paget had led his Hussars on a night march against six or seven hundred French cavalry and captured two colonels and eleven officers and 150 men—'a handsome thing and well done' his general thought; and George was immensely surprised to find all these prisoners far from cast down, playing the guitar and singing in a cellar that evening, and already complaining about English food. From all that could be gathered of these captives, nothing in the situation was promising; all the same Moore was going to have what he called his 'wipe' at Soult, reported to be at Saldaña, slightly out on a limb and unaware of Moore's nearness. 'I was aware that I was risking infinitely too much, but something I thought was to be risked, for the honour of the Service, and to make it apparent that we stuck to the Spaniards long after they themselves had given up their cause as lost.' On the evening of December 23rd Moore was on his charger ready to be off; by the flickering torchlight of Sahagún George handed him his pistols and turned away to mount himself, when dramatic news came.

Napoleon had turned north west from Madrid. He was making one of his leopard leaps, to blot the contemptible little British army off the face of Spain. Pulling back his men from Talavera on their way south, and from elsewhere all over the country, the Emperor had crossed the Guadarrama in a snowstorm, going on foot at the head of his troops when they faltered under the deadly wind. He was already three marches on his way. And though, by threatening his long line of communications with Bayonne, Moore had diverted Napoleon from southern Spain and given the Spaniards a chance to re-group and recover, Moore's wipe at Soult would have to wait. He was off as fast as he could lick for Corunna or Vigo, trailing his coat at the Emperor and hoping for a chance to inflict at least some minor damage on the French forces as he covered the 300 miles. After him zoomed Napoleon, whisking fifty thousand men and their supplies through the wintry countryside of Spain as lightly as if they had been a pack of hounds, and uttering, head down to the blizzard in the Guadarrama passes, some harsh thoughts about the English. The day he met them would be a day of jubilee: he wished that there were 100,000 of them instead of 17,000, 'so that more English mothers might feel the horrors of war!'

By the end of the year William was with his brothers. The two armies had converged at Valderas where the men from Corunna had teased their friends from the south for looking so sunburnt and 'Asiatic'; (so do fashions in complexions change). From Sahagún on Christmas Eve the retreat began; and of its perils and risks perhaps only Moore took full cognisance. It was now midwinter, and between his army and the safety of the British ships at Corunna loomed the Galician mountains; the knee-deep mud of the valleys, the snows, blizzards and icy footholds of precipitous mountain roads that were sometimes barely a couple of yards wide. Food and shelter on the route was so scarce that regiments must proceed singly: at any moment Napoleon might catch up and wipe them all out one after the other. To drop behind meant death from cold, starvation, or French sabres. Steadily Moore strove to keep his men in hand. Horrified to hear how uncivilised the British troops had been at Benavente, fighting drunk and robbing people's houses, he gave them a severe rocket for their 'extreme bad conduct' and their officers another for their 'negligence and inattention'. His notions of how to treat friend or foe were strict but chivalrous; and when a thirty-five-year-old French Hussar general, the Empress Josephine's nephew, was captured at the bridge across the river Esla, Moore bathed his head-wound himself, lent him dry linen and gave him one of his own swords.

It was at Benavente too that a vast disaster was narrowly averted. Some six thousand British soldiers were sleeping in the torpor of exhaustion in the upper part of a huge deserted convent nearly surrounding the main square; on the ground floor below them hundreds of cavalry horses were stabled in tightly packed rows. The whole building had but one door. All was quiet when late at night two officers of the 43rd entering the door saw that far down the building a high wooden shutter was furiously ablaze, and that smoke from the rapidly kindling straw under the horses was beginning to flare up. One of them, Captain Thomas Lloyd, adjuring his companion to keep mum and raise no alarm and stampede, took a standing leap onto the back of the nearest animal, and running from back to back along the closely stalled and terrified horses, was able to break down the shutter and cast it outside before the blaze could spread.

Marches were long, night rests were short; and all the time the pursuing French harassed the rearguard in a continual skirmish. They took worse than they gave: how true the saying was, William thought, that a British army in retreat could be gleaned but could not be reaped.

Moore had commanded his men to leave their women and children behind in Portugal, and had made all arrangements for their care and comfort; but many of the wives and girl-friends had taken no notice of this and had followed surreptitiously, so that the winter march afforded some heart-rending sights: little children with bare legs raw with cold leaning against the fierce upland winds; and women dead by the roadside with newborn babies crying in their cold arms, luckless infants who were immediately adopted by the regiments who came after. Charles, commanding his battalion of the 50th, in the rearguard, noticed also the misery of the Spanish refugee families, fleeing from the French army and crowding the narrow mountain roads with their goods piled on carts; there was no time to do anything but share his snatched lunch with some of them.

Officers had noticed an immediate change in the men's aspect now that they were on the run and saw no chance of a proper wipe at Napoleon. Lack of help or co-operation from the Spaniards turned them sullen and ruthless and they had begun to break open the stores in the villages as they passed through them. At Astorga the British troops, maddened by bellyfuls of Spanish wine, had broken down doors and smashed their way into houses and robbed food; confusion in the narrow streets was worse confounded because the Spanish General Romanos, punished by Soult, had disregarded Moore's request and retreated on Astorga with his typhus-stricken army, greatly complicating Moore's task and adding the danger of fever to refugees and British troops alike. Discipline was slipping with appalling speed from the fine set of fellows who had marched into Spain. Many young officers were less effective than Tom Lloyd: the army in general found retreat from the French 'too galling'. At Bembibre on New Year's Day soldiers had got loose on the huge wine-vats of this little town. Too drunk to move or care, or even to stand up when shaken awake by their mates, they had lain all morning in the snow till the French dragoons caught up and came upon them. They were cut to pieces as they lay, or tried too late to stagger to their feet, with their women, and the babies in arms, the dragoons 'slashing left and right as a schoolboy does among thistles'.

In due course *The Times* would thunder that the passes of Galicia should have been made another Thermopylae; but the truth is that it is not possible to defend someone else's country when they are so proud or indifferent or terrified that they would rather submit to conquest than have it defended for them. On January 1st Lieutenant Boothby wrote to Moore from Puebla—'as to any neighbouring passes, there are no people whom I can call upon to occupy them, or should expect to defend them, however naturally strong they may be, for I see no people who are thinking of the enemy's advance with any sentiments beyond passive dislike, and hopes of protection from God and the English army.' This army, for its part, felt that it had been fed a lot of guff about the burning patriotism and enthusiasm of the Spaniards, for General Fane, after five hundred miles of marching through central and western Spain 'had not been joined by one man, or seen one Spanish corps in arms'; he had been offered no help, no shelter, never a cart, or a guide over the unmapped country—'How our ministers could have been so deceived as to the state of the country is inconceivable.'

Sir John Moore, castigated by many contemporary writers, glorified by William Napier to such an extent that he was subsequently denigrated by an irritated Sir Charles Oman, has finally been allowed his greatness by historians. Was his only fault a tendency to fall into that well-known English vice proudly called keeping oneself to oneself? Though one in eight of the men in some of the regiments he commanded were released felons and few or none could read or write, they were not fools. Could he with advantage have taken both officers and men more into his confidence? All they could see was that they were an unbeaten army flying like scalded cats from an enemy they could outfight in every slight encounter permitted them. Unaware of their deadly peril, they reacted to retreat with appalling bloodymindedness. 'They were so wild and hot for the fray,' one of their officers reported at the Coa crossing, 'that it was hard to drag them from the field.' So dragged, their tails went down. Demoralisation set in: and just possibly need not have done if they had been told that the Spanish armies had collapsed, that the French had 300,000 men in Spain to the maximum British 24,000 and that Moore could not even stand with England's only army in these defensible passes because of the appalling certainty that if he did the outnumbering French would get round behind him and block his exit to the sea. It was quite a simple proposition: hearing the truth the soldiers might have gone less wild.

At Astorga William parted company with Charles and George, Craufurd's division being diverted to Vigo to cover that port in case of need; and it was at Astorga too that a rather more vital departure took place a few days later. On New Year's Day the Emperor gave up the chase. Moore had escaped him; and disturbed by the news from Paris and wishing perhaps to save face, he had whirled away back with his coach headed for the Pyrenees, leaving Marshal Soult with 47,000 men to pursue Moore into the mountains. At Villafranca there was a sombre scene. Some of the men had fallen out, looting and drunk, assaulting civilians, and Moore had a soldier of the Light Dragoons shot in the market square in sight of all the citizens and his halted army. The man had been caught red-handed, maltreating a Spanish civilian, and later that day another soldier so found was publicly hanged. Stragglers who had been mutilated by the French cavalry were paraded as warnings to drunkards and malingerers; some were so badly mutilated that Moore would not have them shewn—without feet or hands, barely alive. The horses, bullocks and mules of the supply wagons were beginning to founder; and the worst hills, with the steepest and iciest tracks lay ahead. But a slight lift to morale was given near Villafranca when the British, with Moore always at their vulnerable rear, turned on the pursuing French and mauled them badly enough to gain a day's respite.

Ahead was the last lap; but the mountains were steeper yet. Wagons broke down, exhausted horses foundered, in the foggy darkness of a wild night Colonel Graham and his horse disappeared over the precipice, whence, miraculously, they were both hauled back with pikes and officers' sashes. The wind was such that it nearly blew men out of the saddle: miserable cavalrymen received in bitterness the order from Paget to shoot their ailing horses. Soldiers lost their boots in the icy slush and went barefoot, and in the whipping wind their

legs were soon as red as their coats. Muskets and boxes of ammunition went crashing down into valleys where rivers roared and smoked
in the spate of winter, even at one point £25,000 of silver (the French
were so close behind), as the British army, slipping, stumbling, and
cursing on the bouldered road, hauled up yet another steep slope.
But it had been nearly as bad for the French; and at Lugo Moore
halted to face Soult's army and gain another day's start.

As his ADC, George had been rarely out of the saddle since
Sahagún, galloping hither and yon with Moore's messages and
orders. Two nights before he had been sent ahead at midnight with a
dispatch to Baird telling him to halt his men at Lugo, and enclosing
others for Fraser and Hope, and for Brodick, commanding at
Corunna. The night for once was fine, with a million stars ablaze and
a hard frost glittering the ground; but as George rode on the stars
were wiped out and the sleet and snow drove blindingly in his face.
He had been urged to great speed, and at daybreak he came up with
Baird at Las Nogales, still asleep in the cold dawn. His orders had
been to find Baird; and his offer to go on to Fraser if Baird could let
him have a fresh horse was gruffly put aside by that officer, not in the
rosiest of moods after being shaken awake. Baird would, he insisted,
send a dragoon orderly. George felt more than doubtful about this
procedure, and so did the dragoon, who fortified himself so well
against the cold ride that he mislaid the dispatch to Fraser who
accordingly had gone another day's march before his orders arrived.
Fraser had fetched up at Santiago di Compostella: he had to turn
round and march his men back: not surprisingly the streets of the
town rang with some very non-pilgrim expressions. He arrived back
at Lugo short of 400 disgruntled stragglers.

The fifty miles from Villafranca to Lugo had been the worst of all;
even tough veterans among the men who had endured the scorch of
India and the chill fogs of the Low Countries had slumped by the
icy roadsides preferring death to further efforts. Captain Alexander
Gordon thought that all the straggling that had gone before was
'a perfection of discipline compared with the retreat from Villafranca . . . a comparison drawn at this period between the British
army and Romana's mob would not have been very much in favour
of the latter.' Men who stumbled and fell were found frozen to the
ground by the rearguard: the temptation to end the agony by lying
down into death was almost irresistible. Men and horses slipped and
stumbled in the frozen snow packed hard by tramping feet: ahead

stretched what seemed an endless route of snowy mountainside stained red by the bleeding bare feet of men and the cut and shoeless feet of horses who had passed that way. The dead and dying lay all along the roadside. Pity failed, and men marched without thought or feeling. Two Highlanders sank to the ground—'we sat down together; not a word escaped our lips; we looked round then at each other, and closed our eyes. I attempted to pray, and recommend myself to God; but my mind was so confused I could not arrange my ideas. I almost think I was deranged.' Still the women toiled on, looking, Rifleman Harris thought, 'like a tribe of travelling beggars': one tough Irishwoman fell out when her pains came on, caught up when her son was born, and carried him safely to the sea. And when the French dragoons arrived, the dazed Highlander rose to his feet, started firing at them, and resumed his march. There were no villages, no houses, no sheltering walls, only the shrieking wind over desolate heights, French bugles in the far distance, and the intact and splendid rearguard repeatedly saving the famished and exhausted army.

To George, who got around a great deal with Moore's messages and orders, the fault for the demoralisation seemed to lie with the generals. The Guards remained an intact fighting force, and so did the Reserve under Paget, but by the other senior officers, except for Hope, Bentinck and Hill, he was unimpressed—they were 'supine' and used 'imprudent language' in open discussion of the conduct of the campaign. At Lugo Moore blasted them. 'Generals and Commanding Officers must be as sensible as the Commander of the Forces of the complete disorganisation of the Army. . . .' He had shot one soldier at Villafranca, but 'there would be no occasion to proceed to such extremities if the officers did their duty; as it is chiefly from their negligence, and from want of proper regulations that crime and irregularities are committed in quarters and upon the march'.

At Lugo fresh stores awaited the army; and on hearing that the French were here to be faced and fought, a great number of stragglers came in, and surprisingly many malingerers staged startling recoveries. They were rewarded by the satisfaction of driving the French back down the hill in such confusion that Soult did not renew the attack, and the retreating army gained a vital twenty-four hours start.

Food after long starvation effected a great lift in morale, and George, riding away down the hillside past Charles and Charles

Stanhope and their infinitely alluring pot of Irish stew on that chill slaty morning, heard their cry 'Dainty Dog!' and their mocking laughter echo loudly after him. He had eaten nothing since early the last night, let alone hot meat. He was surprised a little later to see Mrs Mackenzie, wife of the colonel, surveying the scene from close to the enemy on a large reliable white horse. Next day George had a narrow escape from death at the hands of one of his own side. Chasing some men who were plundering a farm, he was closely missed by a shot from one of them, and felt that he ought to have shot back, but how could one, in cold blood, and when they were all in such a jam? He knew, afterwards, that he should have handed the man over, and was immensely glad that he had not.

No such qualms troubled Black Bob. Dark and small and wiry as a Spaniard, General Craufurd, guarding Moore's left flank, bore his men along towards Vigo with his stern eye and infectious courage, spurring them on with ripe oaths and tots of rum. He had a short way with stragglers. 'If he flogged two,' Rifleman Harris reported, 'he saved hundreds. I shall never forget Craufurd. He was in everything a soldier.' When Harris and his mate were struggling in a bog late one night and had given themselves up for lost, they saw the flickering torches of the local Spaniards whom Black Bob had rounded up to rescue them. Further on things grew worse and Rifleman Harris 'felt something like the approach of death—a sort of horror mixed up with my sense of illness—a feeling I have never experienced before or since'. Beside the way were Sergeant White-body and his wife; he had not been well and had been sent ahead to Vigo but the march had been too much, and he and his wife lay down in the snow to die in each other's arms. Shouts of joy spurred Harris on for the last climb; from the top of the hill the men could see the English ships lying in Vigo Bay. As he went down the hill the longed-for sea dissolved before Harris's gaze. He could hardly make out the outline of the boat which came back for him: the faces of the sailors who hauled him on board with rough kindness and rude remarks about landlubbers were blurred and dim. The terrible privations had sent him temporarily blind.

William was left behind with the rearguard to defend the bridge of Castro Gonsalo over the Esla river; 'cavalry and stragglers being all over the river we commenced destroying the bridge amidst torrents of rain and snow, half the troops worked, the other half kept the enemy at bay from the heights on the left bank', whence John

Walton and Richard Jackson, two sentinel privates of the 43rd, though almost cut to pieces by French sabres, had managed to stagger in and give the alarm. William hung on for twenty-four hours, 'mid-leg in clay and in snow'; but the final lap was the worst, wrestling the wagons full of wounded through swollen streams that dragged the boots and coats off the hauling, shoving, drenched men. Sleet and snow continuously lashed them, mud had sucked them under and bogged them down. William brought his convoy in to Vigo, complete with wounded and ammunition, but the last few days had been terrible, marching with bare feet, and nothing but a jacket and linen trousers against the January cold. He had arrived skin and bone, been carried on board with a raging pleurisy, and was reported dead.

Further north the main body, a weary and disintegrating army, struggled on to Betanzos while the weather grew ever wilder and the rain relentlessly drove in their faces. Here at least there were more stores waiting for them; but by now the army was too spent even to eat. The French cavalry were hard on their heels: even some of the generals were openly disaffected. These were Spanish hills; why did no Spaniards harry the French army? Moore's stern address to them had a bracing effect. Straggling, frostbitten, moving more like sheep than like trained men, they shambled past the General, who shook and angered them into marching these last few vital miles to the safety of Corunna and the waiting British ships. He would rather, he said, be killed by the first bullet than command men who behaved in such an infamous manner; and thus goaded, the army reluctantly, staggeringly, bloodymindedly crossed the last mountain. Some time on this bitter pitch-black night so near to safety Mrs MacGregor, wife of a sergeant in the Gordons, was lost. She had three little boys with her, in baskets slung over a donkey; none of them were ever heard of again.

By noon all but the rearguard were down into the milder plain of Corunna, where the wild flowers were already beginning to bloom and the lemon trees to bud. On January 11th of 1809 they struggled into the town, while Paget's cavalry fought a last delaying action with Soult's advanced dragoons at El Burgo, where the Engineers had failed to blow up the bridge—'What, another abortion! And pray sir, how do you account for this failure?' Along the straight road to Corunna one brigade strode out in regular columns with drums beating and the drum major twirling his staff at their head, their chins

held high against the late light of a setting sun: the Guards had
arrived.

But to what? In all the bay there was nothing but a sprinkling of
ships. Under a north-east wind the waves lashed an empty shore. The
rescue fleet, commanded by Hood, were still beating from Vigo
against the bitter head winds. When the remnants of the army
trailed into the city their aspect was so stricken, ferocious, and ragged
that the people of Corunna shuddered and crossed themselves as the
men passed. Gaol-birds, vagrants, with scarred backs and livers
corroded by grog, the British army had lost their spoils, bullocks,
horses, wagons, ammunition; their wives, women, supplies, boots,
morale, discipline and treasure; everything except their fight: the
French soldiers were overheard by their officers to say they would
sooner face a hundred fresh Germans than ten dying Englishmen.
They had also retained their colours and their guns: now perhaps
they were fatally trapped between the French and the empty sea and
not one would be left alive or free.

Under his gruelling responsibility Moore had never faltered, but
when three days later on the morning of the 14th he saw the bay still
empty of ships, he said to George Napier 'I have often been thought
an unlucky man by my friends, in consequence of being generally
wounded in action—and some other events in my life. But I never
thought myself so till now. And if the transports do not arrive this
day, I shall certainly be convinced that I am an unlucky fellow, and
that Fate has so decreed.' Fate at least had not decreed this; by noon
the bay was full of British men-of-war and its shores were busy with
the to-ing and fro-ing of their ship's boats. And now Moore's great
hope was that the French would attack him outright, and not wait
to maul him in the vulnerable moment of embarkation. All through
the 15th of January came the melancholy noise of ammunition dumps
being blown up, and the worse sound of foundered horses being shot.
George could only comfort his feeling heart with the thought that
this was better for the horses than being worked to death by the
Spaniards. By nightfall all Moore's troops were disposed in their
stations, his wounded and sick and any stores that could be saved
were carried on board; and when, in the black dawn of the 16th,
sounds of action from the French camp reassured him, his staff
noticed that the General's face suddenly looked as young and happy
as a boy's.

XII

Charles would be unable to complain that his first battle was not a proper one. He stood on the slope of the hill outside the walled promontory city of Corunna at the head of the 50th, replacing their absent colonel. Four days of lull had enabled some recovery from the rigours of the retreat. Across the valley, with sharp-shooters in front and a magnificent barrage of artillery supporting them from behind, three great well-disciplined columns of French soldiers were advancing downhill and up the slope upon the thin red line, shouting all the while *'En avant, tue! tue! en avant, tuez!'* in a concentrated menacing roar. Splendidly equipped and trained, filled to the back teeth with revolutionary fervour, they had scattered the armies of Europe like chaff; shrewd confident fighters with their wits about them and a clear idea of what to do and when to do it. In front the voltigeurs, their well-spread sharp-shooters, came on with superb alacrity, taking advantage of every gorse bush and boulder yet never losing their impetus. But the outnumbered British were fighting in their favourite situation with their backs to the sea, of which their navy had command; and they had confidence in their general. Moore knew that Soult must attack his right wing if he wanted to get at the harbour and disrupt the embarkation of the British troops. But he had expected a strong feint at his centre, posted on the hill above the village of Elvina, and this Soult was duly supplying.

Writing forty years later, Charles could still remember the feelings of this first encounter—'I felt great anxiety, no fear, curiosity also. It was unpleasant until the fire opened, and then only one idea possessed me,—that of keeping the soldiers steady and animated. Personal danger did not enter my thoughts until I was cut off, and had to fight man to man, or rather with many men. When overpowered and struggling, thinking my life gone, fear made me desperate.' That moment had not yet come, and laughing, he stood in front of his men—'Don't duck, the ball has passed before you hear the whiz.' As the fire increased, Sir John Moore appeared on a terrified cream-coloured horse with a black mane and tail: 'he came at speed, and pulled up so sharp and close he seemed to have alighted from the air.' Whatever else was going on, Charles could never not notice horses; and the whole aspect of rider and steed riveted his attention—the quivering horse momentarily on its haunches, so suddenly halted with its forefeet slipping and sliding on the loose stones, its widened nostrils snorting terror, and 'ears pushed out like horns, while its eyes flashed fire'. It would, Charles thought, be off in a flash, and he watched with admiration while Moore stilled his animal with legs and hands, his eyes and mind fixed with searching intentness on the advancing enemy: never before had he seen a being so wholly concentrated. As they stood on the hillside, biding their time, the men had been asking for Moore since the firing began—'there was a feeling that under him we could not be beaten'. Having seen, Moore was off as fast as he had come to another part of the line.

French fire from the village of Elvina was now very sharp, and when Moore returned, 'I asked him to let me throw my grenadiers who were losing men fast, into the enclosures in front.

' "No" he said, "they will fire on our own picquets in the village."

' "Sir, our picquets and those of the 4th Regiment also were driven from thence when you went to the left."

' "Were they? Then you are right, send out your grenadiers." And again he galloped away. Captain Clunes of the 50th, six foot five and proportionately broad and strong, had just come up from Corunna. "Clunes, take your grenadiers and open the ball." He stalked forward alone, like Goliath before the Philistines, his grenadiers followed, and thus the battle began on our side.'

It was an age without communications, and George, as Moore's galloper, had been in the saddle with orders and messages since dawn; but whenever there was a pause he had had a chance to see what was going on in the various parts of the field. The fortress and town of Corunna were behind him, to the left the little river Moro wound through fields and vineyards to the sea. In the valley below the British troops was the village of Elvina, a tangle of stone walls, winding lanes, orchards, and low houses; and on the heights behind it were the French swarming down the hillside, the smoke of the skirmishers' muskets, the relentless movement of a well-disciplined advance. Soult, George suspected, would try to turn their flank and get between the English and the sea: if Moore wanted to embark his army safely he would have to teach him a sharp lesson. And how many French reserves lurked behind those heights?

But George knew that the general's only anxiety was lest the light of the short winter day should fail before he had hit the French as hard as he meant. He had been galloping at Moore's side when they heard the signal for the French advance. Thank God, they were coming for it. George heard Moore shout to General Graham that he was 'very happy'. The French had obliged.

As Moore came back along the line once more to the 50th, a round shot hit the ground between Charles and the general's spectacular horse, whose terror he again controlled, while asking Charles if he was hurt. No sir! But a man of the 42nd had been less lucky; his leg was torn off and he was screaming horribly, 'and rolled about so as to excite agitation and alarm with others. The general said, This is nothing, my lads, keep your ranks, take that man away: my good fellow, don't make such a noise, we must bear these things better. He spoke sharply, but it had a good effect; for this man's cries had made an opening in the ranks and the men shrunk from the spot, although they had not done so when others had been hit who did not cry out.' Moore, soon to have to bear these things better himself, rode off to the 42nd, and Charles never saw him again.

The painful, lethal wait continued. Would they never be allowed to push on? Had someone, had George, been hit, on their way with orders? Moore, he knew, with a view of the whole enterprise that was denied to Charles on his patch of hillside, would know the exact moment when the French attack lost its impulse, began to scatter and fail—the perfect occasion for counter-attack. But where now was Moore?

Under a heavy fire on Charles's hillside 'Lord William Bentinck now came up on his quiet mule, and began talking to me as if we were going to breakfast; his manner was his ordinary one, with perhaps an increase of good humour and placidity. No recollection of what he said remains, for the fire was sharp and my eyes were more busy than my ears: I only remember saying to myself this chap takes it coolly or the devil's in it. Lord William and his mule, which seemed to care as little for the fire as its rider, sheltered me from shot, which I liked well enough; but having heard officers and soldiers jeer at Colonel Walker for thus sheltering himself behind General Fane's horse at Vimiero, I went to the exposed side: yet it gave me the most uncomfortable feel experienced that day.' Soon the cool Lord William rode off to the 4th regiment, but without having given any order to advance. He took with him Charles's spy-glass which he had borrowed—'I never saw it more.' Charles regretted this; it was a fine one and had been Lord Edward Fitzgerald's, that fiery young cousin who had died as a rebel in Dublin Castle. Short-sighted himself, Charles badly needed it.

By his side stood the helpful figure of John Montgomery, 'a brave soldier who had risen from the ranks'. Soon they saw the 42nd, advancing in line; still no orders came. 'Good God, Montgomery, are we not to advance?' Montgomery, a Scotchman, said laughingly, 'You cannot be wrong to follow the 42nd.' Unseen by Charles across the brow of the slope, Moore himself had led them—'My brave Highlanders! Remember Egypt!' and they had driven the French down the hill. Behind his slope Charles could see none of this: he gave the word to advance but forbade firing.

' "Major let us fire!" '

' "Not yet." '

Soon they were up with the 42nd, checked at a breast high stone wall and firing across it. Charles called out to his men

' "Do you see your enemies plain enough to hit them?" '

' "By Jasus we do!" '

' "Then blaze away!" and such a rolling fire broke out as I have hardly ever heard since.'

Orders or not, what they must do, Charles knew, was to drive the French out of Elvina village and silence the battery on the hill behind it. The 50th's officers, and a hundred of their bravest men were over the stone wall, but many had stopped behind it and had to be driven over. The line was formed beyond the wall, but now Charles saw that half the men were firing too high; he laid a halberd over the firelocks of the nearest to keep their level low—'being cool, though the check at the wall had excited me and made me swear horribly'. Crossing the marshy ground close to the village was the worst part of the advance; fire from the houses had been terrible and the howitzers had pelted them from the hills. Ensigns Moore and Stewart with the colours had followed Charles closely until they were both hit and Sergeant Magee took on. Charles's sword belt was shot off, scabbard and all, which made him spin, as they entered the village. They had driven the French forth; but Charles never heard Moore's final shout of 'Well done 50th! Well done, my majors!' Nor indeed did Stanhope and Clunes. Elvina was empty, but for a scatter of dead Frenchmen. 'The soldiers cried out "Bayonet them, they are pretending." The idea was to me terrible, and made me call out No! No! there are plenty who bear arms to kill, come on!' This piece of inexperienced clemency cost the lives of four men and nearly cost Charles his.

Elvina was theirs, but the line had been broken and scattered and Charles could only collect three officers and thirty men for his rush up the lane towards the French battery. At its head was some cover, a breastwork of loose stones which the picquet had built; Charles had noticed it when visiting the picquet the night before. But 'my efforts were vain to form a strong body, the men would not leave the rocks, from which they kept up a steady fire'. In the lane the French gunfire was deafening; halfway up it Charles fell, 'much hurt, though at the moment unconscious of it; a soldier cried out the Major is killed. Not yet, come on.' At the end of this murderous lane their diminished numbers found the cover—'and then it appeared to me that by a rush forward we could carry the battery above'. The cover proved less adequate than he had hoped, 'and it was evident that we must go on or go back, we could not last long where we were'. Three or four of his twenty survivors were killed at his side, 'and two more by the fire of our men from the village behind. The poor fellows kept shouting out as they died, Oh God! Major our own men are killing us! Oh Christ God I'm shot in the back of the head! The last man was so, for he fell against me, and the ball had entered just above the poll. Remembering then that my father had told me he saved a man's life, at the siege of Charleston, by pulling a ball out with his finger before inflammation swelled the parts, I thought to do the same, but could not find it, and feared to do harm by putting my finger far in. It made me feel sick, and the poor fellow being laid down, continued crying out that our men had killed him, and there he soon died. This misery shook us all a good deal, and made me so wild as to shout and stamp with rage, feeling a sort of despair at seeing the soldiers did not come on.' Stone walls hid them all from each other; Charles sent the three officers back down the lane to collect help 'and they found Stanhope animating the men, but not knowing what to do, and calling out Good God where is Napier? When Turner told them I was in front and raging for them to come on for an attack on the battery, he gave a shout and called on the men to follow him, but ere taking a dozen strides cried out Oh my God! and fell dead, shot through the heart.' For the scattered British troops in Elvina this was the last straw, and when Lieutenant Turner bravely rejoined Charles he had not been able to collect a single man to follow him up the lane.

The long frustration of the retreat, the death of the soldiers shot by his own men, and his raging disappointment that no one would follow him to storm the battery, now built up in Charles to the point where, by his own account, he went mad. He jumped on top of the breastwork, waving his hat and sword, shouting to the men behind the rocks—'but the fire was so loud none heard me, though the lane was scarcely a hundred yards long'. The French were amazed; and, affording that deference which the very primitive and the very civilised alike accord to madness, held their fire. Afterwards their chivalrous captain, not knowing that Charles had been the man, told him how he had stopped the men's fire: 'instead of firing at him, I longed to run forward and embrace that brave officer'. His own men shouted at him to jump down or he would be killed—'I thought so too, but was so mad as to care little what happened to me.'

At least from the top of the wall Charles could see a little way around the smoke-filled scene. To the left was a copse, and a hedge-topped ridge 'which debarred further sight', and might conceal some more British soldiers—'if fifty men of the 42nd and 50th could be gathered, we might still charge the battery above us: if we failed there was a house near, into which we could force our way, and as it was conspicuous from the English position, Moore would send us support.' Armed with this total confidence in the general, he leapt from the wall and went down a right-angled lane to the left, exposed to English, but not to French fire, 'but being armed only with a short sabre, useless against a musket and bayonet, and being quite alone, short-sighted, and without spectacles, I felt very cowardly and anxious . . . the disadvantage of bad sight is tremendous when alone, and gives a feeling of helplessness'. At the end of the lane lay a wounded French officer: horrified by Charles's smoke-blackened face he thought he came to slay and not to help, and called out to unseen companions; and from behind the hedge from which Charles had hoped so much came a burst of French fire which nearly blew him to pieces. Now indeed he really felt lost. 'The temptation to run back was great, but the thought that our line might see me, made me walk leisurely, in more danger indeed yet less alarmed than when going forward without knowing what would happen. The whole excursion along the lane was the most nervous affair I ever experienced in battle.' When he got back to the stone breastwork there was no one there.

His madness was over, and a terrible flatness and defeat came over him. 'I felt very miserable then, thinking the 50th had behaved ill; that my not getting the battery had been a cause of the battle being lost, and that Moore would attribute all to me. The English smoke had gone back, and my only comfort was that the French smoke had not gone forward. The battle seemed nearly over, I thought myself the last man alive belonging to our side who had got so far in front, and felt certain of death, and that my general would think I had hidden myself, and would not believe me to have done my best.' Moore had ordered the 50th to be reinforced, but he had been mortally wounded and carried back to Corunna, and Bentinck, still cool, had recalled the regiments. Apart from a handful of others, scattered through the houses and vineyards, Charles was alone, and, he felt sure, disgraced.

'In this state of distraction, and still under a heavy fire, I turned down the lane to rejoin the regiment and soon came on a wounded man— "Oh praised be God major! My dear Major! God help you my darling, one of your own 50th". Could he walk with Charles's help? No, he was too badly wounded, "Oh Christ God, my jewel, my own dear major sure you wont leave me?" The agony with which he screamed was great, it roused all my feelings, and strange to say alarmed me about my own danger, which had been forgot in my misery.' Charles bent to lift the man, and as he did so, a musket ball broke a bone in his own leg. Barely able to get along himself, but helped by his sword, and encouraged by the sight of four privates in the middle of the village, Charles left the soldier—'I felt it horrible, yet what could be done by a man hardly able to walk and with other duties to perform? Selfishness and pain got the better.' The four men told him they were cut off; and indeed from the two lanes parties of French soldiers were now converging on them. Selecting the smallest lot, and 'forgetting my leg then, though I had not pluck to do so for the poor wounded man left behind, I said to the four soldiers, follow me and we'll cut through them'. He started forward, and his leg failed under him. Chill but painless, he felt cold steel running into his back. The sham-dead Frenchmen of Elvina had come alive with a vengeance: pouring out of a doorway they had attacked the five Englishmen from behind. The steel plunged in, and Charles fell forward on his face.

*

George had had a day to trouble the stoutest heart. Untouched himself, he had been compassed about by the deaths of dear friends. He had seen the heartening sight of the British troops, in their scarlet and white, their dark green and tartan, charging the swarming close-packed brown French columns at the point of the bayonet, and with loud cheers forcing them to retire uphill, under the protection of their own guns. He had seen his brother Charles, charging at the head of his regiment with Charles Stanhope; but then, in what seemed but a moment after, he had been ordered away by Moore to bring up a battalion of Guards to support Bentinck's brigade. The sun was setting, the light sloped along the valley behind him and dazzled his eyes as he galloped off, seeing over his shoulder the General at the head of the Highlanders being most furiously engaged—what a hell of a time to have to leave! Just as he reached a corner and gave a last look, he saw the general's horse give a bound in the air, and Hardinge dismounting to catch him as he fell. Moore must be wounded; and every instinct of affection and loyalty made George long to be with him, but he must first find Colonel Warde and deliver the message; he galloped on with a sinking heart.

Moore had been hit high up—'a dreadful wound bared the cavity of his chest . . . the blood flowed fast, and the torture of his wound increased; but such was the unshaken firmness of his mind that those about him, judging from the resolution of his countenance that his hurt was not mortal, expressed a hope of his recovery.' Taking a long searching look at what was left of his chest, Moore told them, 'No, I feel that to be impossible.' He was carried towards the town, making the Highlanders who bore him turn him around at intervals to see how the battle was going, 'discovering his satisfaction' when he saw the advance of the British firing line. Two doctors came out to meet him, but he told them they could do nothing for him—'Go to the wounded soldiers to whom you may be useful.' In Corunna the surgeons could indeed do nothing for him, the pain increased as night fell, and as his soldiers, unmolested, began to go on board the warships. No groan escaped him, but to his close friend General Anderson, whose arm supported him, he said in a low voice 'it is a great uneasiness, it is great pain'. He was very strong; he knew that it would take him some hours to die. The chaplain prayed quietly beside him, and as long as he could speak he continued to ask after his men and to make arrangements to promote those who had done well. As the ships in the harbour sounded eight o'clock his ordeal ended. 'Are the French beaten?' he had asked, as one after another his staff and friends had come into the room at headquarters, and all had assured him that they were. 'I hope that the people of England will be satisfied. I hope my country will do me justice.' But it would be long before these hopes were fulfilled; and in their realisation William Napier, now choking with pleurisy on board a man-of-war in Vigo Bay, would be a major instrument.

When George got back to the cross-roads he was given the news of Moore's desperate wound and of his removal to the rear, and again the impulse to go to him was almost uncontrollable. General Baird had been wounded early on and was now on board one of the ships having his arm cut off at the shoulder; George swallowed the misery he felt over Moore and dutifully attached himself to Hope, now in command. He heard that the fiftieth had three times captured Elvina, and that the French, reinforced by fresh reserves under Mermet, had three times driven them out. While Hope was in consultation George, and James Stanhope, sought news of their brothers from the 50th's rear-guard: riding ahead, George met some soldiers carrying the body of an officer shot through the heart. With trembling hands he drew the handkerchief from the dead man's face, and saw the marble features of Charles Stanhope still drawn in the pain of death. There was no time for a tear for this dear friend, his brother was coming up, and George with an instinct to spare him the pain of such a sight, mounted and took James's bridle to turn him around, 'Come along, we must instantly return to General Hope.' Riding back, he told James the news of his brother's fate as gently as he could—'he bore it as every soldier ought, but could not resist the desire of going to take a last look at poor Charles'.

They rejoined Hope, who was riding from brigade to brigade, directing and encouraging; passing through a narrow defile in single rank, Woodford, just in front of George, was hit by enemy sharp-shooters, and Harry Burrard, just behind, was mortally wounded. And when they came up again to the 50th, still in close action, the gigantic Clunes, now in command, reported to Hope 'Sir, our commanding officer Major Napier is killed. We have no field officer left. Our ammunition is expended. What are we to do?' But the French in Elvina too had fought to a standstill; by six o'clock the sound of their drums beating retreat could be heard all along the valley. Foiled in all his thrusts and encirclements, Soult had had enough. He was pulling back. Soon the valley, below its pall of mist and smoke and gathering darkness, held no one but the dying and the dead.

General Hope was off to Corunna to superintend the army's embarkation, but the stricken George followed him no more. Somewhere in that dark and smoky valley Charles might still be alive and lying out in mortal pain: one or two of the young officers of the 50th had told George they thought he might only be wounded. In the cold darkness, with a flaring resin torch in his hand, George went over the whole field of battle, turning over the body of every officer he could find 'in vain hope of once more seeing the countenance, though in death, of my beloved brother Charles, and that I might satisfy my mind that he was dead'. Bodies were lying in heaps where the fighting had been hottest: George's task took a long while. At last it came to him that there might be some point in searching the makeshift hospitals in the town too, but here no one could tell him anything but that they had seen his brother killed.

In the darkness George turned his weary horse towards headquarters house. There was a small crowd of people outside, but no light or sound came forth—'all was silent as the grave. A cold dread chill struck upon my heart as I ascended the gloomy stairs.' He opened the door and beheld a scene he was never to forget. Moore had that moment died; his ravaged chest was still uncovered. 'That lofty spirit had taken its flight to the region of the great and good.' Moore's 'family', all save George, had been around him. By his side leaned General Anderson, his one arm supporting the general's head, his cheeks and lips drained of colour, his looks drawn with anguish. Colborne was standing, head down, overcast and stunned with grief. François, Moore's devoted servant, was bending over his master's body with his hands clasped in a speechless agony. Poor James Stanhope was overwhelmed by the impact of this fresh blow. The only sound that broke the stillness was the convulsive sobbing of that cheerful sandy-haired character, young Harry Percy.

Moore was barely forty-six. A thoughtful, deliberate, well-read man, he had applied his intelligence and experience to his profession, and greatly advanced its capacities. 'The lofty sentiments of honour habitual to his mind, were adorned by a subtle playful wit, which gave him in conversation an ascendancy he always preserved by the decisive vigour of his actions' William considered. Moore was handsome and well-made, with fine hazel eyes under dark brows, and 'a singularly expressive mouth'. He had loved the serious charming young Caroline Fox (daughter of apple-cheeked Harry), and gone often to Lady Hester Stanhope for company, stimulation, and amusement, but the real wife of this attractive bachelor had been his country; a spouse that like some others took many years to realise his worth. There was much angry criticism of his campaign; much indignant pity for the 'betrayed Spaniards': it was mainly to vindicate Moore's memory that William Napier embarked on his monumental history of the Peninsular War. None of the brothers ever forgot him: both George and William christened sons after him; and if Charles had ever been blest with a boy there would doubtless have been a third John Moore Napier. 'You know, FitzRoy, we'd not have won without him' Wellington said long afterwards to his friend Somerset, when he had finally driven the French from Spain. But song is more enduring and potent than flesh or fact; and it was an obscure and hitherto unknown Irish curate who would immortalise Moore, his hurried midnight burial by the sombre shore, and the love that he inspired in the hearts of his friends.

Three days after William was reported dead of pleurisy on board a warship in Vigo bay he was on his feet again, disguised as a sailor for a projected cutting out expedition against a Russian frigate (the Russians at this point were still on Napoleon's side). But the plan was abandoned, and as William lay sweating again in his fever, the news of Charles's death was brought to him. The warship rolled out into the Atlantic, bound for home, bearing him past the triumphant French tricolour on Corunna's fortress, 'without' he bitterly complained, 'having an opportunity either of dying like my darling Charles, or of contributing to revenge his and Moore's death'. The tale came, too, of Charles Stanhope's death, and as the long, depleted form of handsome William groaned and sweated in the rising seas, the days in the drawing-room at Putney with him and his sister Hester, and all the practical fun with Mr Pitt, seemed small and dear and far away, like some delectable nursery with firelight playing on its walls. The weight of Charles's death lay on him like lead. 'We have lost the best friend and best brother and best son God ever made' he wrote to Sarah, his hand shaking with fever, his heart cold with weakness and sorrow and the movement of the sea.

*

Charles was determined not to go without a struggle. Forty years later, he recalled the force of his feelings—'thinking my life gone, fear made me desperate. Had I not lost my sabre, I think I could have cut my way through; but while striving for the man's musquet nothing else was thought of: there was but one weapon for both, and death for the man who lost it.' Somehow getting to his feet, he wrestled the Frenchman's musket away from himself and drove the man back on his companions. But all round him the parties of brown-uniformed men were closing in, he heard the dying shouts of his companions as they were bayonetted to death, while blows from a score of French rifle butts rained down on him. Stumbling from his broken leg, he called out ' "*Je me rends*" (remembering the expression correctly from an old story of a fat officer, whose name being James, called out Jemmy Round). Finding they had no disposition to spare me, I kept hold of the musket.' He was still vigorously defending himself when a tall swarthy man came up to give him the coup de grâce with a heavy brass-handled sabre, 'and struck me a powerful blow on the head, which was bare, for my cocked hat had fallen off.' This, Charles had time to think, must really be the finish; but he ducked his head so that the blow should fall on his back, or on the hardest part of his head—'so far I succeeded, for it fell exactly on the top, cutting into the bone but not through it. Fire sparkled from my eyes, I fell on my knees, blinded, yet without quite losing my senses and holding still on to the musket. Recovering in a moment, I regained my legs, and saw a florid handsome young French drummer holding the arm of the dark Italian, who was in the act of repeating his blow. Quarter was then given.'

Thwarted, the French soldiers then tore Charles's clothes to pieces to get at his watch, and his purse, and a locket with a girl's hair which hung round his neck. '*Est-il pillé?*' asked everybody, as he was taken to the rear. '*Oh pour ça, oui, joliment.*' But two soldiers were shot by English fire while the pillage was going on, and Guibert, the French drummer, told the Italian to take Charles to the rear. Charles could see that the Italian was far from satisfied and would complete his job the moment he got a chance, they had only gone a few yards when the man turned round to assure himself that Guibert was busy before he again drew his brass-handled sabre. Here Charles's French lessons really came into their own, and he yelled out at Guibert ' "This rascal is going to kill me! Brave Frenchmen don't kill prisoners." Guibert ran back, swore furiously at the Italian, shoved him away, almost down, and putting his arms round my waist supported me himself: thus this generous Frenchman saved me twice, for the Italian was bent upon slaying.'

They were going up Charles's old 'murderous lane' when a fresh figure appeared upon the scene. John Hennessy, an enormous Irishman of the 50th and a well-known regimental character, was walking down it at a rapid pace, as though he owned all Spain. Strong as an ox, he had once been a famous malingerer. Insisting that he was paralysed, he had once endured the appalling punishment of the lash, rather than run round the church tower and thus prove himself able-bodied. With frequent pauses to allow him to think again, he had borne no less than six hundred lashes, enough to kill a man twice over, before he had exclaimed Be Jasus, that's enough, and run round the church tower without the least difficulty. This savage treatment had not soured his temper towards officers, and when he saw Charles he levelled his musket and prepared to rescue him singlehanded.

' "For God's sake don't fire, I am a prisoner, badly wounded, and can't help you. Surrender."

' "For why should I surrender?" Hennessy shouted back.

' "Because there are at least twenty men upon you."

' "Well if I must surrender, there," said he, dashing down his firelock across their legs and making them all jump, "there's my firelock for yez." Then coming close up he threw his arms round me, and giving Guibert a push that sent him and one or two more reeling against the wall, shouted out, "Stand away ye bloody spalpeens, I'll carry him myself, bad luck to the whole of yez".'

En route for base, with a guard of a French captain and ten men, 'We passed a large gap in a wall, on which the English fire was still very heavy. The French soldiers cried out Don't cross there except on your knees or you will be shot, whereupon the French officer desired Hennessy and me to do so, but we refused, and Hennessy said low, Be Jasus they're afraid. My desire was to be seen by our own people, and therefore my walk with Hennessy and the officer was erect and slow; but seeing the French guard crawl on their hands and knees, I said to the Captain, Crawl you too, or you will be hit, I can't run away. This anxiety for an enemy greatly amused the Frenchman. . . . However the officer would only stoop and none of us were hit.'

Dark was come on, the pain of Charles's wounds and bruises was now great, and everything passed in a kind of nightmare. His head had been plastered at one point by General Renaud's surgeon, but his leg was too swollen to permit his boot to be got off without cutting it, and this Charles would not allow; he would need his boots to escape in. French officers treated him with kindness but were necessarily occupied; night deepened, he was laid down on some straw near a fire, cast violently off the straw by its indignant owner, taken into the roofless remains of a blown-up house, propped up by the powerful arms of Hennessy in a corner near the fire. His sword had come back to him, sent by Renaud on the grounds that he had used it so well, and Charles had written his name on a scrap of paper, using his blood for ink, and asked an officer to take it with the sword to Soult. The officers had all gone away, and some soldiers came and tossed him into an outhouse full of filth and stood over him taunting him, discussing which of various methods would be the most amusing way to kill him, and he had wished to God they would hurry up and get on with it, when some officers had returned and saved him.

'These officers were very angry'—and he was aware of rage and voices going on round him, and of the icy wind blowing down from the mountains—'but my understanding was faint, and my desire was to be put out of misery, for I thought we had lost the battle and my pain of body was past bearing.' They had taken him near the fire and offered him broth and wine, 'but I could touch nothing for the agony of my wounds, and groaned at times for the pain was no longer supportable even before an enemy'. Hennessy made sure he was dying, and before being marched off, he had, with Charles's consent, unbuckled his silver spurs and taken them with him—'the spalpeens would murder you for them'.

The battle in the valley below had not been lost. Soult, at length attacking where he hoped he was turning the British right flank on the corner of Mount Mero, had encountered Paget and Fraser's divisions full in face and found that far from rounding a flank he was heading into an unengaged centre; he went no further. His diversions round the left flank of his opponents, where Hill's men kept the shore route to Corunna, had ended in stalemate; (here Colonel Alexander Napier of the Gordon Highlanders had been killed: it was not a lucky day for Napiers), and the British soldiers were now splashing out undisturbed to the boats that rowed them to the warships and transports in the dimly-lit mist-covered harbour.

Up on the heights of Penasquedo the fire went out and Charles was alone. All that January night and the long succeeding day and another night he lay unsheltered, except for a ruined wall, on the bare hillside. He was faint with exhaustion and lightheaded with pain; 'what fretted me most was that no flag of truce came in for me. I thought Moore was angry, that myself and the regiment had been disgraced, and therefore he would not send in, nor let George come: and then the fancy came that George was killed, but my thoughts were all wild and sad that night.' On the next afternoon all hope of rescue died: immovable on his high hillside he saw the spread sails of the British fleet as they stood out for the west and north, bound for the open Atlantic and for home.

Charles was an avid reader, devouring history, biography, pamphlets, verse, as some devour food: had he read what Coleridge, just ten years earlier, had written of another soul in torment? 'In his loneliness and fixedness he yearneth towards the journeying Moon, and the stars that still sojourn, yet still move onward; and everywhere the blue sky belongs to them, and is their appointed rest and their native country and their own natural homes, which they enter unannounced, as lords that are certainly expected, and yet there is a silent joy at their arrival.' For him death by exposure or a casual blow now seemed certain: all he had hoped or dreamed would end here in lonely disgrace, on the Spanish hills where it had ended for so many; with no friend or comrade to hold his hand or shut his staring eyes. The cold clamped down on him as darkness deepened into another night.

On the third afternoon he managed to crawl out, not much minding now whether a French poilu knocked him on the head or not, and he was found by a bandsman, treated with the utmost kindness by all the officers he met, and taken to Soult, whose promise he exacted to rescue the wounded and starving English soldiers still in Elvina village; a promise Charles knew that Soult would keep. Next day he was put on a horse and taken into Corunna, nourished and put to bed and nursed in the house of the American Consul, a charming Frenchman with a pretty Spanish wife, lent money by Baron Clouet, Ney's ADC, and generally cherished within an inch of his life. But of all the chivalrous treatment he got, Charles remembered most clearly the few hurried actions of a French officer while the fight was still going on. He had come into the ruined house, a Frenchman par excellence, tall and handsome, his grace and panache undimmed by the long mountain march or the fierce battle, a gallant spirit, body and soul of the Gallic dream. He had leant over Charles, and held to his lips the flask of delicious wine he carried, which Charles from weakness could barely sip. As if he could read right into the loneliness of Charles's bruised heart, he had given him a searching long look from his bright eyes; being the darling perhaps himself of some small green-shuttered house in a provincial French town, of some elegant château amongst its vineyards, destined himself maybe to gasp out his life in the blizzards of Russia, or bleed to death on the hard hills of Spain. For a moment they were brothers, and he had passionately cried out 'War! War! War! My God will this horrid work never cease! Poor young man I fear you are badly wounded.' He had tried again to make Charles drink, and as he bent over him Charles saw that the tears were rolling down his face.

H.M.S. *Audacious*, a 74, was as full of men as she could ride. Beyond her normal complement of six hundred, officers and seamen, she carried nearly as many again of Moore's troops. George lay amongst them; he could not remember how many days it was since he had taken his uniform off. As *Audacious* surged and crashed in a strong south-westerly wind, he had time at last to think; to realise and comprehend all that the last few hard weeks had brought. Since they sailed from Corunna his friend Harry Burrard had died in the sick bay, and another young man who had only been wounded in the thigh; the splash of their bodies consigned to the wild sea had struck George with the weight of accumulated sorrow and tears had filled his eyes, and the eyes of many others. Nor, now he had time to think of such things, was there any joy professionally: as Moore's senior ADC George should have been sent ahead with the despatches, which meant automatic promotion, but Baird had naturally given the job to his own nephew, Alexander Gordon. That was minor. Charles was gone, and no one seemed to know for certain if William were alive. There would be poor old Mrs Moore to visit, whose son John had been the light of her eyes. And he would have to go home alone to his own mother.

All Sarah's eaglets had had their wings clipped; pleurisy had taken its toll of William's fine frame; Charles was due for a lifetime of headaches; George himself 'had gone through such scenes as he cannot bear the recollection of at all'. Never, maybe, would those three redcoats step so lightly down the street to her door, ride so recklessly at the Irish banks, or blaze for the pretty girls in so entranced a mind.

War had bared its ugly teeth at them; its reality had tarnished the glittering picture that Froissart and Malory had painted, had dulled the martial glories of Greece and Rome, the archaic splendours of Troy. Wafting themselves into the pages of Homer and Plutarch in the great light rooms of Castletown, galloping down the long avenue or racing and chasing up Celbridge village street to the grey house at the end that was full of Donny's courage and laughter, the battles and the glories had seemed magnificent things. And though he himself described it only as a necessary evil, following his confidence-inspiring figure striding across the Irish hills, his young sons had come to feel war an affair of splendour. But now they had seen Hector's mouth choked with dust, and Launcelot lying with his chest torn away.

Around George the stout oak of *Audacious* creaked and groaned, overhead the sails strained in the rising south-westerly wind, feet thundered along the deck. Not even the crash and swing of the sea could lull his mind asleep. Lanterns swung dimly, the air was thick with the breath of sleeping men and the mutters of their dreams, and George was not ashamed to turn his face to the wooden wall and weep.

Behind them French armies, like a river in flood, now spread over Spain and Portugal almost from sea to sea. In March Soult stormed Oporto, whose bishop had refused a surrender; stampeding Portuguese defenders into the Douro in such numbers that their bodies rose above its surface; and the French soldiers, discovering six of their comrades tortured and mutilated but still alive in the principal square of the city, went berserk; before Soult and his officers could stop them they had killed ten thousand Portuguese soldiers and civilians, men, women and children—for the loss of five hundred French. The Spaniards still held Seville, and Cadiz; and for a few more months the Portuguese flag still flew over Lisbon.

To the east Gibraltar remained; with the evening cloud on its heights, the lifeline three-deckers in the harbour, the wary red-coats with their guns ever trained on the mainland, the bugles sounding through the sea mists of early morning. And far inland, slowly, one by one, a gathering constellation of defiance to the French, the fires of the Spanish guerilleros pricked out along the hills.

XIII

The human race is remarkably resilient; and the British were back in the Peninsula in less than the time between Dunkirk and D-Day. The people of Spain had finally redeemed themselves in British eyes when the entire population of Corunna manned their walls to fire at the French and protect the last trickles of the British embarkation. 'They braved a superior enemy to assist a friend whom they had no prospect of ever seeing again,' one officer said; and another, 'Thus we became reconciled to the Spanish character'. On the voyage home the transports were so small and crowded that an officer with a lantern and a drawn sword was permanently posted to keep the men from moving when the ship heeled over. The welcome in England was all the more heart-warming. People in the south coast towns and villages, a Highlander reported, did them all manner of kindness, helping the lame and leading the blind; 'we were received into every house as if we had been relations. How proud did I feel to belong to such a people!' The returning army, licking its wounds, rapidly cashed in on the free drinks situation; and the popular Duke of York, not yet sacked from his position as C. in C. on account of the bribes taken by his mistress, Mary Ann Clarke, paid Moore a ringing tribute.

And since, once the battle was over, officers and men of this epoch still felt able, like everyone else, to relieve the shock and horror of war by the efficacious apparatus supplied by nature for such purpose, and shed buckets of tears, they largely avoided duodenal ulcers, stress diseases, and nervous breakdowns. Though mostly brave as lions, the British army and navy wept their way steadily through the Napoleonic wars: Nelson was a proper Lord Lundy,* and even the Iron Duke himself wept over the deaths of Badajoz, was seen with the tears pouring down his cheeks at the bedside of Charles March, thought to be wounded to death, and broke down completely after Waterloo when they brought him the casualty lists. The wars left

* 'Lord Lundy, from his earliest years Was far too freely moved to tears'
                                                             —Hilaire Belloc

222

them one-armed, one-eyed, wasted by fever; many limped and sweated through their remaining lifetime, but not with mental or with nervous troubles.

Sarah entirely refused to believe that Charles was dead. No one had seen his body, so? And Charles, nourished from Soult's own dinner table, and cheered by the company of Ney's ADC and of his host's pretty wife, recovered his *élan* and was presently exchanged for two captured French midshipmen, a bargain whose validity the French afterwards questioned. Napoleon frowned on such exchanges, but Ney, hearing that Charles's mother was old and blind, had generously sent him home. (None of the family ever forgave the French for subsequently chopping this brave and humane Marshal, though he admittedly swerved a bit between Napoleon and the returning Bourbon kings.) Landing at Plymouth, Charles sent a comic message to his mother and then repaired for a week to the house of some friends in Devon where his love, Elizabeth Kelly, the deserted wife of a paymaster, was lodged; she, poor girl, betrayed the strength of their relationship by falling in a dead faint as he arrived. When George, Louisa and Richard met him off the Exeter coach they thought he looked, except for his black whiskers, as aged and gaunt as a Chelsea pensioner, pale and bearded and with his old red coat out at the elbows.

'Imagine' wrote a sympathetic journal-keeper, 'the transports of the poor blind mother.' But Sarah's transports were quite crisp. 'My beloved Charles is *alive* and recovered of his wounds. My joy is too great to say more, so God bless you!' She had wept a great deal, in spite of her non-belief in his death; and obituary letters had whizzed round the family. 'We can only dwell upon all those affectionate traits of character,' Louisa Napier told Susan, 'he always forgot himself when others were in question, and often has deprived himself of indulgence and even necessarys that he might assist those in want . . . George looked for his brother at night among heaps of slain, think what a task for such a heart as poor George's, the remembrance makes him distracted, we must all exert ourselves, . . . Ly Sarah keeps tolerably.' 'She is extremely interesting in her affliction,' Caroline Fox reported, 'dear soul she is trying in every way to occupy her thought.' (Whatever else they worried about, the Georgians never concerned themselves with loss of identity. Sarah, with four sisters called Caroline, Emily, Louisa, and Cecilia, christened her four daughters Louisa, Emily, Caroline and Cecilia; and both Stephen and Harry Fox called their daughters Caroline: this one was Ste's Caroline.)

Of late Sarah had been suffering from that 'they are all gone into the world of light' feeling. In September of 1806 Charles James Fox had died, that ever amusing and amused same-age nephew, characteristically pointing out to his wife, Dearest, dearest Liz, it don't signify. 'What is that fat gentleman in such a passion about?' a child taken to Parliament had asked, seeing Fox on his legs; and though to his friends he was 'incomparable Charley', many quite otherwise sensible people had firmly believed that he was in the pay of France. Lady Hester Stanhope thought he looked like an innkeeper, or, when addressing the House, like a Punch and Judy show. But he had seen through and rejected Napoleon's offer in 1806 to divide the world between France and England (Europe to France and the rest of the world to England); and his last action had been to steer the bill for the Abolition of the Slave Trade through the House (which now seems so obvious but was in fact the first time and place that an institution considered perfectly ordinary and acceptable throughout recorded history had been made illegal). To some Fox was an Awful Warning, to others a Noble Ruin; to his friends he was 'the negation of cant and humbug, an intellectual Titan, the quick and visible embodiment of every lovable quality in man'.

'I try to keep off from my mind accumulating sorrows, for fear its weakness should deprive me of the cheerfulness which I ought and will try to attain for my children's sake.' But the sadness of Fox's death carried her back to Donny's, 'I saw it all again renewed for others as I then felt it for myself.' She was visiting Charles Richmond, 'kind and very pleasant, a brother I love to see enjoying life at 71 like a man of 21. . . . All is as it should be between us, independence on our part, and obliging attentions on his.' But soon he had gone too; and her blindness was making her say goodbye to her confidential correspondence with Susan; all must now be dictated— 'our long long correspondence, from which I have derived so much of interesting, affectionate, and friendly entertainment and pleasure'. She had still with her in London 'my dear sister Louisa and daughter Emily, my sheet anchor in all things', and was about to move out of 'this odious old lodging' in 4 Sloane Terrace and into 'my clean airy small house', 13 Cadogan Place; and 'a settled home, my girls well and thriving in health and spirits'.

The settled home was a brief dream. War was sending prices

soaring, and the buyer of Celbridge had gone bankrupt and was not completing the payments. 'I am not ungrateful for the blessings I enjoy; my two sons are well in Spain, and Charles at home,' she told Susan in 1809. 'His presence was never more useful to me, for it assists me in a difficulty, which, tho' it never can be put into the scale of misfortune, is very distressing, I mean the want of money, which obliges me to retrench in a very decided manner. I propose to let my comfortable house and hire a small vulgar home somewhere in the country where I may part with a manservant, and my whole family to consist of my old maid and myself, my 2 daughters and 2 active young maids; when my sons visit me they must be in a lodging. Thus I may pass a couple of years and pay off all those debts which non-payment of a gentleman in Ireland has occasioned. . . . The concurrence and assistance of my dear children make a heavy task light, still I own it lowers me a good deal, perhaps more than it ought, but the habits of 65 years are not easily changed, particularly by one who has no occupation to engage the attention; for if I could enjoy the country I should be busy. . . .' Her income, and pension, would die with her, unless it were continued to her portionless daughters, 'but no Minister will ever consent to this except it is for his own children . . . I often reflect on the joy it would give me to think my death did not entirely ruin my children as it will.' She had £850 in all, paid £100 in taxes and £200 for Richard at Oxford, but thought they could all live in the country on £550; 'but I will change the subject'.

She switched to public affairs; her passion for politics no whit abated by age and lack of sight. 'The waste of gunpowder, oil, and tallow, which are to evince the love of his subjects to the King, is very tiresome particularly as Ly Bathurst has told me the King particularly desired to have no rejoicing of any kind except gifts to the poor.' 'Never till now' Sarah continued, switching to the Castlereagh-Canning duel, 'did a whole Cabinet agree to stigmatize themselves as false people in the eyes of the whole world . . . there must be much cutting and shuffling before the two wise heads in England unite, and till they do Government will decay daily, and in all probability Napoleon's genius will not sleep.' She had been, she told Susan, quite deaf, 'but it proved accidental, thank God, for it terrified me sadly. I have had very pleasant society this summer in two or three families of relations.' Her long dictated letter (Caroline had now signed on as sole amanuensis, 'the comfort of having but one reader, I am in the habit of reposing my thoughts more truly in her mind') which had begun cheerfully, ended on the same note. '49 years is a tollerable span to remember as if it was yesterday, and yet I am sure my dear Ly Susan, you remember our merry excursions to Pains Hill, diverted with all the wise, important, bustling, looks of sorrow and joy that every face had whom we met on the road and for the remainder of that week till the new *great* people were announced to the public.' (The accession of George III.) 'Adieu, its 12 o'clock and Charles is just come home; says the streets are crowded beyond immagination and the illuminations fine, but that the dullness of English people provokes him. He heard everywhere one and only one observation, and what was it? "It has been a fine day for this." Can you conceive how among thousands the good King's reign of half a century could create no other idea?'

Two further thrusts at Napoleon had been set under way. Charles, always unlucky in such matters, was sent on the failed expedition to capture Walcheren, a Dutch island in the French-occupied Netherlands; an attempt that resulted in the British being smartly returned to store. George and William had been luckier; in Craufurd's Light Brigade they had followed Sir Arthur Wellesley, sent to Portugal to attack the French occupation from the Lisbon bridgehead. Soon after Corunna, Soult had stormed Oporto: in April of 1809 Wellesley made a brilliant and secret march to drive him out. 'The Serra Rock,' wrote William, 'round which the Douro came with a sharp elbow, barred sight of the upper channel, and Soult, thinking it secure, took his station to the westward of the city from whence he could see the lower channel to its mouth: but on the rock stood Sir Arthur, searching with an eagle glance, the river, the city, and the country beyond.' He passed a division across the river by night in boats and barges, took the city with small loss, and drove Soult into the northern mountains of Galicia minus artillery, stores, and six thousand men.

In July he made another bold sortie towards Madrid; a move much criticised at home for its risk and danger. Owing to a departmental error by which they had all been sent to the wrong port, Craufurd's brigade arrived too late for the extremely bloody British victory of Talavera. The lightning march up the Tagus valley under the July sun was described by the ever-optimistic George as being a pleasant one; it was certainly taken at record speed in its last lap of sixty-two miles in twenty-two hours, with each man carrying 50 lb. on his back; a feat thought never to have been performed by infantry before. But

William had already fallen by the wayside, at about the same time as
Wellesley, that dignified general, was on his knees to his Spanish
opposite number, General Cuesta, to induce this courageous old
noodle to retreat from the death trap where he had placed himself
and his army.

William had been in Ireland for the winter, restoring his health as
ADC to cousin Richmond, now Lord-Lieutenant. (Sarah's nephew,
George Lennox's son, had succeeded her brother, who had only left
a number of illegitimate daughters.) But the pleurisy William had
caught in the Galician snows before Corunna was clearly only in
abeyance and at Placencia it had struck him down. He was so heavily
bled by the army doctors that he could no longer stand, and had been
put in the local hospital by George. This delay had caused George to
keep going all night to catch up with his regiment; a solitary effort
which he did not enjoy. 'It was very dark, and a large forest of many
miles long to march through without a guide or companion.' The
worst of it had been 'the devils of wolves howling in all directions'.
The melancholy menace of this sound coming out of the darkness
made it difficult to concentrate on finding the correct route; but he
was up with the Light Brigade in time for their record march, upon
which he embarked without benefit of a night's sleep.

'As we moved on, the road was covered with cowardly fugitives—
Spaniards innumerable and lots of English, commissary clerks, pay-
masters, sutlers, and servants, to say nothing of a few soldiers and
officers who said they were sick; all swearing the British Army was cut
to pieces, Wellesley was killed, the French a few miles off. How we
did swear at them, and hiss every fellow we met!' These, George
noticed, were 'committing every kind of rascality and pillaging with
impunity, as they never fail to do when out of reach of punishment.
It is much more difficult to keep the civilians and followers of an
army in order than twice, ay, ten times the number of soldiers.' The
camp followers were 'the devils incarnate, they disgrace an army
more than anything'. He thought stern punishments essential, for the
sake of the unlucky locals.

The great Soult, that swarthy hero, was on his way south to cut the
British off from their base and to reinforce Marshal Victor, but
Wellesley had joined the Spanish General Cuesta and engaged Victor
before Soult could arrive. Hearing that Soult was nearing Placentia,
William got out of his bed there and, pleurisy or no, walked forty-
eight miles to Oropesa, the first place he could find horses, and

managed to ride to the gates of Talavera before falling off in a state
of collapse. Here he was nearly killed by some Spaniards, on the
grounds that any foreigner so dark and dashing must be French; but
appeared to recover next day, when the grisly task of clearing up the
battlefield fell to the Light Brigade. Fought by the Tagus on the
afternoon of July 27th and for most of next day as well, Talavera had
been a struggle of terrible ferocity, decided in the main by British
bayonets. George recalled its aftermath with horror. 'We were
employed in burying the dead and saving the unfortunate wounded
French from the fury of the Spanish peasants, who murdered them
without mercy. . . . The dry grass had caught fire, and numbers of
wounded of all nations were burnt to death, being unable to crawl
out of the way of the raging fire; the dreadful smell from the half-
burned carcasses of the horses was appalling . . . I never saw a field
of battle which struck me with such horror as the field of Talavera.'

It had finally exposed Spanish inability to fight a set battle; brave
as they were the Spaniards behaved in an incalculable manner in the
fight owing to their overriding fear that someone else might acquire
the glory. Few of their generals could stop fancying themselves El Cid
in person—though the effect was rather more of Don Quixote. Their
wont was to plant themselves plumb in the middle of the chosen
ground and remain there immovable, as if by so doing they could not
fail to win the field: perhaps it came from incessantly defending
narrow gorges against the Moors in old days. Nothing would move
them; nor did they train their men to manoeuvre: the French of
course made rings round them and they were slain in enormous
numbers with nil effect.

But Talavera confirmed Napoleon in his impression that the
British not only meant business but knew how to do it; he made
plans to withdraw a few more divisions from his hard-pressed Austrian enemies and send them into Spain. 'Hard honest fighting with
extreme gallantry by both English and French soldiers,' William
thought. 'In all actions there is one critical moment which will give
the victory to the general who knows how to seize it'; at last, at long
last, they had such a one. Wellington's dispositions 'gained the day;
the British became strongest at the decision point; . . . their fire grew
hotter and their ringing shouts—sure augury of success—were heard
along the whole line.' The British public were pleased with the victory
despite its casualties: as Charles cynically pointed out later in life,
they loved a butcher's bill. Wellesley was made Lord Wellington; and

what was more vital to him and to his army, consolidated his home support.

All the same, after this bold dash up the Tagus, it was back to Portugal again: the French had a quarter of a million men in Spain and Wellington had thirty thousand. At Almarez, on the river Alemtejo, six thousand troops out of this precious total died of fever. Even George's spirits were damped by long delirium and he was left with an ague which troubled him for years. To the young in the army everything seemed to be hanging fire, and this and his hot temper nearly brought George to an untimely and irrelevant end at Pinhel, in northern Portugal next winter. He had asked some German Hussars to dinner, and also Gifford, his lieutenant, with whom, in their cups, he had a near fatal quarrel. Talk had turned on the projected French invasion of Britain in 1803-4, and George, flown with a good Portuguese vintage, had declared that if a single Frenchman had landed in England he would have given no quarter—'I for one would put every soul of them to death.'

Gifford, also slightly pickled, and ashamed of such opinions uttered in front of foreigners, exclaimed—

'Any man who has such sentiments is no Englishman.'

'Do you mean, sir, to imply that I am no Englishman?'

'Yes I do, and I'll be damned if they are the sentiments of an Englishman or an officer.'

These were fighting words, and the German Hussars were now left to finish the port by themselves. George told Gifford to get his pistols ready and meet him at the field outside the town in half an hour.

He collected his own pistols, but by great good fortune met another friend on his way back, who asked him what on earth he was doing with them, and George, on whom the night air had had a beneficial effect, explained.

'The sentiment uttered by you was far too cruel and ungenerous ever to have been the feeling of your heart, my dear friend' George was told. 'Gifford I know loves you as sincerely as you are attached to him. Follow me at once and offer Gifford an apology for what you said, and your hand on it.'

Sobered, George complied. The sun had come within a whisker of going down on his wrath for ever. He sought Gifford and begged his pardon with a warmth as heartfelt as his rage had been, 'repudiating my own language and sentiments'. 'I have acted wrongly and foolishly,' George went on. 'I am a true Englishman with the same

generous feelings as yourself . . . let us be the same attached friends
we have been for years.' Gifford, beaming with relief, had also
sobered up, and declared that he had been to blame, and they ended
happily weeping on each other's shoulders; for open emotion had
not yet become a matter for shame.

To an age more learned and scientific, more cynical and sered, the
lavish male affection of this epoch seems suspect or rum: authors
have been quick to suggest that Nelson and Hardy, kissing each
other goodbye, were up to no good. But it seems to have been just
their way. At fourteen and fifteen years old, when the emotional
compass tends to set its course for life, the men who fought at Trafalgar and in the Peninsula were out in the free-for-all heterosexual
Georgian world as commissioned officers, and had been so for years,
far from insulated schoolrooms or the anxious intrusive eyes of
loving parents. And whatever else Spain and Portugal lacked, these
countries were not short of girls—'the dear little dark creatures with
their sweeping eyebrows' of Andrew Barnard's description; even in
his first weeks in Galicia William had realised that Spanish men
were not so jealous as they were cried up to be. Both Captain Kincaid
and Rifleman Harris, from their different viewpoints, noticed that
whoever else said No, the nuns of these countries could always be
relied upon for what Kincaid called 'an elopement without conditions'. The army marched, oftener than its commissaries liked, with
a cheerful chatty tail of paramours and wives, who were far more
skilled and active pilferers than their men, and incessantly in and out
of cellars, whipping cheeses and broaching casks.

> 'Happy is England,' Keats exclaimed about now,
> 'sweet her artless daughters;
> Enough their simple loveliness for me,
> Enough their whitest arms in silence clinging:'

and then instantly contradicted himself by adding

> 'Yet do I often warmly burn to see
> Beauties of deeper glance, and hear their singing,
> And float with them about the summer waters'

and it was a sentiment which his countrymen in the Peninsula
echoed, though their opportunities for floating were restricted: they
were mainly confined to rolling with them about the autumn heather.
Fortunate Harry Smith, the envy of many, married a lovely and very

young Spanish girl, who, in the holocaust after the fall of Badajoz, was confided by her grandmother to the care of the British C. in C. Wellington himself gave her away, after her two days' wooing by Harry, and they lived happily ever afterwards. The famous siege of Ladysmith in South Africa was no assault on her but on the town named after her.

The point was that a feeling heart, whether it swung north or south, was a necessary piece of equipment for the whole man; and feeling hearts, as the brothers well knew, grew everywhere. The insularity of the English was still at a pitch (William was to be accused of writing his history in aid of the French); but the Napiers, being Scots bred in Ireland and thinking of themselves as Englishmen, were less racially bigoted than some; and the Spanish experience was chiselling away at prejudice. There was a tendency in England 'to affirm that the French were encouraged by their leaders to misdeeds unmatched in wickedness and peculiar to their nation. Such assertions, springing from morbid national antipathies, it is the duty of the historian to correct' William announced firmly. 'All troops will behave ill when ill-governed, and the best commanders cannot prevent the perpetration of the most frightful mischief.' When in small parties on their own, or given half a chance, the British troops had nothing to learn from the French as to drunkenness, robbery, or rape, though not quite up to snuff when it came to torture.

William's radical instincts were outraged by the general Spanish lack of humanity—'the miserable state of the soldiers, the unquenchable vanity of the officers', who 'hated and ill-used the peasantry, and were so odious that the poorer people, much as they detested the French, almost wished for Joseph's success.' But he admired the Spanish guerilleros very much, although put off by their habit of murdering opponents who surrendered upon offers of quarter; for if you once abandoned Queensberry rules war did indeed become impossible. 'There is', he thought, 'always some point of honour reserved even by the worst men, which if rightly touched may be depended upon.' In Europe's ceaseless attempts to commit suicide, William particularly felt sympathy for the Poles, even when fighting on the wrong side—'the Spanish colonel was repulsed by Morozinski, a Pole, with the bravery inherent to his heroic nation: a nation whose glory springs like an *ignis fatuus* from the corruption of European honour.' As for the French, he had an infinite respect for the courage and the chivalry of his opposite numbers among them.

Most particularly must feeling be respected in the private soldier. Passionately, George adjured his sons to do them justice, to attend to and understand their men—'he is as good a man and as good a Christian as yourself, and possessing the same feelings as the proudest peer in the land'. (This in the early nineteenth century was an extremely advanced idea.) Discipline, yes; but a disgraceful punishment for a slight crime simply made a man reckless, 'and from disgust and sulkiness at severe treatment he becomes a bad soldier and a worse man'. He hated the treatment of soldiers 'as if they were mere brute, without either sense, feeling, or character'. An Irishman of the 50th, the day after a battle in which he had lost his brother and had his own arm amputated, had walked twelve miles to see how George and William were after their wounds—'Sure, I thought you was kilt. . . . I pursued the inimy as long as I was able and now I'm come to see your honour, long life to you agin.'

'But John you are wounded yourself, why is your arm tied up?'

'Och, nothing at all to prevent me coming to see your honour, and your honour's brother lying there, Captain William, long life to him . . . sure it's nothing, only me arrum was cut off a few hours ago, and by Jasus I'd rather be shot twenty times.'

'The scum of the earth, enlisted for drink' Wellington once called his army in an exasperated hour, and at times it looked that way, but George knew another side. He had seen his men give away the last of their rations when passing through a Portuguese village full of starving women and children, knowing full well it meant that they themselves would go empty for the next forty-eight hours. Charity, as he pointed out, is generally giving away something we can do without, but these soldiers gave all they had to eat for a gruelling two days of work and marching, and suffered accordingly. 'I have rarely met with a private soldier who has not feelings and keen ones too, though often indeed they had been blunted by bad example and harsh treatment; . . . see that you look upon them as rational beings and as fellow men. The officer who considers himself a better man than the private, except from his superior education and intelligence, is a presumptuous fool' George continued firmly. 'I look forward with pleasure and certainty to the moment when a British soldier will *never* have his back bared to the lash of a cat-o'-nine-tails.' In George's impecunious old age no disabled soldier was ever turned from his door without food and drink and something to help him on his way.

Through this winter, while George and William and other young
sparks danced and argued and carried on generally in Lisbon and
district, hunting, larking, and dressing up as bishops, Wellington was
perfecting his plans. Every time the British had set foot in Europe
the forces of Revolutionary France had driven them smartly back
into the sea. The first essential, it seemed to him, was to establish
an impregnable bridgehead. Events had made it crystal clear that
in spite of individual and guerilla successes Spanish numbers could
not for years be brought to bear in force against Napoleon; and if he
himself were to lose any sizable number of troops in a battle, the
British government would lose heart and whistle him home like a
lost dog. His one hope was to harry and tire Napoleon, that 'grand
disturber of Europe' as he called him; and for this he must have a
sure base.

His answer was the Lines of Torres Vedras; and William wondered
why no one before had thought of it. 'It was Wellington who first
conceived the design of turning those vast mountains into one stupen-
dous and impregnable citadel, wherein to deposit the independence
of the whole Peninsula . . . entrenchments, inundations and redoubts
secured more than five hundred square miles of mountainous country
lying between the Tagus and the ocean. Nor was this the most
gigantic part of the undertaking. Wellington was a foreigner, ill-
supported by his own government, and holding power under that of
Portugal by a precarious tenure; and he was vehemently opposed by
the local authorities, by the ministers, by the nobility. Yet he under-
took to reform the abuses engendered by centuries of misgovern-
ment, and make a slothful people arise in arms, devastate their lands,
and follow him to battle against the most formidable power of
modern times.'

'Did you never observe that idle people have time for very little,'
Sarah asked Susan this winter, 'and quick active people have time to
think of others and of their own business too, and yet are never
hurried? I am not of that cast,' she added sadly, but after this
apology for an unanswered letter proceeds to think a good deal of
others. The *Hussar* frigate was missing, with Francis Napier,
Donny's nephew, on board; could Susan, at Weymouth, find out any
news of her? 'All losses of the kind are heartbreaking to parents, but
I have experienced so much warmth of heart in the character of Ld

Napier, I know so well how he, his wife, and all his family have existed on domestic happiness for years and years back, that the idea of their wretchedness is dreadful to my thoughts. Their eldest son is also in the navy, a lieut., and just gone home to them after six years' absence, but to aggravate his feelings he had just placed this brother in the *Hussar* as a preferable situation to a large ship. . . . Charles is at last exchanged [swopped for two French midshipmen] and his Regiment is now tossing at sea on its return from Walcheren. My two sons in Portugal are well, and I suppose will not stay there very long' Sarah added hopefully. 'Richard has shut himself up at Oxford during the vacation to avoid the temptations of London. I have heard of Henry being safe at Madras last July, so as far as hopes go I have every reason for cheerfulness, but I never can forget that the very essence of reason teaches us to rejoice with trembling.'

She found Caroline a better reader and writer than Louisa, 'making no comparison of merits. Chance makes one more suited than the other; both are trustworthy, both ready to serve me, both capable of it in different ways. Louisa is too quick, too much occupied by other thoughts, too different from me in opinions not to make a sacrifice in devoting her time to me . . . it seems more adapted to Caroline's turn . . . no drawback but her extreme youth, not in years, but in the knowledge of a world that I don't wish her to grow old in, for much happier are those who know least of it I think, so that I often am brought by her perfect natural ways of thinking to reflect on the contrast between her and me, and it makes me appreciate nature still higher as I see the world perverts it. Instead of doating in my old age I grow wiser by living with young people.'

The shadows were lengthening over this relationship too. By February of 1810 fears for Caroline were beginning to prey on Sarah. Writing to Susan at Bath to urge her to be friends with her sister-in-law, Lady George Lennox, she seems herself—'of *course* she must like you, and then you are both very Royall and very good friends to Ministers, tho' both of you have too much sense not to know they are fools this year, tho' neither of you will own it; so I think you will suit together delightfully, but I don't advise Mr. O'B. to put in his little Opposition frigate in the fleet.' Then her half-realised terror takes hold, thinking of 'your poor niece Ly Mary Talbot whose distress Caroline Fox told me of last night. [The Talbots' daughter was in a decline.] Oh! what an unhappy mother! I cannot express how her misfortune haunts my mind continually. God have mercy on her! This is the only thing to be said or thought about her, but in that word *all* is comprized and every hope revives.'

A letter from George with the official account of the battle of Orcana had turned her thoughts. The French under Soult had defeated the Spaniards and taken 26,000 prisoners and 45 guns. 'Sir Arthur is in a rage at them, having done all he could to prevent it. Their answer is, he is an ambitious Englishman who wanted all the glory to himself.' Sarah had moments when she compared Wellington unfavourably with Moore. Openly keeping his mistress at head-quarters (in this she was confusing him with his elder brother), he seemed to her not to bother enough about the sick, or about food for the troops, expecting the Spaniards to produce supplies as promised, 'not as poor Moore who worked night and day to secure what was wanted for the army. . . .'

'I wonder' she demanded at Christmas 'how long we shall hold Portugal?'

Arriving in Lisbon in April of 1810, still thin as a rail after Walcheren, Charles had no doubts, after a look at the Lines of Torres Vedras, now under construction. He had been glad enough to get his annual accident over on January 22nd; his horse had come down on the ice and rolled on his leg, without actually breaking it. Writing a week earlier he had sought to comfort Sarah, still struggling back to courage and hope after Donny's and Cecilia's deaths. Of course she was anxious about George and William; it was natural. But 'riding out to meet evil is bad. . . . Do not make arrangements as if something shocking was decidedly to happen: no spirits can stand that. Your sons come home full of fighting and without clothes; we shall be very merry' he promised her. A week or two later he was grumbling at her in his old confidential manner, as if to stir and anger her out of her quiet sadness. He was disgusted about his promotion; all the other Corunna majors had got theirs, he told his mother in February. Sir David Dundas was hopeless. 'Confound old Pivot! A young captain, famous for nothing but shirking duty has been made major: I would like to roast old Pivot. But don't you make Fox or anyone ask him to promote me, work him up for George if you can. He must however be touched up to let me go to the seige of Cadiz; more thanks for that than for a lieutenant-colonelcy.' But he had had such marvellous letters from people who really knew about such things, extolling his part at Corunna, including Bentinck and Clinton, that it made him feel it was glory enough even to have fought with Moore.

At Lisbon Charles thought the church of San Roque superb, and wondered very much that the French revolutionary armies had left it all its silver and jewels; allowed by the English in the Convention of Cintra to take away back to France their own personal possessions, the French had interpreted this so liberally that they had removed church silver and pictures, palace furniture, and priceless medieval manuscripts from the archives of Portugal. Britannia might sicken at the name of Cintra but probably not nearly so violently as the Portuguese did.

At Sacavem on the ride north Charles passed the olive tree under which he had sat laughing with Charles Stanhope so short a while back, talking of their admiration for Moore and of their hopes of glory. Now he alone survived and his heart saddened thinking of them—memory was a fiend! 'Napoleon talks of peace: would to God he wished for it as sincerely as I do.' Reaching Celorico on June 15th he dined with Wellington, who told him how much he admired the French technique in retreat. What about his own? Charles wondered. One could not always know the motives of generals, and often had wrong motives of one's own in criticising.

'Nevertheless we must think; and I think Wellington committed a great error in that [Talavera] campaign by trusting to the Spaniards after what Moore had experienced; and another in advancing too far when his retreat might be cut off. He was wrong also I think in fighting when victory did him no good, and defeat must have destroyed him: his information was bad, and he trusted it too implicitly. Again—Why did he stay in the destructive marshes of the Alemtejo until nearly all his army fell from sickness? It is not easy to comprehend all this, and I have heard no good answer to it.' (These strictures on the Talavera sortie were afterwards echoed by Wellington himself.) Wellington was right, on the other hand, not to be enticed into Spain by the French siege of Ciudad Rodrigo; if he bogged or failed the game would be up. At Pinhel was General Picton, and a Moorish castle, and a bishop, said to be sensible, 'very hospitable, and very like Charles Fox, but better looking and not so fat; his palace full of prints, all very bad, and some not very decent for a bishop.' At Gallegos, at last, were his brothers—'Saw William, and George, the latter not well, heat affects him: he has I believe the best heart alive and beating, and a right good head. I hope to see both home after this breeze: if not they are well prepared for a longer voyage, but God forbid they should take it now.'

The breeze in question had arisen around the fate of Ciudad Rodrigo, northern gateway into Spain from Portugal; in this walled city the Spanish were holding out with great gallantry. Honour seemed to compel the British, now strengthened by as many men again of trained Portuguese, to go to their rescue. But the French were everywhere in great force. In Salamanca with six divisions was Ney, dining perhaps at that same table where Charles and George had sat so short a while before, listening to Moore's gentle wit, while the candelabra glittered and the Spanish wine flowed. And the famed Masséna had arrived with eighty thousand fresh men and strict instructions from Napoleon to drive the English forthwith into the sea. From Ciudad on June 29th its general's imploring messages were smuggled out—'*O venir luego! luego! luego! a secorrer esta plaza*'; an appeal for instant succour echoed two days later with a final '*por último vez!*'

It was heartrending; but Wellington had not come down with the last fall of snow. His heart could not afford to be rent: he had a war to win, not a battle. He must retreat and fight the huge French armies where it suited him. 'He is blamed for this but he is right and it gives me confidence in him' Charles wrote. 'He is a much better general than I suspected him to be. My persuasion is that the siege was little more than a battle-trap for his lordship which he has not been caught in' Charles thought.

On July 11th a message came over from Ney, what was Major Charles Napier doing back in the battlefield, had he been exchanged? and Wellington sent Charles over with a flag of truce to explain. Where was he going, everyone shouted at him as he went by?

'To spend the afternoon with my friend Marshal Ney' Charles shouted back, unable to resist this cryptic tease.

'At Gallegos I was blindfolded and taken to Loison's quarters. None of my French acquaintance there. Loison offered a large bet that Lord Wellington would not fight to relieve Almeida: is this a quiz, or do they mean to besiege that place? I was not blindfolded coming back, but made to gallop at full speed. Loison is a savage looking fellow, yet was very civil, and much pleased with the brave conduct of the company which beat off our cavalry.' Black Bob had caught a Tartar on the previous night; attacking a French company in an ill-chosen place he had lost Colonel Talbot and thiry-three troopers with smaller damage to the French. William Campbell's horse had been killed and he had slowly disentangled himself within feet of the French sabres and walked very deliberately away, declining to hurry; chivalrous Guache, the French captain, not letting his men fire at this solitary unconcerned figure, stumping off with the stiff gait of a cavalryman out of the saddle.

'We did not allow that we had many men, or that we were beat, but honestly avowed our admiration of his people. No chance of a battle till Buonparte comes; but then his numbers will put battles out of the question: he will not risk his fame against twenty-five thousand Englishmen. . . . Rodrigo surrendered the evening before Colonel Talbot was killed. Old Andreas Herrasti made a rigorous defence, and Loison told me the town was almost destroyed by the bombardment. The French committed no excesses; even the Spaniards allow this. Almeida is preparing for a siege.'

Refreshed by a good French dinner, Charles galloped back to his own side.

Wellington had sent the Light Brigade into Spain with orders to harass the French wherever possible and keep him informed of their movements. All spring the river Agueda, flooding freely, had been their safeguard; and Craufurd had handled them most effectively, sending them patrolling deep into Spain, watching Masséna's every movement. But by late July the Light Brigade was still in the wooded plain between the Agueda and the Coa; and here the uncertain and obstinate character of their general all but put paid to Charles, George, and William Napier, amongst hundreds of others. A stubborn fighter, Craufurd found it hard to understand how effectively Wellington was chiselling at Napoleon by keeping so many of his superb veterans tied up among the Sierras with all this advance retreat technique. Man for man, Craufurd knew that his troops could outfight the French: aware of having a marvellous instrument in his Moore-trained brigade he could not resist the urge to linger and inflict knock for knock. Strictly commanded by Wellington to get his brigade across the Coa river in good time and not risk its destruction, Craufurd delayed, 'deeply enamoured of his separate command as ever youth was of mistress' Kincaid thought. The wily French naturally trapped him in the narrow valley, with its single small bridge across the swiftly flowing Coa.

*

Charles was writing his journal, in the long light of a July evening. Their necks, as he realised, were stuck well out, and George's bad go of fever was worrying; but none of that was any excuse for bad behaviour. Ney, on his way back from taking a look round had been shot at by one of the British picquets: Charles thought this very poor. Ney had already seen what he came out to see—'it is not right to fire at people without necessity, like Indian savages'. (George disagreed: shoot the general and confuse the enemy.) Charles and Brigadier Mackinnon and Pakenham had ridden past that same place only yesterday, and the French had shouted out jokes and cheerfully invited them across the river. Their position was, Charles told his journal, extremely dangerous, well out from the army, and with three thousand men to the French twenty-five thousand, but that was old Craufurd all over. 'Our bivouac is beautiful, like a fête champêtre rather than an outpost close to the enemy. Why is this fine division risked? If the enemy was enterprising we should be cut to pieces.' He found time to grumble about his promotion; Dundas was still blocking it, 'the stiff old brush'. But Dundas could be bullied, and 'No-one can conceive the good to the army when a little rebellion to injustice can be got up.' (When Charles finally visited Dundas to ask him for promotion, the subject was swiftly turned. 'Wear flannel, Major, wear flannel' the old general urged him, at intervals throughout the visit, and on these words the interview finally concluded.)

The trouble with Craufurd was that so much depended on his mood. 'At one time', William thought, 'he was all fire and intelligence, a master spirit in war; at another, as if possessed by the demon, he would madly rush from blunder to blunder, raging in folly: the demon was strong at this period.' All the same, they were fond of the old so-and-so. He was a tiger for securing regular food supplies: on one occasion the commissary had gone to Wellington and complained that General Craufurd had threatened to shoot him.

'Did he indeed?'

The commissary had assured Wellington that indeed he did.

'By God, then he'll do it' Wellington had unsympathetically pointed out. He was fond of Black Bob.

Heavy rain all through the night of July 23rd had made the ground too muddy to lie on; and George had been so ill with a return of the Alemtejo fever (probably malaria) that Charles and the doctor both thought he would die before dawn. On the morning of the 24th George staggered up after a night of burning fever to the sound of firing. In the dangerous half-light between night and day—their favourite moment—the French had attacked. The brigade must get itself away over the one narrow bridge across the Coa or be lost.

'It is needless,' William wrote firmly, 'to describe the first burst of French soldiers—it is well known with what gallantry the officers lead, with what vehemence the troops follow, and with what a storm of fire they waste a field of battle.' He had already noted on other occasions that the British troops in Spain fought 'as if for their existence' even in an attacking battle; and here they were virtually surrounded. 'The British regiments, with singular intelligence and discipline, extricated themselves from their perilous situation. They ... presented a mass of skirmishers, acting in small parties and under no regular command yet each confident in the courage and discipline of those on his right and left, and all keeping together with surprising vigour.' It was the British at their best, saved by individual determination and instinctive cohesion, but 'only Moore's regiments could, with so little experience, have extricated themselves from the danger into which they were so recklessly cast', William thought. 'Their matchless discipline was their protection—a phantom hero from Corunna saved them.' Defending the churned muddy bridge-head as the last of the British guns rolled over the Coa, William was shot in the hip; his men dragged him with them over the bridge as the French cavalry hacked at the rearguard. Losses were heavy, yet Beckwith's counter-attack as the last of the 52nd fought their way down under the pine trees to the safety of the bridge had been so skilled and vigorous that Marshal Foy gloomily confided to his diary that the despised islanders were better soldiers than the French. Wellington was furious at the foolhardiness that had made the fight necessary, but would not censure Black Bob: 'his error was one of judgement, not of intention.' Censure was 'not the way in which any, much less a British army, can be commanded'.

Once over the bridge, George and his party had been sent to guard the ford upstream. Blazing away at the enemy from the far side of the river bank, George found time to feel desperately sorry to have to shoot an extremely brave French officer who had come down to test the swollen river for a possible crossing. 'Not liking to fire at a single man I called out to him, and made signs that he must go back: but he would not, and being determined to try it, he dashed fearlessly into the water. It was then necessary to fire at him.' There could be no letting either man or horse cross the river and thus prove it fordable

Louisa Conolly in middle age

Sarah Napier in middle age

British Light Troops Fording the Esla

The Battle of Salamanca

Charles Napier

George Napier

William Napier

and lead a force across to attack the Light Brigade on its flank. George fired; and horse and man were swept away down the rushing Coa. 'What a pity, poor fellow, God bless his soul' George had involuntarily cried out; and years later he told his children 'one of the great evils of war is that many harsh and to appearance cruel things must be done to individuals for the general good, or rather I should say to ensure success . . . the good being very little that is done by war, so seldom is it carried on for the defence of the weak or the liberties of mankind. And I fear it is vain' George added, seizing this chance to point a moral and adorn a tale, 'to expect the world to control its passions and vices in such manner that universal peace may rule over the earth, so that it is every man's duty and particularly that of officers to ameliorate as far as in his power the dreadful horrors and scourge of war. Little do those who only read of war know. . . .'

William and Tom Lloyd, 'with a bad clink in the head', were put into a bullock cart and bumped over the rocky track to Celerico, where they lay some hours in the sun without water or a doctor, tormented by heat, smell and flies, with the blood of their wounds trickling slowly through their rough dressings. Here they were seen by the Spanish General, Don Miguel Alava, who took them into his house and looked after them. 'That gallant and noble-minded Spaniard' as George called him, was afterwards exiled from Spain, and George recalled with pleasure that he had been provided with a little house in Hampshire by Wellington. 'Fervently do I pray' George added, 'that he may live to see the day when his dearly loved Spain will have energy enough to cast off the shackles of superstition and tyranny, and hold the place she ought among the nations in Europe; for with all their faults and false pride, they are a fine race, and under a good government, with a free constitution, Spain would be a glorious country!' Bathed, sustained, and bandaged in kind Alava's house, William too paid tribute on many occasions to 'this generous, brave, and disinterested Spaniard'.

Charles seethed into his journal on the matter of the Coa action; it brought out all the angry young man in him: 'a long and murderous skirmish, destructive as it was useless, by which many officers and men lost their lives and many were wounded . . . the bloody business closed with as much honour for the officers and men as disgrace for Craufurd's generalship.' He had done everything wrong, 'and kept the artillery and cavalry in a place where they could not act'. Charles had come as a volunteer to the Light Brigade; he had as yet no regiment of his own, and as the summer day failed he joined his brother George, exhausted, soaked to the skin, and bloody-minded at the mess and disaster of it all. But slowly, the pleasure of being still alive took hold of him. 'George and his company were on an immense plate rock; the rain was over, they had a good fire, and a supper of beef-steaks (taken off the poor bullock that had pulled our baggage all day) with tea.' This was a treat; the Light Brigade had been on short commons for a long while now. 'I stripped, and the soldiers who were then dry and had supped took my clothes to dry them. I sat meanwhile naked, like a wild Indian, on the warm rock. It was very pleasant, drinking hot tea and eating steaks half raw.' (He had eaten nothing all day but a bit of bread.) We regretted the poor fellows who were slain—there were a great many—but the excitement of battle does away with much regret, there is no time; it is idleness that makes people grieve long, or rather bitterly.' Dried and fed, Charles and George went on into Celorico in the darkness to see how William and Tom Lloyd did.

Ciudad Rodrigo surrendered: it could do nothing else. Masséna was free now to cross the Portuguese border with his eighty thousand men; and it was back to Lisbon again for the English, trailing their coats, turning back wherever possible for the Parthian shot. 'As this is the last army England has, we must take care of it,' Wellington pointed out; and he was no Napoleon, a dictator able to fight when and where he fancied, but the nominee of a political party that depended on popular opinion and demanded results; if he skedaddled back to Lisbon without a pitched battle he and his army might well be called home. Charles, who had had his doubts at first, was acquiring an increasing respect for him; clinched by Wellington's choice of the ridge of Busaco on which to make a stand, and his dispositions before that battle. Harrying Masséna's advance, the Light Brigade made all speed to follow the main army. Depleted, but still an intact fighting force; infantry, cavalry and guns; wounded, wives and dogs; they rolled once more back up the stony Portuguese valleys, past the poor houses and the ragged peasants tilling scant fields, past the mourning chants sounding eerily from monasteries on crags, past vines in fruit, and rivers running dry below the wolf and vulture-haunted hills. In their ranks was a second Charles Napier, a first cousin of the brothers; a sailor on leave between ships, he had come to see what campaigning was all about, and looked interestedly round him at the marching men. Some were halt and many were bandaged but they moved as men who know that they have given a good account of themselves. Sparky, larky, undimmed, they swung along the Mondego valley and climbed to the right over the rocks and heather, pulling up the steep gorsey slopes of Busaco, and turned at the top of the ridge to look back at the enormous unconquered French army crowding on below them; 'the same laughing invincible tough men, Who gave Napoleon Europe like a loaf, For slice and portion, not so long ago.'* In ever increasing numbers French soldiers swelled into the valley from every direction, like some huge river in full spate, grey-blue and brown with glints of steel, veterans of Ulm and Austerlitz, Marengo, Jena, and Vienna. 'If Masséna attacks me here I shall beat him' Wellington calmly announced; and all knew that he was never one for the rash overstatement.

William's Coa wound was still open, but his eye for the scenery and backcloth of war was undimmed, and on this still September evening before the battle he stood out to drink it in. 'The skirmishing clatter of musketry arose from the dark wooded chasms beneath,' he wrote, looking from Busaco's hilltop across the valley to the French on the opposite heights. 'Only veterans tired of war could have slept while that serene sky glittered above, and the dark mountains were crowned with the innumerable bivouac fires of more than a hundred thousand warriors.' (There were twenty-five thousand British troops, supported by about the same number of newly trained but useful Portuguese troops, to sixty thousand French.)

From far along the line, the sound of the pipes came from a Highland Regiment. Ardent William, stirred by the scene and pained by his wound, was up half the night, but rolled himself in his cloak and dozed through the early hours, awaking in time to witness a strange scene. For shortly after dawn the Light Division was attacked by 'one of those extraordinary panics attributed in ancient times to the influence of a god. No enemy was near, no alarm given, yet suddenly the troops, as if seized with a frenzy, started from sleep and dispersed in every direction; nor was there any possibility of allaying this strange terror until someone called out that the enemy's cavalry were among them, when the soldiers mechanically ran together and the

* James Elroy Flecker.

illusion was dissipated.' Grattan, no great admirer of Wellington, noted that as the General 'passed through the ranks of the different battalions already formed, his presence and manner gave that confidence to his companions which had a magical effect'.

'The mountain was so rugged that no general view could be taken,' wrote William, 'but Ney, whose military glance was sure, instantly perceived that the mountain, a crested not a table one, could hide no great reserves.' He ordered the attack, and the French advance was made in their usual great columns, 'scaling the mountain with astonishing power and resolution'. Hidden just over the crest, the English waited, while their skirmishers harried the advance until the French had all but gained the summit of the ridge. 'The enemy's shot came singing up in a sharper key, the English skirmishers, breathless and begrimed with powder, rushed over the edge of the ascent, the artillery drew back, and the victorious cries of the French were heard within a few yards of the summit.'

The moment had come—'a horrid shout startled the French column and eighteen hundred British bayonets went sparkling over the brow of the hill'. On the right William was aware of George, apparently trying to break the French column single-handed; he was so far in front that the ten men nearest behind him, a more substantial target, were all killed, though he was not. News had come that morning which put a madness of grief into the brothers, which they were not slow to take out upon the unfortunate French. 'William and Lloyd,' George reported 'wheeled up their companies by the left, and thus flanked the French column and poured a well-directed fire right into them,' till even Loison's men, with their alacrity and firmness, their unwavering drive up the hill against the pounding of Ross's guns, had suddenly had enough. They turned, and all six thousand of them were at the bottom of the painfully mounted hill in a few minutes. In the centre a Highlander, Alexander Wallace, colonel of that rough and tough collection of Irishmen, the Connaught Rangers, had repelled a dangerous attempt to cut the ridge in half. The newly-trained Portuguese Caçadores too had done finely: it had given them a taste, Wellington thought, for 'an unaccustomed amusement'.

Long afterwards, when he had forgotten so much else, an old man remembered agile William as he had seen him at Busaco in their youth, 'leading his men into battle, *en sabreur*, as for a dance'; but William's sword dance, although he never lost his clear head, had been a caper in part compounded of private anguish, a Highland fling of grief. Charles March, coming from headquarters, had brought a letter with tidings of bitter loss.

This was the first set piece battle in which all three brothers fought at once, and George remembered its early morning of passionate sorrow, when they heard that their youngest surviving sister, 'charming, beautiful, gentle Caroline', had died. Reading his mother's letter, thinking of her blindness, her recent loss of Cecilia, of her charity and prodigal sympathy for others, and of his own love for Caroline, George was turned right over. 'It went so deeply to my heart at the moment that I cared very little whether I was killed or not.' 'You may smile at my saying George is impetuous' William wrote to his mother 'but your smile will cease when I tell you that at Busaco he attempted to break the head of the French column with his own hand.' Caroline's death, the desire to avenge Sir John Moore, the relief of attack after retreat, all possessed George. He was shot, but was soon on his legs again pursuing the French down the hill. 'We kept firing and bayoneting till we reached the bottom, and the enemy passed the brook and fell back upon their main body . . . it was not above twenty minutes from the charge till the French were driven from the top to the bottom of the mountain like a parcel of sheep. I really did not think it possible for such a column to be so completely destroyed in a few minutes, particularly after witnessing how gallantly they moved up under a destructive fire from the artillery and a constant galling one from our sharpshooters. . . . When we got to the bottom, where a small stream ran between us and the enemy's position, by general consent we all mingled together searching for the wounded. During this cessation of fighting we spoke to each other as though we were the greatest friends and without the least animosity or angry feeling!' George's incurable friendliness was allowed short shrift. 'Very soon Lord Wellington, finding we remained as he thought too long below, ordered the bugles to sound the retreat, and the French having done the same, off scampered the soldiers of each army and returned to their several positions like a parcel of schoolboys called in from play by their master.' After the battle Masséna did what George considered 'a most unhandsome thing' which was to order one of his batteries to fire at Wellington while he was thanking his troops for the way they had fought. Either Soult or Ney 'would have scorned such an act'. What was war coming to if even generals ceased behaving like gentlemen? Masséna, badly mauled, was clearly not a good loser, and George could only cheer himself by the recollection that the fellow was an Italian, and not French.

Charles shared the desperation of the morning: a wild recklessness was on him. 'We three brothers went that day into battle with sad hearts, for our cousin Lord March had told us our beloved sister Caroline, just 22 years of age, was dead. Our hearts sunk with sorrow: we said nothing, but embraced each other and went to our posts.' Charles was with Craufurd, and had the other Charles Napier under his wing (known as Black Charlie in order to distinguish him from his namesake), a naval officer on leave and waiting for a ship, and come to the war in Portugal just for the ride. Determined to make the most of his time, he had insisted on accompanying George into action a day or two before, riding a conspicuous white pony and wearing a still more conspicuous naval uniform with well-pressed white trousers. He had been shot in the leg 'very slightly, and I was delighted at it, the obstinate dog; he deserved it well!' commented George. 'However he was very good-humoured and laughed as much as anyone at his own folly.'

Looking back at it from a great distance of years, Charles thought 'Busaco was the great test, and a very beautiful fight it was. The French were in the valley, shrouded in mist when the morning broke and the running fire of the outposts began; soon an irregular but very sharp musquetry rang through the gradually dispersing mist.' Mingled with smoke, the mist of the autumn day came drifting up the mountain, 'and from it many wounded men broke out'. The picquets then appeared, being driven back, 'but firing so hard that our line loudly cheered them from the crest above'. Remembering it all so long after, on the other side of the world, he could hear the furious shouts and the roll of gunfire, and Craufurd crying out 'Now 52nd, avenge the death of Sir John Moore, charge! charge! Huzza!' but, 'I was hit, woe the while for me. Now, thirty-nine years after, the horrid suffocation of that wound is scarcely endurable.' He did not fear death in battle but he had always dreaded 'to be mangled'; yet when it came to the crunch some demon made him expose himself over and above the call of duty.

A furious fire had opened on the British line when Régnier's corps assailed the position, and Black Charlie, warned by his previous experience, begged Charles to dismount and put a dark cloak over his red one; he was horribly conspicuous amongst the green jackets. He had better have stayed silent. With a curious mixture of panache and desperation Charles had answered 'No! this is the uniform of my regiment, and in it I will stand or fall this day.' Courage, bravado, some childish irrepressible spirit of taking the dare? Grief for Caroline? Some fey death wish from his Scots past? With one of those swift changes of mood that were like Sarah's, he added delightedly 'What an infernal funk my creditors would be in if they could see me now.' Not surprisingly, as the day wore on, he received a bullet in the jaw.

Blood covered his eyes; the shock deafened him. 'I could not see or speak, but heard "Poor Napier, after all his wounds he is gone at last." I felt obliged by this regret, but hoped they would not bury me, being still alive and bent upon living. With a slight twist I intimated —alive but not merry.' As Black Charlie was carrying the wounded Charles out of the battle, they met Wellington, to whom Charles was sufficiently alive to wave his hat in token of congratulation at the way the battle was going—'I could not die at a better moment.' The blood was such that he feared for his jugular vein. Was he dying? The battle, at least on this part of the long ridge, was won.

Charles was carried into the small chapel of the convent of Busaco. George and William sent for news of him; he felt proud that they had not made his severe wound an excuse to leave the battle. But through an arch in the wall he was amazed to hear the voices of people, 'officers of high rank, in the next room, eating and drinking though the battle was not yet over!' It added to the strange dream-like quality of this too highly charged day to hear that the gathering in the next room was discussing, of all things, the extraordinary beauty of Donny and Sarah, his own parents, and extolling them. Charles had a moment of delight, in thinking that they were not forgotten, but soon his rage at these characters who had happily opted out of the battle overcame him, and he tottered up from the pallet on which Black Charlie had dumped him before he went back to the final act of the battle. Charles managed to walk clean out of the chapel and got to the door of the convent, gazing around for his horse. Looking very wild indeed with his broken jaw, and with the flow of blood from his mouth re-started by his sudden springing up, he was met by Edward Pakenham, who had just had a wound dressed and was on his way back to the scene of action. 'My looks were worse than the reality,' Charles thought; but they had been more than enough for Edward Pakenham, who took him by the arm and led him back inside, 'Damn it Napier, are you mad to think you can go back in this state to the action? Be quiet for God's sake.'

Presently Surgeon Kirkpatrick arrived, and Charles was laid on the grass while 'Kirkpatrick and another surgeon worked, and very disagreeable work it was; for the ball was imbedded in the bone, and pull as they would it could not be extracted, though they cut open my cheek for three inches. At last, one put his thumb in my mouth and pushed, while the other plucked, and away it came, tearing innumerable splinters of bone with it. I did not call out, but it was very painful.'

George, who was to lose his arm two years later, was a witness of his brother's operation. 'He never uttered a word or winced,' he reported, 'the surgeon told me he never knew a man who bore pain so patiently and manfully. I must confess I did not bear the amputation of my arm as well as I ought to have done, for I made noise enough when the knife cut through my skin and flesh. It is no joke, I assure you,' he told his sons, 'but still it was a shame to say a word, and is of no use.' The surgeon escaped next day on one of Charles's horses, on an alarm of French attack, leaving Charles's wound undressed; but George was not going to have his sons left with a low opinion of army doctors for all that. They were kind, skilful, indefatigable, well-educated, full of beneficial experience—'Some of my greatest friends. . . .'

Long afterwards, thinking back to Busaco, Charles remembered Edward Pakenham, dead in America—'Poor fellow, he was a heroic man that Edward Pakenham, and it was a thousand pities he died in defeat; it was not his fault that defeat'—and he thought how lucky he and his brothers had been to survive so long, 'all three still alive and old men', and Black Charlie as well, now in command of the Channel Fleet. 'We were then young, strong, and as hardy men as any in the army; we have had fifteen or sixteen wounds amongst us, and being very fond of each other it made a talk amongst our comrades: noble, brave, and excellent comrades they were!' Sitting in an Indian desert, he sighed after that good company with all the bitter nostalgia of lonely old age.

It had been a traumatic day, the misty sunny September 27th of 1810. Charles's wound, agonising and dangerous, would leave him disfigured, with a nervous facial twitch, and many a night of sleepless pain. It did something worse to him, destroying his looks, and at some deep never-expressed level, his confidence in his power to claim and merit an equal love. Though never to be compared in physical splendour with George or William or Henry, he had been personable enough before Busaco, with a sensible confident charm. Totally at ease with women, he had been very well able to please or be pleased. Now he was mangled; it was the fate he had most feared. But he was alive, and his limbs worked: and that was a great deal. His comments were laconic. 'So much for Busaco . . . where I was shot through the stem and George through the stern; that was burning the family candle at both ends.'

XIV

Black Charlie was amazed by the whole thing. When you could beat the French as he had seen them beaten at Busaco, why not press on? 'He is as queer a fellow and as honest a one as ever crossed my path' his namesake recorded. 'He is the delight of my life and should be trusted with any enterprise were I a great man, he being just fit for a sailor—that is bold, decided and active.' After his grandstand view of Busaco, Black Charlie turned his white pony towards Lisbon, and dining with Wellington, asked him why he didn't make 'a boarding dash' at the French? Wellington patiently explained that England had only one army, that it would cost him ten thousand men to defeat the French, and that 'he must fight in a position where the French would lose more men than he'.

Expressing the opinion in a letter to the Admiralty that campaigning was 'a damned rum concern', Black Charlie left for Cadiz, to spend the rest of his leave in dalliance with the Spanish ladies, or talking his Winston Churchill French to the Chasseurs Britanniques, a Free French regiment to which his brother Tom Napier was attached. Cadiz, rather more intriguing and foreign than Gibraltar, had been a happy stamping ground for the British since the October week five years ago when that spry midshipman, Hercules Robinson of the *Euryalus*, had been the first to step ashore after Trafalgar with

Admiral Collingwood and had eaten rather more of the Spanish Captain-General's pineapple than was strictly polite. Rum or not, for the rest of his life it was Black Charlie's unacknowledged dream to lead an attack sword in hand in the mountains, and oddly enough for a naval officer, he did.

Sarah had come round to Wellington; urged perhaps thereto by Charles, George and William, and by the news that filtered back from the Peninsula. In mingled hope and fear, she followed it all; worn by the continuous apprehension, sustained by the frequent bursts of glory. (Don't, Charles had urged her, keep seeing George and William cut clean in half.) After 1811 she was almost completely blind. Susan O'Brien, though occasionally called on to mingle her tears with Sarah's over this and that, probably heard the more cheerful side of the picture; but judging from their replies to her letters, the role of sustainer of spirit had now passed from Susan to Sarah's sons in the natural course. They told her the tale; but she had a shrewd idea of what the war in Spain was like. She could not be ever brave, ever serene. But her philosophy had always been robust; and no one had yet come up with the soothing yet ultimately unhelpful solution that all our difficulties are to be laid at the parental door.

'Oh! how time passes,' she had (unoriginally) noticed at the age of 49, recovering from fever at Celbridge in 1793 and reminiscing over girlhood, 'and yet, my dear Ly Susan, I am a happier being at this moment than I was then with all my thoughtless, wild, and giddy spirits; for tho' nearer my death by 32 years I am more sensible of the wonderful mercies of God towards me, who had ever bestowed blessings on every moment of my life, which till within these 12 years I never knew the value of, for every misfortune of my life is by my own fault; and to my dying day I will justify every mortal accused by my partial friends of being conducive, by their education of me, to my errors.' Unexhausted by this extremely long sentence, she continued—'Happiness was in my reach at all times, if I had had courage to pursue it.' Now, sightless, widowed, and in grief, her realism was still humble, her faith firm. 'Providence does nothing in vain I am confident' she asserted, surrounded by badly wounded sons and mourning the deaths of two sweet pretty daughters.

Caroline's consumption had moved in fast. By the end of May she 'is taking broth much against her will, is carried downstairs to prevent motion, and passes her day on a large sopha moved up to where the small one was, she reads, she looks out of the window, and sees scarce a soul but us. She is in no pain now, but sick 4 times a day after food however little; she is not low, nor in spirits, very patient, and much pleased since yesterday with Richard's return, who, having passed his examination lost not a moment to come and devotes his time to her which you may guess is a comfort to us all. . . . I am in very good health, as one always is when the mind is on the stretch.' 'As to dear Caroline I don't know what to think of her' Richard added in a postscript, 'one day I feel *in* spirits, by the next out; however we must hope the best. She has naturally a good constitution which is a great point.' In July Sarah reported that 'my dear Caroline's illness is by word of the physicians this very day pronounced so singular a nature that they cannot account for it . . . who knows how soon some of these evils may return? I must live in anxious misery . . . a nervous fever may be the end of it all . . . Richard is well but very low, having less sangwine turn than the others. He is devoted to his poor sister, reads to her and waits upon her, bringing her food as often as he can coax her to eat it. Emily as you may guess is an excellent auxillary in all this.'

The torture of hope and fear continued, but Richard knew well what was coming. 'My mother has been deceived by the physicians a little, but much more so by herself . . . it has all the appearance of the last stage. I believe Caroline does not suffer in mind or body; she says not, and the physicians say so too. I am compelled to undeceive my mother lest the last scene should come too suddenly. . . .' And on September the 12th he told this faithful friend Susan 'My last letter only foreshadowed what has happened. Our sweet Caroline is no more: she expired on Sunday last without a struggle. My mother is very calm and her health not injured. My sisters are in tolerable spirits, and appear in good health, but have not recovered their painful watchings yet. It is some comfort to have heard lately from *all* my brothers, who were well. Ever, my dear Ly Susan, yrs, Rd Napier.' Perhaps almost the most striking difference between our lives and theirs is that there were virtually no hospitals, no trained nurses, no skilled help in sickness, and that twenty-three-year-old Richard, Fellow of All Souls or not, never hesitated to come home and comfort his sister through the last months and her sad early death, as she quietly left a world in whose ways her mother had not wished her to grow old.

For the moment Sarah hardly took it in. But years later she recalled the anguish of this, in writing of Susan's sister in like circumstances who had lost an only child, Lady Carnarvon: 'it is not often we admit that others feel misfortune more poignantly than ourselves, but there is a sort of force in truth that admits of no deception even in our own case. I have long thought that to lose an angel daughter wholly devoted to a blind old mother surpassed most losses of that sort, because no day passes that I do not feel and say to my heavy heart, "She is not here." But your sister's misfortune has struck me as of the deepest dye, for what has she left to bring a cheerful ray of comfort, what beloved object is near her to animate her spirits, tho' but for a moment like the flash of lightning, when a sound of happiness from those we love forces on our hearts the animating feeling of gratitude to God for his mercy in our temporary relief; but where is hers? Write me word I beseech you what you know of her.' For the moment, she was stunned and quiet, with that curious calm which is in part spiritual and in part a kind of cushioning of nature.

All was far from quiet on the Peninsula front. Victory at Busaco had slowed and safeguarded the British retreat, but not made it unnecessary; Masséna had been halted and turned, but he would come on. The nights were so cold that Johnny Kincaid of the 95th had to heave his six-foot length up every hour, wet with dew, and dance a highland fling. The Portuguese people were, he felt, 'kind and hospitable, and not destitute of intelligence; but somehow they appeared to be the creatures of a former age'. Alarm and despondency radiated from the home government. Lords and Commons vied with each other in declaring that the British position in the Peninsula was 'untenable, melancholy, and alarming'. The Common Council of London sent an address to the King complaining of Wellington's 'rashness and ostentation' on the Talavera campaign, and of his 'incapacity of profiting by the lessons of experience'. Undiscouraged by the armchair dirge, Wellington plodded back to his bridgehead. Time would show. His way back to the lines of Torres Vedras lay through Coimbra, which the French were trying to reach before he did, to cut off his retreat; and here George, stiff and ill from his Busaco wound, felt again the full horror of war.

'Lord Wellington had ordered all the inhabitants to withdraw and carry all their property and provisions with them; but as they had unfortunately delayed doing this until we were actually on the march through the town, the hurry, fright, and confusion were beyond description, and I never witnessed so heartrending a scene. Beautiful women and young children, the aged, the decrepit, the sick, the poor, the rich, nobles and peasants, all in one dense mass of misery, wretchedness and confusion; some barefoot, others crying, women tearing their hair with loud lamentations, and calling on every saint in the calendar, many of them running to the officers for protection and food, the weather bad, and all drenched with rain; and to crown all, when we who were the last of the troops were passing by the prison, which was also the madhouse, the unfortunate inmates, prisoners and maniacs, were all at the grated windows rending the air with wild shrieks of despair at seeing the whole population of the city driven before us through the gate, and these unfortunate creatures all locked in; a fire having broken out in some houses close by them which they with reason expected every moment to communicate with the prison, and that they must all perish in the flames. The British officers and soldiers could not stand this sight, and we soon broke open the gates and let them all loose.... Their keepers or jailers had left them, the flames were fast approaching, and the enemy entering the town.' George appealed to his favourite section of the community. 'I feel confident that no man of feeling could blame us.

'As we moved along, driving this immense multitude of unhappy people before us, houseless, penniless, and hungry, I could not help cursing war and all its dreadful attributes, and inwardly feeling that I was myself one of the instruments by which so much misery and injustice was inflicted on a poor guiltless race of inoffensive human beings, not one of whom most probably ever had a voice in the decision of peace or war and who were scourged so severely, for what? the inordinate ambition and personal aggrandisement of a ruthless soldier, Napoleon Buonaparte! Much as I admire that most extraordinary man as a warrior, and splendid as were his talents in all things, I can never look back to his deeply cunning and treacherous invasion of Spain and Portugal, the crimes and horrors which in consequence were committed, the seas of blood which flowed, and the absolute misery of millions of a harmless population, without condeming him.' George, who hated to hate anybody, turns with relief to love Sir Lowry Cole, who next night had given him his own bed, found a doctor to dress his wound, and sent him a good dinner: 'he is as kind and generous as he is brave, and a more truly gallant, enterprising soldier never breathed. He would never permit officer or private soldier to want anything that he had.'

At Lisbon George found Charles with his face so swollen that his eyes and nose had virtually disappeared—'I really thought his nose had been shot off. And as you are aware what a fine long one he has, you can easily imagine how swollen his face must have been to hide it.' Here, in spite of days and nights in pain and in Charles's case of some danger, there was the solace of female company. Both brothers were impressed by the difference between Portuguese and English social mores. They were lodged with a French lady, 'a very kind, excellent, clever, dirty, snuffy little old woman, as kind to us as possible, then and ever afterwards' George reported; and from their high room they could chat up two charming Portuguese girls in the house opposite. Could they not come and visit? No, unless they could fly! Leaning out from their third floor window Charles and George begged to be allowed to drop over; and were teasingly told they could only come in if they crossed the street at this level. They lashed two planks together, and when dusk gave cover, lowered them on to the opposite balcony, startling the Portuguese girls by running across them and in at their windows. They were 'very graciously and good humouredly' given coffee and cakes and a merry evening; talking bad Portuguese and producing shrieks of excited laughter. After wounds and campaigns it was meat and drink; no one minded at all how silly or incomprehensible their opposite number was. Hereafter allowed to come in by the front door, they were introduced to 'parents and friends and other young ladies'. Charles and George thought it all 'very agreeable and amusing, such an adventure could never happen in England. Our manners and ideas of society would not permit such a thing' was George's rather wistful comment on the social mores of his native land.

Charles's experiences surprised him still more. He much disliked the Portuguese government, who, among other vices, were intriguing for the dismissal of Wellington, and when an old Italian friend of his was swept into prison on a private grudge, Charles wrote to the British ambassador, Stuart, about his release. It was, Charles supposed, a question of bribes, augmenting steadily until they reached Forjas, the head of state? Stuart was so foolish as to pass this letter on to Forjas; who said it was a lie, and Napier must answer for it.

'I will prove it a truth, said I.' Collecting an interpreter and his friend Charles MacLeod, Charles 'went straight to the palace of government and saw the minister'. Surprised by this slight and fiery apparition with a lacerated and swollen face, Forjas listened in amazement to the interpreter.

'I said he must choose one of three things, 1) making an ample apology. 2) Fighting me. 3) Horsewhipping.

'He said it was very unpleasant to do any one.

'Our tastes are perfectly similar, said I, but having unluckily been born a gentleman I have a character to keep up, which obliges me to desire an immediate compliance.

'Tomorrow you shall have an answer, said he, for I too am a military man.

'This minute if you please, your excellency, quoth I.'

The written apology was duly given, and the Italian friend was let out of prison next day. Charles immediately made friends with his foe. 'Forjas had a beautiful and agreeable Oporto lady for his wife, but the old knave kept two opera girls, being seventy: this was rather outré, and I told him so.

'It is gentlemanlike, said he, and you may make love to them both if you like.

'I'd rather do so to your wife.

'I thought you *did*.

'Not I.

'More fool you, they are all three at your service.

'As I went to the army immediately his family life was all safe for me. His wife was excessively handsome, very agreeable, and had the most beautiful mouth and teeth, but was a great deal too fat.'

He had suffered greatly from the wound that shattered his face; it was months before he could bite, and the pain of it, the nervous facial twitch, the slight disfigurement and what he called 'the suffocating feel' endured for a lifetime. Did it affect his life? All biography is guess-work: we read our own misconceptions into other people. No mention is made; but from henceforth there are certainly no pretty imperious Miss Gages, no entertaining Miss Carters, no laughing demoiselles with the best legs in the islands. Women are still beautiful, still sought; but they are all married: he plays it safe, and enjoys the company of handsome dames. It may be that he felt his disfigurement too deeply to risk a rebuff from a pretty contemporary: he was a very proud man. He married two widows, one much older than himself, and it has been suggested that he was permanently in love with Sarah; but his letters read unlike the letters of a mother-fixated man. Love is of all sorts; and certainly he loved Sarah; but never is he placating, defensive, fearful of being overwhelmed, a suppliant: if he had a fixation it was for the memory of Donny.

During this time of pain and danger his letters to his mother swing between sympathy for her loss and his ironic and incalculable humour. 'You never saw so ugly a thief as I am: but melancholy subjects must be avoided, the wound is not dangerous . . . you bear so nobly the trial you have gone through . . . the loss of our sweet angelic girl. An endeavour to console you would be silly. You have taken the only way—resignation to the inscrutable decree.' 'Children and parents dear mother' he wrote ten days later 'should be friends and should speak openly to each other. Never had I a petty dispute with you, or heard others have one, without thanking God for giving me a mother, not a tyrant. . . . The scars on my face will be as good as medals, better, for they were not gained by simply being a lieutenant colonel and hiding behind a wall. What nonsense, yet better than putting you in the dismals. We are a vain set of animals indeed, yet feel the gratitude you deserve though we don't *bow* and *ma'am* you at every word, as some do. The Almighty has taken much from you, but has left much; would that our profession allowed us to be more with you.' Not all Charles's jokes stand the test of time; but on a solemn age they broke like sunlight. 'All the time I was ill he used to sit with me for hours and make me laugh whether I would or no' wrote Ensign Leslie. 'And ill I certainly was. I thought I would make a die of it.' 'Charles delighted to find himself and others in ludicrous situations, but generally described them with too much of Rabelais' richness for record' William regrettably wrote.

Cheering news was on the way—'Lord March has just come in and tells me you have had your eyes done and can see a little. Is this blessed news true? Great God grant it to be so.' Dr James Moore, the general's brother, had been among the experts who had advised it: 'my mother tried it chiefly to please us and because she could not be worse than blind,' Richard told Lady Susan. 'As to my sufferings,' Charles went on, 'there were none after pulling out the ball: so that matter is settled' he added, with total untruth. 'Perhaps the use of my choppers will never be regained, and stiff jaws are a bore, but only painful at dinner . . . my desire is to join the pursuit, the French will be touched up now, yet there will be no general action which consoles George and me much. What spirits our poor fellows will be in, pursuing instead of the wretchedness of retreating, which preys on the strongest mind and overwhelms men more than anything else.

Poor devils of French, they excite my pity, for they hate this warfare.'
His annual narrow escape had just taken place: a heavy log of wood
had fallen from a high house and just grazed him in passing. He felt
born to be hanged, and meeting some friends, asked them home for
dinner. Was it ready, he asked his servant?

Quite sir.

What is there?

There's no soup.

Anything else?

There's no sosingers.

What more?

There's no visibles.

What next?

There's no pratees.

So it seems, go on.

There's no nothing.

Hum, a good negative dinner: you must borrow.

There's no time.

Buy.

There's no money.

Credit.

There's no tick.

Are there no rations?

Yes sir. I ate the beef.

Why didn't his mother go to Ireland and be happy with Aunt
Louisa? She would hear the war news just as quickly there. Richard
must have her swung into a ship in a chair. Flying our mothers, he
added presciently, might become fashionable. 'Oh God, what nonsense I talk when the fit takes me. . . . How I pity the poor old King,
and all of them, they have much suffering: God restore their poor
father to his senses. For the men my pity is less, they are said to have
little feeling: but the princesses, and the poor old queen, who is said
to be very much attached to him. Well, no more.'

Lack of promotion still irked him, and the more as he was idle; if
Moore had lived he would have seen to it. Promotion was, alas, all
push and interest. Charles at last wrote to Sir David Dundas at the
Horse Guards, Old Pivot as he was mockingly called in the army,
and got a cold negative answer. Sarah was besieged with demands
for her interest for other young men: she told suppliants she had
really not enough to go round for her own. 'My positive injunctions'

Charles told her in February, 'are to say nothing about me to the Duke of Richmond, speak only for George and let no-one interfere with his claims. . . . . If Lord Moira comes in as Commander-in-Chief I have his unsolicited promise to give me a lieutenant-colonelcy, and William a majority: between friends you should take all advantages, for our family have been too proud, it don't thrive, and tis time to change. We have worked through all for our own bread, and I would now have no conscience in asking. It is delightful to hear of Richard's success . . . how does he like All Souls?'

'Anticipation of ministerial change and hopes of promotion were alike vain' William regretfully recorded 'he and his brothers had still to fight their way to fortune, winning rank not through the aid of their high connections, not by the favour of the Horse Guards, but with sweat, and dust, and blood, from Wellington, who was now leading the army to victories as incessant as they were glorious. For Masséna, after exhausting all means of subsistence at Santarem, had retreated early in March 1811, with a skill which balanced the errors of his advance, justifying Napoleon's remark that it was only in danger and difficulty that he became a general. On that retreat, day after day, Ney, the indomitable Ney, offered battle with the rear-guard, and a stream of fire ran along the wasted valleys of Portugal, from the Tagus to the Mondego, from the Mondego to the Coa.'

Sarah had taken Charles's advice and gone to recuperate amongst the trees and the calmness of Castletown, 'a deserted palace which would fill me with gloom could I see those places, where the happiest years of my life were spent, in a neglected state; but my dear, my perfect sister, who does all that is right and unites prudence with all her actions, spends the money she has allotted for its maintenance in doing all that is necessary rather than showy, so while it *looks* neglected the essentials are well done, and as fires are necessary we live entirely on one floor, which makes it more connected and comfortable; but life there is perfect retirement, which is most comfortable to me, but broke into now and then by those we love who come to dine and sleep a night.'

At the moment she was at Vice-Regal Lodge in Dublin this January of 1811, with the Richmonds. 'Inspite of the just attention they pay to being retired during the poor King's illness still a Ld and Ly-Lieut's house must be publick; at least comparatively so to me, but

as I am permitted to be a privileged person and to wear the individual cap and gown I do at Castletown, I feel no inconvenience for
coming here; for I do not care if strangers say, "How can the Duke
have that queer old blind woman in the corner", and I do care very
much that the affection of my dear nephew should induce him to have
me here surrounded by his delightful girls, who absolutely vie with
each other who shall attend most to me, and the Dss is kindness
personified to me on all occasions.' (Sarah's nephew had married
Lady Charlotte Gordon, niece of her old flame, William Gordon,
who had, after all, died a bachelor. Lord George Gordon, eccentric
to the last, had become a Jew; and also died childless.)

Sarah's delight in the young found full scope in this household of
daughters. 'Their minds are as well regulated as their manners, and
their adoration of their father is the most delightful thing . . . he
enjoys their society and seems to depend on it for the comfort and
relaxation of his leisure moments. To catch Papa at a lucky minute
and take him out to walk for his good is the first object of their care,
and the moment he appears in their room all his daughters flock
round him, and he is like a brother with them. His eldest son is in
Portugal, and thank God the love of military glory will not degene-
rate in him; the rest are at school. You may guess there is much half
joking debates . . .' and in this laughter, these soft voices, she could
catch an echo of lost Caroline's, that was at least as joyful as it was
sad. Life goes on, and Sarah was happy to go with it.

'It is impossible not to dread the Duke's removal' Sarah continued,
with her usual firm family partiality, 'from a country which he is
absolutely formed to govern with the even hand of perfect justice
tempered by humanity but never swayed by weak indulgence. Happy
the poor Paddys whom he governs, for when once he goes their own
wild whiskey spirit will break out and ruin them, poor souls. . . .
George's wound was as bad as Charles's with respect to pain, danger,
and confinement, but he is at last well. As to poor Charles, I know not
what to think, for apparently he is well, but inwardly he suffers
much.'

The cruel war in the Peninsula swayed back and forth, and Sarah's
spirits with it. 'I own I am very sanguine,' she wrote a little later in
1811. 'I cannot be a mother when glory is in question, or rather I
hope I am what a mother should be. At all events I am such as my
sons wish, when I feel glad they are recovered in time to partake of
glory, particularly when Charles writes a whole page to prove the

folly of thinking a battle is dangerous when so many people escape; nevertheless I wish it was over and our army snugg in winter quarters. Charles tells me his wound will never turn to danger now, but will remain a plague to him all his life. Poor fellow, it is hard he cannot get a lt. Colonelcy, which Sir David Dundas admits he deserves as a good soldier; but Sir David is a man of words and not of deeds in this instance, which is hard on a Napier, for old Lord Napier my father in law had nine sons in the service and there are now nine of his grandsons in it . . . I have been fortunate in letting my house for three months certain: it will help a little towards my 2 journeys which are very expensive, but I own I feel much gratification in feeling I am not quite a log and can be moved. . . .'

Charles had been feeling quite a log in his turn. Even before the French retreat began he was restive: George had already recovered and had joined the push after Masséna. By early March Charles could bear it no longer, and gave his doctor the slip—'ridiculous— you'll lose your neb' this old Scot scolded him. His horse Rosinante had never been the same since he came down on the ice, but he had acquired a new one, Blanco, destined to be the joy of his heart for the next score of years. From Morocco, and part Arab, Blanco was tireless and spirited, full of character and charm and of just enough contrariness. A new horse always acted on Charles's spirits like a new love without the worry; and riding from Lisbon, with his wound still open and the bone of his shattered jaw sticking out of his cheek, he was free enough from pain to note the beauty of Mafra Palace, but thought that like all Portuguese buildings it lacked consistency; there were odd patchy bits of rubble between the most beautiful pillars. Riding ninety miles on the 12th and 13th, he caught up with the army between Redinha and Condeixa, having paused at Tom Napier's quarters, 'who gave me a positive bad but comparative good dinner'. (This was Black Charlie's younger brother, as fair as his elder was swarthy: he fought at Corunna, Fuentes d'Onoro, Salamanca, Vittoria, the Pyrenees, and the Nivelle without a scratch, and lost his arm in the final battle on the Nive; ending up as General Sir Thomas N., K.C.B., and, not surprisingly, Governor of Edinburgh Castle.)

Charles and Blanco proceeded next day through the wasted countryside. What was the point of such cruelty as Masséna's? He, like George, was baffled by it. The Portuguese villages and little towns were destroyed not in uncontrollable anger but with a kind of regular military ritual by the departing French; all the furniture was piled up on the ground floor and then, to the sound of a bugle, every house was set alight at the same moment; their owners standing by helpless meanwhile. Treatment of animals seemed equally pointless and cruel: George found thirty or forty donkeys left hamstrung by the wayside. Why not kill them outright and not leave them to starve or become a prey to wolves and vultures? All George could say was that Masséna was an Italian, and they, poor sods, had been for centuries either kicked around by Austrian overlords or ruled by petty princelings as tyrannical as these. The nations no-o-o-o-ot so blest as we . . . One must make allowances.

As the afternoon wore on Charles met a litter of branches, borne by soldiers and covered with a blanket.

'What wounded officer is that?

'Captain Napier of the 52nd, a broken limb.

'Another litter followed.

'Who is that?

'Captain Napier of the 43rd, mortally wounded.'

They were set down under a tree, and George, however suffering and shocked, could not but laugh at the fury with which Charles drove off the surgeon who approached his brother with an offer to take off his arm, 'elegantly'.

'A sharp affair between the light division and the enemy's rearguard this day,' Charles recorded in his journal. 'We lost 400 killed and wounded. My two brothers commanded the companies chiefly engaged, and are both severely wounded: the ignorance and imprudence of Sir William Erskine said to have been conspicuous; and Colonel Drummond is not extolled for military qualities. Great want of provisions, continued our route, enemy in full retreat.'

Terrible sights awaited the British as they advanced north through a foggy spring; French soldiers dead and dying of starvation, and a slaughtered, tortured and mutilated population of Portuguese peasants. The reverse side of revolutionary ardour was its inhumanity: if Napoleon was God then all who opposed him put themselves beyond mercy. 'Within a very few years,' Captain Gomm thought, 'the French people seem to have traced back every step that nations make towards civilisation; and they who a short time back were the fine spirits and cavaliers of the age will have degenerated by the close of this campaign in Portugal into something worse than Huns.' It had happened with dreadful speed; but George, a great believer in people being fine spirits and cavaliers, remembered a French officer whom the 52nd took prisoner in these days and who told George how much he hated it all, the unjust war in Portugal, the hangings and torturings of poor people—But what could we do? If we did not find provisions we must ourselves have starved? He had asked in vain to be sent home to France. George was determined to bear no personal malice, and at Redinha, on an evening when a good dinner had come up, and the picquets had all been posted, the 52nd invited the French captain of the picquets over to dinner, when a good time was had by all: next morning they blazed away at each other. In the afternoon George was hit over the heart by a bullet but was only bruised; it was shot from so far away that it was too spent to do more than cut through his coat and waistcoat.

A few days later when Charles met them they had not been so lucky. Craufurd was away on sick leave, and the obstinacy of Sir William Erskine, who replaced him at the head of the spearheading Light Division, cost the lives of nearly four hundred valuable men, at Casal Noval, and condemned 25-year-old William to a life of grinding pain. Strictly charged by Wellington to husband every man, Erskine sent them in to attack in a thick fog, in spite of assurance from his picquet captains that the French were present in great force. He had hardly given the word before a French twelve-pounder opened up and ploughed through the ranged ranks, killing a number of men. 'Still the wise Sir William was sure it could be "nothing but a single gun or two and a picquet of the enemy" ' George reported, even he enraged into sarcasm, 'and desired Colonel Ross to send my company to drive them in on the flank. We made a grand push, and drove the enemy from vinyard to vinyard, keeping up a hot fire.' This went on from three in the morning till three in the afternoon; but half of them were pointlessly killed or wounded in this easily defended country. Erskine, not a quick learner, repeated the error at Sabugal where he sent two battalions over a ford into the midst of an entire French corps d'armée, from whose overwhelming midst they were only extracted by the extreme skill of Beckwith. 'A short-sighted ass' Harry Smith called Erskine, and when Craufurd was restored to it the cheers of the Light Brigade rent the air.

At Casal Noval William had been sent up in the thick fog, without his own 43rd, to support the 52nd, for the sun had suddenly come out, revealing the redcoat companies surrounded by French, like a pimple on a brown face, as Charles inelegantly put it. William had been unable to rally more than a handful of the 52nd to follow him and cut their way out—'the most painful event that ever happened to me'; but he hastened to excuse them. 'Their own captains had not been with them for a long time, and they were commanded by 2 lieutenants remarkable for their harsh, vulgar and tyranical dispositions, and very dull bad officers withal.' He went back three times to try and draw the remnants out of danger, crossing the open fields to do so; finally a shot in the spine paralysed his legs. 'The enemy very ungenerously continued to fire at me when I was down. I escaped death by dragging myself by my hands towards a small heap of stones which was in the midst of the field, and thus covering my head and shoulders. Not less than 20 shots struck this heap.'

He lay helpless till afternoon, when Tom Lloyd and William's own company came up and drove back the French, dumping William under a tree, where John Morillyon Wilson of the Royals gave him a swig of tea and brandy which William felt sure had saved his life. They never met again till they were old men, but Wilson who had been sure William was dying, still remembered him as the handsomest man he had ever laid eyes on, even in extremis.

On the 21st of March Charles was, he told Sarah 'flead, bugged, centipeded, beetled, lizarded and earwigged. Cleanliness is known to me only by name.' The army had got far ahead of its supplies, all of which had to come on mule-back over the mountains, and food was chronically short; but the poor people of the country had even less than the army. There was nowhere to write at, and nothing to sit on except a furze bush; and his breeches were worn too thin for that. But George and William were reported better—'are we cats that we live and bear such wounds?' He played down the atrocities and went on to the animal stories. 'Blanco is the strongest horse ever backed. Still, he thinks a bivouac the worst amusement in the world, as he gets nothing but heather and hard riding. Poor fellow, I pet and coax him but it dont make up for no oats. He is the most delightful animal that ever was, but thinks being admired by the Lisbon ladies with a full stomach is better than my affection with heath.' A scene at the village of Muselha had pleased him—'Colonel Stewart and a Portuguese are trying to cheat each other about a beautiful goat:

Caledonia is too much for Lusitania.' He rather feared his division might become 'headquarter pets, as the guards belong to us, and are favourites of his lordship; deservedly so', although the same might be said of the Light Division. News of the redoubtable John Hennessy was not good. Escaping after Corunna he had found his way to Emily Napier in Ireland and given her back the survivor of Charles's silver spurs: he had had to sell one for food. Reaching Cork, he had been told at the pay office that Charles was freed and back in the war in Portugal. Without even going to see the wife and children he had had no sight of for two years, Hennessy had rejoined the armies in the Peninsula; but he was now under arrest and likely to be hanged. He had gone into a Portuguese cottage and seized their last loaf of bread away from a starving man and wife and their five children; and in Wellington's army this was a capital offence. Charles begged him off, on the grounds that Hennessy had saved his life after Corunna; but this extraordinary character was quite unrepentant, and seemed certain to repeat his theft, and it was almost a relief when he lost his life in battle a month or two later.

'This country is ravaged by fire and sword, we get nothing for love or money, but pass through deserted tracks, the only symptoms of former habitations being the burned walls and dead bodies. . . . We are on biscuits full of maggots. Blanco is starving and curls his nose into a thousand wrinkles, cursing Buonaparte: there, my biscuit has run away on maggot's legs.' Clothes wore out; and nights were spent on rush mats, rolled out on the wet ground with cloaks for cover. The bivouacs, when there was time to make them, were rough shelters made of branches.

Next day there was a halt in the advance and Charles rode back over the mountains to see how George and William were doing. 'Says I to Blanco yesterday, Suppose we walk over the mountains old boy and see the other boys; no sooner said than done.' At Condeixa he found George in 'acute and constant pain, unable to sleep without opium', and stricken by the losses. Major Stewart—'fine, enterprising and gallant'—had died on the night of the Casal Noval action, telling George that he knew his life had been sacrificed in vain by a stupid and unnecessary order from above. George had not been able to disagree; holding Stewart's hand as he died and offering what comfort he could through his own mounting pain, he was distressed to the heart by the death of his lieutenant, Gifford, with whom he had so nearly fought the duel two years back. As the 52nd extricated themselves from their awkward position in the midst of the main body of the French, George had looked round for Gifford and seen him down: he had been fighting with such skill that the French had continually cried out to their sharpshooters, Kill that Officer. George saw that they were pillaging Gifford's body almost before the breath was out of it; the sight was too much: there might even still be some life in him. With four men following him George had gone back for him and hauled him away; though still breathing he was dead in a few minutes, and they had unfixed their bayonets and scooped a grave in the sand and buried him before they left, under fire—'as honourable, generous, gallant and guileless a soldier as ever the fate of war cut off in the prime of youth, health and spirits'. The company had given Gifford three cheers and charged the enemy to avenge him: Charles tried to console George with the thought that 'never was a soldier's death finer, or his burial more honourable'; but on that first night George had been restless and miserable with the shock and pain and the surgeons had cheered him on his way by telling him that William's wound was certainly mortal.

Far from it. William was up in a week and 'runs about in a go-cart like a child'; Charles thought this 'fair proof that his inwards had not been injured by the ball'. There was nothing to eat at Condeixa, but Lieutenant Light of the 4th Dragoons had acquired a loaf of bread, which he brought across miles of countryside still full of scattered parties of the enemy, to give, with some wine, tea, and sugar, to George and William, where they lay in a ruined house. Highly welcome too was Charles March, sent a twenty mile ride by Wellington from headquarters to tell George and William that they had done well and that he had written to Sarah to say they were wounded but all right. George was further cheered by an Irishman of his regiment, John Dunn, who had tramped seven miles to see him —'Sure I thought you was kilt; didn't I see you knocked over by the bloody Frenchman's shot? But myself knew you wouldn't be plaised if I didn't folly on after the villains, so I was afeared to go pick you up when ye was kilt, long life to you! and your honour's brother lying there, Captain William, long life to him, I hope he's not dead?'

'But though it may be confidently said they are not dangerous, they are very bad clinks,' Charles wrote to his cousin Emily Berkeley: William and George should be out of action for months, he thought. Needless to say, William was back in time for Fuentes d'Onoro on the 5th of May, notable as the only major battle in the Peninsular war in which none of the Napiers got wounded—'though the fire of grape and shells was heavy, I made it a point of honour not to be hit', Sarah was told. 'William and I are quite well . . . . and in mad spirits, and long to fight again, but Masséna is not inclined.'

The Marshal, always aware of Napoleon's gimlet eye in the small of his back, had marvellously rallied his men after their starved retreat and now tried to drive the English back into the Coa, in which he all but succeeded. But Wellington was back from Badajoz in the nick of time; the sight of his long nose in a fight was worth a reinforcement of ten thousand men, Johnny Kincaid thought. At one point in the battle of Fuentes d'Onoro four French cavalry brigades had closed in on the open plain on the Light Division with its British Dragoons and German Hussars—'there was not during the war a more dangerous hour for England' William wrote; and in the desperate ensuing fight even the Guards were cut down. 'We were many hours in a severe fire'; and Charles considered that if Bonaparte had been there things might have gone otherwise (though he had a great wish to see this master of war in action). 'Remember now dearest Mother that fight more, or no more fight, a hundred thousand men are in the pickling tub with William and myself: it was our turn to escape and we did.'

Wellington himself was in no doubt: 'If Boney had been there we should have been beaten.' But Napoleon, by the mercy of heaven, had other fish to fry. He wanted a son to inherit his vast empire and who more suitable than a Habsburg as partner in this enterprise? Last year he had been away in Austria, celebrating his marriage to the Emperor's daughter; and whether she was more dazzled at his glory or more disgusted at having to marry one of the party that had chopped her aunt Marie Antoinette is not known. Now he was awaiting the son (duly born on March 20th), in the intervals of twisting the Czar's arm. At Fuentes d'Onoro the British soldiers were so little worried by all these mighty matters and by life in general that they seized the chance to play football during a lull in the battle. 'Our brigade marched first off the position, playing the British Grenadiers which was a little like dunghill cock-crowing, but the men like it' Charles concluded.

George had missed Fuentes d'Onoro on account of a more personal combat. He and William had been taken in an ox-cart to Coimbra, comparatively untouched and comfortable, having doctors, houses, and beds; but here George's arm had gone septic and he was still in fever when William left to rejoin the army. He woke up one night to hear a noise in his room, took down his sword which was hanging over his bed, stepped forward, and was grappled round the waist and expected the instant stiletto. In his one-armed struggle he tried to force the man to the window—'but in this through weakness I failed . . . and finding that he had not made any attempt to kill me I began to suspect that he must be an English soldier'. George struck him with the hilt of his sword and told him to speak out and be let go. 'But speak he would not, and suddenly seized my wounded arm in his teeth and gave me such pain by tearing at it that I let go my sword.'

George's sword dance might well have ended at this point; for he was still deathly weak and dodged under the table as his assailant hacked at him with his own weapon. Fortunately the noise brought help, the intruder cut open a glass door with George's sword and escaped via the balcony. George was annoyed to lose his gold watch but glad the man had got away, as the Portuguese would undoubtedly have hanged him; and 'as he certainly had no intention of doing me any bodily harm when he first entered the room I should never have felt comfortable'. Poor George felt far from comfortable even so: not surprisingly, his lacerated arm went septic again 'and my recovery was much retarded'.

In April Almeida, the last French-held fortress in Portugal, was still holding out, though besieged by the British. The home government, economising on such essentials as siege-trains and heavy guns, had made obligatory the storming of European fortresses with 30 foot stone walls by human bodies alone. 'The British infantry is the best in the world,' one French general was heard to remark, 'but fortunately there are not very many of them': and there was the nub. 'I wish Lord Wellington would give me 60 scaling ladders, and 200 volunteers with a supporting column,' Charles longed, 'and the British standard should fly in Almeida in two hours without losing 50 men. The ditch is dry and not deep, the garrison is weak, and British volunteers are irresistible; they would be on the rampart in fifteen minutes. Once there, the devil would not get them off again.' But these scarce articles were required elsewhere.

At home in England the war still had a certain remoteness and unreality. Her old age, and his illness, had finally softened Sarah's heart towards George III. 'The poor King! My heart feels the sincerest emotion of pity for him.' He was mad and incapacitated, and 'I can't forget that the family of my sovereign should be the most unhappy family in all his dominion'. But others were unhappy about other things. In April Sir Francis Burdett, radical member for Westminster, who had blown the gaff about Mary Ann Clarke and her sale of commissions, challenged the House for imprisoning a seditious printer, was committed to the Tower for breach of privilege, barricaded himself into his house in Piccadilly, and called on the crowd to defend the liberties of England. Huge crowds hurled half-bricks at the constables and Life Guards; and it took horse, foot and artillery to dislodge and arrest Burdett, who dramatically waved a translation of Magna Carta at his assailants. Lord Liverpool complained to Wellington that the war in Portugal was terribly expensive: to which that most careful of generals replied that the war in England which would ensue if Napoleon were not beaten on the continent would be a thought more expensive both in life and prosperity.

Retreating the previous autumn through the quiet little university town of Coimbra, Colonel Colborne had asked his sister to imagine how she would like 'to see your piano, writing tables, chairs and things heaped together at the south end of Sloane Street to impede the enemy?' But no one in England could imagine it; the terrified families murdered in their poor dwellings, the staked bodies of peasants left with their heads in the stream. On the way to look at Almeida, Charles had seen, as so often before, 'numbers of peasants' bodies, many bayonetted, others shot, some were very old men and some were women. I did not think French gallantry would have suffered this—but Masséna is an Italian.' Round Almeida there were 'a multitude of eagles, vultures, and kites eating the carcases of man and beast; I congratulated myself on not making a side dish at their feast: they would have gained little additional good by it, and to me it would have been a great inconvenience'. The stench was terrible, and the vultures so gorged they could hardly leave the ground. A hungry man, riding a hungrier Blanco, he came back to Moita to write with bitter emphasis in his journal, 'England, how little you know of war'. In the cold rainy evenings among these starve-crow hills with their hanged and burned peasants there were times when even the driving forth of the perpetrators felt barely worth the cost. Miserably mutilated, they swung from the beams of their own poor homes, and seemed to make a mockery of the mercies of God and of all human goodness and endeavour.

XV

'I find I have power to conquer my wandering thoughts, and listen to what does not interest me with patience and indifference; it passes time and makes the care of me less burthensome to my friends, which is a great object,' Sarah felt; but there were moments when she feared that her mind might be failing under anxiety and blindness. William reassured her—'My dear Mother, you have an energy of mind that few can boast of, and it has its consequent good effects. The sentiments that caused you to undergo the pain of the dreadful operation on your eye are the original causes that also give to Charles his intrepidity and his ambition of honourable fame, to George his impetuosity and supreme contempt for everything that is not noble and belonging to the character of a soldier.' And in the little house in London to which she was now returned, Louisa or Emily would read her out a letter from Wellington after Casal Noval—'William is wounded in the back, George in the right arm . . . your sons are brave fellows and a credit to the Army; and I hope that God will preserve them to you and their country.' After Busaco Wellington had hoped that it would be a comfort to her 'to reflect that your sons received their wounds on an occasion in which the British troops behaved so well', and maybe it had been: Sarah was a great one for taking comfort in anything that could reasonably be seized on. Louisa would be called on to read the letters out again, until Sarah, sitting in her near darkness, knew them by heart.

A surgeon at Lisbon had told Charles a year back that Wellington deserved hanging for his waste of a third of his army at Talavera and in the Alemtejo marshes. Nevertheless, said Charles, we must think; and his thoughts on Wellington became ever more favourable. 'All lines have this drawback; a soldier who trusts to his firelock alone never despairs while he can use it; but he ever puts too much faith in works, and on seeing them forced thinks all is lost: if ever lines were useful, those of Torres Vedras are so.' That was point one in the general's favour. After Casal Noval the death of Gifford, and William's and George's bad wounds set him back—'does glory repay these losses and pains?' And at Sabugal 'Colonel Beckwith's conduct was in a great measure the cause of such an extraordinary success'. He noticed that 'the French cannot stomach a British attack . . . they stand fire for ever behind walls, but don't like close quarters'. At Ungera on the 5th of April, although 'we arrived last night, wet, tired, and no cover, cursing Portugal, and Portuguese names, and Frenchmen, and English generals, fools and rogues, commissaries and medicos', he thought Masséna was really put to flight—'we have this day been exactly one month in pursuit of him. Where will this interesting campaign close, and how? I can hardly think the French mean to re-enter Portugal, or they would not have destroyed the country so dreadfully. There was a horrible instance of brutality in this village; the French say it was the Italians.'

At Alfayetes, next day, he thought that Wellington's flank movement to force Almeida 'must produce a general action or make Masséna let go his hold of Portugal, leaving Lord Wellington master of the kingdom he has so boldly and skilfully defended'. Masséna might have been starved into retreat: that was skill too, and in a month he had been driven three hundred miles nearer home. 'His (Wellington's) whole conduct has been able: errors may have been committed, all generals commit errors, but this campaign renders him one of the first of his time.' Charles was converted; perhaps only regret for Moore had ever made him critical.

'I can't help wishing for a general action near Almeida,' Charles went on to his journal, 'the ground is perfectly open, and when that is the case our army is sure of victory. Our cavalry can then act, and though less numerous, is so superior that the combat would probably be in our favour. A total defeat of the French would put Ciudad Rodrigo into our hands and effectually stop a second invasion of Portugal for a long time. It would also save the Spaniards if anything can rouse their energies: perhaps it is too late but still worth trial.' The Spanish generals had recently surpassed themselves: in the south one of them had marched his men day and night so mercilessly that when they finally met the French they were too exhausted to move and stood motionless on the shore in large numbers while five thousand British and Portuguese took on seven thousand French on the hill of Barrosa and captured six guns, an imperial eagle, and a wounded French general who spoke severely to them about 'the incredibility of so rash an attack'. And at Badajoz, the great fortress on the Guadiana that was the gateway into southern Spain, the brave Spanish defender had died and the aged defeatist who succeeded him had surrendered it to the French though food and ammunition were plentiful, the walls barely breached, and he had eight thousand men and a British force on the way to his succour. Even Wellington was moved to exasperation with the Spaniards— 'that extra-ordinary and perverse people'. Why must they still live in their Conquistador dream, and not save their lives and their country by pocketing their pride and taking a few lessons in war from their enemies the French or their allies the English?

The fall of Badajoz put paid to all hopes of a real campaign into Spain—'we shall be dispersed in cantonments on the frontier, as Lord Wellington cannot, I think, muster enough men to follow into Spain, and probably more troops will be sent to Alemtejo.' His mother could, Charles told her, rejoice at George and William's lucky recovery 'from two as ugly wounds as could be, short of mortal ones'. His life for the last month had not been perfect for a convalescent: 'cold and sleeping out at night and severe riding made the wound bleed again, but now apart from a splinter of bone protruding from the jaw, all is right.' And Wellington, splendid fellow, at last allowed to promote, had given commissions to three sergeants of the Light Brigade. How Charles longed for a stab at the walls of Almeida!

But alas, Beresford in the south had once again cried Cock-a-doodle do, I don't know what to do, and Wellington had hurried off to tell him. For at Albuera all had been confusion. Foxed by Soult's feints among the olive trees, and impeded by his Spanish allies, courageous as ever but immovable and therefore terribly underfoot (although Zaya did well), Beresford and staff were all but captured by Napoleon's Polish Lancers. A Hanoverian officer with three guns had wandered about asking for orders, what was he to do with them? seeming surprised when someone came up with the original notion that he should fire them at the enemy. But as William kindly if pompously pointed out in connection with Junot in Portugal, 'so many circumstances sway the judgement of an officer in the field, which do not afterwards appear of weight, that caution should guide animadversion on an unfortunate commander'. It does sound the least bit disorganised, but it is easy enough to be brave after the event: we are not there hazed by the gunsmoke, blinded by sheets of rain, and with Polish sabreurs riding relentlessly on us out of the olive woods every ten minutes from the least expected direction. Kincaid was not the only one to think it was going to be that unheard of battle where everyone on both sides is killed.

'Die hard 57th, die hard,' their Colonel Inglis, doing just that himself, advised them; and it seemed about all there was to do. Disaster was saved at a desperate moment, by the few shrewd officers who always seem to appear at such crises, Hardinge and Cole, who launched the Fusiliers in the only direction where the battle could be saved, and with it, the southern road into Portugal. The Fusiliers were accompanied by Worcesters, Northamptons and Middlesex; moved as much by county rivalry as by dislike for the French. It was an occasion that moved William to some of his ripest prose.

'Such a gallant line, issuing from the midst of the smoke, and rapidly separating itself from the confused and broken multitude, startled the enemy's heavy masses, which were increasing and pressing onwards to an assured victory; they wavered, hesitated, and vomiting forth a storm of fire, hastily endeavoured to enlarge their front, while a fearful discharge of grape from all their artillery whistled through the British ranks. Myers was killed, Cole, the three colonels, Ellis, Blakeney and Hawkshawe, fell wounded, and the Fusilier battalions, struck by the iron tempest, reeled, and staggered like sinking ships. But suddenly and sternly recovering, they closed on their terrible enemies, and then was seen with what strength and majesty the British soldier fights. In vain did Soult, by voice and gesture, animate his Frenchmen, in vain did the hardiest veterans, extricating themselves from the crowded columns, sacrifice their lives to gain time for the mass to open out on such a fair field; in vain did the mass bear itself up, and fiercely striving, fire indiscriminately upon friends and foes while the horsemen hovering on the flank threatened to charge the advancing line.

'Nothing could stop that astonishing infantry. No sudden burst of undisciplined valour, no nervous enthusiasm, weakened the stability of their order; their flashing eyes were bent on the dark columns in front, their measured tread shook the ground, their dreadful volleys swept away the head of every formation, their deafening shouts overpowered the dissonant cries that broke from all parts of the tumultuous crowd, as slowly and with a horrid carnage it was pushed by the incessant vigour of the attack to the farthest edge of the height. There, the French reserve, mixing with the struggling multitude, endeavoured to sustain the fight, but the effort only increased the irremediable confusion, the mighty mass gave way and like a loosened cliff went headlong down the steep. The rain flowed after in streams discoloured with blood, and fifteen hundred unwounded men, the remnant of six thousand unconquerable British soldiers, stood triumphant on the fatal hill.'

Bully for John Bull; though Beresford was rightly gloomed at the appalling losses; it had not been his day of glory or success. But Soult was in retreat and something ultimately fatal had lodged in the strong core of French morale. 'This won't do, it will drive the people in England mad. Write me down a victory' Wellington insisted when he saw Beresford's melancholy dispatch. Soult, licking his wounds in withdrawal, was furious with the English soldiers, so totally uninstructed in the art of war—'They were completely beaten, the day was mine, and they did not know it and would not run.'

In the north the French escaped, blowing up Almeida as they went. 'Brennier gave us the slip . . . never was there a more complete blow up; the achievement has been brilliant. Who is to blame we don't know . . . whoever is in fault ought to be shot' Charles felt. It had been Erskine again, most cogent of all walking arguments against Horse Guards influence. 'Lord Wellington must feel it deeply. To have all his operations for securing the town against a large army succeed, to see that army defeated and retired, and then to have the generals under him let the garrison out!' Why had they fought Fuentes d'Onoro? 'Take Lord Wellington away and we are *generalless*' Charles stormed. This botch gave rise to Wellington's famous— 'there is nothing on earth so stupid as a gallant officer'.

Charles was still in some pain and tetchy with it when he wrote. The rain in Spain fell mainly in the plain where the army was. They had been up at three every morning for a month, on the march by four and marching till dark. His wound bled intermittently, and there was nothing to eat except shoe-leather and bread and butter, and less to drink. Enemy manoeuvres when the march was halted, and especially at Almeida, made him grumble 'The French are our masters in war as to all but courage and bodily strength'. He was fed up with the gorging vultures who could hardly get themselves off the ground, and 'I hunted some on Blanco, but he did not half like their looks, thinking they might take to live flesh for a change'.

They had captured some copies of the *Moniteur* in one of the French camps and Charles had been interested to read their account of Busaco, and to hear that *Le Major Napier, déjà blessé à la Corogne, reçut un coup de feu dans la figure.* Sarah chose this moment to write him a severe letter asking him why he was not taking the regency question more seriously? Charles replied rather crisply from Albergaria on May 20th. He thought the dispute laughable. 'The king is mad, and cannot do his duty: he is therefore virtually dead. . . . The prince is, what he ever appeared to be, a milksop for accepting the regency with limitations. What could they have done had he refused?' He was enjoying Prince Eugene's memoirs—'I hope they are authentic . . . towards books and people I feel alike—if they give information or amusement their style is nothing to me.' He could not bear overwriting; nor the elaboration of Georgian manners. 'Gentility, or what is called good breeding, carried beyond a certain point becomes trifling. . . . A fellow comes smirking and smiling with, Will you do me the favour of being so kind as to indulge me etc., and you are conquered unless you get out, I'll see you damned first. . . . I have indeed got pretty well rid of my breeding, it don't now trip me up often.' This was his third entrance into Spain, 'and the cleanliness of the inhabitants is most striking on leaving Portuguese filth'. It was all very well for the military secretary to say 'The commander in chief entertains the highest opinion of your meritorious services,' but here he was five years a major instead of two a colonel; he was practically the most aged major in sight, everyone at Barrosa had been made, and the fighting there had been no tougher than at Corunna. If he didn't get promotion pronto he would resign: 'exit in a rage'.

Wellington was off again to the Alemtejo—'he has to fly backward and forward, and does the journey in five days, hard work this for body and mind'. To renew the siege of Badajoz he had sent for troops from the north: arriving at the head of the first column Charles was sent off to scout around in the area of Medellín and see what the French were about. An active, intelligent officer was wanted—'what a bore to be so clever!' Charles mocked. And he only had two coats; the old one so browned with age that the Spans would take him for a French spy; the other intended for smart occasions and so bright in its new redness that the French would see him a mile off. He would have to rely on getting information from the local Spans—'Blanco and I are like meteors.' He was taking no baggage and so couldn't write, but 'be not uneasy', he urged Sarah from Talavera Real in June. It was dead safe, he assured her—'my orders are not to risk anything and I have no desire to be taken in a ridiculous way', and he set off over mountains where at last the sun was warm and the grass juicy enough even for Blanco's pampered palate.

George was back and a brevet major and the Light Division too was on its way south. He wanted very much to command a battalion: would Beresford give him one of the Portuguese ones that he had brought to such a state of efficiency? Beresford would; but then Craufurd had kicked up a dust and gone to Wellington and said 'if he was to be deprived of his good field soldiers the Light Division would be ruined, and as he was pleased to say I was one of his best officers he positively refused to let me go . . . Marshal Beresford was not pleased and expressed himself in pretty strong terms.' George had ended by getting the first battalion of his own party, the 52nd. He was in bliss, 26, and with all but two fingers of his right hand working again properly. He even had another gold watch. General Ross, leaving for home 'with real grief', had distributed his possessions among his friends: the only compensation for his loss was that Colborne had swopped and now had the 52nd. 'Many happy years I passed in that beloved corps,' George reflected. 'Few regiments equalled it and none ever surpassed it. No need to look behind when at the head of 52nd Light Infantry men!' They would always be there; and a poetical officer compared them to a rill of grasshoppers, flicking from one piece of cover to another with such speed and lightness and keeping up a hail of fire from every gorse bush and boulder, behind 'the grace and intrepidity and lightness of step and flippancy of a young colonel'.

The summer was one of 'continually moving about' which George enjoyed. 'A New Order of things now guides the Universe' Napoleon had told his Senate in 1810; but to a Europe squeezed of men and money it felt a comfortless one; and there were murmurings and rallyings, and prayers for the small British army perched on the stony border of Spain. News of the Czar's mounting anger with Napoleon reached Wellington. In time, he thought 'we may overthrow this disgusting tyranny': meanwhile he had to sit tight on his supply lines of the Tagus, the Mondego and the Douro. He chipped at Badajoz, not much aided by a bare dozen of sappers and seventeenth century Portuguese guns. After losing two hundred and fifty men in two attempts he hauled off: Masséna who had been nonspeaks with Soult had been replaced by Marmont; and this Marshal joined his colleague to relieve Badajoz. Wellington withdrew to the shadeless, dusty, feverish plain between the Caya and the Guadiana, screening Elvas and playing for time until starvation in this desert country and guerilla troubles in their own regions should draw the Marshals away.

Longa and Porlier, famous guerilleros from the Asturias, and Mina from Navarre were active enough, but as Wellington followed the inevitable French withdrawal by moving his army in July for its health's sake into the hill villages whence he could descend on either Ciudad Rodrigo or Badajoz, he wondered once again over the failure of Spanish co-operation. 'One would have thought that there would have been a general rising. This is the third time in less than two years that the entire disposable force of the enemy has been united against me. But no-one takes advantage of it except the guerillas.'

Reinforced in August, Marmont made a dashing move against Wellington's position: he heard rumours that the British government had at last run to a siege train and that it was being moved up to the border from Oporto, and he attacked on the El Bodon plateau. The Light Division was as usual extricated by its eyebrows; almost as if its leader could not forbear to show off its extreme skill and flexibility —'I was in no danger I assure you' Craufurd insisted. 'No but I was, through your conduct' Wellington told him; but Craufurd only reflected that he was being 'damned crusty'. Among Wellington's troops everyone now 'felt the greatest security in his outmanoeuvring Johnny Crapaud'; Marmont retired on Salamanca after a good close look at Wellington's position at Sabugal; and on the evening of El Bodon Wellington received the final accolade from a drunken Light Infantryman—'Here comes the long-nosed bugger that beats the French.'

Good news had come to Charles. The Commander-in-Chief of the forces, old Sir David Dundas, whom Sarah called 'the old stick' and 'a block and impenetrable', and the army a great many ruder names, had been given the push. 'So Sir David is at last turned out!' Charles rejoiced. He had seemed an eternal fixture at the Horse Guards. 'The Duke of York's advent will however do Napiers no good, and indeed Old Davy going to pot is luck enough for ten years.' He was being unnecessarily gloomy, perhaps because he had Guadiana fever and could hardly walk. Sarah had written to the Prince Regent, 'who has none of that stern injustice in his nature', had an answer by return of post and another from the Duke of York three weeks later, thus accomplishing what none of Charles's efforts, skill, courage, or wounds had been able to bring about. He was a lieutenant-colonel: 'the Duke gave it with the most flattering compts, and the Prince announced it to me with a more extended compt to the character and conduct of all my sons, and gave the full share of it as due to the example of their father, of whom he wrote in the most gratifying terms to me.

'While I was rejoicing in this, great news comes to me from Portugal, that Lord Wellington having leave to promote 12 caps to brevet majorities according to his judgment of their merits had named George and William both, who were then made Brevet-Majors in the most honourable manner. It is much the same as were in former days brave men made Knights Bannerets, and the most flattering of all promotions,' Sarah added, slightly carried away. Three generals were arguing over who should have George, and altogether the Christmas of 1811 was a happy one.

Greater luck for the entire British army was now on the way. 'The war in Spain has become to a certain degree offensive on our part' Wellington wrote understatingly to the Prime Minister in August. The stage was set for an attack on the two great fortresses of Ciudad Rodrigo and Badajoz next winter, bastions of the road to Madrid. But Charles, who had seen so much of retreat, would not be there to ride with Wellington into the capital of Spain. Though his longed-for promotion had come, it was to whisk him away from the paths of glory to where the remote Bermudas ride, in ocean's bosom all too un-espied.

He was to command the 102nd, a regiment recently returned from Australia where it had sensibly mutinied in order to be left there. 'To get a regiment that is in bad order is agreeable; my fear was a good one, when no character could be gained and some might be lost.' He too, not knowing what his mother was up to, had finally written to the Duke of York for his promotion, but Sarah was to let no one call it a job: the general comment in the army had been—a damned shame he did not get it sooner. 'I'll doff my beaver, but no gratitude . . . the balance seems clear between George Prince and Charles Napier. . . . Any man who says its a job shall have a fair downright

English box on the ear.' He apologised for his violence but 'a man is bloody-minded when feverish.' Wellington had sent him home ill of Guadiana fever; as he could barely stand he was really not much good, and he and Blanco were off from Lisbon in the frigate *Fiorenza*.

William, who grew sadly suspicious in old age, thought that Charles had been pushed off from Spain for sinister reasons, and that there was no love for his name on high: one cousin, Edward Fitz-gerald having been in open rebellion, another, Charles Lennox, having fought a duel with the Duke of York, and a third been in hot water for chastening a young royal naval officer on board his ship. There was no reason to think this was so; somebody has to cope with mutinous regiments and Charles still looked quite unfit for active service and was known to be both humane and a disciplinarian. He had taken some while to learn to appreciate Wellington and it may be that Wellington took some while to appreciate him. Certain it is that in later life when the English position in India was in great danger and the East India Company asked Wellington to recommend to them the three best generals in the country, he replied crisply

> Sir Charles Napier
> Sir Charles Napier
> Sir Charles Napier.

In any case there had been no British regiment available for him in the Peninsula, and Wellington had refused to give him a regiment of Portuguese Caçadores on the grounds that he would be killed, so conspicuous would he be among them, and the family had had enough of wounds, so thought their generalissimo. 'The Napiers' Wellington concluded to Beresford, not unfairly, 'always get hit.'

At home in London, William had been most pleasurably hit; though some months of illness had to be endured first. Sarah had been gloomed about him when he first came home: in December 'William's health now gives us the greatest alarm.' Such was his ague and his violent coughing that Dr James Moore 'has taken him into his own house that he may watch him closely . . . his health keeps us in constant alarm'. Henry, on his way home from the Indian Ocean, at least was safe—'he will stay some time, as he belongs to the *Chatham*, which is to be launched in January'. By Christmas William was mending, though still a cause for worry; but of all things Henry had been desperately ill without her knowing about it! Two letters arrived by the same post: in one Henry was terribly ill in the far east and his life despaired of (could this perpetual medical despair about people's chances of survival have been a kind of insurance policy against failure to save them?): in the second letter Henry was miraculously back; arriving in the *Diomede* at Deal before anyone had a minute in which to agonise. He was a sailor with a cousin in every port. At Deal was Admiral Foley, married to Lucy, one of the innumerable Fitzgeralds, who tended Henry until he could be moved to Oxford to be nursed at All Souls by Richard (who can but rarely have got time off from blanket-bathing to do a little work of his own).

'As soon as a few months have set him up again Henry will go to sea, for he is a lieutenant near 2 years past, and we hope to get a good climate for him; for to speak truly, which I may venture to do to such an old friend as you,' Sarah told Susan O'Brien, 'he is well worth preserving and I am not sure if he would not take your fancy more than any of his brothers, having the most gentle tone of voice and manners with the same spirit; not spirits, for the being deprived of family society is a hard situation to affectionate hearts, which I do not think a seaman's life rubs off so well as a soldier's. All hate it (the deprivation), but my *soldiers* have such spirits that it makes them go through all the plagues of war in the most surprising way, and yet both are ill, William with a quartern ague and Charles ague and great weakness; but they are like children, the instant the ague or the bile goes off they forget they have suffered: but fortunately their terrible looks have struck the Duke of York, who said "No, no, I see how it is, you shall not go back yet".' And there were other consolations. 'My 2 sisters, my 2 daughters, my 3 sons are actually round me and tollerably well, dare I complain? No, I must be, I am thankful, grateful.'

By autumn 'Richard is at Edinburgh attending lectures'. (Perhaps the only place with no pillows to smooth.) 'Scotland is a new world to him, and therefore an advantage to see, for the mind opens by knowing variety of characters or rather variety of education which makes character appear different.' Altogether the year was ending on a cheerful note, she delighted to hear of the Christmas party at Redlinch. 'They say great witts jump, of this I can say nothing having no experience in witt, but I am sure great friends do, since you wrote me precisely the sort of letter I wanted from you.'

William had fought at Fuentes d'Onoro with a chalk white face and a bullet still nudging his spinal column, and not many weeks afterwards Wellington had taken a firm line with him and sent him off to Lisbon in his own calèche, en route for home and medical attention; for as George said, he was a merciful man. Shortly before this a young left-wing officer had deserted to the French and been given command of a French company: taken prisoner in a skirmish he had been the butt of a great deal of patriotic English rage; most of the army would have been delighted to see him shot. But Wellington had taken his time. He had made enquiries, and found there was a history of insanity, and sent the poor boy home without publicity or disgrace. (And this, as George pointed out, was all the more remarkable in that the deserting young man was nobody's nephew.) In London, where the doctors had pronounced William's bullet to be immovable, he was seen by the novelist Amelia Opie at a party. William was a novelist's dream: his looks, like George's, were rather on Paul Newman lines. Mrs Opie was suitably impressed. 'By Lady Sarah was one of her sons . . . I never saw a handsomer man! I could not help looking at him.' Very dark, and like 'some Venetian by Titian', Mrs Opie found his manner extremely pleasing. He had, she noted, 'his mother's outline enlarged into manly beauty, and he has such fine dark eyes'. Charles II rode again, with better features and rather more respect for other people's wives. William's notable orbs were shortly to be directed, in a purposeful manner, upon Miss Caroline Fox.

Here was an oasis of delight for Sarah: she sat down to share its delectable waters with her fifty-two-years-standing friend. 'My son aged 26 is to be married this week to the daughter of the little rosy-faced Harry who was running about then'—at Holland House when first she arrived there aged fourteen—'and lisped out his partiality to me, so that when I shall take his Caroline to my arms as my own daughter, I shall only lengthen out the early affection that subsisted so uninterruptedly between her father and me.

'Add to this my knowledge of her character, the likeness it has to my beloved Caroline, *their* friendship, the love she has long acquired in the hearts of Charles, Richard, Louisa, and Emily, and crown that with William's reflected love for her, and you will rejoice that in her latter days your old friend is made more happy than it seemed possible she could ever be again.

' "Is William worthy of her?" you will very properly ask. *She* thinks he is, but less prejudiced judges agree with her. Col. and Mrs.

Bunbury,' (Caroline's elder sister had married Henry Bunbury, nephew and heir of Sarah's first husband), 'Miss Townshend, Mr. and Mrs. Clayton,' (Caroline's mother had been Marianne Clayton), 'Ld Holland and I hope Miss Fox,' (the other Caroline Fox), 'but she was taken by surprise and has not yet made up her mind to its very sudden appearance.' Ste's Caroline Fox, forty-four and unmarried, may have felt that not even a war *à l'outrance* should excuse a young man from a gradual, graceful courtship. She was the doubter; 'the bête noire', William ungraciously called her.

'But she knows not William's sharp decerning character, which has been so matured by hard service; he is not to be deceived or likely to deceive himself.' He had loved Caroline for some while, but had held his horses until he had seen enough of her to be sure she was 'what he calls sterling gold, not spoilt by fashion, prejudice, vanity, or folly, but simple in conduct, wise in acting, tender in feeling'. But William was not half a Lennox for nothing. 'He declared he never would try to persuade a woman he loved to be a beggar, and therefore would ask none who was not able and willing to keep herself in her own fortune. This he has met with, and his orders are to settle it *all* on herself and to add his own small nothing, all to go to her . . . they marry next Saturday I believe. . . . There never was a match that promised better, barring his being a soldier, but her mind is made up to that, and I trust in God that one of my dear sons may now look forward to a happy home which suits their domestic turn, all of them loving home in preference to every other place. I hope, my dear Ly Susan, you will *approve* of this to my heart's content. . . .' Caroline justified William's narrow observation by loving him dearly, bearing him nine children, and copying out seven drafts in longhand of his six-volume masterpiece on the Peninsular War.

There were times in the bitter aftermath of battle when William's soul revolted against war, but a part of him remained permanently enraptured with its *mise en scène*. In January of 1812 the British army began their bombardment of Ciudad Rodrigo under a lowering winter sky. 'Then was beheld a spectacle at once fearful and sublime. The enemy replied to the assailant's fire with more than fifty pieces, the bellowing of eighty large guns shook the ground far and wide, the smoke rested in heavy volumes upon the battlements of the place or curled in light wreaths about the numerous spires, the shells, hissing through the air, seemed fiery serpents leaping from the darkness, the walls crashed to the stroke of the bullet, and the distant mountains faintly returning the sound appeared to mourn over the falling city.' As further preliminaries had involved fireless midwinter nights after days of digging trenches up to the waist in water, all were glad when the moment for attack arrived.

Marmont was on the way, and Wellington could not wait for all his heavy guns to come up from Almeida. His orders were simple. 'Cuidad Rodrigo must be stormed this evening.' It was a moony, frosty night: Grattan of the 88th noticed a kind of fierce severity in men's faces as the storming parties assembled in the gathering darkness and cold. George had volunteered and 'had the honour' of leading the left-hand assault: from nearly half the division who wanted to come with him he selected a hundred from each regiment —'in high spirits and determined that nothing should stop us from carrying the breach'. A senior officer had tried to improve on George's arrangements, but no, Wellington had said, leave him alone, he knows what he is doing.

As the January darkness thickened the attack began. 'I knew if I failed it must be my own fault, as I had at my back three hundred British bayonets, wielded by able hands, and as stout hearts of oak as ever faced the enemy! that I had only to lead, to give the word, and all would be carried by British steel, let the opposition be ever so great. If I fell I should fall as I wished.'

Thus philosophised, George was nearly at the top of the breach, flooded almost as by daylight with whirling French fireballs, when his arm was shot away at the elbow and he was knocked over: there was a moment's check, and George was heard shouting, 'Recollect you are not loaded, push on with the bayonet!' Still shouting them on, and a good deal bruised and trampled in the darkness and confusion, he heard the storm going according to his plan; the men foamed up and over the top like some irresistible tide; the main forces poured through the breach, and soon the shouts of Victory! and England for ever! echoing in the streets reassured George, as he staggered up through the blood and dust. Gurwood, leader of what was known as the forlorn hope, had arrived at the top after being briefly stunned and went on right through Ciudad Rodrigo till he received the sword of the governor of that city, just about to sit down to dinner and greatly surprised at the interruption. 'The milk of human kindness was flowing richly through the veins of these

Englishmen who stopped to draw breath in the breach and gave terms there to Frenchmen' one German eye-witness thought; 'the loss of the besiegers doubled that of the besieged.'

Once through the terrible bloodshed of the ramparts and into the city another passion prevailed, and officers lost control of their men. The same shrewd German observer noted that the English vice was not bloodthirstiness but greed: they went mad ransacking the Spanish houses for things they could not possibly either use or carry home. (It is a strange thing that the Christian Church has banged on down the ages about lust, and largely kept quiet over greed, the one sin against which Christ raised his hand in violence, the one sin that is now destroying the human habitat.)

Friends tied up George's arm with their sashes, a sergeant helped him down off the wall and he went to join the queue outside the surgeon's tent. Here, in the icy darkness, sitting on a stone was General Vandeleur—'I never heard him say or do a harsh thing'—hit in the shoulder. George joined him and they sat together for half an hour or so whilst unencouraging sounds came from the surgeon's tent, and George contemplated for the last time the remains of his puissant right arm.

There was this to be said; it had been hit before. And he had had a kind of fatalism about it. He was going to lose his fin: so sure was he that he had come almost to want to lose it. The fatalism, or the precognition, that haunted so many fighting men and yet seemed in no way to daunt their courage, had been on him; and in the chill of this nervous wait George remembered others who had felt this uncanny foreknowledge as he himself had. Light-headed now with shock and pain and loss of blood, with the reaction from such violent effort, his mind wandered off into the realm of the unaccountable. Was everything ordained already, as the Calvinists said, and the Moslems, and the Hindus? Or was the way we should ourselves ordain things ordained? The lot men guessed at did not bring fear or avoidance or recklessness: it seemed sad but ordinary and necessary, almost in the day's work, as his coming fate had seemed to Nelson as the ships slowly neared each other at Trafalgar. Death, to George Napier's generation and many before, was only an important event in a continuing life, like marriage; subsequent happiness, as in marriage, depending upon the nature of the choice made earlier. They did not, accordingly, shut their eyes to its coming.

William Pakenham, who had been with Charles and George in

their cheerful parties with the Portuguese girls, was another instance of this eerie prescience. Appointed to a ship, he had told the brothers at a farewell dinner in Lisbon, 'I care not where I am sent so that it is not to cruise in Lough Swilly on the Irish coast, for if I go there I am sure I shall be lost.' He would not be laughed out of it; and a few weeks later the ship was sent to Lough Swilly and lost with all hands. 'Poor Pakenham, a gayer or more kind-hearted fellow never wore a blue coat,' George thought. His father had told him of a like experience at the siege of Charlestown. He had a very brave lieutenant whom he found one day in a state of deep silent sadness. He told Donny that every time before being wounded he had had a dream haunted by a peculiar kind of stag. On the previous night four of these strange stags had appeared in his dream, and this time they had turned on him and attacked; he knew he should be killed that day. In vain had Donny tried to reason, to reassure, to laugh him out of it. They went to their posts, and 'the night passed quietly with scarcely a shot fired,' Donny related: their relief arrived in the morning, they were all but back in camp. 'There you are' Donny said, standing within a few inches of him. At that moment four random bullets from the town hit the lieutenant and killed him. He was in the thick of many others, none of whom were touched.

On the other hand, no one ever recounts the times when people have had presentiments of death that are *not* fulfilled.

At length it was George's turn for the knife. He had a friend called Walker, a junior surgeon; he had seen him at work and asked him if he would take his arm off for him, as the senior surgeon, Guthrie, had already taken off so many limbs that his knives were blunted. This request, owing to the niceties of medical etiquette, was refused. The task took twenty minutes, and George, having cursed Guthrie like a trooper while he was doing it, was heard thanking him politely when it was done. He was some while wandering the town before he could find shelter and warmth. All around him Ciudad was being sacked; for men who had seen their comrades blown to pieces before their eyes on the deadly breaches had thrown off all discipline and were helping themselves, though for all their drunkenness they did not kill. 'John Bull, though heartily fond of fighting, is not a man of blood, but he is a greedy fellow and he plundered with all the rapacity of one to whom such liberty is new,' one eye witness reported, and George staggered through men dressed up in French cocked hats and uniforms, strung with ladies' shoes, and waving wine bottles and delightedly clutching hams, bird cages, and empty glass cases. No one could stop them; the officers had had to content themselves with saving lives. Not surprisingly, those Spaniards who could, withdrew behind strong walls and barred their doors, and it was long before George found a roof.

Cheerful sounds attracted him to an inn, 'after stumbling about the suburbs for upwards of an hour'. Here were a lot of soldiers, a warm fire, and his friend Colborne, sitting on a stool and in great pain with a bullet in his shoulder: this seasoned veteran burst into tears when he saw magnificent George with a stump where his right arm had been. On the top floor George found a bed into which he fell and was delirious for twenty-four hours. His fever was not soothed by the groans of General Craufurd; for poor Black Bob was dying in great anguish from chest wounds in the room below, and harrowing George by sending up hourly messages to know how he did, praising his behaviour in the breach and regretting he should never see him again. 'I never shall forget this: I should be an unfeeling brute if I did.' Though clever and dashing as they come, Craufurd's sullen and incalculable temper had at times called down curses from his men; but charitable George thought him in a fair way to master this defect, had he been allowed a little longer to live.

Still in high fever, George was borne out next day in a blanket, and passing through his own regiment 'I was greeted by many a kind exclamation of approbation and pity from the men who had so gallantly supported me in the assault. Nothing is so sweet, so soothing to a wounded officer. . . . You may perhaps laugh at it, but it made me cry with pleasure and joy to find myself among the men . . . looking at me with every expression of kindly feeling.' Wellington came to see him, told him he was highly pleased with him, and that he was made lieutenant-colonel and given a medal, and that his battalion of the 52nd were going home. 'No commander ever felt more for his officers and men,' George had thought with a swelling heart. 'He never failed to visit his sick and wounded when it was possible.' There had been mutterings the winter before when Wellington had some French deserters shot: they had signed on in the British army in order to get away from the Spanish prison hulks at Cadiz; and back at the front were unable to resist a midnight attempt to swim the river and get back to their countrymen. But, George insisted, Wellington was kind as well as 'of transcendent abilities'; it was his 'short manner of speaking and stern look, which people mistake for want of heart'.

'My dear Bill,' wrote Charles MacLeod from Ciudad Rodrigo to William, still at home and with the surgeons having another probe at his backbone for the Casal Noval bullet, and anxious for firsthand news of George, 'your extraordinary and inimitable brother does well; he beats you all out and out—in as good spirits as ever I saw him, writing letters and impatient for soup, which he drank with his left hand. . . . Adieu my dear Bill. I hope you are getting well, but sick enough to keep you quiet for some time'; for MacLeod himself, thin and poor physiqued and delicate, but 'with enough heart and spirit for two', was off with the army for an assault on Badajoz, the huge walled city that still guarded the southern way to Madrid, and had a shrewd idea of what that performance would be like.

By slow stages George and Colborne proceeded via Coimbra to Lisbon, both still in pain and some fever. At Lisbon Colborne was too ill to go further, and George sailed down the Tagus river in the *Agincourt*, 74, without him. They spent six weeks beating up against contrary gales to get to Plymouth; during which George, no sailor, and unbalanced by his armless state, probably endured the worst yet.

XVI

The next *coup de foudre* to strike George was a pleasant explosion on his home ground north of the Border. His impetuous courtship of Miss Craig was as characteristic of him as the deliberately controlled pace of William's advance on Caroline Fox had been of William.

Margaret Napier, pretty, newly married and just nineteen, was fresh from the chill and regularity of Edinburgh life, and felt a little guilty at sitting down in the morning for such an indulgence as letter writing. 'My dearest Friend,' she addressed her stepmother, from London, 'there is a great deal of time for doing as one likes here, so do not think when you see this long sheet that I am scribbling when I should be giving my attention to others.' Even a place like London did not immediately induce a well brought up Scots girl to start playing the giddy goat, but she *must* just tell a very kind step-mother what a relief it had all been.

'I cannot tell you how delighted I am with Lady Sarah, and how very kind she is to me, she is so affectionately so, and in her whole manner to her family there is a tenderness and indulgence I have never seen before; so very mild, and when she finds fault, or any little thing happens which she cannot approve of, her opinion is given in a manner quite her own. Then her approbation is so warm, and the smallest thing done right and well-timed gives her so much pleasure; I perfectly see how her approbation should be felt by her sons as their greatest reward. She seems very cheerful and perfectly happy, and draws everyone around her; in short, there is something about her that seems to soften and improve every one within reach of the influence of her manners.

'Louisa has not been quite well for two days; she is as kind and friendly as possible, and I like her much—very showy in appearance, and certainly more like a woman of fashion than anyone I have yet seen, though a great many of the friends of the family have called for me. I shall not here give a string of names, but shall only say I am delighted with my reception; it is quite cordial, and I have felt more at ease than I thought it possible I could in a room full of lords and ladies.'

Her clothes, so rapidly gathered together, had also passed muster. 'I even felt satisfied I was making a very good appearance, and Lady Sarah introduces me so kindly by the appelation of "dear Margt", or "my dear daughter, George's wife", or something that at once shows the footing I am on with her. George is so beloved too that seeing him so happy seems assurance enough of my title to their regard.' Colonel Lorrence (sic) had told George that 'we go on the Staff very soon, and he believes the northern district, Yorkshire, but it is not fixed. George, I knew, was not quite at ease about accepting the situation, and Lorrence has in the kindest manner set aside all his doubts, assuring him that he has a full right to remain at home, and that it cannot be mistaken by anyone for hanging back.'

And William's fashionable wife turned out not to be terrifying at all. 'I am very much pleased indeed with Caroline, and we are quite friends already. She is quite superior to what I was led to expect; her manner is innocent, kind, and engaging, at least towards me, and to all my husband's family; then she is very sensible and well informed, and by no means so silent as George represented her; she has quite taken to me, which perhaps adds to the favourableness of the impression. Indeed, my dearest Mrs. Craig, I am surrounded by kindness, and feel received into the very bosom of George's family and whole conversations.'

The Moore family were friends of the Craigs, and 'they seem so glad to see me, and have held me higher than I can possibly deserve ... they have been so kind in talking favourable of us all.' Old Mrs Moore, mother of the hero who had died three years past at Corunna, had sent for her and soothed her remaining fears, and talked highly of her father, and assured her 'how kindly Lady S. had expressed herself towards me all along'. She seemed to understand what a plunge it had all been, but told Margaret she could dispense all her apprehensions. Even tough and worldly Holland House approved: 'my father is held very very high from Mr. Allen's account of him.' The only jar was that George's arm was threatening a little, 'but I trust it will not break out.

'You would be quite pleased if you could see how completely the style of this family corresponds with your own: table, and appearance in every way. In short, I can hardly call up my former feelings or fears. This morning I have been sitting for some time quietly with Lady Sarah, and am convinced that I can meet all her wishes with regard to her son; it is impossible that rank or fortune could for one moment enter her mind.' (Well done, Sarah.)

All the same, Margaret was not going to forget all she had been taught, and burst out into wild extravagance. 'Louisa and I, and Lady S. too, have had a great deal of conversation about our menage, and I am to have two women servants: less cannot be attempted in England, particularly on the Staff, but, to comfort one for the extravagance, one is to work to be a complete dressmaker and to take her share of the housework besides, and I have one of that description in view. Louisa says that washing and saving dress-maker's bills will make it a great saving on the whole.'

It was all smashing; and Lady Sarah was just going to write to Mrs Craig (and perhaps be nice about Margaret to her parents); but a little pang of homesickness would creep in all the same, into the most unbounded happiness. Edinburgh was so far! And there were her two half-brothers. 'Keep up the remembrance of me I do intreat with my little boys: I cannot reconcile to giving them up, often thinking of them so long as my greatest interest. I write to you not to my father, because to you I tell every sort of thing, and you can cull for him.' Signing her new name was still an excitement, and with best and dearest love to them all, she was theirs, Mt Napier.

Sarah's sight had wholly gone: she had now to subsist on friendship, affection, and glory; of which there was quite a lot about just now. Wellington had written to her after the storming of Ciudad Rodrigo, to tell her himself of the loss of George's arm. 'Having such sons I am aware that you expect to hear of these misfortunes, which I have had more than once to communicate to you; and notwithstanding your affection for them, you have so just a notion of the value of the distinction which they are daily acquiring for themselves by their gallantry and good conduct, that their misfortunes do not make so great an impression upon you.' Sitting upright in a stiff Georgian chair in the little rented house in London, Sarah would listen to Charles's lively and amusing scrawls, to Wellington's measured prose, with its strengthening refusal to pity. She appreciated that, and was all for glory; but how could the Duke, or any other man, know how it felt to hear that one's darling son had had his arm hacked off? From such close range she could not see that a great gate into Spain was broken down, that Madrid would be taken in time to hearten the desperate Russians driven out of Moscow and beyond, that what Fichte called 'a Europe sunk in the abyss of one arbitrary will', was on the way to resurrection. And if she had, though mind and spirit would rejoice, the heart would still cry out My son, my son.

She turned to Susan, who had unfailingly understood everything about her except her marriage. 'The very great honor that my son George has acquired by leading up 300 volunteers to the top of the breach, he and his lieutenant, Gurwood, being the first men on the top of the wall, will am I told by everybody entirely compensate him for the loss of his arm. I shall be glad if he comes home to tell me so himself. . . . The danger and loss of an arm fills me with horror, but I am assured by his brother William that he will not consider it so, and that no man in the army will bear it better. I will therefore tell you all the few consolations I can find . . . there can be no doubt of the necessity of the amputation, that arm was much weakened by former wounds, and I have a letter from Lord March, dated the third evening after the operation, with a message from two surgeons of the Regt assuring me there was not the least danger, and Ld March says he appears in the greatest spirits, and that he was to be removed to

Ld March's house at the headquarters in Galligos. Adieu, I thought
an account from me however short would be better than none. . . .'

She would ask her step-daughter to read out the letters from Spain
again; and unmarried Louisa, helpful, joke-seeing, and rather over-
dressed, would comply; with a pride and pleasure in her half-
brothers nearly as great as Sarah's own. One letter had been sent on
by Charles. 'He did it in a style second to none that ever went up a
breach—Believe me with the greatest veneration for everybody that
bears your name, Charles Rowan.' But many had come straight to
Sarah. 'Everybody in the army admires his gallantry,' Charles March
had written; and Charles Stewart had brought in her other sons as
well, which was best of all; his was handsomer almost than Wellington's letter, which was saying a lot—'His conduct equalled that of
his brother Charles, to surpass it would be hard; but the gallantry of
the Napiers is as proverbial in the army as the fame of our chief.'
Laying it on a bit thick, maybe; but how soothing when one thought
of George with a lifetime of one-handedness in front of him. Arm or
glory? George himself would give an unhesitating answer.

And soon, to the joy of William's marriage, was added the pleasure
of George's. For another of George's dear friends, William Craig,
had died of fever caught in the Alemtejo marshes, and he had a Scots
family whom George had always meant to visit to tell them of their
son's last months of life; and now that his lost arm had made a long
leave necessary, he had time. After his six weeks passage from Lisbon
to Plymouth in the *Agincourt* 74, Captain Kent, and a month of
basking in Sarah's affection and care, George took the Edinburgh
coach and set off for the north. Here, in the space of forty-eight hours
spent with her family, he fell madly in love with the beautiful and
intelligent daughter of the house. Nineteen-year-old Margaret Craig,
cautious but kind, was quite unable to resist gorgeous George with
his out-going heart, his red coat, and his empty sleeve. Not yet had
dawned the days of obligatory bridesmaids and fuss, and they were
married at the end of the week.

'I like her much' Susan O'Brien was told by Sarah, 'and George is
happy tho' not rich, yet not quite a beggar, for their present income
is more than £800 pr anm. . . . I am well off to have found uncommon
good sense, a well-informed education tho' not polished, a perfect
temper, a disposition to love me because I am the beloved mother of
him whom she perfectly adores, so judge if I may not be very thankful
that a sudden match of fancy should turn out so well.'

Appointed to York, and urged by the military authorities to stay there, George was unable to resist returning to Spain after eight months, on succeeding to the first battalion of the 52nd. Luckily for him he was ambidextrous, and could write and use a sword with his left hand, though firing was difficult and managing a horse *and* sword not easy either. 'My dearest girls,' George instructed his daughters years later, 'if you marry soldiers or sailors, like your mother, never permit your feelings so much to get the better of your duty as to influence or try to influence your husbands in acting contrary to what their honour, character, duty point out.' For Margaret, after weeping buckets, had said that of course he must go.

In Bermuda, no longer able to contrive to be foremost, Charles was suffering a return of his blue devils. He had joined his new regiment, the 102nd, in Guernsey, where it was training for Spain, having just returned from Australia via Cape Horn, the first regiment in history to circumnavigate the globe, though this may not have consoled it, as it bucketed through the roaring forties. It had however mutinied in Botany Bay, sensibly wishing to remain and settle there, and was not in very admirable trim; and all, from Charles downwards, were furious at being sent offstage at this dramatic moment, and to Bermuda of all dead ends. Only the behaviour of his horse had given Charles real pleasure at the Guernsey manoeuvres—'at a sham fight our general in the flush of victory got with his ADC into a field where Blanco was feeding'. Blanco had jammed them up in a corner, they had drawn their swords but to no effect, 'setting his ears back he kept them prisoner while the fight went on: at last they were found in durance, but could not be released for he would only surrender them to my servant. Was there ever such a matchless horse!' He was glad Sarah had at last sold Celbridge, but 'You owe me nothing, pay others. *Je suis bien riche*, and am going to buy a cow for myself which will give suck on the voyage to some soldiers wives and children—hang the imps, poor things.' He was not looking forward to the journey, but sailors had always been excellent fellows to him. 'Some army bucks complain of them, because, forgetting they are in a man's house when in his ship, they give themselves airs, and are taken down.'

'Plymouth, 28th July. Forced in here by stress of weather, and my seasickness horrible: with enough to make the pot boil in England, no other country should see my pretty face. Unable to eat, my spirits are low, and six weeks, perhaps two months, of this before me; oh murder! We have six ladies on board and two on the point of being confined. Poor women! Why do I complain? Jonathan [current slang for an American] has declared war. We reckon ourselves equal to two frigates; three we should fight hard, and even four would have a tug; we have seven hundred men on board.' But he would rather dig potatoes at home than give Jonathan a licking—'an American war is a miserable thing'.

After defeating at Plymouth an attempt by officialdom to send 500 troops on a two months' journey across the Atlantic without bedding, he arrived at Bermuda on September 12th. 'Island beautiful to look at, but food and all things but rogues scarce,' and the ensuing weeks did not encourage him. Nor was the Governor impressive—'yellow fever, starvation, and minor evils under the reign of King Horsford, a man extremely dull, and feeble of mind . . . no man ever gets yes or no from him.' In October came the news of the Salamanca victory; Charles felt more than ever frustrated to be out of it all. 'These glorious deeds in Spain make me turn with disgust to the dullness of drill, and it is hard to rouse myself to duty: yet duty must be done . . . my greatest fear is that the idleness of others will corrupt my gents.' He was disgusted to hear that only two Spaniards had been killed at Salamanca and four wounded. 'A decisive battle fought in the very heart of their country for their liberty! Thousands of British fell. . . . Could a friendly Spanish army have fought such a battle in an inland county of England, and only six Englishmen fall?' He could not know what execution the tireless guerilleros were doing to French communications and to French morale.

But by November Charles was beginning to like Bermuda, though he found himself the only person in his regiment who did, with its 'wet climate, nothing to eat, no fruit, no vegetables, no wine, no good company'. Why were there no vegetables? He started gardening, drawing, reading, planning better harbours, more agriculture; why couldn't Horsford get a move on? 'About 14 whales are caught each season, a good one being worth £300. The whale steak is like veal, some like it better, few find it any different.' That would be something to build on, if anyone had the energy. In December the news of George's marriage delighted him, and 'you may now, in time, have a dear animal of some kind with you' he told Sarah, 'instead of being left in your old age by a pack of vagabond itinerant sons.' He occupied himself with writing; sticky with heat, his pen covered page after page; on the principles of war, care of men, lessons learnt from the French, conquest—'when a great nation has conquered another nation it should never despoil it of its treasures of art' (Napoleon had gutted Italy)—care and kindness for the people over whose country war is fought, Alexander the Great, Hannibal, the use and equipment of cavalry, disposal of booty—'should be made over in presence of the army: the Romans did so, and they clearly understood war better than we do'—training of officers, baggage of an army, freedom, Gibbon, Rienzi Gabini, languages, lawyers, strange dreams, other nations, the press. On he went, through the year, with the crickets shrieking in the mild darkness, and the smell of the cedars floating in. 'The more I see of the countries of the world the more certain it appears to me that morality, public and private, is the sine qua non for good government; and the sine qua non of morality is a free press . . . whatever evils spring from a free press will in the long run be remedied by a free press . . . in all things human there exists a perfect arrangement, a truth, because God creates not imperfections. I speak as a believer not a sceptic. . . . A free press is an emphatic term for unceasing enquiry, unceasing pursuit of truth and right, unceasing exposure of wrong. My opinion is that if the earth is to be regenerate and goodwill towards men to be universal, which I do not altogether believe, it is by a free press that the Almighty means to work. War indeed it may put an end to, if it gains ground all over the earth.' From war he turned to booty, and his sardonic turn of mind bubbled uppermost. 'Plunder or booty is absolutely needful in some shape or other to urge the soldiers to enterprise, because interest is the great stimulant of human nature. A guinea is of all heroes, of all politicians, of all clever fellows, the most heroic, the most politic, the cleverest: he has no superior except two guineas.'

All the same, 'books do not make up for the want of curiosities to be found in other lands'. At times Bermuda was claustrophobic: 'an island so small that the smell of cedar is overpowered by that of rum.' 'We have the curses of banishment without its freedom, or its instruction, or the comfort of being "suffering patriots". Our officers and men sigh for Botany Bay,' Charles wrote on New Year's Day of 1813. Yet the boys were coming on; and for Sarah's diversion he sat down to write reports on some of his young officers—'A. is a fine young fellow and will make a good soldier: a little of a spoiled child now, and don't like drill so well as the Opera; but you may tell mamma that he is going on very well, and stands a fair chance of losing the genteel slouch he has at present. He is a very fine lad indeed, and no one is more convinced of that than himself: but I like him because he don't sulk at drill though clearly to him a bore. H. grows tall, broad, fat, ruddy, attentive and steady: he is one of the best subalterns in the regiment, makes a point of being seldom in the wrong, and of never admitting it if he is. I make counterpoints, of proving to him that he is in the wrong; which proofs though in black and white before his eyes he always rejects: but then he notes down for himself that he was in the wrong and does right another time which is just what I want. K. wants promotion. Is one of the best officers in the regiment: he is nearly six feet high, is in love, and in debt: what greater claims can an ensign have? L. is always wrong, but means to be always right, and he will be so at last.'

Hearing Charles's letters was a great amusement. 'Family connections alone give comfort in old age, when the heart clings to relationship with redoubled tenderness,' Sarah had felt, as early as 1799; and now, as the long long war drew to its climax, she was growing further from the great world she had enjoyed so much, and was unable to resist an occasional mild pontification on that subject. 'I perceive that their comforts' she told Susan, referring to people of their own age, 'are so entirely guided by their situations in their own families that it evinces the truth that all is vanity and vexation of spirit except adherence to what is right, and as family affections are virtues so they meet with their reward in old age, and the mere followers of the world remain sadly neglected.' She found herself 'compleatly and pleasantly occupied with George and his Scotch wife, who have lived some time with me and are now at York, where he is on the Staff . . . you know I could not allow myself to be so spoilt by my dear Caroline as to expect to find another like her.' All the same she liked Margaret immensely, and thought herself very lucky. 'Louisa Napier has been really ill a long time by the drawing of a strong tooth, but is better. My sister Leinster is not well, and naturally low at parting with her grandson Edward Fitzgerald, gone to Spain.' Was everyone gone to Spain, or going?

Neither in her letters or in the thoughts of others does Sarah sound like a blind woman. At first she 'did so hate to sit in the dark, musing', but when the operation failed she came to treat her blindness as if it did not exist. Her sons assured her that any fame they had come by was due to the widespread knowledge of her own fortitude—'most of our friends know you, and the firmness with which you support your misfortunes. . . . Many officers are as brave and have more talents than us without meeting with the same attention.' She loved still to go about; no longer able to bask in her own beauty, she could bask now in the glory of her sons. As she grew older, her pleasure in the very young increased, as it generally does. Caroline was gone and Cecilia was gone; something also had gone from her sons, away in the world with their right hands showing them terrible things. But there were great-nephews and great-nieces, the Bathursts' little girl Georgina, 'something very winning in the warmth of a childish mind, she combines infantile zeal with a much older judgement'; and there was Isabella Fitzgerald who had just lost her baby and whose husband was due back in Spain; they were at Weymouth and would Susan be kind to them? 'He is Col. Viscomte Chabot of the Ninth Cavalry. As a foreigner, yet born, educated, naturalized and married in Ireland, still he feels such gratitude for his preferment that a fine spirit carries him out again, I fear to his death; he is in very delicate health if not bad health, but one must make the best of it to her poor soul. I am sure you would be a great comfort to her at the sad parting hour.'

A year later there was George Lennox, quartered at Dorchester and knowing no one in the neighbourhood; he was her nephew Richmond's son, would Susan be kind to him? 'He is a perfect stranger even to the officers of his own regiment, the 9th Dragoons . . . I have prepared him to expect so little from you, that every attention you show him will be an unexpected favor, so I hope it will not be troublesome.' Claiming Susan's and her husband's kindness for him, she added a description, seeming not to have lost her perceptiveness with her sight. 'He has been, very unwisely in my mind, kept at Westminster School till 18, and I suspect that there is a great deal to ammend in his ideas, which have been allowed to run in their own way as a full-grown man at school in a metropolis. All his family call him shy and childish, but boys who know him better say he is up to anything! I know not where the truth lies, but to us women he appears handsome, pleasant, a little sudden, and too tenacious of his opinions for good company, having a horror of being advised or directed, in which he rivals his brother Ld. March, who left school about the same age to be Aide-de-Camp to his father in Dublin, where the Dss tried to civilise March, and made him very obstinate to her and to all appearance, but in fact his natural good sense and very delightfull heart led him to addopt everything that was right. The Duke then fearing a Ld. Lt.'s son would be spoilt, sent him off to Lord Wellington, and there never was a son of whom a parent had more reason to be proud of than this dear and most delightfull March. His father naturally expects George will follow his steps and has kept him in Dublin to polish him a little . . . you will judge him fairly and with your usual perspicacity, and I should like to know your opinion of him *truly* given for myself and civilly given for the Dss of Richmond, who loves to be flattered about her children as most mothers do, but she has been spoilt because those who have grown up do deserve much praise. . . .

'You will find that though lately come from Ireland George has not been sufficiently dipped in the Shannon to be perfectly at his ease, besides which the recent loss of his brother (who was unfortunately killed by falling from the rigging into the sea at Minorca) has left a natural impression of lowness upon his mind, which one wishes the change of scene from his afflicted family should remove. Poor Henry Lennox was a very fine boy of 14 on board Captain Codrington's ship, who wrote the Duke so feeling a letter on the occasion that it has been a great consolation to his parents. The poor Dss of Richmond's mind was sadly worn out by a month of close attendance in her mother's melancholy sick-chamber; however, she received great comfort in the latter end by seeing her mother express much gratification in having all her children round her, in seeing the Duke of Gordon very kind to her, and in the Dss's perfect resignation to her death.' (Sarah never quite lost interest in William Gordon's family.)

'The news of poor Henry's sudden death is a shock of so different a nature, that she is very much to be pitied: indeed, it is the first she hast lost of fourteen children.' (Was infant mortality looking up?) 'I am still in expectation of my son George's arrival, who very probably will have met William just landed at Lisbon, so whatever news comes from Badajos I am sure none of my sons have been there, but my affection for my dear nephew Ld March keeps up my anxiety on the full stretch, for he is terribly like his cousins in contriving to be foremost on all occasions.

'We have discovered that one leads a much more dissipated life by being devoted to a large family and to friends than by what is called living in the world . . . we are in constant and very pleasant occupation.'

*

In the August of 1812 Black Charlie, now Captain R.N., was on the move; in command of H.M. Ship *Euryalus*; this time not to Spain but following Captain James Gordon in the *Sea Horse* up the Potomac river, warping, sailing and bumping their way towards Washington. Going ashore through the wooded country, they were given glasses of peach brandy by an American farmer who seemed to have little idea of what was going on, but begged the Britishers not to make off with his negro slaves. His two daughters, Black Charlie disappointedly noted, were 'rather uncouth and homely'. The garrison at Alexandria surrendered at the first shot; and an evening or so later the squadron saw the glow of great flames blazing beyond the curve of the river: Washington had capitulated to the British forces who had set the public buildings and the arsenal on fire. Black Charlie disapproved: everyone knew that this action, in full summer, was in reprisal for the American burning of an entire Canadian township in mid-winter; but behaving barbarously ourselves was no way to teach others not to be barbarians. A strong British guard had been put round Washington's house at Mount Vernon, Black Charlie noted with approval. It was, after all, a gentleman's house: the Washingtons were respectable squires from Northamptonshire, bearing on their modest coat of arms an interesting device of stars and stripes. (Now so soon to fly over the moon, it had been first chipped in the local stone on their small midland manor of Sulgrave near Banbury.)

On their way down the squadron was attacked. 'The Americans fought under a white flag bearing the words Free Trade and Sailor's Rights and behaved remarkably well, but their efforts were useless' Black Charlie reported, a thought patronizingly; and by September the 27th the squadron and prizes were well away in the open sea. Captain Gordon received a K.C.B. and Black Charlie a glancing bullet in the back of the neck from an American sharpshooter.

In Bermuda the days wore on. The high collar of Charles's red coat chafed him, boots and breeches irked his limbs in the sticky heat. Do what he would, the men were drinking hard in their boredom and frustration: the company on the island was not conducive to jollity; most of them had never moved out of their islands and never wanted to. 'There is a large lake, seventeen fathoms deep in every part, and cutting away a little earth would render it one of the most perfect

harbours in the world: it is called Harrington's Sound. . . . The soil
is favourable for cultivation, but the indolence of the people is great,
and everyone lives by petty traffic.' The blacks were musical, but idle
too and drunk: 'in short what slaves must be'. Bermudian whites
were ill-looking, but—at last a ray of light—the women were pretty.

The shopkeepers were fearfully grand, and immediately affronted
if you called their store a shop; butter was three shillings a pound,
and you had to bow and scrape to get served, listen to a long speech,
and not argue with his 500% profit on eggs and candles. The soldiers
went hungry: Charles gave them the full government allowance of
flour instead of selling some, and bought proper fuel for baking and
was known as baker Napier. At least the regiment was coming on.
'My gents are now good, and proud of their military knowledge,
which keeps up the military spirit. But to what end is all this work?
To be starved in Bermuda, and become pioneers when tools come
from England: it is hateful to think of. Every officer of mine, except
three young ones, can now exercise a battalion, yet . . . in one year
the men will be ditch-diggers! How can we pester men with drill for
that end? I only do it to keep them from drink and myself from rust.'
Yet 'these battles [in Spain] keep me cock a hoop despite of reason'.

All around, on the dazzling coral, an underwater world of inconceivable beauty flashed and trembled unregarded, like a kingdom of
heaven unperceived. To the sweating troops Bermuda was no paradise of colour and gleam, of cedar and breeze, but a death trap to life
and hope; damp with spray and mist, riddled with fever and inertia,
with languid blacks and scrounging shopkeepers; it was a place where
glory failed and boredom clamped down like an everlasting fog;
where time stood still and yet where the grave insistently gaped:
'consumption's throne is here: the Bermudians all die of that hateful,
horrid, cursed disorder'. 'King' Horsford went on as usual. 'He
seldom speaks, never to the purpose, and is indecisive on all occasions.' Yet he was very pompous. 'Poor man he tries to look sensible,' Colonel Lloyd said, 'and no man can do more: he never
succeeds indeed, but how can he help it?' 'Oh to come home for the
rest of my life and drive old Blanco in a buggy!' Charles mourned.
If he must be far abroad he would like to be governor of Botany Bay.
'Man! thou art certainly vile: let me speak of my cow. She gave milk
during the voyage for all the women and children on board the ship.
She has a fine little calf, and there are hungry fellows about me who
wish to kill it.' Not on your life, she was to be allowed to grow up

and give milk like her mum, even if Henry had to fetch back a bull from Nova Scotia in his frigate. Charles went to sea with Henry and —typically—was at once assaulted by a hurricane. Henry's captain was ashore and he saved the ship with great skill, many others being sunk or stranded.

And why, just when Napoleon's power was beginning to crumble, his armies thinning and the terrible weight of encircling sea-power beginning to press upon him, must the Americans need intervene? A long while they'd stay independent if Bonaparte conquered all Europe! They were casting sheep's eyes at the empty plains of Canada, largely undefended and affording a tempting prize now that Mamma Britannia was at full stretch in Europe. A desultory sea war had begun, and several British ships, outgunned and outmanned, were beaten in single ship actions—events which had no bearing upon the main war, but which caused at least some of the hard-pressed soldiers in the Peninsula to grin sardonically: the Navy had been too big for its boots since Trafalgar. Charles was not of these. 'Yankees fight well and are gentlemen in their mode of fighting. Decatur refused Cardon's sword, saying Sir, you have used it so well I should be ashamed to take it from you. Though much abused they are really fine fellows. One, an acquaintance of mine, has just got the Macedonian: he was here a prisoner, and dined with me.'

The second unfortunate outbreak was not war with America but yellow fever, infinitely more menacing. A vicious circle locked the troops; for fear of this dreaded and generally fatal scourge the men drank to excess; and excessive drink weakened them to a point where they became more prone to the disease. 'The drunkeness of my regiment is beyond endurance' Charles felt in February. He kept them exercised, bathed, and as far as was possible within the narrow limits of the island, amused: nothing kept them from the rum. 'After doing all that was possible I warned them that the lash would be used, for drink was killing them.' He had always loathed the lash; its use was only possible as a life-saver. Nursing a friend through yellow fever, he was profoundly depressed by the death of the friend's wife just as he seemed to be recovering. Not even the arrival of Henry, in command of his fine frigate, had cheered him. 'Peace is not for us on earth, at least not for those who love more than themselves. Is not this enough to terrify one from marriage? Who can dare to be in love?' The suddenness, the danger, the ferocious climax and agonising death of the disease chiselled at all their nerves. (We can never long enough or loud enough pay thanks to medical science.) 'You cannot imagine the dread here created by the fever: terror is visible with the most determined fellows. Not being one who expected to have the fever, my mind has not been tried like those who have: but even those who had no fears were depressed in spirit beyond description.'

The drinking and the deaths went on through February and March. Everything irritated Charles, even the news that Lord Camden had been made a marquess at the same time as Wellington; for Lord Camden it was who had refused to allow Aunt Louisa Conolly to visit her dying nephew, Edward Fitzgerald, in prison in Dublin Castle, though she had gone down on her knees to him. He was 'a stupid despot', and it simply debased the currency of honours to give him the same one as Wellington—'a hero, a defender of two countries, and the greatest living ornament of Great Britain and Ireland' Charles grumbled.

He poured it all out into the ever sympathetic, ever interested ears of Sarah and Louisa—'We buried a poor ensign and the ceremony from being at night was more depressing. All present except myself, went to a party to cheer their spirits.' But Charles, in some ways a glutton for punishment, would not do this. He lay in bed while one candle burnt itself down and 'the snuff of another grew as long as my nose,' wrestling with his daemon. 'At midnight my lowness was overcome: then quoth I, Lo, I am master, let me sleep. It is easy to nerve myself in such cases, after Corunna: but I feel myself failing in self-command as to anger. It is good to be in a passion intentionally; very bad to be unintentionally, and that has grown on me from the brutal drunkenness of my men.'

'Pat fears Odium for getting his comrades into trouble, more than punishings. He does some *bloody mischief* in his cups, but it is horrible to flog him when you know he is as sorry as possible himself. There are however some ruffians: One of the 98th was lately wounded by me with a bayonet, and beaten besides, which saved him from a flogging. Before my eyes the ruffian, after beating his wife—he was not drunk, she had merely contradicted him—gave her a kick which absolutely lifted her from the ground, and then, before he could be reached, jumped twice upon her breast with thick shoes, leaping high up to crush her.' An attack upon a woman always drove Charles perfectly wild. 'Had he struck me I would have killed him on the spot, and even wished he had given me occasion . . . had you heard the horrible shrieks of the woman until her breath was stamped out!' In calmer moments he reflected that the Irish 'with all their sins are fine soldiers'. He was encouraging them to work their fury off in boxing bouts—'Oh Pat thou art a very odd fish.' William thought that salt meat, and a monotonous existence when the world was everywhere convulsed, were strong incitements to drink.

By the end of March the fever was over, but lowness continued— 'would we could remove anxiety like bile. My friend Stewart is dead: I wonder how he likes it? I am alone, for Henry is on board, which is not amiss, as he makes me idle when business is necessary to keep me up; besides his mad spirits are too much: not that my lowness is apparent, others are not damped by me, if hanging is my fate you shall have a joke at the gallows and probably not a decent one.' Through April he rumbled on exhaustedly: pestilence had been a new experience and must have tautened his ever responsive nerves like bowstrings. Had the English settled yet whether Napoleon Bonaparte was to be boiled or roasted? he mocked in May. 'Everyone says he is done for at last. As to the Yankees; if you wish to know American politics, read Cobbett: all Americans acknowledge him to be master of the subject.' Even Sarah's tales of a happy Christmas spent at Castletown brought only a momentary gleam—'A year's pay to have seen aunt dance at Christmas—the idea is delightful. God bless her. Oh, my wish is to be dancing with those I love . . . and to pitch my sword where it ought to be—with the devil. Gardening from morning to night would be my occupation if there was anyone to command the regiment: it is a madness with me.' Why had nature made him love such things, and 'the sweet red and blue birds that swarm around, and women's company, more than the sublime pleasure of cutting people's throats, and teaching young men to do so?'

'Henry is wrong, I would not be tired of home. My craving for rest is such that twenty years would hardly serve to satisfy me.' He could accept hardship and danger with great cheerfulness but inactivity sent him up the wall.

'What a cursed life is a soldiers, no object, no end, without *appui* for head or heart, unless that unnatural one of military fame, which to a British soldier is so trifling that it is not worth gaining.' It was the old insoluble military problem: no one without an active nature could or would be a soldier; yet how employ that part of his life that must perforce be inactive? Sailors, however cramped, had that permanent and lively enemy, the sea: must use a wariness against wind and weather that permitted no slackening of attention. On this far island soldiers felt but passengers: 'Bermuda is a ship in the ocean without the feeling that the journey must end.' He was still ill and exhausted, doubting his power to tackle another campaign: still divided and driven, ambitious and home-loving.

Bellyachings fell to the lot only of Sarah and Louisa: Charles's ennuis were known only at home. Charles Robertson, a gunner who became his friend in Bermuda, derived a very different impression, the reverse side of this dual nature. 'There was such earnestness of character,' he wrote of Charles, 'such a high estimate of his profession, such enthusiastic stern devotion, that he could not fail to influence all who had a spark of chivalry in their nature. He made soldiers of all under him, and had the rare quality of rendering the most familiar intercourse compatible with absolute authority. His men he was wont to address individually as comrades . . . with the fraternity that should exist among brother soldiers; but he held the true sceptre of command, mental superiority . . . there was no part of a soldier's duty which he could not teach, and with infinite care, and a peculiar happy manner he taught.'

The obliging Americans were about to effect Charles's cure. Rumours of expeditions against their continent were now to be heard. 'To be afloat with a thousand light infantry and two pieces of cannon and allowed to land where it pleased me and be off again is my wish. A force of that kind might pay itself, not by plunder, which leads to every dreadful crime, but by contributions levied by the magistrates.' The war against Napoleon was saving America just as it was saving Europe, if the Americans could only see it. 'The King has the right to make the enemy defray the expenses of war, and it would be delightful to have the Americans paying taxes for us. I am not a hater of Yankees though, they are fine fellows; liars it is said, but so are we. You English wise ones hold Yankee cheaper than he merits, you take him for a dollar when in truth he is a doubloon.'

By the end of the month of May rumours became certainties. 'Sir Sidney Beckwith has come with a force, to "whop" the Yankees. I go second in command, and am in most excellent tranquil spirits, having much to do.'

The event brought disillusionment. 'We were five months cruising along that hostile coast, acting with so much absurdity and so like buccaneers that I should be ashamed to refer to it had I not protested with disgust against everything that was done' Charles wrote to a friend nearly forty years later. Even at the time the goings on seemed to him pretty silly, the arguments between admirals and generals and the consequent sulks. The rebuff at the landing on Craney Island was due to just this: after it Charles himself had been able to insist on having complete command on shore and giving complete obedience on board. He found no difficulties: 'I was 5 months on board the *San Domingo* 74, always acting with navy officers and so far from quarrelling we never had a difference; on the contrary I there formed some of the most intimate friendships I ever had.' Forty years on he noted that the inter-service problem had still not been settled and led to unnumbered failures in efficiency.

'My fear is' he wrote on June 1st 'that my gents may be too eager: all young soldiers are dangerous in that way. The marines, being ever on board ship, are necessarily under-drilled, and the foreigners under me are *duberous*. Fight these last shall, all men fight when they begin, but delay enables rogues to evaporate.' (This happened; the bulk of the free French troops deserted and disappeared into the American hinterland, having enlisted just for the free ride.) 'My self-confidence makes me wish for the chief command; yet am I fearful of estimating my powers too high, and much I dislike sacking and burning of towns, it is bad employment for British troops. This authorized, perhaps needful plundering, is very disgusting, and I will with my own hand kill any perpetrator of brutality under my command. Nevertheless' he added flippantly 'a pair of breeches must be plundered, for mine are worn out, and better it will be to take a pair than shock the Yankee dames by presenting myself as a *sans culotte*.'

It had been altogether a flop: a needless war ill-conducted. The only ray of light was the gunner, Captain Robertson, a kindred spirit, brave and skilled; he and Charles became great friends. Fine as it was to be on the move, the bungling and confused counsels of the admiral and two generals in command ruined all. 'A general in a blue coat or an admiral in a red one is mischief!' Admiral Cockburn in particular had a deep conviction that he was another Wellington and had only to step ashore and vanquish. The American coast, Charles noted with interest, was flat and wooded; and not defended with high cliffs as England was. The woods worked just as well; the Americans simply disappeared into them—'Yankee never shows himself, he keeps in the thickest wood, fires, and runs off; he is quite right.' Like the French, the Americans would not meet the English in open battle, but blazed away effectively with their guns on Craney Island, a botched expedition if ever there was one. 'I think,' Charles remarked, with unwonted mildness, 'one of our naval leaders is a little deficient in gumption; much hurry and little arrangement . . . Cockburn's confidence in his luck is the very thing most to be feared: it is worse than 1000 Yankees.' On shore 'I would have attacked three times our number of Yankees with confidence, but Beckwith was resolved to let nothing take place . . . he was not free to do what he thought wise, and run sulky when required to do what he deemed silly.' To complete the picture of unrelieved ineptitude, Mr Croker, civil lord of the Admiralty, advised that all naval ships be sent at once to the American lakes, brushing aside the tiny difficulty of getting them up the Niagara Falls.

The sack of Hampton made Charles furious and ashamed: 'Whatever horrible acts were done at Hampton they were not done by the 102nd, for they were never let to quit their ranks, and they almost mutinied at my preventing them joining in the sack.' He thought the marine artillery 'glorious soldiers. They had it in their power to join in the sack and refused. I said to that noble body of men, I cannot watch your conduct, but trust you will not join those miscreants. They called out, Colonel, we are picked men, we blush for what we see, depend upon us, not a man will plunder. We are well paid by his majesty and we will not disgrace him or ourselves by turning robbers and murderers.'

A boat load of 'the duberous foreigners' had stranded at Craney Island and all been killed by the Americans: their mates took it out on the luckless people of Hampton. (Oh dear, the Free French.) Later on a Frenchman 'robbed a poor Yankee and then shot him in the back: I would rather see ten of them shot than one American' Charles raged. 'It is quite shocking to see men who speak our own language brought in wounded; one feels as if they were English peasants and that we are killing our own people.' He hated fighting Americans every bit as much as his father had done: why was this the luck of the draw? 'Strong is my dislike to what is perhaps a necessary part of our job, viz. plundering and ruining the poor peasantry. We drive all their cattle and of course ruin them; it is hateful to see the poor Yankees robbed and to be the robber . . . it is certainly a most unnatural war. If the Yankees are worth their salt they will give us a thrashing yet in one of our landings, going ashore as we do like a flock of sheep . . . had Jonathan come down to the water's edge or to his waist in it, he would have destroyed half our men; our soldiers themselves grow frightened at the evident want of arrangement. . . . Seven thousand men are at Baltimore, and we have no such force; still my opinion is that if we tuck up our sleeves and lay our ears back, we might thrash them: that is if we caught them out of their trees, so as to slap at them with the bayonet. They will not stand that.' All the same—'We despise the Yankee too much.'

As a diversion the Chesapeake attacks seemed to Charles a bit empty; 'but whether doing more would be doing good is a point to dispute'. There was talk everywhere of a landing at New Orleans; Charles felt it had little hope of success as the Americans would not be so foolish as not to dig themselves in. 'The stupid Craney Island blundering has indeed damped us all, but the 102nd have a good spirit and will, like all young soldiers, dash boldly. . . . Even now the notion of attacking New Orleans is only known to me from officers who hear it talked of in the streets. We always take care to knock at a man's door and say, Good sir barricade and load your blunderbuss, we are coming to rob and murder you at night.' 'I have luck,' he thought. 'Luck is a good thing on a pinch, but it sometimes gives a pinch. I suspect it is inclined to follow good arrangements.' After an expedition to Ocracoke he wrote off Cockburn: 'no doubt an active good seaman, but has no idea of military arrangements; and he is so impetuous that he won't give time for others to do for him what he cannot or will not do himself . . . before an active enemy he would get his people cut to pieces'.

'My regard for the navy officers in general is very great, they are open-hearted generous-spirited men; but their life is one calculated to injure the mental powers, and turn them from enlarged views of things, and judgment of human nature, to the minutiae of their profession. . . . Tyranny not discipline is their system generally speaking; and their habits of life appear to me to contract their ideas and destroy their judgment. I find however more mind, more expansion of ideas in the younger officers of the navy, who have not been long enough in it to suffer from the system. . . . A captain rules by force; no-one speaks to or dare be familiar with him: the terrible confinement of a ship renders this necessary they say. In the army officers are eternally forced to use their judgement in command, and from habitual familiarity have to support themselves against wit and satire, and even impudence at times.' All the same—'my feeling is that they are generally more open and generous than soldiers in moral character'. And 'I have learned much on this expedition; how to embark and disembark large bodies in face of an enemy; how useless it is to have more than one commander; how necessary it is that the commanders by sea and by land should agree and have one view; finally never to trust Admiral Cockburn. Nothing was done with method, all was hurry, confusion, and long orders.' When Beckwith went north Charles was left with a thousand men and three guns—'I expect to be up the Missouri and Mississippi rivers in three months. . . . Now wherever we land the Yankee runs away; but when he is, in his opinion, able to face us, he will have not less than 5000 men, with strong works and heavy artillery. These 5000 in the open field might be attacked, but behind works it would be throwing away lives: yet I speak as one willing to try much. . . .' Alas for Moore, 'who thought of everything but himself. Fortunately another hero has come forth, but we want both.'

Altogether it was a vile situation: everybody had friends or relations on the other side. Beckwith had cousins he was very fond of, and quite a few of the naval officers had American fathers. 'It is certainly a most unnatural war, a sort of bastard rebellion. . . . This trans-atlantic service sickens me'; and whenever he was not totally absorbed by work or plans he felt 'a soldier is a miserable exile, labouring in a bloody vocation, living to destroy, destroying to live'. Without a very strong reason in which a sensible man could believe, it was sheer bloody nonsense.

The American negro slaves indeed almost gave him a reason; the escapers clinging to his feet and imploring him to take them to the freedom of an English ship distressed his heart profoundly and made him feel certain they must be ill-treated, whatever the propaganda to the contrary. As against these miseries there were the mocking-birds and the fire-flies, and another new sight—'a bird like a bat, covered with beautiful green plumage'; and needless to say Charles was adopted by a large dog which followed him everywhere ashore and then swam a mile and half after his boat. It would have needed a a far stonier heart not to have adopted *him*: there was nothing in the King's Regulations and Admiralty Instructions against that, impossible though it might be to accommodate several hundred runaway slaves. A captured American 20-gun ship whose ammunition consisted of jagged pieces of iron, broken pokers, and locks of guns, set him off on a characteristic piece of mockery. 'Man delights to be killed according to the law of nations; nothing so pleasant or correct: but to be dowsed against all rule is quite offensive. We don't then kick like gentlemen. A 24lb shot in the stomach is fine: we die heroically: but a brass candlestick for stuffing, with a garnish of rusty twopenny nails makes us die ungenteelly, and with the cholic.'

This crisis of non-leadership sent Charles to his journal: 'Let the commander do his own duty, that is the great secret. In battle a leader who cries Forward may see his men fly disgracefully; but he who sword in hand rushes on the enemy will generally be followed. Nothing more useless than scolding—it is weak and contemptible ... an occasional touch-up is invigorating: only let it come out at once like the devil, hail, rain, thunder and lightning! When this is justified by the matter, it never creates enemies or discontent. British officers won't bear insult, but they know that duty must be done, and idle fellows are thus worked up. The soldiers are the same, and this makes them fight so well. They all go into action as comrades, not as despots and slaves.' All that he had liked about the war, the only excitement, had been the rowings ashore in the silence and stillness of the night, the loud hurrah as the British soldiers leapt on land; what one had to do there went dead against the grain. 'A war of folly and piracy, uniting all that is bad without a redeeming point, not even that of success' he wrote twelve years later. The real war was being fought around the Danube, or in Spain where George and William were still involved in the move and counter move around the high hills and to and fro across the rushing rivers.

Henry at least was nearby, cruising for two successive winters with his brig, the *Jaseur*, off Boston, 'watching to try his strength with some American ship, being well-prepared for the encounter'. He never met one, but narrowly missed capturing the Vice-President of the U.S.A. who came forth for a boating picnic with some ladies and had to make swiftly for the shallows. Henry had refused to make money out of his convoys, as was then the custom; and had in consequence been given a handsome present of silver plate by the captains and merchants of St John's, New Brunswick, which he did not accept. This seems ungracious; but a childhood in bribe-ridden Ireland and Donny's example, had steeled their hearts against any form of perk. Charles when in Spain was offered the sinecure governorship of the Virgin Islands (which did not involve going near that pleasant group), on account of his wounds and good service: he accepted for a year and then thought better of it and gave it in; whereupon it was offered to George, who would have none of it either.

At Halifax, new-made a commander, Henry had had an adventure in a fire. 'One house was destroyed to stop the spreading conflagration, but a long narrow beam remained, connecting the burning quarter with the untouched buildings, and it was flaming, at a height of fifty or sixty feet: then from the roof of the menaced edifice Henry Napier was seen to step, axe in hand, upon the lofty blazing beam, and with a few powerful strokes at that dizzy elevation cut through the burning beam at his feet and dashed the flaming mass down, cheered by the gazing crowd below: certainly it was a very daring act.'

Fortunately for Charles, he was sent home before the fiasco of British arms at New Orleans that he had predicted; a well-heralded assault of which long notice had been given to the Americans, and which resulted in the death of two of his great friends, Samuel Gibbs and Edward Pakenham—'that most delightful of all characters', George had thought him. Charles had exchanged back into the 50th, now fighting in the Pyrenees, but by the time he reached home with his handsome presentation sword from the 102nd Napoleon was on Elba; and he went to the Staff College at Farnham, where he was presently joined by William, wounded once again, but freed at last for England, home, and the calm beauty of Caroline. Peace: but for how long? What went on inside that impressive over-excited brain, mildly guarded on an island within fishing-boat range of the mainland of Italy?

XVII

Charles might grouch away in Bermuda at the inactivity, and at the futility of the American war, but in Spain this spring of 1812 the British army had really a tough nut to crack. Secure above the rain-lashed Guadiana, the great fortress city of Badajoz, southern gateway into Spain, was still, after two vain attacks, in French hands. Through a wet and boisterous March, with gales catspawing along the river, the British probed and hammered at it, under-equipped as ever with the tools of their trade. George and William, as if relieving each other, passed going in opposite directions at Lisbon; George with his severed arm returning home and William more or less recovered of wounds and ague, returning to the fight. On the evening of March 27th the final assault on Badajoz was launched.

Like a garish unrestful hotel in the small hours of morning, the centre of the city was brilliant and still. Even the roar of the attack had died down. There was not a soul in the bright streets as the small parties of British soldiers made their way to the main square. The silence was eerie, broken only by an occasional shot from under a heavy door or a thin infant cry from high windows. 'The great square itself was as empty and silent as the streets, and the houses as bright with lamps: a terrible enchantment seemed to be in operation, they saw only an illumination and heard only low whispering around them.' By the sinister but accepted laws of war, a city that resisted once its walls had been breached laid itself open to sack. Badajoz lay under the strange electric silence of a stormed city awaiting its fate.

The lull was soon broken—'the tumult at the breaches was like crashing thunder'. The conquest of the city was appalling. Phillipon, its French governor, had further strengthened the thirty-foot walls and added the dreaded *chevaux de frise*; sword blades welded three inches apart into the embrasures. The drop into the surrounding ditches had been deepened, and they had either been flooded or sown with mines, harrows, caltraps, and other uninviting devices. The fortress city, insufficiently mined or bombarded through the usual British lack of equipment, had been taken by human bodies with dreadful loss of life. The assault had begun in darkness, with a faint mist rising from the Guadiana river; wave on wave of British troops had surged on, and had in turn been slaughtered by a murderous fire from the walls, until one third of the Light Division alone had been killed. In the attack on the far side of the town the scaling ladders, slippery already with blood, had again and again been flung down full of British soldiers who fell in the ditch exposed to fire and stones from the walls, until hundreds lay dead and dying. It was a scene of unparalleled horror; and Wellington had called off his main attack, when he heard the shouts from the centre of the town from the British who had stormed in by the back door while the French were all occupied by the terrible assault on the front.

Everyone had known it would be a horrific battle: to one officer the faces of the waiting men had worn a tigrish look; and once in the town across the bodies of their slaughtered mates, tigrishly they ravaged. This was the third attack on Badajoz and all had been bloody: to the troops it was a town full of Spaniards who were but French collabos. They broke open the wine vats and from then on for two days there was no mercy. 'Hundreds risked and many lost their lives in trying to stop the violence' William recorded; but it was like trying to stop a tempest. Even their own wounded mates were stripped and left to lie out naked for two long nights in the winds of March. The Portuguese and Spanish camp followers who had suffered so horribly themselves were foremost in the murder and the rape.

Fresh from three weeks of an unimagined happiness, newly-married William arrived upon this scene still steaming with blood, and reeking to high heaven with unburied dead. Vulnerable as never before to these heart-sickening sights, and further anguished by the loss of Charles MacLeod and of so many of his regiment in the appalling shambles of the ditch and ramparts, he was stung into his bitterest words yet. All except seven officers of the 43rd had been killed or badly wounded: and by this beastly process he was now in command of the regiment; its destruction seered him. 'It was my home; I knew no difference hardly between it and my mother's house; it is now a desolate deserted dwelling. . . . The barbarity of our soldiers extended to that pitch that they would not for two days carry off the wounded at the foot of the walls—our own men! They also stripped them naked. . . . The town was dreadfully plundered, and the inhabitants murdered of all ages and sexes. The French were the only people to whom they gave quarter, out of a spirit of honour, not humanity. They even killed each other. Such is war. . . .' 'We are licensed murderers; the nature of war is misery,' he raged to Caroline. Charles MacLeod had been his friend since boyhood: 'if I could have seen him once before he was killed—' and William's head reeled and split 'with the painful images that are passing before me'. If he could have been with MacLeod when he died, spoken to him once again, lent him his own strength for that rough lonely ride! Mac-Leod had been with him at Corunna, at Busaco, through the spring campaign chasing Masséna, at Fuentes. It was Macleod whom he had long ago lectured against gamesters. MacLeod who had long ago forgiven him, MacLeod who made him laugh, MacLeod who within his puny bodkin frame concealed a lion's heart, MacLeod who was the only person who ever called him Bill.

'He was the best of my friends, when can I find another like him? You must be my friend and wife and everything' he entreated Caroline.

Next day he pulled himself together. 'I was in great agony of mind at the time, you must not let anybody see my letter nor allow it to hurt your spirits. If I could have seen him once before he was killed! What comfort or pleasure can I have in filling the place that belonged to him?' for MacLeod would have been in command. 'I am perfectly dead to all the feelings of glory that I used to have: without aspiring of a very strong nature it is impossible not to be disgusted with war ... I am condemnd to a profession I dislike, by religion, honour, and necessity. .... I tell my thoughts to you because I feel them, but I put a different face upon it here and am very gay.' Disciplining the regiment with an iron hand, after its lapse in the aftermath of Badajoz, he told Caroline 'There is a pleasure in being unhappy with people we love, as well as merry: I feel it so with you, and hope when you are low it will not prevent your writing to me.'

Slowly the 5000 dead were buried, the wounded cared for, the shattered battalions reorganised. 'I made a mistake about England, in trying to conquer it,' Napoleon afterwards admitted. 'The English are a brave nation.' Harry Smith at least was happy, married a week after the assault to the lovely Spanish girl whom her elder sister had saved from the sack of Badajoz and put in Wellington's care, the eventual godmother of South Africa's town of Ladysmith.

The men who died at Badajoz had at least enjoyed their last months. The waiting army, lodged high in the hills, had watched the French movements; and betweenwhiles, played football, chased wolves, and held donkey races and cheerful dances that were lively with strumming guitars and twirling senoritas. Grattan had had a narrow escape from a novel enemy; loaded up with the St Patrick's Night dinner he had bought in a local market, he was chased and almost devoured by a pack of wolves. After the fevers of the summer and the Guadiana ague, the winter lull restored them all, and Johnny Kincaid, permanently zestful, wrote afterwards that the delight and avidity of it all was beyond his words to convey. He made a good shot at it: 'we live united, as men always are who are daily staring death in the face on the same side and who, caring little about it, look upon each new day added to their lives as one more to rejoice in'.

Napoleon's imbalance of mind had now become more pronounced. He was so long used to astonish and deceive mankind that he had come at last to deceive himself, Wellington said. The Emperor rushed 80,000 troops to the Pas de Calais on the chance that the British government would lose its nerve and recall the troops from Spain, blind to the harsh fact that his men had no chance of getting across. He commanded Marmont to conquer Portugal. Finally he turned his back on the whole problem and went east: checked in the Mediterranean, he could only reach India through Russia. So intoxicating was the sensation that he found it difficult to stop conquering. When spring came, for the English it was at last, at last, a pause in Fabian tactics, an occasion for attack and not defence. The fall of Badajoz made it possible for Wellington to keep Soult and Marmont's forces apart, and although he still had only 45,000 men in Spain to the French 250,000, enough of these were pinned down by the admirable guerilleros and in holding the restive Spanish provinces elsewhere. All through May and June Wellington and Marmont, at last not unfairly matched, sparred for an opening; a couple of wary, well-hardened fighting cocks.

'Your letters are the comfort of my life,' William assured Caroline in May. 'Do not let anything check the current of your feelings when you write to me. If they should be nonsense it is no matter, for I am a stern animal as a commanding officer (although, I trust, not an inhuman one); and the pleasure of unbending from my dignity to talk nonsense with you is greater than you can imagine.' He was still only twenty-six. 'I have sent you the music of four boleros, and I expect that you will dance much with George.' He had found his horse in a bad way and was sending him home to convalesce. 'Make a pet of Tamerlane for me; he certainly is the most beautiful of horses, even now in his bad condition.' William was restored. Ordinary life was claiming him back, after the shame and horror of Badajoz that had almost dulled the glory of its immense courage.

Newly introduced to married bliss, he still trembled for its fragility. In June he heard that Anna Staples's twelve-year-old son had died. She was a young widow, Tom Conolly's niece, and a great friend of all the Napiers—'the most amiable, excellent and interesting creature that it is possible to meet with'. How desperately vulnerable a thing was human love: 'I hate this life which keeps me from you and prevents us from enjoying the few short days of happiness that may be allowed us. . . . I know your tender affectionate soul need never

be reminded to take an interest in any of your friends' feelings—
soothe Emily's mind. . . . Marmont had certainly better look about
him' William added, suddenly cheering up, 'or we shall be disagreeable.'

But Caroline had awoken and softened his heart, and reft him
from the love of fame, his old amour, who hung around now in
the middle distance, as old loves do. No one guessed his feelings:
his hand and nerve were still as firm: like Charles he retained the
vigour of his love-hate relationship with the army; only Caroline
and his mother knew how he had come to feel. He comforted his
heart with the thought that in serving his country abroad he was
saving it from the miseries he saw in Spain. None could see into the
future and guess the headlong descent of the pale brilliant little man
whom Wellington called the grand disturber of Europe—'should
Buonaparte beat the Russians, as is probable, the game will be up
in the Peninsula,' William thought. (Far into the night of this June
21st of 1812 Napoleon was watching his troops crossing the river
Niemen into Russia in the bright moonlight, transfixed by their
numbers and splendour—a Midsummer Night's Dream, if ever there
was one.)

'I was once glad that I was born in these times, when great minds
are at work, and the whole world in arms; now I regret it, and sigh
for the quiet of peace, when I could without loss of honour live in
retirement, and only look to you for my reward in this life,' he told
Caroline. 'Go more into company than you do, George was right to
scold you . . . write to me Caro, all the news, true or false, which you
hear; flatter me up to the skies, it is very pleasant . . . get your picture
painted . . . I hope you have not taken the benefit of the times and
divorced me. . . .' Caroline's letters were 'a food to my mind that
relieves it of sickly longings to which it has been subject ever since
I left you. . . . Reading them over again does not do: I want something new about you every moment.'

The hot summer days passed, while the two armies jockeyed for
position in the arid light of high Spain, through country that seemed
to William 'like the open downs of England, with dry hollows and
bold naked heads of land', while overhead, tireless in the remote blue
sky, the waiting vultures watched and wheeled. Whoever won or lost,
they at least must be gainers: one young officer's great fear was to lie

in the open field too badly wounded to drive them off. By the end of July Wellington had caught Marmont where he wanted him. Near Salamanca, William, employed by the general to drive back Foy's division and seize the ford of Huerta, led the 43rd, 'advancing three miles under a disagreeable fire with a degree of correctness I never could persuade them to on a field day'. To his second in command his jokes about the cannon balls came across as though he had no care in the world.

They saw Pakenham's division cut through the encircling French lines 'like a meteor'. Maucune, so unwise as to leave his young, surprised poilus in a square where they were fatally exposed to the direct impact of British bayonets, saw them broken and scattered: the veteran French squadrons were far away on the plains of Russia. The French army fought with its habitual dash and skill, but in spite of a violent thunderstorm the night before which had killed several people and made the cavalry horses stampede, great clouds of dust were blown in the Frenchmen's eyes by the south-westerly wind, and as the hot day declined the sun shone blindingly into them. A charge of Le Marchant's dragoons and a follow up by Leith's infantry destroyed more than a third of Marmont's army in forty minutes; and now the road to Madrid was open and it was *Viva los Heroés Ingleses los Salvadores! Viva el gran Capitán!* from cheering Spaniards as the British marched east through the Guadarrama villages to roses roses all the way; pausing only to re-bury General Tierney, 'for the honour of the 43rd'; the Spaniards having dug him up in order to bash his skull in. French general Foy, a survivor, gloomily told his diary that Wellington looked like being another Marlborough: he could do more than defend. All of drowned Europe noted and took heart.

In Madrid the church bells were ringing and the fireworks were soaring; and the pro-British Spaniards were celebrating, in the intervals of chasing the pro-French Spaniards for their lives. 'Madrid is an enchanting and enchanted town,' William told Caroline. Even their eventual entry had had a charmed quality about it, with the spires of the city appearing out of a haze while the men on the Guadarrama ridge gazed down on them crying out Madrid! Madrid! as if in a kind of dream. The evening at the Escurial had seemed quite unreal with six bands playing in the gardens and the fountain jets soaring against a background of blue mountain. William thought the Palace of St Ildefonso 'the richest thing both inside and out, that ever was reared by the hands of man. How it came to be in Spain

God knows.' The world of fantasy continued in the capital itself. The marching British soldiers were wreathed in flowers and the officers, 'old or ugly, young or well-looking', were nearly pulled off their horses by tumultuous embraces from the Spanish girls. Grattan was amazed: it seemed to him that the Spanish men 'totally shunned the company of the fairer sex', and sat around talking to each other at café tables; and he was unable to imagine how they had come by their reputation for jealousy. 'In Madrid a married woman may go to any house she pleases, or where and with whom she wishes.' The great blazing candles on all the balconies were such that night seemed turned to day. The British army, as far as was possible to men five months in arrears with their pay, gave itself over to happiness.

'I have been a whole night at a ball at the palace,' William told Caroline, 'the Spans all as gay and confident as if there were not a Frenchman in the country.' After the ruined poverty of the country-side it was unbelievable: light and water sprayed into the sky night after night as the fireworks and the fountains continued to soar. Gazing at the pictures, William was in another world; and Caroline duly sent off his paintbox. Another young soldier, John Morillyon Wilson, already had his, and was blissfully at it copying the Van de Velde seascapes. 'Get your picture painted' William urged Caroline late in August: 'Should you want anything from Paris let me know, the Staff say we are going there directly' he mocked. Fantasy had infected the staff also.

'Since I last wrote we have been quiet, if dancing and other sports can be called quiet,' William contributed on September the 5th. He had been to a bull-fight and thought it 'more cruel by chalks than bull-bating', though the expertise of the bull-fighters was such that he wondered whether it were not all a put-up game. 'Your letters come to me constantly and always with the greatest welcome and joy' he assured Caroline on the 12th of October. He was, he told her, merry; but what was she up to? 'I don't understand the cause of your growing thin and pale.' Could it be the right reaction for some-one expecting a first baby? And Wellington's siege was not succeeding. 'Burgos goes on ill, very ill . . . we have lost 420 men storming *one* of the outworks.' Britain was still spending men—instead of money for a proper siege-train. A copy of Marmont's dispatch on Salamanca had come and William thought it a vast improvement on the generality of French dispatches—'scientific, modest, and true to the utmost extent . . . Marmont was a brave fellow and a good officer and had the best of the business until the 22nd when he extended his left wing too much and Lord Wellington seized the opportunity like a hawk.' But alas the bright days in Madrid were done—'I cannot describe to you the grief of the people when the English left Madrid.' They would have the guerilleros among them again—night murders, draggings from houses, burnings, knifings, no matter whose side they were on. Because the guerilleros tackled Napoleon so effectively the people in England were inclined to think of them all as first eleven heroes, clean as a whistle and worthy of all acclaim. A wave of love and pity for the incomprehension of his daft and distant land smote William—'Happy, stupid, credulous England!'

He had suffered his usual reaction after the Salamanca battle. 'We had not as much of it as we wished, yet I am pleased with the conduct of the regiment.' Yet, 'I am really tired of seeing people butchered in a skilful way, and the more so as I do not see how we are to be ultimately successful, but that must be a secret. I might perhaps do as much good to my country living with you in quiet and peace as here; and I really do not think my wonderful military genius would be very much missed in the army.' Why not retire and remain forever a very very promising soldier, a marvellous future general if he hadn't unfortunately left? 'How the Club would stare when I told my stories! and the children would say La, papa! did you see Buonaparte? Hath he got mustachios? Instead of which I am obliged to punish men for being tired of marching 20 miles a day with 60 pounds weight on their shoulders and nothing to eat, and I am every day getting more of a savage in body and mind. Write to me, Caro. . . .'

Soult, now Duke of Dalmatia, had been enjoying life in the south of Spain. Like some great wearied Norman crusader carving out a piece of the Peloponnese for a pleasing domain, this craggy marshal had set up a kingdom for himself in sunny Andalucia. Now that Wellington was actually in Madrid he was obliged to make a move; trundling northwards in the autumn days with his still immense army. Wellington retraced his steps once more to Portugal, and Soult's removal left all southern Spain open for the activities of the ever-strengthening guerilleros, now being armed and supplied from Britain by the Navy from the sea over which the British now had complete command.

One great French army had been beaten in the 1812 summer, and Napoleon had launched himself into his most grandiose and fatal mistake.

But the autumn was anti-climactic, as the army left a weeping Madrid and trudged back across the great golden plateau of Spain, loath to leave the gay capital, loath for another static winter in the safety of Portugal. The French were on their heels in a flash, a new Quartermaster-General sent all the British food supplies ahead by the wrong route, and for four blasphemous days the army marched foodless over the high hills back into Portugal. Soult was a shrewd character who had not for nothing been at war with the British army for four years; one sniff of a wine-store and the men would break it open for two days of helpless sozzlement: he would drop on them then: he knew its weaknesses, thought Grattan, as well as its strength. No pitched battles: but a British army in retreat could be gleaned if not reaped, and Soult proceeded to glean it, aided by disease and the weather, to the tune of 3,000 men. 'We have had a retreat of 68 leagues, bad roads, rainy weather, no provisions, lying out at nights,' William reported from Ciudad Rodrigo on November the 20th. 'The retreat to say the truth was badly managed, the loss immense.'

Harried all the way by the French cavalry, spent with hunger, drenched with ague and rain, fresh young men from England and tough veterans alike fell by the wayside. Soult knew that a British army could never have a week's rations given out in advance because the men, unlike the frugal French, would either eat all the food in the first two days or sell it for drink. Therefore it would now be very weak and hungry, and he would harry it till it dropped. Through weeks of incessant rain the army plodded on: Grattan thought his Connaught Rangers better off than most: as they were used to tattered clothes and bare feet at home, losing their boots in quagmires made little difference to them. This was not the demoralised force that had slogged its way to Corunna: the veterans of the 95th still offered their precious biscuit to a young man found palely munching acorns under a tree, and who turned out to be Lord Spencer. 'Lords found they were men, and men found they were comrades' said Rifleman Costello; and as they battled on towards the safety of Portugal with tight belts and tight cohesion, women found they were men as well: one of the riflemen's wives at one point plodding dauntlessly on with her better half over her shoulders like a sack of potatoes.

William privately described an odd affray just above the Huebra fords. One early morning he reported 6,000 French cavalry only a mile away from the bivouac; 'some of their light parties had already passed our flanks and were in our rear'. When Wellington rode back to see what went on, he found that General Alten, now in command of the Light Division, instead of hurrying them over the river had incredibly formed them into squares. Although Alten was a few yards away, Wellington turned on William, perhaps the only available intelligence.

'What the devil are you about here with your squares?' he shouted, getting at Alten through William.

'They are not my squares' bawled William, doing likewise.

'Get into column and retreat with the division.'

'There is General Alten, Sir.' William was beginning to think Wellington couldn't see him.

'Don't reply' Wellington countered briskly. 'Order the division to retreat—and do you hear sir? cover it with four companies of the 43rd and Riflemen.'

'I took the hint,' William recorded, and he defended the woody ridge with his four companies while the division plus wounded and stragglers crossed the fords in the valley below. 'We had then to cross an open and smooth though steep descent of half a mile to the nearest ford . . . the French cavalry were close behind their skirmishers in our front, waiting to charge us when we should retreat down the open descent. But by giving a quick and well sustained fire and then running down before the smoke cleared away, we gained the fords in safety; Ross's guns firing shrapnel shells over our heads as we descended, and thus keeping the enemy in check. General Alten was present during this operation, but he gave no orders and did not in any way interfere with me except at the moment we were descending the hill, when he ordered me to halt half way down and form a line.' They had already lost 27 men, the French cavalry were breathing down their necks, William's horse had been grazed by a bullet and his ragged old coat had had two more bullet holes shot in it: he was unable to see the force of lingering when all but they were over the fords. 'I convinced him that as there was nothing to wait for we should only lose men without an object: Charles Beckwith also joined in remonstrating with him on the inutility of stopping.' At last they got him moving. 'General Alten,' William reported later, steering just to windward of the laws of libel, 'was a very obstinate man under fire, his remarkable courage overwhelming every other faculty.'

There was in William a harsh and unforgiving streak: he refused to subscribe to Alten's presentation sword when this general retired, on the grounds that he had needlessly sacrificed men's lives. Alten, on the other hand, said that William Napier and Baring were the two men out of the entire Light Division to whom he would have entrusted any daring enterprise. Either William was a great concealer, or, more probably, his spirits veered, rising always after writing to his wife. To his regiment he did not seem grim. Whatever his own spirits might be, he had, like Charles, the power to animate. 'Men under his command were equal to anything' one officer thought, and a soldier wrote home that William always knew what he was about and was not afraid of anything. 'There was not a soldier in the Light Division that did not admire and love him' another declared. Observers noted that Wellington would talk and listen to William when he was only 23 and had 'no military position'. Sparked off by the shrewdness of William's observations and questions, 'Lord W., one of the most secret of men, would have confidential military discussions with him'.

One way and another, it had been a bit of a straggle, 3,000 men had fallen out from exhaustion and hunger, and Wellington told the army on its arrival in Portugal that they were 'a parcel of the greatest knaves and the worst soldiers that he not only ever had to deal with but ever read of'. From this he verbally excepted the Light Division and the Guards: William thought it might have been a good idea to say so outright in the general order, and the regimental officers muttered freely at being blamed for the food situation. 'We are the funniest cripples you ever saw, and in uncommon pain,' William told Caroline from Gallegos on December 1st, 'our toes feeling as if they were always out of bed on a cold winter night . . . we hobble along.' For some it was less funny. 'Poor Rideout who was so badly wounded is dead,' William sadly recorded. 'He bore the amputation with the most admirable serenity and fortitude, and two days after died of a gangrene in the *well* foot from cold. We regret him much. It was astonishing how the recollection of his unoffending manners seized upon everybody during his funeral, and people who seldom thought of him before actually wept then. He was so inoffensive, so hardy, and so willing to do everybody service.' Tough as he was, William could sometimes halt in his tracks to pay tribute to gentler natures.

'Your present letters just received are full of fun and uncommonly diverting' he assured Caroline from Gallegos in December; and he was writing sketches for the boys to act, now that they were safe in winter quarters in Portugal.

And at last William was made happy. Caroline had had a little girl: she was alive and well and so was his daughter. This triumph of continuing life in the midst of so much death rejoiced his heart, as the autumn rain lashed down on the Portuguese hills and the British army waited for yet another—and how many more?—of the seasons of deathly war. Both France and England fought for their different visions of liberty; and it is impossible to read of it without an appalled wonder that two such countries, the flower of western civilisation, should go on, year after year, with such devotion and heroism, decimating each other. If ever Europe is reduced to nothingness, it will be by her own hand that she has died.

During this terrible winter of 1812–13 Napoleon's soldiers were trudging through blizzards in retreat from Moscow: the Grande Armée, the largest body of men under arms ever launched in the history of the world, was on its way out; 'distracted, spiritless, benumbed, and blind, Whole legions sink' Wordsworth relayed, with almost Old Testament glee. Wellington, leaving Portugal once again for his spring assault, was able to wave his hat in farewell and declare he would never see it again. He had had enough of this pleasant country with its sardines and its sea-breezes, its twanging voices and its echoing crags, though he took most of its now admirable army with him. Nor did he see Portugal again, though the French armies in Spain were by no means beaten. Although they had by now cleared this country of all its food stocks, the French soldiers were so self-sufficient that they could all reap the corn as soon as the Spaniards grew it, grind it into flour, and bake their own loaves. (Why do the Spaniards grudge us Gibraltar? but for us the French would be all over them still.) The British never reached these heights of self-help: but their enemies now had a near madman at their head. Ever more consumed by *folie de grandeur*, Napoleon sent out commands that were fantasy in face of the dour realities of the situation. Like Hitler, he issued bulletins to the newspapers proclaiming that the British were surrounded and annihilated; like Hitler, he declared that if he fell he would drag down the world in ruins round him;

but there the resemblance ended. For Napoleon was a genius of organisation and administration, and in his prime, an unbeatable soldier.

But this was not his prime; nor was he in Spain. And Wellington, at one moment hauled in a basket high across the foaming upper Douro, while the Hussars, with infantrymen hanging onto their stirrups passed the swift and foaming Esla in its spring spate, rolled the French armies inexorably back towards the Pyrenees. He had new guns, a siege train (now that it was no longer so badly needed), and his army now enjoyed an incredible luxury, tents, instead of the straw mats on which they lay out in all weathers. Taking full advantage of his observation that the Frenchmen, so fly and intelligent, were always windy about their flanks, he was turning them by skirting round the north of Spain to make Santander instead of Lisbon his port of supply; for Portugal was now safe. 'Here was a noble army driven like sheep before prowling wolves,' William wrote of the French, 'yet in every action inferior generals had been prompt and skilful, the soldiers brave, ready, and daring; firm and obedient in the most trying circumstances of battle. . . . Sixty thousand veteran soldiers though willing to fight at every step were hurried with all the tumult and confusion of defeat across the Ebro.' Wellington swept round the upper sources of this river; and guns, supplies, even horses, were hauled and roped over the steep passes and down the narrow ravines for six days 'through those wild but beautiful regions till on the seventh, swelled by the junction of Longa's division and all the smaller bands which came trickling from the mountains, they burst like raging streams from every defile and went foaming into the basin of Vitoria'.

Thus William, looking back from twenty years later at this June day, the longest in the year, when Wellington, aided now by large Spanish forces, met and routed the French Marshal Jourdain at Vitoria and drove him into the foothills of the Pyrenees. The party, alas, was by no means over, for Napoleon had just won another central European victory at Lutzen; but Spain was all but free, and even the Russians, gathering for another assault on the French, sang a solemn Te Deum in honour of British arms, and in Vienna, Beethoven took 'Rule Britannia' as the theme of his new overture.

The 43rd had learnt their lesson after Badajoz, and William was pleased to note that his regiment had not picked up 'so much as a coat or a chair' after Vitoria, though other regiments were luckier and a good deal of spoiling of the foe went on, for the French had been caught with coaches, baggage, jewels, spoils, mistresses, and silver chamber pots. Such was the confusion of their flight that if a good cavalry general had been there, he might have chased their armies into non-existence, but Le Marchant was dead at Salamanca, Cotton was held up by contrary gales in the Bay, and incomparable Paget, now Uxbridge and soon to be Anglesey, was in disgrace after having run off with one of Wellington's sisters-in-law. (He was re-admitted into the fold in time to lose his leg at Waterloo.) But all along the coast the Basque guerilleros in league with the Royal Navy were sweeping up the French in an irresistible movement; and wrote Ensign Bell, 'we fired our last shots into the parlez vous as we slashed them over the hills into their own country, while they carried along with them the curses of a whole country'.

In a brave dash to relieve Pamplona, Soult, at last prised out of his happy home-from-home in Andalucia, pushed back two British generals, hesitant in the foothills; but when from across the rise he heard the Portuguese troops shouting Douro! Douro!, the cry echoing along the valley as Wellington rode up to take charge, Soult thought better of his projected attack and dug in for the winter along the strong line of the Nivelle river, constructing a small but powerful little Maginot, and with as little ultimate result. Countries tend to fall too deep in love with their successful weapons: the British went on with their bayonets long after there was anyone near enough to poke; the French stuck much too long to those stone walls behind which Charles Napier had noted they fought so admirably; and in 1939 the Poles were still using their matchless cavalry to confront Hitler's Panzer divisions.

Soon the tattered British troops could look down from Pyrenean heights across a great spread of southern France, on to fair plains wooded and well-watered; spellbound as Moses gazing on the promised land. Who, having such a country, could want more? To their left, they saw something more. Reassuringly, always on their flank, always at command, the British fleet could now be seen active in the Bay. Sea-power was hugging Napoleon to death.

But not without further titanic struggles. The Emperor of Austria had hitherto believed that Napoleon, married to a Habsburg, might still become civilised; and he hated the idea of encouraging the Russians and Prussians, those uncivilisable beings, to push further into Europe. But as Napoleon had clearly now gone mad, the

Emperor joined the others to push 'the grand disturber of Europe' back behind his own frontiers. Refusing to accept the Rhine, the Pyrenees and the Alps as such—for wars once begun are remarkably difficult to stop if you are a dictator—Napoleon was met and defeated by the eastern powers at the monumental battle of Leipzig. His dream was still unbroken: he counted on sowing discord and dividing them up; and indeed virtually only Castlereagh's patient persistence stopped him.

William had been on leave; and parting from Caroline had been worse than ever—'how curious it is that when I want to say most to you I can say least'. 'Why' he demanded from Plymouth as the transport lay in the Hamoaze, and the troops and horses were slowly loaded on, 'do you thank me for my kindness to you, when I have been as cross as a devil half the time we have been together?' He thought Pasajes, on the north coast of Spain, 'the most beautiful place I ever saw', but what about Caro, left lonely and flat and with another baby on the way? 'Being by yourself is likely to give you gloomy thoughts. . . . Your arrangements are all very good, but I wish you would not let the word economy enter your head at all when you are upon your comforts or convenience in any way.' On September 13th he dined with Wellington who told him that, to date, 'deceiving the French and passing the Douro . . . was the most difficult move he ever made—it was touch and go. He made me laugh much.' William was also amused by a friend who came to dinner with him and told him among other things that 'he liked me best, because Charles and George were too good, and liked beef-steaks as well as they liked pies, but that I liked good living'. But sometimes his recurrent fever and the often present pain in his back made him feel that life was a burden; and 'we are tormented here by constant desertion to the enemy'.

Caroline sustained him. 'The sense, the arguments, the tenderness of your letter gave me a sensation that I cannot express to you. Certainly my darling Caroline there is nothing now that can either add to or diminish the love I feel for you.' It was early October and 'the plains of France lie before us, cultivated, enclosed, rich, and beautiful beyond description. The Spaniards, Portuguese, and I am sorry to say the British, are exulting in the thoughts of robbing and murdering the unfortunate possessors of what they see before them.

Lord Wellington says they shall not do it, and I have great hope in General Pakenham.' There was comfort in being commanded by such sensible men; and Archibald Hamilton, an eighteen-year-old cornet in the Scots Greys, recorded another merciful dispensation: 'dress was one of the things about which the Marquis of Wellington did not tease his army. Everyone dressed just as he liked, and his lordship showed the example by wearing a pepper and salt coloured coat, a white neckcloth, and sometimes a round hat.' El gran Capitán had been awarded an income of £12,000 a year by the Spanish and Portuguese governments combined, which he had refused to accept from states so devastated by war: at home the Commons, dragging their feet somewhat, awarded him £2,000.

The winter began, and wept unceasingly upon the army strung out along the high hills. 'It seems to be my fate' William grumbled on October 17th from their camp above Verra, 'to remain with the unfortunate right wing of the regiment on the tops of the bleak mountains on rainy nights . . . I do not feel the same man that I used to do, and I am gallant enough to attribute it to love of you . . . my head is exceedingly conglomerated with love, war, politics, rain, and headache.' The Central Powers had signed a truce with Napoleon which could only prolong the war: no consolation here. He seized one nearer to hand. His grey mare had been badly bruised in disembarkation from England; but General Pakenham had taken her under his protection. She would be able to live it up, softly, in snug stables: William entertained hopes of her recovery. 'Pakenham makes me think there are some good men in the world.' By November he had command of the regiment again but 'nothing can compensate me for the loss of your society'.

It was difficult to feed the armies in the mountains so far from the sea, Wellington found; and the spectacle of lush France was too much for 1200 hungry Spaniards, Germans and Englishmen, who trickled down the hills to desert to the French; while the Portuguese who had fought so well, rather naturally started to trickle home. But what remained was enough; and though Wellington had no wish to invade France, pressure from home ministers and allied sovereigns sent him on. After a series of probes along the line, the British were on the move again in November, rushing the high passes above the Nivelle and through Soult's little Maginot line. 'Six years of uninterrupted success had engrafted on their natural strength and fierceness a confidence which rendered them invincible,' William thought;

and looking back on that bitter day his imagination invested it with its due of colour and gleam.

'On the left the ships of war slowly sailing to and fro were exchanging shots with the fort of Socoa; and Hope, menacing all the French lines in the low ground, sent the sound of a hundred pieces of artillery bellowing up the rocks, to be answered by nearly as many from the tops of the mountains. On the right, the summit of the great Atchubia was just lighted by the rising sun, and fifty thousand men, rushing down its enormous slope with ringing shouts, seemed to chase the receding shadows into the deep valley. The plains of France so long overlooked from the towering Pyrenees were to be the prize of battle, and the half-famished soldiers in their fury broke through the iron barrier erected by Soult as if it were a screen of reeds.' Swept on by the remembrance still so sharp and deep, William continued. 'Hill, after a long and difficult night march, neared the enemy . . . Clinton turned the ravine with the sixth division . . . Hamilton, passing the ravine on Clinton's right, menaced the next redoubt . . . Byng stormed the third redoubt . . . Beresford, brave Kempt, . . . Colbourne, always at the head. . . . In the end Soult was driven in a few hours from a mountain position he had been fortifying for three months.'

William himself had been leading the 43rd in the storming of the heavily defended Rhune fortresses. They had first to cross half a mile between marsh and crag, before a final assault on the steep rise crowned with a fort and leading to a long hog's back serrated with defence works. He set a steady pace so that the men should not arrive below the steep rise too breathless to go up. But Gore, a young and excited ADC, mishearing what he was told, had galloped up from behind and given the order to charge. There was then no stopping anyone; and seeing this, athletic William concentrated his efforts on keeping in front of his men: the pace was very hot and he was just pipped by an enormous Irishman yelling like a banshee. But he had been first up to the fortress, slightly wounded by a rock rolled down at him en route by a determined French grenadier officer, still fighting on the burning hill whence all but he had fled.

This rushing of the fortress had been, Harry Smith thought, 'one fell swoop of irresistible victory', but the subsequent casualties among the narrow paths and stone walls were terrible; and the breathless men halted for a breather at the foot of the final rock had afforded far too good a target from the fortress above. To William the

aftermath brought a near despair; for nearly all his friends who had
survived Badajoz died in this Nivelle fight. Tom Lloyd, now commanding the 94th, and a lifelong friend, had died; Andrew Barnard,
and Murchison, 'a friend and companion of eleven years standing
with every good quality who died in great agony from his wounds'.
Young Freer, too had gone; one of Shakespeare's 'fiery voluntaries,
With lady's faces and fierce dragon's spleens': so fair and good-
looking that the Spaniards thought he must be a girl dressed up, but
so shrewd and brave in action that everybody instinctively looked at
him in a battle to see what he would do next. He was only half-way
through his education, 'yet were his natural parts so happy that the
keenest and best furnished intellects shrank from an encounter of
wit'. The night before the fight, when they had lain out on the bare
ground under their cloaks, he had crept up to William and cried as
if his heart would break, not for himself, but for the mother whose
only son he was, and for his sisters, knowing for a certainty that he
would be killed next day. 'He was nineteen, and had fought in as
many battles.' Very different was Tom Lloyd, a large majestic Hercules; a generous laughing thirty-year old, so funny and clever that his
jokes were a by-word. He it was who had leapt along the horses'
backs to put the fire out on the way to Corunna and thus saved all
their lives. He too after innumerable fights had known that this
would be his last; a fact he accepted in a matter of fact manner.

Not so did William receive the news of Tom Lloyd's death. When
at the end of the day he was told of this last loss, he flung himself
down full length on the ground and wept as a knight of King Arthur's
might have wept—'then was there weeping and dolour out of
measure'—not at all like a sophisticated English gentleman, nor the
colonel in command of a crack battalion; but like the primitive being
that he was not afraid to be, cast down in uncontrollable grief like a
young child, or some Homeric hero on the dusty plain outside the
walls of Troy.

Quickly next day William sat down to write to Caroline. 'I am safe
after a good deal of hard fighting. This I hope will reach you before
the news of the battle, and save you the danger of a shock. I am much
afraid that some foolish report will reach you, as I had a very narrow
escape and it was reported during the action that I was killed. I am
not; my head is actually turning round with the misery I suffer from
the death of friends . . . the very number of my losses have left me
hardly a point to fix upon to rest my grief. Lloyd is the deepest; but

I cannot understand that every friend is dead, whom I loved, and spoke to in health but a few hours back. . . .' As if still moving on through a haze of fire to seize the fortress, his passionate sentences grope through a fog of pain towards the strong tower of Caroline's love. He was twenty-seven, and seemed to have lived more than a lifetime. 'How little should I feel the value of living longer myself if it were not for you . . . but there is a sensation for you that I feel keenly above any other feeling, which breaks through that dead horrible sensation that this crush of feeling has caused. God bless you. . . .'

Again his courage and self-discipline came to the rescue and he wrote a few days later in restored strength to beg himself off with Caroline for his poured-out sorrow. 'I believe I am a very weak-minded man to let the disposition of telling my feelings get so much the better of me as to run the risk of doing you harm. But . . . it is the particular happiness of my life that I have a tender good friend in whom I can confide.' By December his concern for her was such that 'I could now with a great deal of pleasure compound for having no child to be assured of your safety.'

At Arcanges William was again wounded in the thigh, but morale had been restored. He did not report the wound for fear of alarming Caroline with her imminent second baby—'so you see I am not so vain as you imagine, having given up that feather in my cap. My horse was wounded also the day before I was, so you must divide your sorrow between us. Some vanity lies at the bottom,' he had to admit. 'We Napiers are supposed to be always wounded,' but as William was already walking about a few days later, it would look as if they were 'a humbugging set. I am as vain as my neighbours, and nearly as besotted about the name of Napier as some of my cousins can be about the name of Fox,' he teased her who had lately been Miss Fox. He had met a muleteer really torturing a mule and had nearly killed the muleteer before he got his rage under control —'You know I am a beast about animals.'

Tom Napier, brother of Black Charlie, had had his arm shot off: would Caroline order for him 'a silver fork like George's with a cutting edge on the side for one-armed people?' It was the greatest fun to have George so near, and the joke was that 'Margaret has persuaded George that he has no money and must starve in a little while, and it is very funny to see the distress he is in between his fears and his natural disposition which leads him to be more than liberal.' He had had first hand news of Caroline: 'March is come out again; you never told me that he had called upon you and saw you. If it were not that you are so ugly that I can trust him, I should be jealous,' he teased Caroline. All the same, when he went home, he was going to give George his now recovered grey mare, and to Charles March his chestnut; 'without exception the best in Europe', William added doatingly. In January one worry was over—'I have seen in the papers that you are safe. I am so happy at this that I was not in a passion above an hour at your having a daughter!' For with so many friends dead he had dearly wanted a son.

His relief spills over the paper during the winter weeks of comparative inaction. Aunt Fanny (Miss Clayton), an opposer of their marriage, had turned up trumps and been extremely helpful. 'I owe Aunt Fanny all the fine good speeches possible . . . for her goodness, and the more especially as I took her for a bête noire, like a Goth and a Vandal as I was. What can I say to thank her? Nothing! And when a man is very much obliged to a pretty woman, and has from the fulness of his feelings nothing to say, he can only kneel and make love with his eyes; being 500 miles off I can't do this, and if I could I suppose it would not be pretty behaviour, as she is too handsome and young to pass it off as the duty and affection of a nephew who was bred up in the most moral and proper manner. . . . Does the baby continue refractory after the manner of its paternal race or not? If it gives way an inch, it is not mine. . . . Don't take any house for a long period, as I shall live at the seaside when I go home, and I suppose you will like to live with me?' Caroline could have anyone she liked as godparents except the editors of the *Courier* or *The Times*, 'as I hate them both. Don't give the girl ten thousand names for goodness sake; get her vaccinated as soon as possible, by Jenner if you can.' The weeping out of measure had made him whole again.

They were on the move after Soult once more; their task made infinitely easier by the fact that Wellington had held his army in such strict bounds that the local French, rudely despoiled by their own returning troops, were on the English side, and all communications were safe. Attacked by Soult's men on the left bank of Nivelle, where he and the 43rd were on picquet duty in front, William had withdrawn to his assigned post at the church of Arcanges without the loss of a single man, and defended this and its churchyard for three days against repeated attacks until Hill had won the battle of St Pierre on the right bank of the Nive. It had been touch and go, between Soult's columns fighting in their own land, and 'the thin red line of old bricks', and was finally decided by Wellington's reserves of High-landers, swinging into a counter-attack with all pipes playing. The French retired to Bayonne and Wellington proceeded east, keeping Soult permanently on the guess about what he would do next.

At Orthez, in February of 1814, neither William nor George was wounded. William's regiment was not in action, but as he sat under a tree on the battlefield with the head of apparently dying Charles March in his lap, his thoughts were bitter. Galloping up at the end of the action George just had time to leap off his horse and press Charles March's cold hand and kiss his forehead in farewell: that night even Wellington rode many miles into the hospital at Orthez to see him before he died—'a figure in a white cloak and military hat walked up to the bed, drew the curtains quietly aside, leaned over and pressed his lips on the forehead of Lord March, heaved a deep sigh—it was Wellington! his cheeks wet with tears.' 'I fear much that he will die' William told Caroline that night, 'he is wounded very badly. The only thing in his favour that I could see yesterday was that his face had no immediate death about it; people mortally wounded have a very livid look about the lips, which he has not.' Apart from family sorrow, 'it is doubly sad that he is the only person of rank I ever saw with everybody his warm friend and nobody envious of him. Day after day the best of us go down, and still no remorse, no check of conscience to those ruffians who are constantly calling out "War!" ' The Russians, the Austrians, the Prussians, as well as the English were all actually inside France: why could not Napoleon now throw in the sponge?

The cares of fatherhood cast their long shadow. 'I don't think London is a likely place to improve a delicate child, as she will have to swallow at least a pound of sulphur every day in consequence of the smoke.' Could Caroline not take a country cottage somewhere near London? William asked her in February. But a month later William was a carefree young man again—'This night I give a ball at the castle to the village of Banco, of which I am the sole governor at present' he announced grandiloquently from Château Papreon on March 7th of 1814. There were moments when even war had its compensations.

XVIII

George had spent New Year's Day of 1814 tossing in a menacing gale after leaving Falmouth, the ship clawing off a lee shore where the fanged black rocks of Cornwall were hidden in torrents of spray. To have been devoured by them would have been a sad reward for again leaving his young Margaret in the course of duty, but the ship was narrowly saved, and five days later George was reporting to Wellington at St Jean de Luz. Joining the Light Division next day, he found Colborne in command of the brigade and himself consequently in command of the regiment, which was delightful; but unluckily just as the incessant rain of the Pyrenean winter was clearing up and advance into France seemed imminent, a senior to Colborne appeared on the scene and he and George accordingly each moved down one.

Kind Edward Pakenham, shortly to be whisked off to his death at New Orleans, offered George the job of assistant adjutant general, but George preferred to stay with the Light Division as second in command of the 52nd. Before he left, Pakenham told George how doubtful he thought the New Orleans expedition was, neither wise nor politic; a plan based, he felt sure, on false information. George begged him not to stick his neck out by always being right in front, as was his wont. 'George my good friend, I promise you I will not unnecessarily expose myself'—and George remembered his expressive eyes as he spoke—'but you are too old and good a soldier not to be aware that a case may arise. . . .' A year later Pakenham was dead, after ferrying his men seventy miles across the swamps and inlets of the Mississippi mouths in rowing boats from the fleet. The forewarned Americans, as Charles had predicted, had dug themselves in in a position where only a frontal attack was possible, and drove the English back with heavy losses. The regimental officer who initiated the retreat was cashiered, Pakenham and Samuel Gibbs were killed trying to retrieve the situation. The battle had two important results; it made the name of a young general named Andrew Jackson, and it persuaded the Americans that they had won the war, an effect ultimately detrimental to their sense of reality.

The feet of some others had also fatally parted company with the ground. Our worst enemy, religion and psychology unite to tell us, is the worship of a glorified image of ourselves: just now over Europe such an image was being born in Germany, such an image was holding France in its lethal grip; although the frantic boast and foolish words would not really get into their stride in Britain for another eighty years. War on their own soil had bared any illusions still left to the French people, whose schoolboy sons had been hauled to the colours from plough and bench, to die almost before they knew which way up to hold their muskets. Their own retreating troops had stripped Aquitaine bare of food, and though the English and the Portuguese under Wellington's iron hand behaved well and paid for dinner, the Spanish had not surprisingly given back in France some of what they had received from Frenchmen in Spain, until Wellington sent them home again. A sense of stalemate prevailed: when does a brave defence transform itself into a dree of senseless slaughter? When there's no hope; but the little emperor from Corsica was still dancing his fantasia of a sword dance, dashing hither and yon for a slight useless triumph, sending imaginary legions on impossible missions, leaving invaluable veterans to guard outposts of an empire whose centre was already in the quicksands.

After Nivelle orders had come that the war must continue right into France: soonest begun, soonest over, and Wellington was off in pursuit of Soult. After some of the arduous Spanish advances it seemed to George a delightful march through 'a most beautiful country about Pau'. People were civil and even kind, they had 'famous quarters in the Basque towns and villages where we got plenty to eat and drink'. Thus sustained, they struck at Soult with a right good will at Orthez, where the roads from Bayonne, Bordeaux and Toulouse met. The marshal had lost heart, George thought; he allowed the British to cross the fords unmolested, and neglected the marsh, which he thought impassable. But George and his 52nd passed it, 'up to our knees every step in bog, the enemy pouring a heavy and well-directed fire upon us from the height above, which we could not return'. In spite of their line being a bit straggly and George's poor horse having to be abandoned in the bog, they formed on the other side, where they swept up the hill under a hail of bullets with review precision, preceded by their fringe of sharpshooters: Harry Smith thought it 'the most majestic advance I had ever seen'. Its triumph was saddened for George at once. Riding to

the right he was hailed by Charles March—'George, you see I am
not hit yet, though you swore I should be as soon as I left the staff
and joined my regiment.' 'Don't holloa till you're out of the wood'
George urged him, and had hardly gone a hundred yards before a
sergeant came running after him to tell him Lord March was killed.
'I found my gallant high-spirited young friend lying with his head in
my brother William's lap, to all appearance a lifeless corpse.'

During this last and seemingly unnecessary campaign even
Wellington's temper sometimes betrayed a hint of fray. A piece of
negligence on the part of Colonel Sturgeon, 'one of the cleverest most
clear-headed, experienced officers in the British army,' George
called him, 'and a man . . . whose opinion Lord Wellington (if he
ever took any man's in preference to his own, which I doubt) is said
to have often asked and sometimes followed,' received such a violent
and harsh public dressing down, that poor Sturgeon 'sank completely
under it, and a few days afterwards took the opportunity of the
affair at Tarbes to gallop in among the enemy's skirmishers and got
shot through the head.' Even benevolent George was shocked when
the C. in C. confined his report to 'killed by the enemy's sharp-
shooters'; disregarding Sturgeon's long, distinguished, and faithful
service—'but he has always kept to that system of never acknowledg-
ing he was wrong or mistaken'. At the Garonne an engineer mis-
calculated the width of the river and failed to bring up enough
pontoons to get across. 'Lord Wellington was furious. I never saw
him in such a rage—and no wonder; for this unpardonable mistake
was the cause of many days' delay'; all the same George never
doubted that Wellington was 'one of the greatest captains that ever
lived': he did not know which of his attributes to praise most.

Spring was on the way, the sun shone on a marshy meadow country
as the British drove eastward towards Toulouse through the March
days, with chickens to roast at their camp fires, wine at 15 sous the
bottle, and even, wonder of wonders, an occasional bed to sleep in.
Beresford was now in Bordeaux, and the French people of Aquitaine were declining entirely to obey Napoleon's command that they
should imitate the Spanish guerilleros and fall upon the British; they
were far more inclined to wreathe them with flowers and ask them to
dinner. Although Wellington did not know it, Lyons fell to the
Austrians just as he himself neared Toulouse: he had always said that
Napoleon lacked the patience for defensive operations. The Emperor's army was in rags and bare feet: and the 70,000 veterans who

might have saved him were forbidden to leave the fortresses beyond the Rhine that he still believed he could hold. In the end there was hardly anyone but the gallant boys of the Ecole Militaire to defend Paris against 180,000 Russians and Prussians. They died on Montmartre in great mounds; their bodies being preserved by their frugal fellow-citizens for display to tourists at 4 sous the peep.

In the south the canny Wellington knew better than to relax: Napoleon with his battered remnants might well be retiring on Toulouse, where Soult's still intact forces were about to be joined by Suchet's from Catalonia. Toulouse was the magazine of southern France; behind its stone walls the French might bang on forever: Wellington thought Soult was best attacked before reinforcements rolled up from south or north. But the Garonne was swollen this Easter to a formidable width; and when half his army was over, the bridge broke and they were left in a most vulnerable position on the far side. Urged to attack them, Soult gloomily said, 'You do not know what stuff two British divisions are made of,' and sat tight. Only one side of Toulouse was approachable and at dawn on Easter Day Wellington approached it; though he knew that his troops would have to flounder through three miles of marsh under fire with an unfordable river behind them. Soult had only to advance down the slope to destroy them; but Wellington had a hunch that Soult's nerve was not what it had been and he was right. George was interested to hear the Spanish General Freyre demand 'in rather a haughty tone' the honour of attacking first; he then rushed the northern end of Soult's fortified ridge without waiting for orders—the watching George saw the Spaniards going 'steadily and boldly on, to my astonishment and delight'. He was expressing these sentiments to Colborne, who told him to watch it, when a French column attacked the Spaniards as they emerged onto open ground, and a startled George had barely time to throw the 52nd into open column of companies so as to get them out of the way, before the Spanish troops 'rushed through the intervals like a torrent and never stopped till they arrived at the river some miles in the rear'. Why get killed just to bolster General Freyre's pride when the war was all but over? Let the stooge English get on with it. Wellington drily remarked that he had never before seen ten thousand men running a race, while the 52nd re-formed themselves and advanced on the fortified crest.

Next morning Soult evacuated Toulouse, retreating southward in good order. The British army was just crossly preparing to chase him

back into Spain again when dispatches came for their Gran Capitán
which at long last halted the march. This last bloody battle in which
the Black Watch alone lost more than half its strength, need perhaps,
had communications been better, never have been fought. Napoleon
had abdicated and French resistance was over.

English reactions were predictably various. 'We live and breathe
again,' thought some. Dorothy Wordsworth thought it like a dream;
and a number of biblically minded persons told each other that it was
the Lord's doing and marvellous in their eyes. Others, more crisply,
just plain thanked God. Byron thought that a Prometheus had been
bound in chains by the dim-wits of Europe. 'You don't say so, upon
my honour,' was Wellington's comment when he heard the news,
though he went so far as to say Hurrah, and to snap his fingers.
'I hated thee, fallen tyrant!' exclaimed another old Etonian of rather
different calibre; but little as he cared for Napoleon's 'dance and
revel on the grave of liberty' Shelley concluded in his sonnet that the
alternatives were even worse—

> 'I know
> Too late since thou and France are in the dust,
> That virtue owns a more eternal foe
> Than force or fraud: old Custom, legal Crime,
> And bloody Faith, the foulest birth of Time.'

But not many compatriots were in tune with this fine piece of Papa-
bating; particularly as the Czar grandiloquently proclaimed that he
came to Paris not for conquest but for peace. Everyone in England
who could afford it filled their window-sills with blazing candles, and
quite a lot who could not did just the same. The church bells rocked
the steeples and the coaches ran garlanded in laurels while on their
long horns the postboys sounded a triumphant Gone Away! that
rolled from hill to hill. The poor drank beer and the rich drank
claret and Scotland swam in a great surging foam of whisky. For
no one could remember what the aftermath of war is like, and if they
could, they knew that it is a poor heart that never rejoices. After twenty
years of so much blood and sweat it was over! Boney was cotched!

George recorded no comment, beyond an appreciation of the
marvellous way Wellington had played it. Appointed to command
the 71st, whose colonel had misbehaved in the face of the enemy,

George found them in poor order, his predecessor having been 'Weak, overbearing, and insolent'; (George never cares to employ less than three adjectives). He disciplined them so firmly that he was sent anonymous letters, threatening to shoot him: George's reply was to remove the sentry from outside his tent and tell them to come on, as, one arm or not, he would give a good account of himself with either sword or pistol. Carried away by the success of his efforts and the good effect on the 71st, George adjured his sons later on to keep their tempers, remember that soldiers were as good men as themselves, try gentleness and reason first when dealing with recalcitrants, never abuse officers in front of men, and insist on obedience, 'but then on your part do not give orders of no real consequence in themselves, and which only tease and irritate others'; which notions were quite novel at the time. Among the British troops all longed for home but feared to be pushed off to America to continue the pointless war there.

The infantry were mainly shipped home or to Ireland from Bordeaux, while the cavalry, drinking champagne at a shilling a bottle and living it up all the way, were allowed to ride right through France and out at Boulogne; the short sea voyage sparing the horses. George found the maytime tramp to Bordeaux through the vineyard country pleasant enough: no guns boomed from the woods, and no assaults waited at the end, bar the assaults on married virtue at balls and parties given for the British at every town where they spent the night. Charles March had recovered in time for the battle of Toulouse; far from being dead he was about to marry and have ten children (though his father, poor man, subsequently died of rabies, of all terrible deaths, from the bite of a tame fox when he was Governor General of Canada). The young officers danced all through the dewy nights till dawn; but George at twenty-eight was a respectable old married man: he kept his bold black eyes ahead. He found the daytime extremely hot, marching along through the sunny vineyards in his battered red coat, and only wanted to get himself onto the Edinburgh coach and back to Margaret. Yet at Bordeaux the break up was sad: 'Many a bronzed face was moistened with a tear,' Grattan recorded.

It seemed unbelievable that they were over, the haunting sights and sounds and smells of war; that the men were back in 'our own fair

land of fair and handsome faces, well-fed inhabitants, richly cultivated and enclosed fields' as Harry Smith saw it. They were free of
death and typhus and wounds, amputations without anaesthetics,
bloodlettings by surgeons when what were needed were transfusions;
free of long thirsty marches in tight red uniforms along the broiling
roads of high summer in Spain, of rain-lashed nights in the open
with no fuel to dry by, winters on the hills with a rock for pillow and
cloak for cover and nothing but a maggoty biscuit to comfort the
gnawing stomach. All this had seemed in the day's work. But the
carefree twenty-year-olds, marching behind their horn bands to
Dover as George and William had done on the road for Deal like
Johnny Kincaid 'with a donkey-load of pistols in my belt, and my
naturally placid countenance screwed up to a pitch of ferocity beyond
what it was calculated to bear', buffing out from Cork or Plymouth in
the transports, had not foreseen war's full realities; the searing agony
of friends, men of imagination and courage dying in the full flush of
youth in a torture unsolaced by any drugs, comforted only by faith
and friendship and sometimes unable not to cry out under the
intolerable pain. They had not foreseen the heavy vultures, too
gorged on human flesh to rise, nor the wolves creeping out as dark
fell to prey on dead and wounded alike; nor the typhus-ridden
villages where half-dead people dragged themselves about without
succour, the ghost children with their swollen bellies and match-
stick legs, the Portuguese peasants on their scant farms with their
eyes gouged out by French troops to make them tell where their
family's last sack of corn was hid. They had not imagined the
reeking gangrenous hospitals, naked bodies of Frenchmen nailed up
on broken trees by Spanish guerilleros, the helpless wounded on the
battlefields as the flames crept nearer, their own men turned bestial
and unrecognisable in drink and loose on the defenceless people of
Badajoz. They had not reckoned on the refugees, their faces drawn
with defeat and hopelessness, the old and ill, women with child,
terrified girls with babies clutching their skirts, driven out of burnt
homes into the winter nights to walk the snowy hills and die in the
griping dawns without food, shelter or help. For the poor peasants
of every country the sword dance was nothing but a sarabande
with no martial music to light it on its way; a *danse macabre*
indeed.

There was the rub: the sword dance was not for the swordsmen
alone: it was from the innocent that the fiercest tolls of war and

revolution were exacted. And only maybe from this fact would men in time come to see that war must cease in all the world.

For between combatants, and dulling their sense of horror and outrage, the Queensberry rules still faintly held, for the last time in a great European war. The Napier brothers clung to their belief in French chivalry. (Though they did not go much on Charles II, they gloried in descent from his grandfather, Henry IV of France, who, however lecherous and underwashed in later life, had been, as Henry of Navarre, a bonny fighter.) Where there were French outrages they were quick to pin them on Marshal Masséna, an Italian; and Charles never forgot the tall French officer who gave him broth and wine as well as sympathy when he was lying in pain on the hillside after Corunna, nor Ney's dangerous kindness in sending him home. When this Marshal sent over after a skirmish at Gallegos in 1810, in Portugal, to know why Major Napier was fighting, had he been properly exchanged? Charles was able to go among the French army under a flag of truce and explain that two French midshipmen had indeed been sent back to France in exchange for his release; and although the French thought this an inadequate bargain they never hesitated to send Charles safely back. French and English picquets would shout and joke across the rivers, the men swopping brandy and tobacco for beef and biscuits, the officers making and accepting invitations to dinner, and then blazing away at each other next day. 'Look sharp; here comes old Trousers' the English would say, when the famous rub-a-dub of the French *pas de charge* was drummed out, and they in their turn had as many mocking and admiring names for the bifsteks. Their wars were time-honoured fixtures that had been going on for six hundred years and seemed likely to go on for as many more; and they respected each other. In the minds of educated Frenchmen lurked the thought of Bayard and du Guesclin: the English harked back to the Black Prince, who in spite of his behaviour to the people of Limoges had once been the flower of European chivalry, and to Henry V, lonely and outnumbered at Agincourt. Towards the end of the war the French and British sergeants developed a kind of code, banged out with muskets on the rock and conveying Your turn to drive us off the hill this time; though this they never did unless the hill was indefensible. Moore, in spite of the extremity of his position, found time to bind up the wounds of his captured French general and gave him his own sword; and when this general broke his parole and escaped, George Napier told his sons

that if ever they broke their parole he would never see them again—
'a man's word once given is *sacred*', and even Napoleon had had this
general disgraced. Unspeakable wrongs were endured by civil populations unlucky enough to be in the path of war, but between principals a kind of immemorial uncoded Hague Convention still mitigated
the worst falsehoods and meannesses of war; an old old dream of
noble warriorhood, shared by Greeks and Trojans, shared by Crusader and Saracens alike and echoing faintly down from them; a
belief that true courage must scorn cruelty and faithlessness and lies.
These feelings perhaps alone made it possible to endure and to
inflict; these, and the curiously vivid humour that such times bring
out. Members of some vast but exclusive international club that
anyone could join if he would pay the high subscription—kill or be
killed—soldiers and sailors tended to make friends again almost
before the ink on the treaties was dry, and to re-live their wars in long
detached discussions, as who should return to some hard fought Cup
Final or glittering rivalry of a past Olympic games. No doubt war
would have ceased centuries ago if there had not been so many men
who genuinely enjoyed it: the technical developments that have put
such enjoyment out of men's power are the best hope for war's
ending.

'England how little you know of war!' Charles had bitterly exclaimed as he rode through peasant bodies from Almeida; but it was
to keep England from this horrific knowledge that they accepted
death and maiming on these arid hills. And looking back, the pain
and grief was blurred; and they remembered more clearly the feeling
of being, for once in a lifetime, at full stretch. Seeing his comrades
'so jolly and fearless', Ensign Bell had 'come to like my trade'.
'I knew no happier times and they were their own reward' Kincaid
said simply; 'there was a buoyancy of feeling animating all, which
nothing could quell.' Grattan, of the redoubtable Connaught Rangers, echoed him—'Years of hard fighting, fatigues and privations
that we now wonder at, had a charm that bound us all together . . .
our days in the Peninsula were amongst the happiest of our lives.'
George Napier 'looked back with pride and delight to the many
happy years' he spent with the 52nd. Rifleman Harris 'enjoyed life
more on active service than I have ever done since'. War, per se, was
inglorious: only a fool could want it; it could and did degrade and
destroy; but there was a glory in the men who endured it undegraded,
in their carelessness of self, their out-going love for each other, their

jokes and liveliness, and the alert response to joy that danger mysteriously brings. Would there never be a time when such qualities could be called forth in some less dreadful way?

The waking up from the bad dream was over: the clearing up had now to begin. Like the people of Hanover after Hitler, the people of Aquitaine had serious thoughts of resuming their allegiance to the British throne. They said goodbye to the British army with sadness, fêting them, embracing them, and more remarkably still, lending them money. 'I was in hopes' Sarah said, 'the peace would secure all my sons at home, but William is on the point of going to America; poor Caroline looks mournful and says nothing, her little Fanny Napier has delicate health and she herself is to be confined soon. George is with his wife and child at Twickenham. Henry has got a ship at Halifax, and not a little happy as you may guess to command the *Rifleman*, sloop of war. Adieu, my dear Lady Susan, my health is much mended by having passed two months at Farnham on a visit to my son Charles, who is settled there in the Upper Military College, and studying fortification etc, with all the ardour of a young student. He is on half pay, and wanted to make use of his time, of which he gave me but two hours a day, but I thought them precious.'

London this summer resounded with balls and parties, and the countryside with fireworks, songs, and drinkings—there being a general desire to put off the hard work of reconstruction and prolong the party as long as possible. England had never been more beautiful, would never be so fair again; a rich and rural landscape of incomparable verdure occupied by only ten million people none of whom yet knew how to make an ugly building. (No use being nostalgic: if it had stayed that way it would certainly have been pocketed by Hitler, if not by Kaiser William, and we should all now be hoeing turnips in Pomerania. The price of liberty is Harlow New Town.) Sarah rejoiced in the jollities again to be had; though she thought the general carry-on over the visiting Emperors in London was a bit over the odds—'eight hundred thousand souls were collected in and about London for two months, and it is universally allowed they all went mad'.

The Richmonds had settled for the while in Brussels where they were to give that celebrated ball, and the duke and his sixteen-year-old son, William Lennox, were to ride briskly round the battle of

Waterloo rather as if it had been a point-to-point; though William
was considerably overhorsed and hoped that when his mount finally
did bolt it would bolt into the English lines rather than the French.
Sounds of revelry by night also issued from newly-released Holland.
'My sister and my two daughters were amazingly pleased at the
Hague,' Sarah wrote at Christmas, 'for exclusive of its novelty, living
at an Ambassador's house with a moderate but good society without
the least trouble cannot fail to please. They like all the Orange
family, who are really and truly as amiable and agreeable as if they
were a private family, and thats saying a great deal for Royalty; they
say the Dowager is the cleverest of women, and the younger Prince
Frederick has his full share. What a pity he was not the eldest son.'
(This opinion was sometimes shared by the British army, for Slender
Billy, as the Prince of Orange was known to the troops, made a great
boob at Waterloo and sent many veterans to their deaths.)

Like many others, Sarah had little confidence that the last had
been heard of Napoleon, or that he would stay on Elba. 'We old folks
enjoy our homes,' she wrote in January of 1815. 'I shall remain in
mine till March and expect to pass Febry very pleasantly for George
being on Tower duty during the whole month has liberty to dine here
every day to see his wife and child, who are to be with me.' Caroline
was nearby also, expecting her third baby. 'I expect Henry home in
the course of the summer which is bad for his profession and good
for me; for I can hardly pursuade myself that the year 15 will pass
without war or rumours of war, and at my age its a good thing to
secure them when I can.'

She found London little changed. 'Older people seem more in the
background than they are used to be, but the same objects in society
seem going on. In the political circle it is consequence, in the fine one
it is superiority, in the generality of circles it is diversion, religion, and
propriety of conduct somewhat tinged by fashion, which makes a
great variety, and upon the whole I do not believe that the present
generation are worse than the last, except that excess of dissipation
leads more to blind their natural good feelings, but the moment they
are taken out of it by an union with a good man they return quickly
to their good dispositions.'

But would Europe return to its good dispositions? Though the
continent was still reeking with unburied dead, her halls and hospitals and indeed her highways still crawling with untended wounded,
her crops unsown and thousands of her people starving, at least the

menacing little military genius who had refused to settle for anything less than total domination was put away, and the clearing up could begin. The Czars, emperors and princes had gathered in London to make peace, and even the Czar's sister, firm as are all Russians in claiming recognition for their own excellence, had exclaimed to the over-adulating English 'Oh no! the emancipation of Europe is owing to the steady and persevering conduct of this great and happy country! To this country Europe owes its deliverance!' Everyone was entranced by this observation; but when the venue for the peace conference moved to Vienna, where 'our balls, masquerades and whirligigs appear very flat . . . the Emperor, who was *la coqueluche des dames*, falls off a little in fine feeling about poor Poland' the cynical Sarah commented.

Any peace settlement was bound to provoke English mutterings: why should they gain nothing from a war they felt sure they had paid for by their subsidies to every European power, most of whom had been only too ready, in Wordsworth's view, 'to gaze On prosperous tyrants with a dazzled eye'. Poets are apt to be ideally in the right; but no one knew better than Castlereagh that politics is the art of the possible: to free Poland was the wish of all western Europe, but the Czar had 600,000 men under arms and declined to budge. In the view of this patient statesman 'it is not the business of England to collect trophies but to restore Europe to peaceful habits'. (Napoleon thought they were perfectly daft; expressing later at St Helena his opinion that the English would never have such a chance again in a thousand years: they should keep every single French or Dutch possession in Asia for themselves and allow no other European vessels so much as to pass the Cape of Good Hope.) But to Castlereagh it was worth giving back their West Indies to the French, their East Indies to the Dutch. (The notion of returning any of these to their indigenous populations never even faintly crossed anyone's minds, as they would not have stayed free for five minutes if they had.) It was worth tinkering with the frontiers of Saxony and continuing to subject parts of Italy to Austria, in order to get the whole bunch of eight powers to agree to England's main points—the abolition of the Slavery Trade and a general set-up most likely to maintain stability and peace in Europe. The alternative to such concessions was Russian domination and the object of this long and bitter exercise had not been to swop 'a Corsican brigand for a Calmuck chief'. A kind of wild splendour laced the worst extremes of Russian savagery, a ringing beauty from those ultimate plains; but no responsible statesman could hand Europe over to men to whom human life and individual rights meant nothing; who cut off their prisoners' heads and piddled all over everyone's drawing rooms. Yet the disappointed young of England felt that liberty was being dowsed once more. 'Here we are' complained Byron, 'retrograding to the full stupid old system'.

'It is impossible,' Castlereagh hopefully wrote in the early months of 1815, 'not to perceive a great moral change coming on in Europe, and that the principles of freedom are in full operation.' This dream castle floated on shaky foundations. Early in March, catching the Viennese waltzes in mid-bar, and halting the Czar, Metternich, Wellington and all, dead in their tracks amongst the violins and the chandeliers of the balls in Vienna, Napoleon escaped without difficulty from Elba, crossed the Alps and appeared in Lyons on April the 10th, and was received with open arms by a great many Frenchmen for whom a year of Bourbon rule and allied occupation had been quite enough.

'Is it in the power of language to describe the evil?' demanded Sir James Mackintosh, a Liberal, in the Commons on April 20th. Boney's tiger leap had set Europe back into the twenty years' war 'which had wasted the means of human enjoyment, destroyed the instruments of social improvement, and diffused among the European nations the dissolute and ferocious habits of a predatory soldiery'. This was not just Whig self-righteousness at the gallop: chaos had indeed come again, the grand disturber was at large once more.

Part IV

A Rain-washed Country

'The harvest island quivering under rain.'

XIX

Luckily by this time the allied powers had acquired enough sense of self-preservation to entrust the chief command to Wellington, who achieved his close run thing at Waterloo. It was a grand finale won with a scratch allied army, several regiments of which hurried home to the north when the going got rough. If he had had his Peninsula Army, Wellington would, he said, have fought an offensive battle instead of sitting tight and enduring the hard pounding, and gone straight in at Napoleon without waiting for Blücher, in the certainty of scuppering him—'I should have swept him off the face of the earth in two hours.' But these reliable veterans—such as had survived—were scattered, or at sea, or in Ireland. Napoleon moved with the tiger speed that had been his of old, over the river into the Netherlands when everyone thought he must still be in Paris; and Charles and William Napier, coming from England, arrived too late, though Charles was in time to see the piled dead at Hougoumont: he had never seen so terrible or so brave a sight. Angry or not at being reft from Caroline, William could not help being touched when his regiment cheered him loudly on his rejoining them at Ghent; and it was good to hear that the first battalion of the 52nd had done magnificently under Colborne; this was George's regiment and one that William called in its Peninsula exploits 'a regiment never surpassed in arms since arms were first borne by men'.

Having missed the bus through Napoleon's lightning leap across the Sambre, Charles took part in the storming of Cambrai, and joined Neil Campbell (who had allowed Napoleon to escape from Elba) as a volunteer for the last bit of fighting in the suburbs of Paris, he and William riding with Wellington into that city—the first British army to do so since Agincourt. The Czar was so impressed by the natural way in which the British troops marched that he ordered his army to abandon the Prussian goose-step and their own knees-up strut, a sensible decision later overruled.

After a quick look round the delights of Paris, Charles was off back to Farnham: but the annual accident must have been due; the packet boat sank in the harbour mouth at Ostend and he was rescued in the nick of time after clinging to the base of a wave-washed pile for a couple of hours. At Farnham he sat down to the problems—'Soldiers' marriages. This subject requires much arrangement and attention and receives none . . . most soldiers' children die for want of care. . . .'

William, reunited with the 43rd, stayed on; mounting a guard unenthusiastically when the reinstated Bourbons returned to their capital. By the end of the war the British army had fallen in love with Napoleon, as they had fallen in love with Turenne and were to fall in love with Rommel in the western desert, the disinterested affection felt for a gold medallist in an opposing team. 'The feelings of the British soldiers were unequivocally shewn' William reported. 'Proud of their long victorious course against the French, they yet respected the latter as brave enemies, and had a profound admiration, even love, for Napoleon. They thought of him not as a foe but as a hero standing alone; a soldier to be hailed by all soldiers; as a man who had enabled them to gain the greatest possible glory by fighting him: a master in war, and the fast friend of warriors.' Not even Nancy Mitford, with all the enchantment lent by distance, could have made them regard the Bourbons as other than a load of old fancy-dress stuck-ups. 'When Louis the Eighteenth entered Paris, the writer' William went on, 'his post being at the head of the picquets guarding the Barrier of St. Denis, was asked by the captain on duty there, if he was to salute? I have no orders on that head and give none, was the reply. The king came up, crowds thronged forward, and the words vive and Roi were heard on all sides; but the last was generally preceded by the words l'Empereur et, pronounced in a low tone. The British soldiers being left to themselves brought down their musquets from the shoulder, and placing their hands on the muzzles, fiercely regarded the approaching king. He seemed surprised, but soon his countenance assumed a look of such malignant ferocity, so fixed, so peculiar as never to be forgotten. A number of mousquetaires in burnished cuirasses, their faces convulsed with anger, then rode up, shouting, gesticulating, and brandishing their swords: but close behind the picquet was a wall, and the swarthy veterans, hard as the steel of their bayonets, and with wits as sharp, knew the advantage. Keeping their bronzed faces bent over their hands, their eyes glared sternly, yet no movement indicated that they were even sensible of the mousquetaires' presence, until the latter closed within a few paces and seemed dangerous: then suddenly, all their heads were lifted and streams of tobacco joice flew towards the shining cuirasses, whereupon the courtier soldiers followed the chariot of the king. A shout of delight arose from the crowd, and many well-dressed women embraced the British veterans.' Tight cohesion indeed, when without orders everybody could even spit in unison.

The English were struck with the beauty and lay-out of the Paris Napoleon had designed—if only he had confined himself to the arts of peace! In comparison with the Russian, Austrian and Prussian troops the British behaved themselves so well that they were described as '*Doux comme demoiselles*'; but they could afford to be, with their country unravaged and themselves unbeaten for six years. The Highlanders made a great hit—'*actuellement rien qu'un petit jupon, mais comment!*'—and were in big demand as billetees. The Prussians in Blücher's army had wanted to destroy the beautiful bridge of Jena, as being insulting to their national pride: they were stopped by a platoon of the Coldstream Guards and Wellington kept a sentry permanently posted there, involving a good deal of high blood pressure amongst the Junkers. Sent with a message to Wellington, William found him sitting in the back of his box at the Opera, while a party just below were discussing in loud voices which branch of the cavalry had won the battle of Waterloo. It was, Wellington told William, the British infantry who won it; and added that he expected soon to be told that he hadn't been there and couldn't possibly know.

In the autumn of Waterloo year William O'Brien died, lamented by many. He had 'sailed his little opposition frigate' in amongst the fleet of great Georgian 74s, and far from being sunk by their broadsides, had cast anchor and lived happily ever after. It is difficult to see now why Lord Ilchester and Henry Holland had been so bitterly opposed to him: Lord Ilchester had allowed his eldest son's romantic but unprofitable marriage with Elizabeth O'Grady to go through, and had welcomed this penniless Irish charmer. Perhaps it was because O'Brien was a bit flash, and because he and Susan had double-crossed her father, promising to part and begging for a last meeting at which in fact they arranged their elopement. But perhaps Susan's pride and her tossing head had also been in part to blame. In any case she and her husband had enjoyed '51 years of unbroken happiness', and Susan was utterly stricken by his loss.

Sarah longed to hurry to her. Susan's happiness had often shed a comforting glow—'are you and Mr. O'Brien sitting snug by a warm fireside and enjoying the visits of your numerous family?' But now Susan was suffering as Sarah herself had suffered, and ill herself, she could not even go to her. In this crisis her helplessness and dependence really oppressed Sarah. She felt herself, 'a mere log, totally incapable of helping anybody . . . God bless you' she ended, 'my dear, my first, my constant friend, remember how unalterably I am yours, S. Napier.' There was nothing she could do but write. The Ilchesters, Susan's nephew and niece, were being kind and understanding to her; God bless the Ilchesters . . . 'the most beautiful part of good minds is drawn forth by sympathy with affliction . . . confidence in those hearts will create parental feeling in you, and I trust in God you will find it increase interest in life, that sort of interest without which we cannot exist. You say you can be of no use to anybody. Oh! my dear Ly Susan, do you say that to me who am by Providence so marked to be in that sad and sorrowful state? Remember that your natural powers of the mind are in no way abated nor your faculties impaired by age, and who in that state can say they are not useful? But it requires judgment to find out the best line, and judgment never yet accompanied the first emotions of distress. . . .

'I am sorry to hear that your income will not admit of your doing what might be of use to you. I too well know how this circumstance puts everything in the imperative mood, and when one's wishes seem reasonable and useful one is apt to think it a hard case, whereas nothing is hard which Providence has ordained for us. If we examine it closely' Sarah continued bracingly, 'we have but few wants in the world, not more than the situation of life we are in gives us, and all further comforts of life are luxuries to which we have no claim; the greatest I know of is to serve one's friends, but if this is denied to us we must be patient under dissappointment, and not envy those who have the power of indulging themselves in helping others if we see they acquit themselves of this duty well, but if not we can scarcely help wishing the riches were in other hands, at least I catch myself often criticising others, which is wrong.' Out of breath with this long sentence and perhaps aware of having been rather pontifical, she remembered the bleakness of having no one to whom to pour out the little nonsenses of every day, and concluded 'Pray tell me every minute circumstance about yourself, for there is nothing that concerns you that can be indifferent to me.'

Death the devourer had become indifferent to her, as it does to the faithful old. She who had seen so much could accept it with equanimity. She had been to see a very old friend—'not a tinge of hypocrisy in Ly Mary Fitzgerald's zealous hopes that others should enjoy the same feelings that made her bear life with cheerful activity at ninety. She talked to me of our late loss in my dear sister Leinster, and in her brother, and she seemed to rely so much on the certainty that their change of situation was received by them with thankfulness, and I am sure she felt herself perfectly ready for her long voyage. Her preparation for it was very short; the fire caught her clothes about 9 o'clock in the evening, she complained of no pain, and by 8 in the morning she was no more. Ld and Ly Liverpool [her niece] never left her bedside, and she conversed with them to the last moment, blessing them and praying that his honest endeavours for the public good may meet with success. It is not possible for me to lament her death, I think of it without extreme lowness.'

Her friend's loss was quite another thing. She begged Susan to be told 'if I can in any way contribute my small share of power to your service in any way'; repeating herself with sympathetic energy: 'I wait without impatience but not without the greatest anxiety to learn more of you.' Would Susan's friend 'indulge me with a letter . . . all details relating to you interest me too warmly not to be welcome, however minute they may be . . . I must insist on your not attempting to write to me yourself, for I well know how such an exertion produces unnecessary emotion which ought to be avoided.'

So also was infirmity worthy of all sympathy. At a service in St James's Piccadilly, the Dean of Canterbury preached a sermon in appeal for the Eye Infirmary, reminding his congregation that the old King was now totally blind; and Mr George Tierney, the Whig leader, observed a stately white-haired figure, still bright-complexioned, listening closely in the front pew, and recognized Lady Sarah Napier. After a while he looked again; and saw that the tears were now pouring and streaming down her face. Did she weep for her own eyes now blind, that once had done such execution? More likely she wept for the old King, whose bright blue gaze had shone on her with longing and who now was mad as well as sightless; old and lost and wandering, with difficult unmarried daughters and a pack of graceless sons. She wept perhaps for human weakness; for the honest hopefulness, the plodding desire to do right, that turns, in human eyes at least, to failure and to ash.

William stayed on in France for three years with the army of occupation; after which the colonelcy of his regiment was bought over his head by someone with the necessary ready money, to its considerable indignation. War-weary after the bitter battle of the Nivelle, and more than usually plagued by the bullet near his spine, he had once written to Caroline, 'I find myself more than ever inclined to quit the army. My health is really so bad that my life is a perfect burden to me; pain and lowness of spirits are my constant companions; and this, added to an eager restless impatience about you, totally unfits me for a military life. God Almighty bless you my own darling wife, you are the only comfort I have in the world; and I am determined that no silly hankering after fame shall prevent me from profiting from that comfort.'

Now that peace had come the impatience grew. Should he retire at once? 'Speak out to me upon it; I have no doubt but of propriety; I do not mean nicety, but real propriety'; and he was thinking of what would be honourable, and of Emily and Fanny, his two little daughters, and the possibility of their being looked askance at. 'A nice sense of honour unfounded would be an injustice to the little beasts.'

It was the season of accident-proneness: Charles had just had his shipwreck, their sister Emily had fallen on her head, and William's horse had come down on the Paris cobblestones and rolled on his leg. He was astonished at French demoralisation—'the French nation has lost all sense of shame, and my admiration for Buonaparte is increased tenfold when I find what very contemptible stuff he had to work with'. All too soon Caroline's post-Waterloo visit with the children to Paris came to an end; it was 1816, and he was still in the army. 'Does Emily hold by her beak like a parrot? if she does she will be my favourite, I always wished for a child who could do that' he told Caroline who was deploring their eldest's hereditary nose. 'Kiss my little babies for me; I want very much to see you and them.'

His time passed slowly in the army of occupation, riding races, looking at pictures, buying a Martin Vos; and after six months at home he found Bapaume still more 'uncommonly stupid', even with Henry to keep him company. He rumbled on to patient Caro; his horse was away and he had left his skates in England, and he liked plenty to do and there was not enough to do. 'I bear the loss of your company less well than ever . . . no place and no company ever fills up the void or satisfies the longing . . . I am vexed every day by new specimens of treating or rather ill-treating the soldiers, of the complete indifference to their comfort.' Would she send him Cobbett's *Glory against Prosperity*? He complained next month of weak health and a mind dissatisfied with itself, made no better by riding 50 miles between breakfast and 4 o'clock dinner and being kept up till half past two at cards by his host, followed by another day's riding wet through all day. 'Grant has been as civil and good-natured as it is possible to be, but he, like all other people, mistakes my disposition, and imagines that a large party of what are called good fellows must be delightful to me.' William of course increased the misapprehension by habitually being delightful to them, in spite of his moans.

The distress he read of at home worried him deeply. He was sending money to Caroline for distribution to people in want, and she was quite right never to let the servants send away anybody until she had seen and talked to them herself. 'Could you not get Dick to walk now and then upon Westminster Bridge and give something for you and me to the poor creatures Cobbett describes as lying there? . . . I am not well, but part of it I attribute to a fretful disposition which gains strength upon me every time I quit you, the only real good I possess in the world . . . every day convinces me of my own inability to attach friends, and of my natural gloomy unsocial disposition; and my surprise and gratitude to you for loving me is in proportion' mourned poor William, truly down in the dumps, and a walking argument for married quarters.

The new year of 1817 found him more jovial, or simply more well. 'I love you so much that my poetical brains have been called into action by it,' and he enclosed an Ode to Love—

> To beauteous Love I bend the head
> The God of exquisite delight;

and William rolled happily on for six stanzas; not Keats perhaps, but no mean verse, and more gratifying than the bellyache he sometimes could not help emitting. Caroline was to burn the verses if she didn't like them; 'I wrote it from a fulness of mind that I felt when thinking of you and all the goodness of your disposition . . . I believe that the liver is a great steadier of people's minds, as I have been remarkably well these three weeks back, and so I am a poet.' Their longed-for son had arrived in 1816, John Moore Napier, known as Mr Puck, and cunning little Pucky, gorgeous to behold and not yet known to be deaf and dumb.

For all domestic joy, there was still another side to it. 'I feel a charm in command, even though it be during peace.' It was something to be in a position to outwit skulduggery from on high. He had been ordered to reduce the second battalion of the 43rd by 200 'inferior' men. 'At all risks I am determined to keep on a good many worn out poor men who have served thirteen and twelve and eleven years, who would not get a pension under fourteen years' service, but whom it is expected I should thus cheat [by discharge]; I would sooner be hanged.' Still and all, nothing could compensate for the loss of 'your face and conversation and my little Fanny and Emily talking to me'; and, he assured her, 'if I did not already love you as much as it is possible to love, your last letter would excite it; so natural, so frank, so tender.' How did she manage to combine so much gentleness and feeling for him with so much sense and judgment? (Caroline had sensibly liked his verses.) In April he bought a picture, the Marriage at Cana, by a Dutchman; and the following New Year he swopped six maps for a small Castiglione—'the picture mania has seized me again'. John Moore was now two; and the fact that he didn't speak made him no different from many other little boys of two. 'The description of my funny little Puck pleases me much, and I would also be very proud of Fanny's promising beauty, if I believed in it.' Caroline was not to think he had lost interest in the girls because Puck's pranks made him laugh so much—'I love the girls as much as him, be he never so pretty.'

Separation, as it does, was making him bitter about all the other women he saw around, who obstinately weren't Caroline. One particular family sharpened his tongue—'the mother has two large gooseberry coloured eyes; they follow and speak plainly to every man of rank in the garrison. (The father, a brigade major, being dead has become a Major General.) She is tall, raw-boned, and stalking; she is a wild and untameable hyena who entices little heedless officers into her house, and afterwards gives them to be devoured by her cubs; the last two rather fine girls, with strong symptoms of the mother's savage disposition in them.' Or the general's wife—'the old puffin was obliged to leave off her airs and she behaved middling, was rather glad to see me, and did not talk of above half a dozen kings and princes when she first came into the room; however she looked very like a pig that had strayed into a parlour. The two young ladies came late for dinner, peering and stealing into the room like two young sick pea-chicks, looking very ugly and very much afraid of some of the officers pulling out their tail feathers' William concluded sardonically.

At last the regiment was ordered away from France; but to Belfast. And of the people he had most wanted to see again at Celbridge, old Lock had just died, that 'true-bred Irishman of the best kind, full of noble feelings and pride . . . very eloquent, very clever, and very frequently drunk. His attachment to all of us was of a nature that made it impossible not to like him again . . . a wild, bard-like man. I have more recollections and associations of early ideas, old stories, and attachments to horses and dogs, connected with him than with any other person now alive.' He was all the same happy to be back in Ireland, whose charm, eloquence and violence, his childhood had bred into him. But in 1819 came the moment of decision: the colonel of the 43rd retired. It was the turning point of William's life.

Lord Fitzroy Somerset offered to lend him the necessary thousands needed to buy the colonelcy of the regiment; and it was tempting. The world was wide, still offering many a field of glory. When it came to the point, William was loath to go. He had been a lieutenant-colonel at twenty-three, had commanded the regiment on and off since Badajoz when he had been twenty-six; and in spite of his melancholy carry-on he was devoted to them. He knew enough about war now to fight it with skill, and economy in lives, and was sometimes yet haunted by the dream of military fame; had become in some sort an addict. 'The worm,' as he put it, 'still gnawed.' Like Allenby after the South African war, he was tempted to stay on because he could not bear to leave the army in the hands of such noodles.

Practical considerations won through. He now had four children, and despite all the best endeavours of nineteenth-century ladies with pocket handkerchiefs stuffed inside, was unlikely to stop there: he feared he would never have the money to pay kind Somerset back. The regiment was bought over his head, and right furious they all were at such a system; the chances of a military take-over had faded but it is a weakness of the English that regulations once pointful are allowed to linger on in sacred cowhood. William's leaving sword and his parting letters were heart-warming: he particularly appreciated 'your honor's deeds of justice and vaulor witch will always be thought of by them that noes you'; 'you was admired and loved by every soldier of the Light Division'; and James Considine's 'you first made a soldier of me, and confirmed in me what I deem my best and most chivalric feelings'; while another's 'Whenever I hear of a noble deed I exclaim Thats a Napier', brought the ready tears to William's still flashing blue grey eyes.

'Preserve, O Lord, within our hearts
The memory of thy favour,
That else insensibly departs
And loses its sweet savour!'

Wordsworth entreated in his victory ode of 1816; but this prayer misfired. Post-war Britain was involved in far too many complicated problems—what to eat, for one thing—and felt the lassitude of having run very hard for twenty years just in order to stay in the same place in terms of freedom and independence. In some ways it was a Pyrrhic victory, a social and financial Verdun. Unemployment, starvation, the drift from the land: hard times were ahead for sailors and soldiers, as for most people in victorious Britain. The grand veterans of the Peninsula drifted foodless and homeless through the land in their tattered red coats: one-legged sailors who had fought at Trafalgar and for years blockaded Brest stumped the coastal towns begging their bread. Peace emphasized unemployment; industry slackened off, and those whom the enclosures had dispossessed now hungered in the miserable slums to which industrial revolution had drawn them. People wanted to forget the long anxieties of war in an orgy of pleasure, and those who owned anything seemed to strive only to get more. To many it seemed that the fabric of society was about to collapse; and quite a few felt it wouldn't be a bad thing if it did.

Sarah had hardly been able to believe that the long war was really over. Charles and William thought it unhandsome to send Bonaparte so far off to that desolate island in the South Atlantic where he would most surely die of boredom; but to Sarah the unknown antipodes or the moon itself would scarcely have been far enough.

Because of his insensate folly and ambition four of her sons were maimed or broken in health, let alone the loss and misery elsewhere. Long ago she had backed Fox in thinking the first war with France was wrong; but only, she had stipulated, so long as the French stayed within their own boundaries; and how far and wide they had burst beyond!

But at least her five sons were still alive, and she wrote from Cadogan Place in January of 1816 to tell Susan how they were doing. 'I tell you of the birth of my only grandson as an excuse to divert your attention to the happy ménage of my son George, whose Scotch wife suits him so perfectly that it endears her to me exclusive of finding in her all the kindest affections of a daughter-in-law, not given entirely from duty, but made pleasant to me by the persuasion of the most steady desire to have me with them continually, which people do not do if it is not comfortable to them.

'My other married couple are at Paris still buffeting with the plagues of service, for danger is over; but poor Caroline has found a soldier's wife's lot bad enough even in Paris, tho' there never was a person with fewer events than herself, but she says the pleasure of being with William and their joint admiration of the Louvre is quite enough to counteract a thousand plagues. . . . My son Henry is at Castletown with Louisa and Emily, all three enjoy each other's society (not having met comfortably for a long time), together with my sister. Henry has repeated attacks of the liver, which was his constant desperate illness in the East Indies and not much mended in America, but we hope it is now getting better in his own native air and the good care of Castletown.

'He is Capt. and Commander, and has leisure to attend to his health, which I trust in God will make him to recover this horrid complaint.

'Before I finish my family gazette I must tell you my poor old friend and servant Susan Frost is ill, of old age I fear, and Doctor Bain attends her; he is a great friend of mine from the high respect I have for his character these twenty-five years.' 'I want to know' she requested in November, 'how this early and severe setting in of winter agrees with you?' Was Susan going about and seeing people? 'A gloom on the spirits requires society to shake it off.' 'The Ilchesters' kindness to you proves they have right notions of that sort of family affection, which gives a pleasure none but the truly kind can know.'

Family love meant most to her, but she still enjoyed meeting interesting men. At Brighton was 'Dr. Allen, very full of information on politics'; Mr White, 'whose clear and sensible account of the Spanish revolution is very instructing'; and 'General Flahaut, favourite and A.D.C. to Napoleon, and come to England for safety'. The waters at Cheltenham had eased Henry's East Indies liver; he had gone to join William in France while waiting for that elusive prize at the end of a war, a ship to command. 'William goes back to France as a boy to school, for he is a very domestic person, and delighted with his third child, lately born, being a boy, and the mother nursing it herself. Poor soul, it is a great consolation to her in his absence. . . . Emily and my sister go much to Holland House and it secures their meeting with the best society.' George was now colonel of a Guards regiment, Charles at Farnham, and Richard 'at the Temple, pupil to Mr. Dodeswell, member for Worcester . . . Richard delights in him.' Sarah's comments on life became no less crisp with age. 'Nothing can exceed the attentions of Lady Holland or rather flattery to me. Why? I know not; time will show.'

At Melbury in October of 1817 the Ilchesters were entertaining the Duke and Duchess of Gloucester. Married to his first cousin, Princess Mary, daughter of George III, the Duke was the son of the Prince William of Susan O'Brien's youth; and Susan, still rather bruised and stiff from her widowhood, was asked to stay to meet them. 'The Duke treated me as an acquaintance he was glad to find here. Before dinner all met in the saloon. He called me to sit by him, and talked a great deal, and as all the Royal family that I have met with, incessantly returning to the subject of Lady Sarah and the King's admiration of her and confidences with me. Like everything else,' Susan added drily, 'time and distance have added somewhat to the truth.' Not everything the Gloucesters had been told had been said 'in the strong and clear manner he supposed; if they had, they could not have stopped there.

'I showed him her picture, which he and the Dss thought beautiful.'

But really, why should they keep on? 'I always get out of the subject as well as I can, as it is an unpleasant one' Susan recorded severely in her diary. 'I really cannot remember things that were said in the unconnected and loverlike style, sometimes half joking, sometimes with more seriousness, so many years ago.'

The next subject was received still more starchily by Susan. 'He talked too of his father's *great attachment to me*; how we sat at the Oratorios in boxes that joined, and what great friends we were. It seems surprising to me that all this youthful nonsense still gets talked of. I should not have thought a father's flirtations likely to be transmitted to his son, or that ever it sld be thought of or mentioned when once at an end.'

In February of next year she spent much time with Sarah in London, but unlike Sarah she did not think that things were no worse than they had been in her youth. Every Tom, Dick and Harry and their ladies now went to Court, the theatres were so full of 'prostitutes and men that go to meet and talk with them that people are liable to see and hear some very improper things; apartments are fitted up for company that never think of seeing the play.' There were now innumerable balls and assemblies in small houses, and if the parties were not badly crowded everyone thought them not agreeable. Instead of dinner 'universally at four o'clock', people had taken to having it at seven or even eight, and balls began at all hours. 'Thus everything is done by candle-light, which adds greatly to the expense in large families, is hurtful to the health of young persons, and the morals of the lower classes.'

These were getting terribly uppish too. 'Every man, tradesman or farmer is Esqr., and every prentice girl a young lady. Servants speak of their masters in the third person, instead of My Lord, or My Lady, My master or My Mistress.' Time was when 'none but by parents or the greatest intimates were ever called by their Christian names. . . . Now there is a certain rudeness or carelessness of manners affected both by men and women. Ladies pretty and young may go and seek their own carriages, persons with or without titles are called by their Xtian names . . . all follow this laudable humility, and every rank contributes its mite to equality.'

'As morals grow worse language grows more refined. No-one can say "breeding" or "with child" or "lying in", without being thought indelicate. "Cholic" and "bowels" are exploded words. Stomach signifies everything: this is delicate, but to many unintelligible. . . . In trade, character is little attended to, and the cheating swindler has sometimes more advantages than the honest trader. At one time "A woman of doubtful character was shy'd; if bad, decidedly avoided. *Now* the very worst are countenanced by many." '

As for politics, heaven knew where it would all end. Time was when 'Englishmen admired the Constitution as much as all but Englishmen do at present. . . . No ale-house club but meets to descant on the conduct of the Royal Family, or the Constitution, the state of representation, the use that Kings are to the people, the inequality of ranks and riches, and everything that can tend to raise discontent in minds quite unfit for such discussions. Every parish has its committee to arrange something or other.' Really, they would only addle their brains and upset themselves, and where would it all end? Where it had ended before of course; Oliver Cromwell and all that lark. The French Revolution had a lot to answer for. 'Religion was injured and opinions shaken by the writings of the philosophers in fashion. This mischief was not so counteracted as might have been expected; the Bishops were too negligent of their clergy and the clergy too negligent of their parishes; this gave great openings for the introduction of Methodists, who are indefatiguable in their pursuits.' For Methodists read Communists, and dear, stiff, sensible, stuffy Susan might be with us yet.

At the end of 1817 Sarah was very ill; but recovered enough to go to Castletown, that well-known restorative, next year. But she wrote no more letters; her correspondence with Susan ended on a note of joy 'on a topic that is endless to me in point of satisfaction and comfort'. Richard was to be married! Anna Louisa Staples, born Stewart—'tallent, and superior mind and great cultivation'—had been widowed at seventeen and had subsequently lost her only child at the age of twelve; a tragedy which had caused her almost to opt out of human society. 'The business of all Napiers was to try and get her out of this dejected state . . . notwithstanding her multiplied difficulties, Richard . . . succeeded.' And soon Henry followed suit. Sunny, calm, reassuring, with his quiet manner and his fairness he had been as a little boy the most like Donny of them all. Fever had now made him gaunt and dimmed the brilliance of his looks though George, arriving twenty years later as Governor at the Cape of Good Hope, found that Henry's charm and his way with the girls made him still remembered there. He married Caroline Bennet, natural daughter of the third duke of Richmond and thus his first cousin, but affectionate and gentle, and so lovely that whenever she came into a room people stopped talking to gaze at her. The danger of marriage between first cousins had not yet been understood; and sad troubles were in store for both William and Henry.

But what about her eldest, his mother wondered; Charles with his battered, twitching face and his loving heart? All very well in his Bermuda letters to go on about Mrs Byng's radiant beauty, about clever and agreeable Mrs Horsford, and pretty Mrs Butler who was so gentle, so winning, so delightful that Charles had never met her equal; but where were all the spirited Miss Masseys, pretty Miss Vandeleurs, the imperious Miss Gages? Defaced or no, such lively company, such a capacity for loving, such a need, must not go waste.

Before Waterloo, Charles and William and Caroline had been sharing a house at Farnham, where Charles stayed on alone. Both he and William chafed at the miseries of their countrymen in post-war England, and at their impotence to alter or ameliorate. In later times they would probably have entered Parliament, become journalists or broadcasters, or general stirrers-up of the greedy and selfish in power; but journalism was in its slightly shady infancy and Parliament was the prerogative of the well-to-do. Both were trained only for war: both were half-pay soldiers and William had an ever-increasing family to keep. They had given their youth and health, the best years and energies of their lives, in serving not only their country but what they felt to be the cause of humanity; and they and Henry were all about to be thrown on the scrap-heap. Under any conceivable system this tends to happen, cushion the fall how you will: like Donny, like Sarah, their sons presently got up and did something else. Such was William's fire and eloquence that his fame as a public speaker grew, and during the thirties he was asked to stand in the radical interest for Bath, Devizes, Birmingham, Glasgow, Nottingham, Westminster, Oldham and Kendal. In view of the force and charm of his personality and the pressing need for social reform before and during the hungry forties, it seems a pity that he had to refuse; which he did not solely on financial grounds: the Radicals were often republicans and William remained firmly royalist, however much he pressed reform.

His home life, though blessed with mutual love, was beset by tragedy. Years brought the realisation that William and Caroline's only son, a boy of exceptional beauty and splendid physique, was deaf and dumb, as were two of their eight little girls, one of whom died as a five-year-old, from an accident caused by her inability to cry out: the blow struck William with terrible force, and in his agony of mind he blamed himself. The pain of his spinal wound was such that he sometimes had to spend weeks on his back. These things did not improve a temper naturally wild and impetuous. Once on the march in Spain he had lammed into a muleteer who was viciously beating his prostrate wife, and been enormously surprised when the apparently lifeless wife rose briskly to her feet and lammed into him. His tendency to react to cruelty with violent action did not abate over the years. For all his looks and charm, his humour and intelligence, William can never have been an easy husband, with his causes and his passions and his total refusal to truckle in a truckling age. He and his John Moore Napier were fishing a stream one day, and William left his son, aged nine, while he went to inspect a higher beat of the river, when the water bailiff arrived on the scene. The little boy was of course unable to hear what he said, or to explain that he was fishing by permission of the owner: the water-bailiff cuffed him, took his rod from him, broke it in pieces and threw it in the stream. The spectacle of his speechless little boy thus abused was too much for William returning to the scene; the bailiff was so mercilessly beaten up that he was fortunate to survive. Such actions did not make life smooth; but on the other hand, when someone in the village went dangerously mad, it was William who was sent for by the doctor, it was William who with great courage and infinite patience soothed the sufferer into calm. His home was a place of radiant happiness remarked on by all who went there; and his lively, arguing, laughing, intelligent daughters were the delight of his life.

William did not at first think of writing. When he retired from the army on half-pay in 1819 he and Caroline took a house in an unfashionable rural thoroughfare called Sloane Street while he studied to become an artist, under George Jones the academician, and another pretty little daughter appeared with clockwork precision every year. Though made an honorary member of the Royal Academy for his statuette of Alcibiades, and taking a lifelong pleasure in the arts, he came to realise that his talents lay elsewhere; and he was finally spurred into his great work by the cloud which had fallen over the fair name of Sir John Moore by a series of publications condemning his conduct of the Corunna campaign. Inclined as it was to boil readily in a good cause, William's blood came seething up at these attacks. Sent ill-equipped on a fool's errand by a sentimental gullible government, Moore had brilliantly extricated his country's only army from certain destruction and died to see it safely embarked: had he failed the British government might have lacked the nerve for another attempt on the continent until a generation had passed and Napoleon become unconquerably strong. Yet lesser men were daring to yap over his grave: would no one who knew the truth defend him? Walking with Lord Langdale over 'the fields of Belgravia', William was persuaded that the task should be his. For some while diffidence held him back: he remembered his dullard days at school and knew he was no scholar. But persuasion prevailed; Caroline's support encouraged; and William had found his life's work.

'I am quite sure' Sarah had told Susan, thinking back on all the people she had known in her long life, 'that uncommon sense travels from generation to generation and never loses ground, added to excellent education.' Charles's uncommon sense was troubling his heart as he regarded the post-war world, and the Britain for whom so many of his dearest friends, such troops of his bravest soldiers, had died or suffered lifelong maiming. Many of these latter were still tramping the streets as beggars; even for the hale there was no work and no welcome. Used in the hour of desperate need they had been financially forgotten before the fireworks of victory were cold. 'Dear mother,' Charles wrote in June 1816 'as to public affairs it is hard to judge. There are about two millions of people in Great Britain and Ireland in a famishing state, to enable Lord Camden to receive thirty-eight thousand a year, and expend it on game and other amusements insulting to those who provide the money.' (Lord Camden was a permanent bête noire to all Napiers: he had refused to allow Aunt Louisa Conolly to see dying Edward Fitzgerald.) 'It is hard therefore to say how long poor rascals, who think their children's lives of as much consequence as partridge's eggs, may choose to be quiet; or how soon, actuated by an ignorant impatience of taxation, they may proceed to borrow from Lord Camden.

'Your account of the Regent's being so occupied with dress made me laugh: yet he is nearly sixty years old, his people are starving, his government feeble, and at these things I cannot laugh. . . . Our ministers begin by retrenching the incomes of those who have nothing else to live upon, and who have previously fought and worked hard on almost nothing, to gain that provision. Retrenching there, but refusing to curtail the thousands they enjoy in the shape of sinecures, besides their large salaries and large private fortunes: and for those profits doing nothing, unless it be telling men with starving children that they are ignorantly impatient of taxation when demanding that their wives and children may not famish.' The angry pen of a jobless soldier bit into the page. He did not cry *à bas les aristos*, many of whom pulled their weight and the worst of whom at least cherished the people who worked for them: his shout was Down with the canting high-ups of religion and the political parties, down with smug and callous merchants, down with petty oppressors, and with all who condescended to their fellow creatures with that repellent tone of *de haut en bas* he noticed now creeping even into the army.

'Lord Cochrane has by honest courage done more good at the great meeting than ever he did before; Wilberforce's canting speech was hateful.' Charles was sorry that Wellington was going to France —'we want clever fellows for we are getting on the rocks.' It had been 'pleasant to observe that there had been nothing insulting to royalty [in the speeches in the House] but the ministers put all attack on themselves in that category: they are going down the rapids, may they come upon a fall like Niagara!'

Writing on August the 10th, his thirty-fourth birthday, of his love and gratitude to Sarah, he went on—'for those who we have lost there should be no regrets: the best lot is their lot, we may be assured. We should not weep over the graves of the good: to grieve and pine for that which is taken away is to be thankless for that which remains; and for which, ommitting meanwhile to enjoy, we shall not fail also to mourn. And on no point is there greater cause for satisfaction than the perfect union which exists among your family: there has never been a schism, nor even a day's coolness amongst us.' Yet over all their lives and letters an exhausted sadness seems to hang; a post-war lowness born of extreme personal and national fatigue.

'You are the most provoking woman alive,' Charles teased her in September, more as of old; 'you tell me you have been ill in a copper-plate hand, and of your being better in a scrawl like mud where a hundred chickens had been walking. As to Lady Bellamont, [yet another Fitzgerald] you have chopped her and the Bible together so that I fear for her character; she cannot well be separated from Solomon's concubines by the best decypherer of telegraphic dispatches: you see the impropriety of your carelessness!' He promised not to attack Castlereagh when Aunt Louisa was there, knowing how devoted she was to him as a friend. But reform went on so slowly! If there was no going beyond justice then there would be no reaction, and 'the glory of England will become brighter than the battles of the last twenty years have made it. . . . The reformers, Cobbett at the head, tell the people not to riot, not to be personal, not to commit excesses; but to petition daily, hourly, one and all, for in that is their safety, their remedy. They see this is true, and the great security against bloodshed and revolution is to tell the multitude truth. Shew the real evils and the real remedy, and they will not be half so dangerous, or so unjust, as when suffering in ignorance of the cause; for it is then they go furiously ahead and nothing can stop them.'

But by 1819 the Reform Bill was still many bitter years away, and reform of social abuses still further: Charles had grown weary and angry with waiting and voices a familiar complaint. 'We are starved at home and lose our character abroad; we injure, we insult, and gain nothing! We broke faith with the little republic of Genoa; we let the great republic of America hang two innocent British subjects. At home our people hunger and our best men fly to America. . . . Shall we never have a fair representation of the people, and a parliament that will chastise the present government? Surely the king and people of England will not long submit to be thus fettered by men who have disgraced them abroad and ruined them at home?' Poor Castlereagh, hated by so many, took his own life in 1822; but his monument was the nineteenth century, a slow but steady growth of liberty and happiness, and Europe unconvulsed by any major strife for a hundred years.

In April of 1819 Charles was off abroad, to a new job, to the remoteness and sunshine of the Greek islands; away from an evil situation he was powerless to remedy, and into one that he could. Sent as inspecting field officer (French for spy), to Greece, to see what could be done to help them throw off their Turkish yoke, he became governor in the meanwhile of an island in the Ionian Sea. Cephalonia, lovely as a dream but torn by feud, rapine, and murder, and riddled by feudal injustices, was in need, Charles felt, of a little English organisation. His spirits rose with every mile of the journey. The French were recovering their morale, in the resilient way they always do; the view of Mont Blanc from Geneva enchanted him, 'the imagination whispers Live here'; but on further thoughts—'the people call themselves free but are by no means so.' The road over the Simplon pass was beautifully engineered and the landscape dazzling; 'the eye and the mind alike grow weary with admiring.' Milan was a fine town, but 'of its sights all traveller's books give full accounts, but one to me curious, which no book mentions—six field pieces with Austrian gunners having lighted matches ready to sweep the streets with grape-shot, should the Milanese express themselves in a way displeasing to the Tedeschi. What a father of his people this Emperor Francis is. What a happy family! Hate the most inveterate exists.' The Austrians had appalling manners and supplied themselves wholly from Vienna: not a shilling was spent in Milan, to sweeten the pill of their occupation.

Bologna rejoiced him, 'after Milan and Florence the town I should most like to live in: it is a very fine place with an excellent museum. The women looked very pretty and wicked; and the streets have arcades which defend one from sun and rain. Dry cool walks, learned men, good books, good philosophical instruments, and sinful women, but holy withal, being under the pope! what can one wish for more?' On June 24th he was at Rome, 'lost in admiration of Michael Angelo's genius'; and rather less impressed with the eternal city's ecclesiastical aspect. 'Saw Pope Pius Seventh, seated on his throne with his crown on, looking as if he thought he and his parsons were to cajole the world eighteen hundred years longer. Seeing him environed by his own troops, and his fat, red-faced, drunken, fornicating, gluttonous, gambling, priests, I thought it would be fine to read him an account of the life, the power, the splendour of the meek, the humble Jesus! who was no priest or He would not have been crucified.'

Politically, French and Italians were hamstrung. 'From Paris to Milan one only feeling pervades the middling classes and poorer folks, and that is enthusiastic affection for Napoleon.' The Swiss 'place him above all other men with all his faults', and 'in Italy they have the same adoration for him as in France, and express it openly, fearlessly, and without disguise; saying he was the only man capable of raising their country above its debasement . . . under him all had bread, commerce flourished: he fell and their hopes and prosperity fell with him. Now enslaved, divided, and decaying, they seem to despair, as if the yoke of the Holy Alliance was eternal, and the onward course of mankind held spell-bound for ever.' Why could not some prince of Italy arise who would make the gentry live on their estates and improve farming, and 'have the goodness of heart and nerve to grant a free press?' 'They are a fine people and a free government would make them teach the Austrians a lesson.' Their freedom had been 'taken from them by men without talent, honesty, or courage; who have combined to deprive the human race of the little liberty and happiness left untouched by former tyrants.' Thus brooding upon some of the unlucky side-effects of his country's hard won victory Charles launched himself from Otranto upon the cerulean splendours of the Ionic sea, and was borne away from the wounds and headaches of post-war Europe and into the happiest epoch of his life.

Wandering thoughts troubled Sarah after he had gone, as she sat on in her blindness. Did she escape what she herself in her thirties had described as 'the low prejudices of old age', and its 'crossness and discontented ways'? We know only that family and friends continued to love her and to frequent her house. In 1816 her 'dear and faithful maid Susan Frost' had died, she who had been with Sarah on her Knole elopement with William Gordon, and who had driven off the Irish rebels nearly single-handed at Celbridge in the troubles. Two years later Susan O'Brien, visiting her for a long spell in London, found that the beauty which had been Sarah's standby for so long was at length leaving her; but Henry Fox and his father (Ste's son), riding over to Castletown in 1819 to see Sarah, found her 'perfectly clear-headed and cheerful; her language very well chosen and her quickness and wit very remarkable for one of her age and infirmities'. She and Louisa were two old women now, looking out through the long windows towards the blue hills of Wicklow; feeling the morning sun on their faces; remembering together; Sarah glad in her blindness to be again in a house whose every step and corner she knew. It was her last visit.

Maria Edgeworth the novelist, plain and intelligent and perceptive, thought Louisa, even at seventy, 'the most charming person I ever saw or heard . . . full of that indulgence for human creatures which is consistent with a thorough knowledge of the world, with a high sense of religion, without the slightest tincture of ostentation, asperity, or bigotry.' In the beautiful saloon, which so long ago Louisa had had painted in a cerulean blue picked out with gold and crimson and had hung with Venetian glass chandeliers (oh dear, they had arrived to be found just the wrong blue, and pink instead of crimson, but never mind, they were so pretty anyway), the old lady glowed with an aura of amiability which at the same time demanded respect. Emily seemed to reflect the light: to Maria Edgeworth she was 'graceful, amiable, and very engaging'.

In days of youthful prosperity Louisa had built an ornamental cottage in the woods three-quarters of a mile from the house; 'I am sitting in an alcove in my cottage with a porch before it, a lovely fine day, the grass looking very green, honey suckles and roses in abundance, mignionette coming up, seringa all out, the birds singing, the fresh air all about; Mrs. Staples playing upon the guitar in the porch, my work and my book by me. Inkstand as you may perceive and a little comfortable table and chairs, two stands with china bowls filled with immense nosegays.' Here now the two old women would sit; drinking in the flower smells, the birdsong and the freshness; pierced by the intense sweetness with which old age invests each leaf, each summer cloud, the sway and tremble of far water, the movement of each single blade of grass.

Louisa was failing. She was weaker every day, floating off to Heaven on a tranquil tide. There were no harrying decisions to trouble her peace. Castletown was to go to Tom's niece Louisa Pakenham and her husband, and they were to take the name of Conolly. The executors were those two level-headed and reliable characters, her own nephew and niece, George and Emily Napier.

She lay now in a tent set back from the front of the house, where she could gaze at it all day. Every Lennox loved houses and their beautification; it was their form of creation. Maybe that Tom Conolly had lacked what the Georgians called bottom, a kind of indefatigable integrity; but his house did not. It stood there in four square elegance and strength and to Louisa it was more beautiful and satisfying than any house great-grandfather King Charles had owned; in its restrained yet generous symmetry it made even Blenheim, even Versailles, look over-blown and nouveau-riche. Louisa's soul was made; yet dearly had she cherished the delights of this world. Her dying eyes regarded Castletown with love, and Emily sat by her in silent sympathy.

Since dawn people had begun to collect in the park in front of the house at Castletown; first in little knots, and then in gradually thickening groups. Louisa Conolly, who had been among them for sixty-five years, was to be buried that day. For two days past weeping people had filed past the bed where she lay in death; 'serene and beautiful' for all her eighty years. George and his brothers, taking their turns to watch unseen, had heard their murmured grief: 'You'll clear the way for an old sinner like me, and God will receive me from you', 'if she, the poor man's friend and comforter, has not gone to heaven then there is no God, no mercy for human beings', 'Protestant, Catholic—what is it but a name? We have no friends left since you are gone'. By late forenoon the space outside the house was black with people, from as far as thirty or forty miles away, and as the doors of Castletown swung open and the coffin appeared at the top of the great stone staircase, there was 'one long loud cry of despair' from them. All hats were off and all sank on their knees in total silence. Young Leinster, George, Richard and Henry Napier came after. 'Upon the word to move forward the people rose from their knees; again issued forth that one loud cry of grief, and we moved on without noise or wailing except from the sobs of the women (this being so contrary to the custom of the Irish that it made a deep impression on us all).

'When the clergyman met us at the church door and began the burial service, again the hats were off, and this Catholic multitude were on their knees in fervent sincere prayer for the soul of their Protestant friend.' The deep silence continued all the long way to the family vault, when again arose that long wild cry as the coffin was lowered. Sad Emily had followed in a carriage, and the crowds parted to let her pass on George's arm; 'May the Father of mercy look down on you, the poor darling child of her we loved', and they besought her not to leave Castletown, not to abandon them.

It was, George thought, Louisa Conolly's plain simple sweetness, 'derived from the fountain of Christianity and humility which sprang spontaneously from her heart', that had endeared her to so many in the sixty-five years she had been at Castletown since first she came there as a bride of sixteen. 'I never met one who formed a clearer or sounder judgment on all difficult questions, or was more just in her perception of character.' She had had 'a perfect simplicity of religion and unbounded tolerance on that subject'; and friends, relations, or poor people had only to be ill or in grief or trouble and she would hasten to them with help. As her kinsmen wound back to empty Castletown there felt to be a kind of bareness even in the air.

Margaret Napier, George's wife, was bringing up three little boys now, George Thomas Conolly, John Moore, and William Craig

Emilius, as well as Sarah and Cecilia, and she was not too proud to ask her mother-in-law's advice. Sons are apt to marry and wander off: how, above all, had Sarah contrived her lifelong hold upon the affections of her sons? Recording the answer in rather more pompous terms and with considerably better spelling than Sarah herself would have used, Margaret Napier wrote—'the great and primary source was seeing me from their infancy the object of their father's tender love and care, and high in his estimation as his friend and companion. This taught them that I was to be loved, to be greatly considered, and to be respected. My own conduct gave them evident proofs of tender affection. I was steady in denying them what I considered wrong, eager to indulge them when I conceived it right they should be indulged. As they rose out of infancy I left them to their father's management, and studied to be the friend, not the tutoress, of my sons. In me they trusted to find sympathy and kindness, with no idea of mollifying him or changing his views by their application to me . . . they knew that their confidence in me delighted him. My opinion or advice was unaccompanied by the necessity of adopting it, and when left to me at the most dangerous period of life, little able to conduct themselves, little disposed to be directed, I found the happy effects of the system.

'I continued the same practise, and while I secured to them a friend to whom they could and did confide their actions, feelings, difficulties, follies, sorrows and pleasures, it gave me the best opportunity of influencing them by repeating and recalling to them their father's sentiments, and suggesting my own; and then, left to decide for themselves, their actions (probably even unknown to themselves) were somewhat of the hue of what they had just heard.

'The rest of my sons' education was their father's system, growing as they grew, and communicated to me, as I was always the joint partner of the care of our children and made the source through which all indulgence and pleasure flowed.' 'I certify the above to be correct in all points' George added in a footnote.

Emily Leinster too had died, still queen of the ball, still lively, a career begun sixty years earlier at Sir Thomas Robinson's famous dance, given when Emily was ten years old, four years before Sarah was born. This infant début did not seem to have spoilt her, and in old age she was still firmly training up her grandchildren in the way they should go: 'I am more and more convinced every day that the true, benevolent Christian system is the very best that can be adopted even in the affairs of this world; and that nothing else can give true greatness of mind, without which no man can conduct himself well thro' the bustle of contention, passion, jealousy, envy. . . .' Emily had borne twenty-two children, mourned the death of many, rejoiced in the life of many more: married again when her dear-loved husband died, had more children, rejoiced in them. Life was for living. She thought her sister Louisa 'as near perfection as any mortal can be', but allowed herself to be different.

Visiting Sarah in London for the last time in 1825, Susan O'Brien was distressed to see the change in her; she was 79 and seemed suddenly very old. She had many grandchildren now, Henry's two sons had been added to George's three splendid ones, and William's pretty little girls enchanted her with their liveliness and fun. It was a pity that Donny's Louisa had never married, but one could not have everything; and Sarah never had a married daughter. (Emily was to marry later on. The Bunbury family, strangely faithful to the Napiers in view of their first experience, married Emily, and later on, George's daughter Cecilia.) Charles's letters from Greece were a delight. Richard's wife Anna Louisa had no children but she was so charming that one could not complain. Sarah was not without a touch of vanity at being the last surviving great-granddaughter of Charles II.

Nothing in life had turned out quite as Sarah expected. She had had no plan to marry the King of England; and in the event had only missed it by a whisker. She had had quite a plan to marry an intelligent, social-success country gentleman who liked hunting and horses; and it had turned out a dead flop. She had had less than no intention of marrying a penniless soldier; and yet there she had been at the ripe age of thirty-six, walking up the aisle of a little Sussex church in trembling happiness towards one; on legs that seemed to carry her whether she would or no. Her hand to mouth life with Donny had had its glooms and panics; but none of them had really impinged on its deep happiness. In her jet-set days with Bunbury she had met the most attractive men in Europe: a basis of comparison had not been wanting, and she knew when she was lucky. When she was forty, and had added Charles, Emily, and George to the Louisas of their own that she and Donny each had, she had never meant to have any more children. Five was enough, on their income; a fine compact mobile family. But William, Richard, Henry, Caroline and Cecilia had insisted on being born too; and not once had she regretted any of them, and nor had they regretted each other.

'Retrospect don't suit me,' she had once declared, stoutly keeping up her spirits after Donny's death; but as she lay sleeping herself gently out of life it may be that retrospect walked in without knocking. It was August; from outside in the summer warmth the sounds of harvest drifted in, and through the slow nights the moon shone over stubble, over the heaped corncocks of the gathered wheat, over the smells of pasture cooling after heat. August was the month of happiness, the month she had married Donny, the month when Charles, Richard and Cecilia had been born. There are some people, souls perhaps more advanced, who find God on their own; and there are some who like Sarah find him through other people. 'My dear home so long sought after. . . . Mr. Napier has l'esprit et rage du service beyond immagination . . . a steady attachment to those principles he was bred in . . . he has made me prosolyte to his sentiments . . . he turned my mind to see the truth, from him I have derived the way of thinking which alone could procure me peace.'

She lingered on in the warm air of late summer, the sum of her faults and graces, her rash actions and her wayward musings, her illusions and her truth. On August 26th of 1826 Sarah died peacefully; aged 81, surrounded by the family to whom her warmth and spirit had been so bright a central light; leaving them all a sensation that the world had become a colder place.

Rockingham, 1968.

Short Bibliography

ALDINGTON, RICHARD: *Wellington*

BARNARD: *Letters* (ed.) A. Powell

BOYLAN, LENA: *Castletown and its Owners*

BRUCE, H. A.: *Life and Letters of Sir William Napier*, 1864

BRYANT, SIR ARTHUR: *The Years of Endurance*
The Years of Victory

BYRON, LORD: *Letters* (ed.) John Murray

CHURCHILL, SIR WINSTON: *History of the English Speaking Peoples, Vol. III*

COOPER, LEONARD: *The Age of Wellington*

COSTELLO, EDWARD: *Adventures of a Soldier*

CREASY, SIR EDWARD: *Decisive Battles*

CREEVEY, THOMAS: *The Creevey Papers* (ed.) Sir H. Maxwell

CURTIS, EDITH ROELKER: *Lady Sarah Lennox, an Irrepressible Stuart*

DICKINSON, W. C.: *Scotland from the Earliest Times till 1603*

FORTESCUE, SIR JOHN: *Wellington*

GOMM, SIR W.: *Letters and Journal*, 1881

GRATTAN, WILLIAM: *Adventures with the Connaught Rangers*

GUINNESS, THE HON. DESMOND, and LINES, CHARLES: *Castletown, Co. Kildare*

GUEDALLA, PHILIP: *Wellington*

GWYNN, STEPHEN: *A Brotherhood of Heroes, being memorials of Charles, George, and William Napier*, 1910

HAMILTON OF DALZIEL: *Mss.*

HARRIS: *Recollections of Rifleman Harris*, 1829

HIBBERT, CHRISTOPHER: *Corunna*

HOLLAND, ELIZABETH: *3rd Lady Holland's Journal* (ed.) Lord Ilchester, 1908

HOWARTH, DAVID: *A Near Run Thing*
Trafalgar, the Nelson Touch

ILCHESTER, LORD: *Henry Fox, First Lord Holland*, 1920

ILCHESTER, LADY, and STAVORDALE, LORD: *The Life and Letters of Lady Sarah Lennox*, 1901

KINCAID, CAPTAIN JOHN: *Adventures in the Rifle Brigade*

LAWRENCE, ROSAMUND: *Charles Napier, Friend and Fighter*

LINES, CHARLES *see* GUINNESS, THE HON. DESMOND

LINKLATER, ERIC: *The Survival of Scotland*

MAXWELL, CONSTANTIA: *Dublin Under the Georges*

MONTGOMERY, VISCOUNT: *A History of Warfare*

NAPIER, MARK: *The Lennox of Auld*
Life of John Napier of Merchiston

NAPIER: A History of the Napiers of Merchiston, privately printed, 1923

NAPIER, GEN. SIR WILLIAM: *History of the War in the Peninsula and the South of France*, 6 vols., 1839
The Life and Opinions of General Sir Charles Napier, 4 vols., 1857
Life and Letters of Sir William Napier (ed.) A. Bruce

NAPIER, LT.-GEN. WILLIAM: *Passages in the early Life of Sir George Napier*, 1884

OMAN, CAROLA: *Sir John Moore*

OMAN, SIR CHARLES: *A History of the Peninsular War*, 7 vols., 1902

PRYDE, GEORGE S.: *Scotland from 1603 to the Present Day*

ROSEBERY, LORD: *Pitt*

SEDGWICK, ROMNEY: *The Letters of George III to Lord Bute*

SMITH: *Autobiography of Lt. Gen. Sir Harry Smith*, 2 vols., 1901

STAVORDALE, LORD, *see* ILCHESTER, LADY

TREVELYAN, G. M.: *British History in the Nineteenth Century*

WELLER, JAC: *Wellington in the Peninsula*

WILLIAMS, NOEL: *The Life and Letters of Admiral Sir Charles Napier*

WHEELER: *The Letters of Private Wheeler* (ed.) Captain B. H. Liddell Hart

Elizabeth Longford's admirable *Wellington, the Years of the Sword*, now such a valuable authority on this period, was unluckily not published until after this book was completed.

Index

Addington, Henry, Viscount Sidmouth, 123
Addison, Joseph, 173
Agincourt, 337
Agincourt, H.M.S., 286
Agueda, river, 238
Alava, Don Miguel, 241
Albemarle, Lady (born Lady Anne Lennox; Sarah's aunt), 67, 70, 73, 82, 87–8
Albergaria, 274
Albuera, 271
Alemtejo marshes, 236, 239, 269, 271, 274, 290
Alexandra of Russia, Princess, 190
Alexandria (America), surrender of, 297
Alfayetes, 270
Allenby, Field-Marshal Lord, 353
Almacks, 61, 77
Almarez, 229
Almeida, 237–8, 267–8, 270, 273, 282, 338
Alten, General, 318–19
Amelia, Princess, 26
America, War of Independence, 51, 52, 53, 71–4, 78, 127, 134, 162–3, 209, 292, 302–8, 330, 335, 363
Amiens, Peace of, 154
Andalucia 316, 322
Anderson, General (Moore's friend), 212, 214
André, Major John, 73
Aquitaine, 331, 332, 339
Arbroath, Declaration of Independence (1320), 18
Arcanges, 327, 328
Archill (earliest Napier), 17
Armistead, Elizabeth (*m.* Charles James Fox), 99, 100, 149
Assaye, victory at, 176
Astorga, 197, 199
Asturias, 276
Atholl, Earl of, 18
Aubigny (Duchy), 23, 75
Aubigny (town), 47
Aubrey, John, 20
Audacious, H.M.S., 220–1
Austerlitz, battle, 169
Australia, 163, 164, 291

Badajoz, 142, 222, 231, 271, 274, 275–6, 277, 286, 296, 308–12, 321, 326, 336, 353
Bain, Dr, 355
Baird, General Sir David, 188, 200, 213, 220
Baltimore, 305
Banco (France), 329
Baring, Colonel, 319
Barnard, General Andrew, 230, 326
Barrosa, 271, 274
Barton (Suffolk), 38, 51, 58–9, 64
Bath, 59, 234
Bathurst, Countess, 165, 225, 295
Bathurst, Earl, 83, 165, 295
Bathurst, Lady Georgina, 83, 295
Bayonne, 329, 331
Beauclerk, Mr, 53
Beckwith, Colonel John Charles, 270, 318
Beckwith, General Sir Sydney, 240, 262, 302, 304, 306
Bedford, Duchess of, 34, 46, 49, 52, 80, 94
Bedford, Duke of, 49
Beethoven, 321
Bell, Ensign, 322, 338
Bell, Lady, 51, 53
Bellamont, Lord, 80
Belloc, Hilaire, 222n.
Bembibre, 198
Benavente, 196
Bennet, Caroline (*m.* Henry Napier), 358
Bentinck, Frederick, 172
Bentinck, Lord William Cavendish, 207–8, 212, 236
Beresford, Mr, 121, 122, 123
Beresford, Viscount William, 271, 273, 275, 278, 325, 332
Berkeley, Lady Emily (born Lennox; Sarah's niece), 83, 265
Bermuda, 65, 76, 277, 291–3, 297–8, 302, 308, 359
Betanzos, 203
Black Watch, The, 334
Blake, William, 115
Blakeney, Colonel Sir Edward, 272
Blanco (Charles Napier's horse), 260, 263, 264, 268, 273, 274–5, 278, 291 298
Blücher, General, 345, 347
Bologna, 364

Boothby, Lieutenant, 198
Bordeaux, 331, 332, 335
Botany Bay, 291, 293, 298
Boufflers, duc de, 58
Boulogne, 159, 335
Bouverie, Mrs, 174
Boyle Farm, Thames Ditton, 115
Brennier, French officer, 273
Brest, blockade of, 354
Brian Boru, 41
Bristol, 105, 136, 151, 161, 165
Brodick, commanding at Corunna, 200
Brudenell, Anne (*m.* 1st Duke of Richmond), 33
Brunswick, Princess of, 46
Brussels, 339
Buccleuch, 19
Buenos Aires, 175
Bunbury, Sir Charles, Bart (Sarah's first husband), 36–9, 43–5, 49, 51, 53, 58–60, 62–3, 65, 66, 67, 85, 160, 369
Bunbury, Louisa (Sarah's daughter), 65, 68, 79–80, 88, 95, 97, 98, 102, 139, 369
Bunbury, Lady Sarah, *see* Lennox, Lady Sarah
Bunbury, Sir William, Bart (Sir Charles's father), 37, 45
Buonaparte, *see* Napoleon
Burdett, Sir Francis, 268
Burgh, Charlotte, 133
Burgos, 315
Burgoyne, General, 73
Burke, Edmund, 99
Burrard, Harry, 213, 220
Busaco, battle, 242–3, 248–9, 252, 269, 274, 310
Bute, Lord, 16, 26, 28–9, 34, 66
Byng, General, 325
Byng, Mrs, 359
Byron, Lord, 63, 182, 334, 342

Caçadores, Portuguese, 244
Cadiz, 221, 235, 249, 285
Cadogan, Lady Sarah (*m.* 2nd Duke of Richmond; Sarah's mother), 23, 33
Cadogan, Lord, 37
Camden, Lord, 128, 134, 300, 361
Cameron (Charles Napier's friend), 154, 156–7
Campbell, Neil, 345
Campbell, William, 238
Camperdown, battle, 122

Canada, 127, 299, 335
Canning, George, 225
Cape St Vincent, 73, 122
Carlisle, Lord, 36, 46, 55, 56, 58, 61, 63
Carnarvon, Lady, 252
Carolside (Berwickshire), 65
Carton (Leinster), 24, 126, 150, 166
Casal Noval, 262, 264, 269, 270, 286
Castejena, 177
Castlereagh, Lord, 132, 148, 177, 225, 323, 341–2, 362, 363
Castletown (County Kildare), 25, 29, 69, 101, 102–3, 108, 116, 125, 128, 130, 131, 142, 147, 161, 167, 168, 173–4, 221, 258–9, 307, 355, 358, 365–7
Catalonia, 333
Catherine the Great, 95, 190–1
Catholic emancipation, 116–17, 121
Cavendish, Lord George, 96
Caya, river, 276
Celbridge House (County Kildare), 104, 106, 118, 119, 125, 128, 136, 137, 144, 146, 161, 166–7, 174, 221, 225, 250, 291, 353
Celorico, 236, 242
Cephalonia (Greek Island), 363
Chabot, Colonel Vicomte, 295
Charles II, 22–3, 114, 118, 280, 337, 366, 369
Charlestown (America), 73, 162, 209, 284
Charlotte, Queen of George III (born Princess of Mecklenburg-Strelitz), 29, 33, 36, 39, 46, 176, 257
Chartres, duc de, 56
Chasseurs Britanniques, 249
Chatham, 156
Chatsworth, 77
Cheltenham, 356
Chesapeake, 305
Chesterfield, Lord, 79
Chimay, Princesse de, 48
China, Chinese, 190
Churchill, Sir Winston, 138, 160, 249
Cintra, 182, 191, 236
Cirencester House, 166
Ciudad Rodrigo, 236–8, 242, 270, 276, 281, 284, 286, 289, 317
Clairon, Mlle, 48
Clare, Lord, 128
Clarke, Mary Ann, 222, 268
Clayton, Frances (Aunt Fanny), 328
Clinton, Sir Henry, 73
Clinton, Sir Henry, the younger, 236, 325

Clontarf, Battle of (1014), 41
Clotworthy Upton, Mr, 47, 53, 63
Clouet, Baron, 219
Clunes, Captain, 206, 213
Coa, river, 238, 240–1, 243, 258, 266
Cobbett, William, 301, 351, 363
Cochrane, Lord, 362
Cockburn, Admiral Sir George, 303–4, 305–6
Codrington, Captain Edward, 177, 296
Coimbra, 252–3, 266, 268, 286
Coke, Lady Mary (born Campbell), 58, 61, 65, 67, 68
Colborne, Colonel Sir John, 191, 214, 268, 275, 285, 286, 330, 333, 345
Colchester barracks, 177
Coldstream Guards, 347
Cole, General Sir Lowry, 253, 272
Coleridge, 115
Collingwood, Admiral, 250
Compton, Lady Betty, 73
Condeixa, 260, 264, 265
Connaught Rangers, 244, 338
Conolly, Lady Anne (Tom Conolly's mother), 44
Conolly, Lady Louisa (born Lennox; Sarah's sister), 24–5, 29, 31, 37, 38, 39, 42, 44, 47–9, 51, 52, 55, 62, 65, 67, 68, 69, 81, 88, 97, 98, 101, 102–4, 106, 108, 111, 125, 126, 128–31, 132, 133–4, 144, 149, 161, 165, 167, 168, 175, 176, 181–2, 224, 257, 258, 300, 361, 362, 365–7, 369
Conolly, Tom (Louisa's husband), 25, 31, 39, 44, 52, 69, 81, 88, 101, 104, 106, 108, 116, 125, 128, 130, 134, 137, 140, 144, 149, 150, 161, 167, 312, 366
Considine, James, 354
Conti, Louis François, Prince de ('Conty'), 48
Conway, General Henry Seymour, 49
Coote, Sir Charles, 46
Copenhagen expedition, 178–9
Cornwallis, Charles, Marquis, 130, 134–6, 140
Corunna, 141, 188, 191, 196, 200, 203–4, 205, 222, 260, 274, 288, 300, 310, 317, 326, 337, 360
Costello, Rifleman, 317
Cotton, Sir Stapleton, 322
Craig, Margaret, see Napier, Margaret
Craig, William, 290
Craney Island (America), 303, 304, 305

Crauford, General ('Black Bob'), 189' 199, 202, 226, 237–40, 241, 246' 262, 275, 276, 285
Creevey, Thomas, 158
Crewe, Mr, 51, 53, 101–2, 121
Crewe, Mrs, 45, 51, 53, 101–2, 116, 121, 136, 175
Croker, Mr (Civil Lord of the Admiralty), 304
Cromwell, Oliver, 22, 93, 358
Cuesta, Spanish general, 227
Cyprus, Archbishop of, 114

Danton, 108
Darnley, Lord (16th cent.), 18
Darnley, Lord (18th cent.), 111
Dashwood, John, 167
Daubigny, 24
Decatur, American General, 299
du Deffand, Mme, 62, 56, 57, 58, 66
Delaval, Sir Francis, 46
Delaneys, 46
Derby, Lady, 85
Derby, Lord, 160
Devonshire, Duke of, 29
Devonshire, Georgiana, Duchess of, 83
Digby, Colonel, 136
Digby, Lady, 47
Digby, Lucy, 79
Dillon, Lord, 58
Dorchester, Lord, 165
Dorset, Duke of, 65
Douro, river, 221, 226, 275, 321, 322, 323
Drummond, Colonel, 261
Dublin: Napiers in, 145–7, 162
Dublin Castle, 121, 128, 208, 300
Duff, General Sir James, 147, 153
Dundas, General Sir David ('Old Pivot'), 235, 239, 257, 260, 276
Dunn, John, 265

Ebro, river, 321
Edgeworth, Maria, 365–6
Edinburgh, 18, 22, 260, 279, 286, 288, 290, 335
Edward I, 17
Egremont, Lord, 84
Elba, 308, 340
El Bodon, plateau, 276
El Burgo, 203
Ellis, Colonel, 272
Elvas, 276
Elvina, 205, 206, 208–9, 213, 219
Erroll, Lord, 35, 63

Erskine, Sir William, 261, 262, 273
Escurial, Madrid, 314
Esla, river, 196, 202, 321
Eugene, Prince, 274
Euryalus, H.M.S., 249, 297
Euston, Lord, 84
Exeter, 75
Exeter, Bishop of, 75

Fane, General, 198, 207
Farnham Staff College, 308, 339, 346, 359
Fitzgerald, Lord Charles, 126
Fitzgerald, Lady Charlotte, 126
Fitzgerald, Lady Edward (born Pamela Seymour), 83, 127, 128, 131, 133
Fitzgerald, Lord Edward, 44, 68, 79, 83, 126–33, 145, 164, 208, 278, 300
Fitzgerald, Lady Emilia, 80, 126, 138
Fitzgerald, Lord George, 126
Fitzgerald, Lord Gerald, 79, 126
Fitzgerald, Lord Henry, 126, 128, 129
Fitzgerald, Lady Isabella, 126, 168, 295
Fitzgerald, Lady Lucy, 126
Fitzgerald, Lady Mary, 136, 138
Fitzgerald, Lady Olivia, 126
Fitzgerald, Lord Robert, 126
Fitzgerald, Lady Sophia, 126
Fitzgerald, Lord William, 126
Fitzpatrick, Lady Mary (*m.* Ste Fox, 2nd Lord Holland), 51, 53, 60, 63, 68, 76
Fitzroy, Mrs, 46
Fitzroy, Lady Charles, 160
Fitzwilliam, William, 4th Earl, 115, 116, 121–2, 123–4, 149
Flahaut, General, 356
Forjas (Portuguese minister), 254–5
Fox, Lady Caroline (born Lennox, later Lady Holland; Sarah's sister), 15, 16, 25, 31, 34, 36, 37, 41, 47, 60, 63, 65, 67
Fox, Hon. Caroline (Ste's daughter), 223–4, 234
Fox, Caroline (Harry's daughter; *m.* William Napier), 190, 215, 280–1, 286, 287, 310–11, 312–13, 314–16, 319–20, 323, 326–9, 350–1, 355, 359, 360
Fox, Hon. Charles James (Sarah's nephew), 15, 27, 36, 40, 47, 49, 52, 55, 67, 77–8, 94, 96–7, 98, 99, 100, 108, 115, 148–50, 165, 174–5, 224
Fox, General Sir Henry (Hon. Harry; Sarah's nephew), 15, 71, 73, 78, 149, 190, 215
Fox, Henry *see* Holland, 1st Lord
Fox, Hon. Henry Richard *see* Holland, 3rd Lord
Fox, Stephen (Henry, 1st Lord Holland's father), 15
Fox, Hon. Stephen (Ste) *see* Holland, 2nd Lord
Fox, Stephen (Henry, 1st Lord Holland's brother) *see* Ilchester, Lord
Fox-Strangways, Lady Susan *see* O'Brien, Lady Susan
Foy, Marshal Maximilian, 240, 314
Frampton, Mr and Mrs, 146
Franco, General, 93
François (Moore's servant), 214
Fraser, General, 200, 218
Freer (a young soldier), 326
French Revolution, The, 99, 100, 107, 110, 126
Frere, Hookham, 193
Freyre, Spanish general, 333
Froissart, Jean, 137, 221
Frost, Susan (Sarah's maid), 109, 111, 118, 119, 355, 365
Fuentes d'Onoro, 260, 265–6, 273

Gage, Miss, 154, 155
Gallegos, 236, 237, 290, 319–20, 337
Garonne, river, 332, 333
Garrick, David, 48, 61, 86
Garrick, Mrs, 86
Genlis, Mme de, 127
George II, 23, 26
George III, 52, 95, 96, 99, 114, 116, 147, 162, 169, 170, 191, 226; and Sarah Lennox, 16, 26–30, 31–3, 35, 37, 63, 69–70, 135, 150–1, 176; engagement to Princess Charlotte, 33; wedding, 35; and American War, 71–2; illness, 105, 160, 257, 267–8, 349–50, 369
George IV *see* Prince Regent
George VI, 119
Ghent, 112, 345
Gibbs, Samuel, 308, 330
Gibraltar, 73, 221, 249, 320
Gifford, Lieutenant, 229, 264–5, 270
Glorious First of June, The, 110–11
Gloucester, Duchess of, 356
Gloucester, William, Duke of (son of George III), 44, 46, 356
Gloucester, Duke of (grandson of George III), 356

Goldsmith, Oliver, 78
Gomm, Captain, 261
Goodwood (Sussex), 24, 30, 67, 74, 89, 95, 131, 174, 175
Gordon, Captain Alexander, 200, 220
Gordon, Lady Charlotte (daughter of 4th Duke of Gordon; *m.* 4th Duke of Richmond), 259, 295–6
Gordon, Cosmo (scurrilous writer), 68
Gordon, 3rd Duke of, 46
Gordon, Lord George, 86, 259
Gordon, Captain James, 297
Gordon, Nat, 22
Gordon, Lord William (son of 3rd Duke of Gordon), 63–7, 85, 139, 259, 296
Gore, aide-de-camp, 325
Goering, Hermann, 93
Grafton, Duchess of, 46
Grafton, Duke of, 46, 49, 52
Graham, Colonel (later General), Sir Thomas, 187, 193, 199, 207
Granby, Lord, 40
de Grasse, French admiral, 97
Grattan, Henry, 124, 282, 311, 315, 317, 335, 338
Gray, Thomas, 163
Greece, 123, 363, 369
Greville, Mary *see* Crewe, Mrs
Greville, Mr, 40
Greville, Mrs, 52
Guache, French captain, 238
Guadarrama, 195–6, 314
Guadiana, river, 271, 276, 277, 308–9, 311
Guernsey, 177, 291
Guibert, French drummer, 216
Gurwood, Lieutenant John, 282, 289
Gustavus IV (King of Sweden), 190
Guthrie, surgeon, 284

Hague Convention, 338, 340
Haldane family, 18, 21
Halifax, 308, 339
Halnaker (Sarah's Sussex home), 74–5, 85, 87
Hamilton, Archibald, 324
Hamilton, Lady Caroline, 42
Hamilton, Duchess of, 46
Hamilton, General, 325
Hampton (America), 304
Hans Place, No. 21, 174, 175
Hardinge, Colonel, 212, 272
Hardy (and Nelson), 230
Harland, Mrs, 39

Harrington, Lady, 46, 51, 53
Harris, Rifleman, 182, 201–2, 230, 338
Hawkesbury, Lord, 170
Hawkshawe, Colonel, 272
Hayes, Peter, 178
Hennessy, John, 217–18, 264
Henry of Navarre, 23, 337
Henry V, 337
Henry VIII, 69
Hermione, 27
Herrasti, General Andreas, 238
Hertford family, 48
Hervey, Lady Caroline, 61
Hibernian, 124
Hill, General Sir Rowland, 201, 218, 325, 329
Hitler, Adolf, 112, 320, 322, 339
Hoare, Henry, 30
Hobart, Lady Amelia (*m.* Lord Castlereagh), 132
Holland, Henry, 1st Lord, 15–16, 25, 26, 28, 29, 30, 31–2, 34, 36, 37, 38, 39, 40–1, 42, 45, 47, 48, 49, 52, 54, 55, 60, 63, 64–5, 66, 76, 77, 347
Holland, Stephen, 2nd Lord (Ste), 15, 25, 27, 34, 36, 37, 45, 47, 49, 51, 52, 53, 55, 60, 68, 77–8
Holland, Henry Richard, 3rd Lord, 78, 96, 188, 281, 365
Holland, Lady Caroline (wife of 1st Lord Holland) *see* Fox, Lady Caroline
Holland, Lady Elizabeth (wife of 3rd Lord Holland) *see* Vassall, Elizabeth
Holland, Lady Mary (wife of 2nd Lord Holland) *see* Fitzpatrick, Lady Mary
Holland House, 15, 25, 27, 40, 65, 67, 68, 70, 78, 80, 280, 288, 356
Holyroodhouse, Palace of, 19
Homer, 221
Hood, Admiral, 204
Hope, General Sir John, 200–1, 213–14, 325
Hopkins, Major, 171
Horsford, 'King', 292, 298
Horsford, Mrs, 359
Hougoumont (Belgium), 345
Howe, Admiral Earl Richard, 96, 110
Howe, Sir William (later Viscount), 72, 78
Huebra, fords, 318
Huerta, ford, 314
Hume, David, 71
Huntingdon, Earl of, 29

Huntly, Lord, 173
Hussar, frigate, 233-4

Ilchester, Lord, 33, 40-2, 45, 50, 76, 100, 347
Ilchester, Lady, 33, 40, 42, 45, 50, 54, 76, 77, 105, 170
l'Ile d'Adam, 48
Iliad, 137, 171
India, 99, 115, 173, 176, 278, 312
Influenza epidemic (1782), 95
Inglis, Colonel, 272
Ireland, 15, 22, 24, 72, 78, 100, 116-37, 161, 171, 335, 345, 353

Jackson, General Andrew, 330
Jackson, Private Richard, 203
Jane Shore, 27
Jéna, Bridge of (Paris), 347
Jenner, Edward, MD, 328
Jervis, John (Earl St Vincent), 122
Johnston, Dr Samuel, 37
Johnston, General, and Lady Cecilia (Donny's uncle and aunt), 95
Johnston, Mrs (Donny's sister), 165
Jones, George, RA, 360
Jones, Inigo, 101
Jones of Bridport (Richard Napier's tutor), 170, 171
Josephine, Empress, 196
Junot, French general, 182, 271

Katherine of Aragon, 69
Keats, John, 230, 351
Kelly, Elizabeth, 223
Kempt, General, 325
Kennedy, Shaw, 142, 171
Kent, William, 15
Kepler, German mathematician and scientist, 19
Keppel, Admiral, 36, 73, 82
Kerr, Lady Louisa *see* Lennox, Lady George
Kerr, Lady Mark, 147, 175
Kerr, Lord Mark, 147, 170
Kildare, Lady (Emily's mother-in-law), 69
Kildare, Lady Emily (born Lennox; later Duchess of Leinster; later *m.* William Ogilvie; Sarah's sister), 24, 25, 26, 27, 28, 29, 31, 34, 38, 39, 50-1, 65, 67, 69, 76, 79, 80-1, 88, 98, 104, 108, 115, 126, 127, 128, 129, 165, 166, 168, 181, 294, 365-6, 368-9
Kildare, James, 20th Earl (later Duke of Leinster), 24, 27, 31, 34, 38, 49, 50, 80, 116, 126, 137
Kildare House (Dublin), 24
Kincaid, Johnny, 230, 238, 252, 266, 272, 311, 337, 338
Kirkpatrick, surgeon, 248
Knatchbull, Sir Neddy, 179
Knole, 65, 365

Ladysmith, siege of, 231, 311
Langdale, Lord, 361
Las Nogales, 200
de Lauzun, duc, 56-9, 63, 68-9
Lawrence, Colonel, 287
Lee, Charles (American revolutionary leader), 72
Leinster, Duchess of *see* Kildare, Lady Emily
Leinster, Duke of *see* Kildare, James, 20th Earl
Leinster House (Dublin), 126
Leipzig, battle, 323
Leith, infantry commander, 314
Le Marchant, 314, 322
Lennox, Lady Anne *see* Albemarle, Lady
Lennox, Lady Caroline *see* Fox, Lady Caroline
Lennox, Lady Cecilia (Sarah's sister), 24
Lennox, Charles (Sarah's brother) *see* Richmond, 3rd Duke
Lennox, Charles (Sarah's nephew) *see* Richmond, 4th Duke
Lennox, Lady Emily (Sarah's sister) *see* Kildare, Lady Emily
Lennox, Lady Emily (Sarah's niece) *see* Berkeley, Lady Emily
Lennox, Lady George (Sarah's sister-in-law), 25, 30, 34, 38, 74, 83, 234
Lennox, Lord George (Sarah's brother), 25, 30, 34, 67, 70, 82, 83, 94, 98, 105, 160
Lennox, Lord George (Sarah's great-nephew), 295-6
Lennox, Lady Georgina (Sarah's niece) *see* Bathurst, Lady Georgina
Lennox, Lady Louisa (Sarah's sister) *see* Conolly, Lady Louisa
Lennox, Lady Louisa (Sarah's niece), 83
Lennox, Lady Sarah (later Bunbury; later Napier), early years, 15-16, 22-5; marriage to Donny Napier, 17, 22, 86-9, 369; presented at Court, 25; and George III, 27-38;

proposal from John Newbattle (later Lothian), 30; reaction to George III's engagement, 33–5; marries Charles Bunbury, 36–40; correspondence with Susan O'Brien and others, *passim*; visits to Paris, 47–50, 55–8; tries to reconcile Susan O'Brien with the Ilchesters, 50, 76–7; 'affair' with de Lauzun, 56–9; affair with Lord William Gordon, 63–7; birth of Louisa Bunbury, 65; divorce, 66, 67, 69–70, 86; meets Donny Napier, 70–1; secluded life in Sussex, 67, 69, 74, 78–80, 85; forgiven by Bunbury, 85; as Donny's wife, 88–94; children born to, 100–6; loss of Louisa Bunbury, 102; in Ireland, 102–15; Dublin, 145–7, 150; increasing blindness, 151, 174, 176, 224, 250, 256; after Donny's death, 165–71; fight for pension, 166, 169–70; reassured by Sir John Moore, 173; reconciled to her brother Charles Richmond, 174, 176; settles in Hans Place, London, 174–5, 224; sons return from Spain, 220–1, 223; recuperates in Ireland, 258–9; wins son Charles's promotion, 277; described by her daughter-in-law, 287; total blindness, 289, 294; mourns with Susan, 348; ill, 358; death, 26th August, 1826, 370
Leslie, Ensign, 256
l'Estoret, Monsieur, 36
Light, Lieutenant, 265
Limerick, 41, 140, 147, 152–3
Lisbon, 191, 221, 226, 233, 236, 242, 249, 254–9, 278, 280, 284, 286, 290, 296, 309, 321
Liverpool, Lord, 123, 148, 268, 349
Livingstone family, 21
Lloyd, Captain Thomas (later Colonel), 197, 241–2, 244, 263, 298, 326
Loch Lomond, 17, 19, 21
Lock (from Celbridge), 353
Loison, French officer, 237–8, 244
Londonderry, 116, 122
Londonderry, Lord and Lady, 141
Longa, guerillero, 276, 321
Longleat, 30
Lothian, Lord *see* Newbattle, John
Louis XIV, 112
Louis XV, 49

Louis XVIII, 346
Lugo, 187, 200–1
Luton Hoo, 20, 21
Lutzen, 321
Lyons, battle, 332, 342

Mackenzie, Colonel, 172, 202
Mackenzie, Mrs, 202
Mackinnon, Brigadier, 239
Mackintosh, Sir James, 342
MacLeod, Charles (William Napier's friend), 142, 254, 286, 310–11
MacLeod, Major (at Copenhagen), 178
Madrid, 179, 193–4, 277, 286, 314–17
Magee, Sergeant, 208
Maiden Bradley, 30
Malory, Sir Thomas, 137, 221
Mao Tse-tung, 126, 163
March, Charles (Sarah's father) *see* Richmond, 2nd Duke
March, Charles (later 5th Duke of Richmond; Sarah's great-nephew), 222, 245, 246, 256, 265, 289–90, 295, 328, 329, 332, 335
Marie Antoinette, 102, 266
Marie de Medici, 23
Marie Louise, Napoleon's second Empress, 266
Marlborough, John Churchill, 1st Duke, 314
Marlborough, Spencer-Churchill, Duke of, 29, 34
Marlborough, Duchess of, 34, 146
Marly, 49
Marmont, Marshal, 276, 282, 312–15
Mary, Queen of Scots, 18, 21
Mason on Self-Knowledge, 173
Masséna, Marshal André, 237–8, 242–3, 245–6, 252, 258, 260–1, 266, 268, 276, 310, 337
Massey, Miss, 153
Maucune, French general, 314
Melbourne, Lady, 99
Melbury, 50, 77, 82, 88, 356
Merchiston (Edinburgh), 17, 21–3, 71
Mermet, French general, 213
Metternich, 342
Meynell, Mr, 40
Michaelangelo, 364
Milan, 363–4
Mina, Navarrese guerilla leader, 276
Mississippi, river, 306, 330
Missouri, river, 306, 330
Moira, Lord, 108, 112–13, 115, 116, 167, 176, 258

Moita (Portugal), 268
Monaco, Princesse de, 48
Mondego, river, 258, 275
le Moniteur, 274
Mont Blanc, 363
Montgomery, John, 208
Montmartre, 333
Montrose, Duke of, 99
Montrose, Marquis of, 21-2, 105
Moore, Ensign, 208
Moore, Mrs (Sir John Moore's mother), 288
Moore, Dr James, 256, 278
Moore, General Sir John, 113, 141, 143, 158-9, 164; praises young Napiers, 172; 172, 175, 176, 183, 187, 191-204; on Spaniards, 189, 194; in love with Caroline Fox, 190, 214-15; in battle of Corunna, 205-12; death, 212-14; burial, 215; 220, 235, 240, 245-6, 270, 306; magnanimity in war, 337; fair name under a cloud, 360
Moore, Laughlin (servant at Cel-bridge), 118
Morning Post, 68
Morse, Mr, of the War Office, 113, 115
Moscow, 320
Mountbatten, Lord Louis, 160
Mount Vernon (Washington), 297
Murchison (died at Nivelle), 326

Napier, Sir Alexander (15th cent.) and his chapel in St Giles', 18-19
Napier, Colonel Alexander (killed at Corunna), 218
Napier, Sir Archibald of Merchiston, 17-18
Napier, Archibald (16th cent.), 19
Napier, Archibald, 1st Lord, 21-2
Napier, Caroline (William's wife) *see* Fox, Caroline
Napier, Caroline (Sarah's daughter), 104, 118, 138, 169, 175, 183; and sister's death, 181; 234; death, 245-6; 250-2, 295, 369
Napier, Cecilia (Sarah's daughter), 118, 138, 169, 170, 175; death, 180-1, 183, 295, 369
Napier, Charles (Black Charlie), 242-3, 246-50, 297
Napier, Charles James (Sarah's son), 97, 100, 103, 109, 117, 118, 119-20, 124, 138, 139, 140-1, 144, 150, 152-8, 159-60, 164, 165, 172-4, 175, 176-7, 178, 179, 180-1, 182-3;

in Spain, 187-91; at Corunna' 199-212, 235-6; 213-15, 223, 225; prisoner of the French, 216-20; home, 223; Walcheren expedition, 226; Peninsula again, 235 ff.; wounded at Busaco, 247-50, 259-60; 254-7, 260-8, 271-4; promoted, 277; Bermuda, 277, 291-3, 297-302; in American War, 302-7; 308, 337, 338, 345, 346; shipwreck, 350; 354; Farnham, 356; 358-9, 361-5; Cephalonia, 363; 369, 370
Napier, Donald (12th cent.), 17, 21
Napier, Donny *see* Napier, Colonel George
Napier, Elizabeth (Donny's first wife) *see* Pollock, Elizabeth
Napier, Emily (Sarah's daughter, adopted by Conollys), 100-1, 103, 104, 118, 128, 132, 138, 147, 150, 175, 224, 251, 264, 350, 366, 369
Napier, Francis, 6th Lord (Donny's father), 260
Napier, Lieutenant Francis (Donny's great-nephew), 233-4
Napier, Hon. Colonel George (Donny), 70-1, 99, 101-5, 106-7, 132, 133, 134, 138, 170, 221, 224, 256; marries Sarah Lennox, 17, 22, 86-9; in America, 73-4, 162, 209, 284; unemployed, 93-6; rejoins the army, 97-8; serves against France, 107-14; commands Derry regiment, 115-19, 123, 130, 134; helps Fitzgeralds, 128; Army Comptroller under Cornwallis, 135-6, 144-5, 147; illness, 150-1; death and appreciations of, 158-65; hated fighting Americans, 304; 358-9, 369, 370
Napier, George Thomas (Sarah's son), 100, 105, 111, 117, 118, 124, 136, 138, 139-41, 144, 150, 152, 153, 154, 155, 158, 159, 163-4, 167, 171-2, 175, 176, 258; in Spain, 187, 191, 195, 199, 204, 235-50; in Sicily, 189-90; at Corunna and after, 206-7, 212-15, 220-1, 223; in Portugal and Spain under Wel-lington, 226-30, 235-47; champions the private soldier, 232; fever in Spain, 236, 239-42; at Busaco, 244-9, 259; at Coimbra and Lisbon, 252-4; wounded, 261, 263-7, 269, 271; promotion, 275, 277; on Wellington, 280; assault

on Ciudad Rodrigo, 282; loses right arm, 283, 327; marries Margaret Craig, 286, 290; 296, 327, 329, 332, 333, 334–5, 338, 355–6, 358, 366–9
Napier, Henry Edward (Sarah's son), 104, 118, 136, 138, 143–4, 163, 170, 175, 178, 249; in Madras, 234; at sea, 278; Oxford, 279; 299, 301; off Boston, 307; Commander, 308, 355; marries Caroline Bennet, 358; 366, 369
Napier, John (at siege of Stirling Castle, 1298), 17
Napier, John (16th cent.; invented logarithms), 19–21
Napier, John Moore (Mr Puck; William's son), 352, 359, 360
Napier, Louisa (Donny's daughter), 73–4, 108–9, 138, 147, 150, 162, 223, 234, 287–8, 290, 294, 369
Napier, Margaret (George's wife), 286–9, 290–1, 335
Napier, Hon. Patrick, Captain R.N. (Donny's brother), 107, 110–11, 112
Napier, Richard (Sarah's son), 104, 136, 138, 143–4, 168; at Oxford, 170–1; 175, 177, 180, 183, 223, 225, 234, 251, 256, 258; in Scotland, 279; at the Temple, 356; marries Anna Louisa Staples, 358; 369
Napier, Sir Robert (17th cent.), 20
Napier, Lady Sarah *see* Lennox, Lady Sarah
Napier, William (15th cent.), 18
Napier, William, 7th Lord (Donny's brother), 233–4
Napier, William Francis Patrick (Sarah's son), 101, 102, 111, 117, 118, 119–20, 134, 136, 138, 139, 141–4, 154, 162, 164–5, 170, 171–2, 173, 180; meets Pitt, 147–9; estimate of Charles, 158; writes history, 171, 215, 231, 266; at Copenhagen, 178–9; in Spain, 188–9, 196, 198–9, 202–3, 213; praises Moore, 198, 214; pleurisy, 213, 214, 220, 227; in Portugal and Spain under Wellington, 216–31, 236, 240; wounded, 241, 261–7, 269, 271; Busaco, 243–7; Brevet-Major, 277; marries Caroline Fox, 280–1, 286; 287, 289, 290; Lisbon, 296; Badajoz, 307–11; letters to Caroline, 310 ff.; 312–16, 318–20, 321, 323–9; wounded, 327; 332, 339; Belgium and France, 345–7;

daughters, 350; son born, 352; Paris, 355; Radical speaker, 359; elected R.A., 360; family griefs, 359–60; begins book, 361; 369
Napoleon, 114, 134, 147, 149; threat of invasion by, 158–9, 173, 174; in Russia, 176; 177, 179; in Spain, 179–80, 183, 192–6, 237; 223, 224; Portuguese expedition, 226, 233; talks of peace, 236; 258, 261, 264, 266, 268; Polish Lancers, 271; 'disgusting tyranny', 275; gutted Italy, 293; power crumbling, 299; abdication, 334; 338, 340–1; escape from Elba, 342; 'with tiger speed', 345; Waterloo, 345–7; 350, 361; the people's admiration and affection for, 364
Nasser, President, 93
Navarre, 276
Nelson, Horatio, Lord, 122, 160, 163, 222, 230, 283
Netley (Southampton), 113, 119
Newbattle, John Kerr, Lord (later Lord Lothian), 29, 30, 36, 47, 74, 147
Newman, Paul, 280
Newmarket, 40, 49, 55, 60, 77
New Orleans, 305, 308, 330
New York, 42, 45, 51, 53
Ney, Marshal, 219, 223, 237, 244–5, 258, 337
Nieman, river, 313
Nile, Battle of the, 160
Nive, battle, 260, 329
Nivelle, river, battle, 260, 322, 324, 326, 328, 331, 350
Nompareil, Jean *see* Napier, John (16th cent.)
No Popery Riots, 86
North, Sir Thomas, 137
North, Lord, 96
Northumberland, Lady, 36

O'Brien, Lady Susan (born Fox-Strangways), 25, 28, 30, 31; correspondence with Sarah Lennox, 31 *et passim*; elopes with William O'Brien, 40–1; in New York, 42, 44, 45, 46, 49–50, 51, 53, 59, 64; scolds Sarah, 62–3, 87–8; returns to England, 71, 76–7; reconciled to family, 77, 79, 105; Sarah's reliance on at Donny's death, 162, 165–70; 295; husband's death, 347, 348, 356; on manners, 357–8; visit to Sarah, 365

O'Brien, William (Susan's husband), 40–5, 50, 53–4, 63; appointment in Bermuda, 65; returns to England, 71, 76–7, 80; tries to become a barrister, 88; 99, 102, 105; Sarah seeks job for, 115, 123; dies, 347
Ocracoke (America), 305
Odyssey, 137, 171
Ogilvie, Lord, 19
Ogilvie, William (Emily Kildare's second husband), 80–1, 98, 106, 126, 128–30
O'Grady, Mr, 41–2
O'Grady, Elizabeth *see* Stavordale, Lady
Oliphant, Sir William, 17
Oman, Sir Charles, 198
Opie, Amelia, 280
Oporto, 221, 276
Orange, House of, 340
Orange, Prince William of (Slender Billy), 340
Orangemen, 124, 134
Orcana, battle, 235
Orloff, Count, 95
Orthez, battle, 329, 331
Ossory, Lord, 39
Ostend, 111–12, 346
Otranto, 365

Paget, General, 111, 193, 195, 201, 203, 218, 322
Pakenham, Edward, 239, 247, 308, 314, 324, 330
Pakenham, Louisa (born Staples; wife of Tom Pakenham), 111, 128, 366
Pakenham, Thomas, Captain R.N. (later Admiral), 111, 128, 140, 167, 366
Pakenham, William, 283–4
Pamplona, 322
Papreon, 329
Paris, 38, 47–50, 51, 56–8, 60, 70, 100, 333–4, 345–7, 350
Pasajes, 323
Pau, 331
Peninsular War, 176, 179–80, 182–3, 187–9, 191–222, 226–69, 250, 252, 281, 313, 338, 345, 354
Percy, Harry, 214
Petre, Lord, 39
Philip II (King of Spain), 112
Philippe Egalité, 127
Pichegru, General, 112
Picton, General, 236

Pitt, William, 39, 52, 99, 112; and the Irish question, 122, 123, 125; William Napier meets and describes, 147–9; death, 149; 158; and Sarah's pension, 166, 169
Placencia, 227
Plutarch, 137, 156, 221
Plymouth, 286, 290–2, 323, 336
Pollock, Elizabeth (Donny's first wife), 70, 73–4
Pope Pius VII, 364
Porlier, guerillero, 276
Portland, Duke of, 116, 121–2, 124
Portsmouth, 73
Portsmouth, Duchess of, 23, 32–3, 114
Potomac, river, 298
Powell, actor, 61
Prince Regent, 95, 99, 120, 125, 154, 277, 361
Pultusk, 176
Pyrenees, 260, 308, 321–3, 325, 330

Quérouaille, Louise de *see* Portsmouth, Duchess of

Redhina, 260, 262
Redlinch, 30, 50, 279
Régnier (at Busaco), 246
Renaud, French general, 218
Rhine, river, 323, 333
Rhune, fortresses, 325
Rich, Sir Henry, 15
Richmond, Duchess of (Sarah's mother) *see* Cadogan, Lady Sarah
Richmond, Duchess of (Sarah's sister-in-law), 48–9, 75, 87, 88, 100
Richmond, Duchess of (Sarah's nephew's wife) *see* Gordon, Lady Charlotte
Richmond, 1st Duke of (Charles II's bastard), 22–3
Richmond, Charles, 2nd Duke of (Sarah's father), 23
Richmond, Charles, 3rd Duke of (Sarah's brother), 25, 36–7, 39, 53, 65, 66, 67, 71, 80–1; builds Sarah a house, 67, 74–5; 87–8, 95–6, 98–100, 105, 125, 130, 131, 134, 143, 160; refuses loan to Sarah, 167; reconciled to Sarah, 174, 176; death, 176, 224, 227
Richmond, Charles 4th Duke of (Sarah's nephew), 94, 227, 258–9, 295–6, 335

Richmond, Charles, 5th Duke of *see* March, Charles (Sarah's great-nephew)
Rideout, 319
Robertson, Captain Charles, 302, 303
Robert the Bruce, 17–18
Robespierre, 108
Robinson, Hercules, 249
Robinson, Perdita, 96–7
Robinson, Sir Thomas, 368
Rockingham, Lord, 40, 49, 149; death, 95
Rodney, Admiral, 73, 97
Romanos, General, 194, 197, 200
Rome, 364
Rommel, 346
Rosebery, Lord, 149
Ross, General Sir Charles, 136, 244, 275
Ross, Colonel, 262
Rosse, Lady, 39
Rousseau, Jean-Jacques, 24, 52, 66
Rowan brothers, 172, 290
Royal Society, 20
Russia, Russians, 173, 176, 190, 215, 312–14, 320, 334, 341–2
Russell, Bertrand, 46
Russell, Lady Caroline *see* Marlborough, Duchess of
Russell, John, 46
Rutland, Duchess of, 73
Ruthven, Lord, 158

Sabugal, 270, 276
Sacavem, 236
Sahagún, 195–6, 200
St Cyr, convent, 48
St Giles', Edinburgh, 18
St Helena, 341, 354
St James's Palace, 26, 28, 31
St James's, Piccadilly, 349
St Jean de Luz, 330
St John's, New Brunswick, 307
St Leger, Captain, 105, 160
St Pierre, battle, 329
St Vincent, Earl *see* Jervis, John
Salamanca, battle, 260, 276, 292, 314, 315–16
Salamanca, British troops in, 192–3, 195; French under Ney in, 237
Sambre, river, 345
San Domingo 74, 303
Sandwich, Lord, 83
Santander, 321
Santiago di Compostella, 192
Saumarez, Admiral Sir James, 191

Selwyn, George, 57, 60–1
Seringapatam, 115
Seville, 221
Seymour, Michael, Lieutenant R.N., 110
Seymour, Pamela *see* Fitzgerald, Lady Edward
Shelburne, Lord, 37, 46, 96, 98
Shelley, Percy Bysshe, 334
Sheridan, 119
Shorncliffe, 143, 150, 158
Shute, Mr, 39
Sicily, 173, 175, 176, 189–90
Siddons, Mrs Sarah, 94
Skeffington, Harriet, 181
Slave trade, 191, 224, 341
Sloane Street, 360
Sloane Terrace, 174
Smith, Harry, 230–1, 262, 311, 325, 331, 336
Socoa, fort, 325
Somerset, Lord Fitzroy, 215, 353
Soult, Marshal, 159, 187, 195, 197, 199–201, 203, 205–6, 213, 218, 221, 223, 226–7, 235, 245, 271, 276, 312, 316–17, 322, 324–5, 328–9, 331, 333
Southampton, 109–11, 113, 153, 182
South Africa, 181, 182
Spa (France), 59, 60, 63, 64
Spectator, 173
Spencer, Lord Brent, 317
Stanhope, Hon. Charles, 147, 187, 202, 209–10, 212–13, 215, 236
Stanhope, Lady Hester, 144, 148, 166, 170, 193, 215, 224
Stanhope, Hon. James, 213–14
Staples, Anna Louisa (*m.* Richard Napier), 312, 358, 368
Stavordale, Lady (later Ilchester), 41–2, 77, 347, 348, 356
Stavordale, Lord (later Ilchester), 31, 41–2, 347, 348, 356
Stewart, Colonel, 154, 263–4, 290
Stewart, Ensign, 208
Stewart, Major, 301
Stinsford (Dorset), 76, 77
Stirling Castle, 17
Stoke, 67, 70, 111
Stourhead, 30
Strangways, Miss *see* Ilchester, Lady
Stretton (near Wolverhampton), 101, 102, 103
Stuart, British Ambassador at Lisbon, 254
Stubbs, George, 94
Sturgeon, Colonel, 332

Sturt, Mr, 120
Suchet, French general, 333
Suez, 1956 attack on, 123
Sulgrave (Washington family home), 297
Sweden, 190–1
Swilly, Lough, 284

Tagus, river, 226, 228–9, 233, 258, 275, 286
Talavera, 195, 226, 228, 235, 269, 275
Talbot, Colonel, 238
Talbot, Lady Mary, 234
Tamerlane (William Napier's horse), 312
Tarbes, battle, 332
Tavistock, Lady, 46, 47
Tavistock, Lord, 47
Tedeschi, 364
Thurlow, Lord, 99
Tierney, French general, 314
Tierney, George, 349
Tilsit, Peace of, 177, 178
Times, The, 198, 328
Torres Vedras, 233, 235, 252, 270
Toulouse, 331, 332–3
Town & Country Magazine, 61, 68
Trafalgar, 168, 169, 173, 177, 249, 283, 299, 354
Turner, Lieutenant, 209–10

Ungera, 270
Urquhart, Sir Thomas, 20

Valderas, 196
Vallière, Duchesse de la, 48
Vandeleur, General, 283
Vandeleur, Miss, 153
Vassall, Elizabeth (*m.* Henry Fox, 3rd Lord Holland), 126, 127
Vernon, actor, 61
Verra, 324
Versailles, 366
Vesey, Mrs, 37
Victor, Marshal, 227
Victory, H.M.S., 191
Vienna, 364
Vigo, 196, 199, 202–4, 213
Villafranca, 199–201
Villiers, Lord, 40
Vimiero, battle, 182, 208
Virgin Islands, 307
Vittoria, battle, 260, 321

Walcheren expedition, 226, 234

Waldegrave, Dowager Lady (afterwards Duchess of Gloucester), 46
Waldegrave, Lady Maria (later Euston), 84
Walker, Colonel, 207
Walker, Surgeon, 284
Wallace, Colonel Alexander, 244
Wallace, William, 17
Walpole, Horace, 24, 27, 31, 37, 58, 77
Walton, Private John, 202–3
Warde, Colonel, 212
Washington, 297
Washington family, 297
Waterloo, 222, 322, 340, 345, 347
Wellesley, Sir Arthur, later Duke of Wellington, 113, 115; in Ireland, 139; 159, 163–4, 164, 172; in India, 176; in Portugal and Spain, 182–322 *passim*; receives dukedom, 228; in France, Belgium and at Waterloo, 323–47; 362
Wentworth (Yorkshire), 149
West Indies, 73, 97, 122
Westmorland, Lady, 108
Westmorland, Lord, 35
Weymouth (Dorset), 233, 295
Weymouth, Lord, 49
Whitelocke's expedition to Buenos Aires, 175
Wilberforce, William, 362
Wilde, Oscar, 160
Wilhelm II, 112, 339
William, Prince *see* Gloucester, Duke of
Wilson, John Morillyon, 263, 315
Windham, 177
Winterslow (near Salisbury), 76
Wishart, 21
Woburn, 40
Woodford, Lieutenant, 213
Woolwich Arsenal, 94, 95, 97, 162
Wordsworth, Dorothy, 115, 334
Wordsworth, William, 115, 320, 341

Yarmouth, Lady, 26
Yates, Mr, 61
York, Duke of, 39, 46; duel with Charles Lennox, 105; against the French, 112, 134; popular C.-in-C., 222; promotion for Charles Napier, 276–7; 278–9

Zaya, Spanish Commander, 271